MORLEY AND INDIA
1906–1910

MORLEY AND INDIA

1906-1910

STANLEY A. WOLPERT

1967
UNIVERSITY OF CALIFORNIA PRESS
BERKELEY AND LOS ANGELES

168724

University of California Press
Berkeley and Los Angeles, California

Cambridge University Press
London, England

© by The Regents of the University of California
Library of Congress Catalog Card Number: 67-14118

Designed by John B. Goetz
Printed in the United States of America

To Dorothy

To Dorothy

PREFACE

My interest in John Morley's impact on India was first aroused almost ten years ago, when, while doing research in Poona on my study of *Tilak and Gokhale: Revolution and Reform in the Making of Modern India* (University of California Press, 1962), I found so many glowing tributes and laudatory references to Morley among Gokhale's private papers, and almost as many sarcastic and derogatory comments about him in Tilak's *Kesari* editorials and speeches. Morley's papers at the time were still unavailable for scholarly perusal, but the centrality of his role to Indian History between 1906 and 1910 seemed so evident from the reactions of Indian political leaders to all he said, did, and failed to do, that in writing my dissertation chapters about this period I felt as though I were attempting to stage *Hamlet* without the Prince of Denmark.

I was soon to discover that Morley had as many ardent partisans and virulent enemies in England as he did in India, and the more I read by him, as well as about his constitutional reforms for India during his half decade as secretary of state in charge of the India Office, the more intrigued I became by the puzzling question of what his actual policy for India was. Unable to find any convincing answer to this riddle in any published source by 1961, I embarked upon this study. Thanks to the support I received from an American Council of Learned Societies–Social Science Research Council fellowship, I was able to start my research into Morley's papers, preserved at London's India Office Library, during sabbatical leave in the fall of 1961. I wish to express my warm appreciation to the ACLS–SSRC for their generous grant-in-aid, and to those colleague-friends who so kindly encouraged me in embarking upon this project by supporting my proposal for this grant: Professors W. Norman Brown and Holden Furber, of the University of Pennsylvania; Professor Richard L. Park, now of the University of Michigan; Professor Gustave von Grunebaum, of the University of California, Los Angeles, and Chancellor John S. Galbraith of the University of California, San Diego.

The collection of more than forty volumes and manuscript boxes of Morley Papers at the India Office Library was "opened" for scholarly use in 1959, and with the cordial cooperation and kind assistance of the librarian, Stanley Sutton, C.M.G., I was given full and immediate access, not only to these papers, but to all other relevant primary source materials so carefully preserved at his fine library. I am deeply indebted to Mr. Sutton for his felicitous, patient, and prompt assistance over the past five years. Mrs. Molly C. Poulter, who has recently completed a two-volume *Catalogue of the Morley Collection* (India Office Library, 1965), was particularly helpful in assisting me through the maze of manuscript materials entrusted to her excellent care. Miss J. Lancaster, keeper of the India Office Records, was equally cooperative, and thanks to her comprehensive command of the vast collections of official documents in her charge, greatly expedited my search for relevant data, as did her assistant, Mr. Martin Moir. I wish also to express my personal thanks to Miss K. Thompson, and to the many other members of Mr. Sutton's staff, who so kindly facilitated my research on this project.

Minto's letters to Morley from India are included among the Morley Papers, as are his telegrams, and many of the most important dispatches sent by the government of India to the secretary of state at Whitehall, but in addition to these, I have used microfilm copies of part of the Minto Papers preserved at the National Library of Scotland in Edinburgh. I am most grateful to Mr. James S. Ritchie of the NLS for his cooperation in making these Minto manuscripts available to me, and to the Director of Publications, H.M. Stationery Office, for granting me permission to purchase and use these reproductions of Crown copyright material.

There are several other manuscript and document collections containing Morley primary source materials at the British Museum, the Public Record Office, and the British Library of Political and Economic Science of the London School of Economics, and I gratefully acknowledge the prompt and courteous permission I received to consult all these during both of my visits to London, while at work on this study, in 1961 and 1963. I wish to express my special appreciation to Mr. C. G. Allen, librarian of the Library of Economic and Political Science, for his learned assistance; to Mr. J. G. Ryall of the Foreign Office for granting me permission to use the papers of Sir Edward Grey, containing correspondence with Morley, at the Foreign Office Library at Cornwall House; to Mr. K. W. Humphreys, librarian at the University of Birmingham, for sending me microfilm of the Morley-Chamberlain letters deposited at his library; and to Mr. Gustavo Duran, who so generously gave me copies of his private letters from Morley to Mr. Henry Crompton.

I wish to acknowledge the gracious permission of Her Majesty, Queen Elizabeth II, to make use of the papers of King Edward VII in the Royal Archives, Windsor. I sincerely thank Mr. Robert Mackworth-Young, librarian of the Windsor Archives, for his helpful cooperation, and his assistant, Miss Langton, for her expeditious aid in my research.

Morley had no natural heirs, and when his wife died just a few weeks after he did, his private papers were left with his adopted nephew, Guy Morley, who passed most of them on to Morley's close friend, the biographer of his early life, Francis Wrigley Hirst. Hirst deposited most of the papers, which now compose the Morley collection, in the Records Department of the India Office. There were many other private letters and papers, however, not concerned with Morley's India period, which he retained, intending perhaps to use them in writing the second half of Morley's "Life," though he never completed that projected work. Since Hirst's death in 1953 these private papers have been held in trust by several people, including Mrs. Hirst, who left them in the care of Professor A. F. Thompson, of Wadham College, Oxford. I learned of this strange odyssey of Morley's literary legacy after a lengthy search, but when I wrote to Professor Thompson, appealing for permission to consult these papers, I was curtly informed that "the Morley papers in my possession are not available." Sir Edward Boyle, who also possessed some private Morley papers, was most cooperative in discussing Morley with me, but regrettably enough, he too has left his portion of Morley correspondence with Thompson. It is hoped that the latter may someday decide to release these precious papers for scholarly use, or else deposit them with the Morley collection at the India Office Library, where they will receive the archival attention they deserve.

I wish to express my personal thanks to Mrs. Ruth Waley, Edwin Montagu's niece, for her kind assistance, and, although belatedly, to her now deceased husband, Sir David Waley. To the South Asia Center of the Institute of Internatioanl Relations at Berkeley, and to the Research Committee of the Academic Senate of UCLA, I am indebted for financial assistance over the past four years, which has helped me complete my research. I am also most grateful to the excellent Central Stenographic Service at UCLA for their prompt, efficient, and always courteous assistance to me in the typing of my entire manuscript. I gratefully acknowledge the encouragement and unstinting cooperation I have received from the University of California Press, and wish to note my special appreciation to Mr. Robert Y. Zachary, Los Angeles Editor, for his generous and cordial assistance in expediting the publication of this work. I warmly thank Mrs. Grace H. Stimson of the Press, for her expert editorial aid. My friend and colleague in Indian history, Professor Blair Kling, of the University of Illinois, kindly gave of his time in reading the completed manuscript, and I am indebted to him for his valuable editorial suggestions. Finally, to my wife, who has shared my travail at every stage of this manuscript's preparation, my heartfelt thanks.

S. A. W.

CONTENTS

INTRODUCTION 1

1 JOHN MORLEY 10

2 CURZON'S LEGACY 30

3 WHITEHALL VERSUS SIMLA 41

4 THE ARMY AND FOREIGN AFFAIRS 75

5 PILLS FOR THE EARTHQUAKE 98

6 AN ACT OF REFORM 129

7 RACIAL RELATIONS 167

8 SEPARATE AND UNEQUAL 185

9 UNFINISHED SYMPATHY 201

10 LAISSEZ FAIRE VERSUS SVADESHI 211

11 THE PAST AS PROLOGUE 229

NOTES 239

BIBLIOGRAPHY 285

INDEX 295

INTRODUCTION

> True history is the art of rapprochement—bridging distances of place and circumstance.
> Morley's *Recollections*, II, 67

The surging tide of Liberalism which swept over Britain in 1906 ushered in an era of change for India as well, change so fundamental and pervasive that within half a decade the pattern was set for one of the most momentous historical transitions of modern times, the transformation of Britain's Indian Empire into the nation-states of India and Pakistan. For recent Indian history the years 1906–1910 were in many ways a watershed era. Constitutional reforms then fashioned and introduced mark the turning point between the frost of the old raj, whose centralized bureaucratic autocracy reached its peak during Curzon's reign, and the gradual thaw of decentralization and devolution of British power toward the goal of parliamentary self-government for India. These same reforms, moreover, stimulated a sense of political communalism among India's Muslim minority, transforming what had hitherto been a socioreligious and cultural conflict between Hindus and Muslims into a separatist national movement under the Muslim League, which resulted in the birth of Pakistan. The era was one of revolutionary discontent as well as reforms, and for the Indian National Congress marked the open split between Gokhale's "moderate" Conventionists, and Tilak's "extreme" New Party. Never before, since the Crown's direct assumption of power in 1858, had so many currents and countercurrents of agitation and political consciousness filled the Indian atmosphere. The turbulence generated by new ideas, new demands, and mass discontent over the partition of Bengal, generally labeled "unrest" by the government of India, evoked harsh and arbitrary measures of repression, adding a bitter taste to the pills of reform. Cries of *svadeshi*, boycott, and *svaraj* were muted by deportation without trial, and by trial without the safeguards of British justice. Terror of incipient revolution turned bureaucrats into tyrants just as British liberal democracy took its first steps toward transplanting its most cherished parliamentary institutions onto Indian soil. Political assassination developed into a nationwide cult together with the dawn of representative government for India. Never in the half century of the raj's existence were the beneficent policies of British rule in England so darkly obscured by the autocratic actions of British rulers in India. This era of change was thus one of ambivalent actions and aspirations also, replete with paradoxical promises, of hope and fear, reform and repression fixed like the two faces of Britain's Janus head, inextricably locked together while constrained to confront opposite horizons.

The British Indian Empire at this time embraced a population of almost 300 million, spread over 14 provinces and more than 500 princely states from Baluchistan to Burma, from Kashmir to Travancore. In the capital at Calcutta alone there were more than a million people; in Bombay city, the premier commercial center, almost as many. Of the 200,000 Europeans (mostly British) then residing in India, less than 2,000 made up the elite corps of Indian civil servants, who ruled over the predominantly impoverished peasant population of that "brightest jewel" in the British Crown. The hill station "summer capital" of Simla, perched more than a mile above sea level, ensconced like an eagle's nest in the Punjab hills more than 100 miles north of Delhi, was for most of the year headquarters of the raj, where the viceroy and his council, and the commander in chief with his staff, surrounded by their bureaucratic beehive, lived aloof from the blistering plains. Almost half the world away, some three weeks remote by the fastest land and sea route, though within a day's communication by cable, stood Whitehall's India Office in London. There, from his spacious office facing St. James Park, the secretary of state for India, one of His Majesty's five secretaries of state in the British Cabinet, ruled the roost that ruled over the Empire. Throughout this half decade of travail that secretary was John Morley (after April, 1908, Viscount Morley of Blackburn), heir to the mantles of Gladstone and John Stuart Mill, the leading anti-imperialist, antijingoist intellectual of the Campbell-Bannerman and first Asquith cabinets.

The personification of Liberalism, and acknowledged "conscience" of his party, Morley at the helm of India's empire was keenly aware of the irony of his own position. During his five years at the India Office, he wrestled relentlessly with the insoluble problem of trying to find some equitable formula through which British democracy could continue to rule its largest dependency. Responsible as he was to Britain's first truly Liberal and democratic House of Commons, while autocratically empowered with full administrative control over India, Morley became the focal point of critical tension and conflict between the freedom-charged environment of Westminster's lower house, and the bastion of bureaucracy entrenched at Simla. His position was even more anomalous because of the veto power on legislation retained by the still overwhelmingly Tory House of Lords throughout this period. When the strain of India Office work at his advanced age obliged Morley to abandon the Commons for a seat in the less hectic upper house in 1908, many radical friends deplored his "elevation" to the chamber he once had vowed "to mend or end."[1] In 1911, however, as Lord President of the Privy Council, Morley was instrumental in bringing the Lords' veto to an end by announcing that he held George V's warrant to create enough new lords to enact any legislation carried by the Commons unless the peers present agreed to accept Asquith's Parliament bill. This threat by the Crown to pack the Lords was so extreme a measure for British parliamentary government that it could hardly have been resorted to earlier, but it came too late to ease the path of Morley's own Indian reform legislation. He was, nonetheless, the first secretary of state for India who labored to bridge the polar gap between the political systems of the Commons and Simla; who, despite the obstacle of the Lords, significantly breached the walls of the government of India's bureaucracy. Previous secretaries, even the "liberals" Kimberley and Fowler, had neither Morley's personal inclination and talent to attempt this herculean task, nor nearly his number of radical gadflies in the Commons to goad them to reluctant action.

Throughout this turbulent half decade of change, Morley played a unique role in the articulation and formulation of the reforms for which it is most famous, despite the paradoxical ambivalence of his position, which seems microcosmically to reflect the greater paradox of the British Indian raj, replete as it was throughout this time with ambivalent ideals, aspirations, policies, and pronouncements. Then, too, Morley's prestige in India as well as in England, his fame as an author and philosopher, his notoriety as a radical and agnostic, his peculiar power in the Commons as a front bencher to whom those below the gangway looked with reverence rather than antipathy, and his unrivaled position as the last living "master" of India's Liberal elite, endowed his name and actions, his monumental and paltry failures and successes alike, with a charismatic quality of importance far greater than that of any other individual involved at this time with India's destiny. Only Kitchener at the one extreme, and Tilak at the other, came close to being his rivals in fame, but Morley kept the old soldier in close rein, allowing him to retire without the coveted viceroyalty Kitchener desired, while for the latter half of this era Tilak languished behind prison bars in distant Mandalay. Several attempts have been made by his family and friends,[2] and some by scholars,[3] to elevate the role of Lord Minto in this era to that of at least copartnership with Morley in the making of policy; and to date, for the lack of a better rubric, the period itself is usually referred to as that of the "Morley-Minto Reforms." I consider this designation so exaggerated and erroneous a historical exaltation of the image of a viceroy, who was at best a mediocre representative of his peers in that office, that I have dealt at some length in subsequent chapters (especially iii and vi) with the myth about Minto's greatness. The accident of history which has linked his name to Morley's need hardly be perpetuated, certainly not from the perspective of more than half a century.

Time, moreover, has cleared many of the clouds of intellectual partisanship raised by the nationalist struggle. After almost two decades of Indian independence the history of British India may now be viewed more as the prelude to self-government for India and Pakistan, than either as the fulfillment of Empire's "destiny" or as a monolithic obstacle to Indian freedom. The inspirational, cooperative, and educational role played by some British statesmen throughout this epoch of transition can no more be ignored by Indian scholars, than should the degrading, repressive, and tyrannical role of other British officials be denied by British students. No nation can afford to forget the rich legacy of its past, and for Britain and India that legacy in great measure was a common one during some ninety years of direct British rule over

INTRODUCTION

the subcontinent of South Asia. Nor is the history of British India so exotic a subject as to be without special relevance to modern America. Perhaps foremost among the crucial problems of Morley's era was the question of whether a democracy, which cherished freedom at home, could in fact successfully rule an Asian empire by autocratic machinery. The racial question, moreover, was a heated issue of this time, and one of Morley's major reforms was to bring Indians into the hitherto inviolate sanctuaries of official white supremacy, the executive councils of the viceroy and the secretary of state. The struggle between civilian and military rule was still another matter brought to the forefront of British Indian consciousness by the titanic battle between Curzon and Kitchener, from which the general had emerged the victor in 1905, leaving him in a position of unmatched power and prestige on the Indian scene when Morley came to office. Had Morley been a weaker secretary, or less adamant about preserving the constitutional primacy of civil over military rule, Kitchener could easily have become India's "Iron Viceroy" in 1910. Questions of civil rights, the political demands of special minorities, centralization versus federalism, laissez faire versus protection—all add a peculiarly modern ring of contemporary interest to the problems daily demanding Morley's attention, urgently calling for some measure of legislative or administrative resolution. It is always fascinating, often illuminating, but at times depressing, to see how one of the greatest intellectuals and statesmen of his day tackled these problems, seeking practical formulas of long-range policy and immediate action by which they might be ameliorated. The sympathy, insight, and wisdom that Morley brought to his work were unique in the history of his predecessors and successors at the India Office, though his own disciple Edwin Montagu came closest to rivaling Morley's manner. Yet it is perhaps but faint praise to note that in the nine decades of British rule over India from Whitehall, no other secretary of state left so indelible an imprint upon the India of his times, set so distinctive a tone to his tenure. If any Englishmen were Morley's peers in their impact on Indian history they were rather viceroys like Ripon and Mountbatten, and the "father" of India's National Congress, Allan Octavian Hume.

Although four important studies on this era have been published since 1917, I believe none to date has adequately grasped its historic significance, or properly assessed the roles of its leading figures. The first illuminating picture was drawn by Morley himself in part of the second volume of his *Recollections* (New York: Macmillan, 1917). Book V of that memoir, entitled "A Short Page in Imperial History," deals with India from 1906 to 1910, reproducing excerpts from Morley's weekly letters to Minto in chronological order without any retrospective narrative link between the selected passages. Although Morley had retired from public office by this time (he resigned from the cabinet in 1914 when its majority decided to enter the First World War), the still secret nature of many of the subjects mentioned in his letters to the Viceroy dictated the highly selective use he made of them, just as discretion obliged him to delete the names of living officials discussed in any derogatory way in these documents. While remaining the best published primary source, therefore, for his era, Morley's volume is hardly a history of it, nor does it pretend to be. In 1934 Mary, Countess of Minto, published her volume entitled *India, Minto and Morley, 1905–1910* (London: Macmillan, 1934), which, by quoting at some length from Morley's letters to Minto as well as from Minto's to Morley, and including copious extracts from her own Indian diary, does pretend to provide a well-rounded history of this era. As a primary source of information about some facets of Indian life at this time, especially the official ceremonial éclat and viceregal-princely relations, which Lady Minto knew so well, this book is of value. Used together with Morley's *Recollections*, moreover, it has given us a broader view of many of the affairs discussed between viceroy and secretary of state. By itself, however, Lady Minto's memoir is as biased a eulogy of her husband's viceroyalty as any so brilliant and ambitious a woman might have been expected to write after his death.

After the Morley and Minto papers were opened for scholarly investigation in 1959, several students and fellows at London's School of Oriental and African Studies used them for dissertation and monographic research. The first fruit of such revived interest in this period was published in 1964, when two studies appeared: one by the Pakistani scholar Syed Razi Wasti, entitled *Lord Minto and the Indian Nationalist Movement, 1905 to 1910* (Oxford: Clarendon Press); the other by the Indian scholar M. N. Das, entitled *India under Morley and Minto: Politics behind Revolution, Repression and Reforms* (London: George Allen and Unwin). Wasti's study is most valuable as a contribution to the early history of Muslim politics in India, but unfortunately accepts Lady Minto's uncritical view of her husband's role, grossly distorting its overall historical perspective, and practically ignoring the positive role played by Morley. Das has produced the best general analysis of this era to date. He comes much closer than Wasti to understanding the dynamic complexity of the era and appreciating its full significance to Indian history, though he too has failed to grasp the far-reaching import of Morley's policies, especially with respect to legislative council reforms. Das's best chapter, his fourth, entitled "Politics in India," has, however, dealt so comprehensively with the Indian side of "unrest" and "repression" that in my treatment (chap. v) of these important problems I have found it unnecessary to retrace the same ground.

I have not attempted in this study to write a comprehensive history of India from 1906 to 1910, but merely to place in clearer focus what I consider to be the basic policies and inadequacies of British rule during this era, to clarify the motives and personalities of the rulers of the raj, and, by dealing topically with the important issues raised in this half decade, to illuminate its significance to recent India's historical development. To students of South Asian history the most controversial questions raised by the study of this era are whether or not the Indian Councils Act of 1909 was meant to pave the way for parliamentary self-government in India, and whether the separate electorates granted to Muslims under the same act were in fact inaugurated as part of an officially sponsored British policy of divide and rule. I have devoted much of chapter vi to the first question, and deal with the second in chapter viii. The equally vexed, though somewhat broader, problem concerning the relative roles, in law and fact, between His Majesty's government at home and the government of India, in many ways central to the understanding of the changing pattern of British rule in this period, is considered in chapter iii. The fourth chapter deals with military and foreign affairs seen together because of the inseparable connection between the policies governing both matters. Chapter v is a study of the volatile internal disputes that evoked such severe measures of repressive response from the bureaucracy, grimly revealing not only the unpopularity of British rule, but the basic incompatibility of the two political systems it artificially sought to unite. Chapter vii is devoted to the Anglo-Indian racial problem, and the controversy that raged around Morley's measures of council desegregation. Here too, the fundamental hypocrisy of British rule, professing to follow one code of law and morality, while practicing its opposite, highlights the weakness of the world's seemingly most formidable and mighty empire. In a separate chapter (ix), consideration of decentralization and other reforms begun in this era reveals the full extent of Morley's reform aspirations and the ultimate goals of his policy. The tenth chapter is concerned with the key area of required reform for India—economics and finance—which was neglected almost entirely. The lurid plight of India's peasant population in this time of famine, plague, and depressed trade evoked no long-range proposals for official ameliorative action. The conflicting economic self-interests of Britain and India prove more clearly than all the political and civil strife of the time the real failure of the raj, its historic inadequacy and eventual untenability, even when led by the most sympathetic, liberal, and best-intentioned of rulers. The second and concluding chapters of this study note the dominant tone of Indian society at the dawn and after the end of this era, indicating those respects in which the mood of disharmony at the close of Curzon's reign was transformed to a new and more hopeful state for so large a segment of India's politically conscious leadership. In other, more fundamental ways, the cross of empire weighed even more heavily upon India's burdened frame, thorns of contention digging still deeper into her body politic, as she moved up the long and arduous route toward freedom.

My first chapter is a brief biographical study of Morley's pre–India Office career, in which I have stressed those currents of thought and action which contributed to his unique development, and helped prepare Morley for his most challenging and important historic role. In an age of increasing statistical and "scientific" historiography, my emphasis upon the biographical, the humanistic, aspect of historical causation may seem somewhat anachronistic, but the longer I study history the more impressed I have become with the importance of the human, individual factor in its total equation. This is not to deny the impact of impersonal "forces," the reality of institutional momentum, or the validity of such amorphous entities as group dynamics, communal allegiances, or national interests, but merely to affirm my own conviction that above, or behind, all these is man himself. No social scientific formula is sufficiently elastic to label him. No punch card can predict the capricious, perverse, contingent causation, whose resolution will help determine the vector of his action at any point in time. I have therefore stressed, wherever my sources have made it possible, the personal motivations, the individual personalities of the people, whose actions and interactions made this era as significant as it was to recent history. Morley, who was considered enough of a historian

INTRODUCTION

himself, by Edward VII at least, to have been nominated[4] for the chair of regius professor at Cambridge in 1902, concluded in the last year of his life (1923) that "history always misleads,"[5] and that because "far more depended on the conversations of half an hour, and was transacted by them than ever appeared in letters and despatches,"[6] the truth could "never" be known. This may be the worst way to conclude an introduction to a book based primarily on letters and despatches, but seems all the more justification for devoting at least one chapter to an attempt at better understanding the central figure of this era before embarking upon my topical analysis of his government's official actions and policies. Ideally, of course, the art of history should leave no corner of the past unexplored, no event unexplained. In practice, I fear, the writing of history, like politics, is ever but a second best.

I

JOHN MORLEY

> Public life is rather an arid pursuit compared with one's dreams as an ambitious collegian . . .
> Morley to Minto, July 18, 1907

> I was reading the other day . . . the saying of a divine—"Besides a man's professions, and gifts, and many of his sayings and acts—there is something else: there is the *man himself*." That is what one is apt to forget . . .
> Morley to Minto, October 30, 1908

Fog, dense and blinding as that of London alone can be, rolled impertinently past the gates of Buckingham Palace as the procession of elegant broughams clattered away from the royal grounds that afternoon of Monday, December 11, 1905. His Majesty's newly appointed Liberal cabinet soon found itself trapped in fog. The carriage bearing the foreign secretary, Sir Edward Grey, and his old friend, the new secretary of state for India, John Morley, was forced to a standstill on the Mall. Perhaps the ironic symbolism of Morley's plight, no sooner launched on his India Office career than lost, appealed to his wry Lancastrian humor, though this could hardly be called an auspicious beginning to the most important and difficult job of a long and active life.

Suspended limbo-like between Buckingham and Whitehall, on the threshhold of assuming responsibilities weightier than any he had ever shouldered, Morley might well have cast a reflective eye back over the strangely winding path that had brought him in sixty-seven years from the modest surgeon's home in Blackburn to an office commanding more power than was ever possessed by the grandest of Moghul monarchs. "A heavy load for a virtuous man of conscience,"[1] he would soon say of his new job.

For Morley life began on the night before Christmas in the second year of Victoria's reign, 1838, in the bleak Midlands mill town of Blackburn. Priscilla Mary Morley, nee Donkin, gave birth to her second son John, while the proud father, Dr. Jonathan Morley, no doubt watched the midwife's work with more than a professionally concerned eye. Reared in the heart of Lancashire at a time when England's Midlands were fast becoming the workshop of the world, young John imbibed doctrines of laissez-faire economics and Puritan diligence with his mother's milk, remaining a freetrader and tireless worker all the eighty-four years of his life. Although he was born and brought up on the right side of his mill town's tracks, John's hardworking, middle-class heritage (his mother was descended from a family of Northumbrian shipowners; his father was a self-made West Riding surgeon) no doubt predisposed him from childhood to sympathize with the plight of the downtrodden and overburdened among mankind. Certainly throughout his political career he was most popular among working-class artisans and miners, like his sturdy constituents of Newcastle, who more than admired his greatness, revering him indeed for the important ministry he commanded, yet loving him also as one of their own.[2]

Fortunately for India, John was born second among the three sons of Dr. Jonathan Morley. Had he been first he would have inherited his father's thriving practice, which went instead to elder brother Edward. If he had been third, on the other hand, he might have fallen victim to disease early in manhood, the fate of his younger brother William, who died in India, exiled there to seek his fortune, like so many youngest sons of mid-Victorian, middle-class families. As the second son, John was destined for the clergy, and thanks to that goal he received the best available private schooling in the hope that he might qualify for admission to Oxford. Two years at University College in London were followed by another two at Cheltenham, where, as was devoutly expected, young John won a scholarship to Oxford's Lincoln College in 1856. What better training ground, after all, for a boy preparing for the Methodist clergy than the very college once graced by John Wesley? But when he arrived at Lincoln, Morley found it in a state of "sad intellectual dilapidation," thanks to its rector, whom he remembered as "illiterate and boorish to a degree that was a standing marvel."[3]

Instead of stimulating his interest in theology, three years at Oxford served to convert John to agnostic positivism. He rejected all the formalities of religious ritual for the remainder of his life, insisting, among other things, that his initiation into the peerage (in 1908) be by affirmation rather than by oath, and specifying in his will that his body be cremated. Morley's repugnance for the trappings of religious doctrine and dogma, however, by no means softened the moral fiber of his character or undermined the lofty plane of simple piety on which he chose to live out his life. "Cut him open," his dear friend George Meredith once quipped, "and you will find a clergyman inside."

Like many of the brightest intellectual youths of the late 1850's and 1860's, Morley found more inspiration and vital message in John Stuart Mill's *Dissertations*, especially the essay *On Liberty*, than in all the tomes on theology which uninspired teachers had set before him. He translated *On Liberty* into immediate personal terms by informing his father in 1859 (the year the essay was published) of his decision against entering the clergy. Dr. Morley attempted to apply economic pressure, promptly stopping his son's allowance, but instead of relenting John quit Oxford without taking a degree, and moved to London to sink or swim there on his own. The new career he chose was free-lance writing, then as now no doubt one of the most perilous and precarious of occupations. He soon learned, as he later reminisced, the lesson early inscribed on every penurious young writer's mind and stomach, that if his "knack, whatever it amounts to, should cease to please, he starves." Happily, however, by 1861 he proved himself craftsman enough to become editor of the short-lived *Literary Gazette*, thanks to which he was asked to contribute to the more prestigious *Saturday Review*. The best of Morley's essays from the latter journal were published anonymously in two small volumes: *Modern Characteristics*, appearing in 1865; and *Studies in Conduct*, in 1867. When later advised to reprint these books, Morley promptly declined the honor, insisting that no one should be held responsible for ideas expressed in print before he had attained the age of forty. Yet, if none of these early essays were particularly distinguished for expression or content, all were competently written, somewhat in Baconian style, and reflected the rebellious spirit of radical youth striking out at the stodgy mores of middle-aged society, and the pompous pretentions of "Middle-Class Morality," the title of the best essay in the second volume.

For John Morley these monetarily lean years of his London literary apprenticeship were among the richest in intellectual stimulation and growth. His new friends included such men of genius as Meredith and Mill. Although he first met the latter in 1865, Morley quickly became a regular guest at John Stuart Mill's Sunday dinner "seminars" at Blackheath, remaining Mill's devoted disciple till the end of his days.[4] In so many ways the reflection of Mill, Morley seemed almost more like a natural son of the Saint of Rationalism than his intellectual heir alone. In appearance, manner, and intellectual style, master and student were tuned to the same pitch. Morley's own descriptions of Mill could as easily serve as self-portraits. Both men were quite short, or "spare in build,"[5] as Morley put it, with "voice low but harmonious" and "eye sympathetic and responsive." Both were high-strung, sensitive, and rather reserved, "to a fault," thicker-skinned critics like Joseph Chamberlain insisted. Even as Mill was denigrated as "Spinster" and "Finishing Governess" by those who, like Fitzjames Stephen, mistook him to be as "cold as ice," and a "walking book," Morley was mocked as "that old-maidish Priscilla" by Campbell-Bannerman, and condescendingly labeled an ideologue by the less intellectual Asquith. More discerning eyes looked past the superficially cold visages of both to, as Ramsay MacDonald recognized in Morley's case at least, the "warm heart."[6] With Mill as well as with Morley, what was at times mistaken for lack of passion was in fact the strenuous, often precarious, harnessing of intensely passionate spirits by even more powerful mental discipline. The briefest perusal of Mill's correspondence with Harriet Taylor would suffice to dispel entirely so naïve a misconception of his personality as betrayed by phrases like "cold as ice." The same holds true with respect to what little is known of Morley's marriage.

In commenting on Mill's marriage to Mrs. Taylor, Morley noted the "pregnant melancholy truth" of Scott's observation that "the wisest of our race often reserve the average stock of folly to be all expended upon some one flagrant absurdity."[7] Here he might as appropriately have been referring to his own marriage to Rose Ayling. Like Mrs. Taylor, Mrs. Ayling already was married when she met her eminent second spouse-to-be, and remained so till her first husband died of an illness several years later. It is hardly exaggeration to speculate that, but for the socially unpardonable circumstances surrounding his marriage, Morley might well have become Britain's foreign secretary, possibly even prime minister. He was quite well aware, moreover, when he married his "very pretty and graceful girl" shortly after his mother died in 1870, that "for family and other clearly political reasons"[8] the marriage was "not prudent." Impulsive and warmhearted as he was, however, Morley felt at the time that "in some aspects, life is too short for prudence." Yet he and his wife were to be vouchsafed more than half a century together, for she died less than two months after him in 1923. Mrs. Morley rarely entertained and almost never accompanied her husband on his social engagements. Even when invited to dine with friends as close as Mill, she declined, and Morley had to explain that "she is unfortunately so much of an invalid, that she is forced to deny herself the pleasure."[9] They lived in quiet seclusion from society, pariahs as much by choice no doubt as by necessity. Although she bore him no offspring, Rose brought the children of her first marriage to be reared in his household. During Morley's tenure at the India Office, adding personal tragedy to his massive burden of public responsibility, his stepson, John Ayling, was to be indicted on five charges of forgery and sentenced to ten years in prison.[10]

Mill's death in 1873 left Morley bereaved for the "best and wisest man that I can ever know," one whose memory would "always be as precious to me as to a son."[11] Mill's influence on Morley was all-pervasive, as only that of the greatest of teachers could be, inspiring emulation at every level, from petty mannerisms of dress and behavior to lifelong goals and ambitions. As author, philosopher, and politician-statesman, Morley walked in the steps of his master. *On Compromise*, his most important philosophical essay, was clearly modeled after *On Liberty*, and published within a year of Mill's death as an enduring memorial to the teacher whose inspirational life's message Morley defined thus: "Try thyself unweariedly till thou findest the highest thing thou art capable of doing, faculties and circumstances being both considered, and then do it."[12] Like Mill, for years the Liberal member from Westminster, Morley stood for election to Parliament at Blackburn in 1869, but lost as he did again, in more direct emulation of his deceased master, when he tried for the Westminster seat itself in 1880.

Perhaps the most significant way chosen by Morley to emulate Mill, or rather to attempt to complete the prematurely unfinished labor of his guru's lifetime, was by accepting the position of Indian secretary. As examiner of India correspondence, Mill's rank at India house after thirty-five years of service had been second only to that of the "Honourable Company's" secretary when Parliament assumed direct control over Indian affairs in 1858. Mill personally was the "chief manager of the resistance which the Company made to their own political extinction,"[13] and was left so embittered by his defeat before the forces of Palmerston that, though twice offered a seat on the newly created Council of India, he chose instead to retire. It was one decision in which Morley obviously considered his master mistaken, not only because Mill "undoubtedly knew more of India than all Secretaries of State ever installed there put together,"[14] but because by refusing council membership he eluded the old acid test of the Greeks that "office shows the man." Morley himself never shrank from that test, though this time he must have sensed he was about to face the hardest trial of his life.

Less immediate, yet almost equally potent, sources of inspiration to John Morley in his pre-Parliament period of early manhood included individuals as diverse as Benjamin Disraeli and Edmund Burke. Though politically one of Gladstone's leading lieutenants, Morley's mercurial temperament, cosmopolitan intellectual taste, and epicurean predilections bore closer affinity to the "Great Tory" than to the "Grand Old Man of Liberalism." Indeed, as he noted in 1865, Dizzy's "strange career" had much to do with the "political ambition of so many clever lads"[15] of the day, including John Morley himself. "About the most intimate friend"[16] Morley had in the 1870's was the poet-diplomat George Bulwer, later Lord Lytton, who served Disraeli's government as Indian viceroy from 1876 to 1880. Although their friendship was strained to near rupture[17] by Lytton's reactionary India policy, Morley was close enough to the most artistically talented and Bohemian of India's viceroys to confide how "unwell, depressed, morose, and flaccid" he felt on achieving the age of forty. "Quarante ans! It make me feel very solemn and didactic,"[18] he confessed. Yet for all his years, gout, and chronic dyspepsia, and "in spite of Tory government and prospect of a sevenpenny income tax," Morley concluded that life was worth living. In the 1870's he met and befriended Arthur Balfour and Joseph Chamberlain, both destined to become leaders of the opposing political party, though they remained close personal friends of Morley's till the end.

If the examples of Mill and Disraeli sparked Morley's political aspirations, however, he turned to no less a master than Burke for deeper instruction in politics. The subject of Morley's first full-length book, published in 1867, Edmund Burke remained his lifelong mentor "in the strategy and tactics of public life." From Burke he learned the "profound lesson," that "in politics we are concerned not with barren right, but with duties; not with abstract truth, but with practical morality."[19] Just as Comte and Mill weaned him from theology, the study of Burke's life lured Morley to the "empirical art" of politics. He could never again rest content with "a narrow Utopianism—the besetting weakness of most other great writers on politics,"[20] but was, thanks to Burke, inspired to test his moral principles in the cauldron of public action. Burke's abhorrence of the revolutionary chaos of his time served to temper Morley's radicalism to the extent at least of infusing a healthy measure of respect for legal procedure and parliamentary practice into the young man's political philosophy. With Burke, he recognized that "living, after all, must be the end of life, and that stable peace must be the end of Society."[21] Critics who accused Morley of "abandoning the principles of a lifetime" during his India Office career when he sanctioned certain repressive measures failed to appreciate how deeply ingrained and fundamental was his reverence for law and order. He was both a radical and a democrat, but never an anarchist or a revolutionary. His heart recognized in a Mazzini the "voice of conscience in modern democracy," but his head judged Cavour's statesmanship of far greater value to Italy and the progress of mankind. Beneath all the trappings of Burke's conservatism, Morley identified the "one supreme idea" that animated his hero as "the adaptation of the established order of government to the wants and the interests of the governed."[22] However unconsciously, Burke's labors, he felt, did prepare the way for "true Democracy" by insisting that "government existed for the people, and that the will of the people is the irresistible master of those to whom it has entrusted the guardianship of its rights."[23]

Morley was indebted to Burke, however, for more than the general principles that helped guide his public life. Burke introduced him to Indian history as well,[24] and made him conscious of the desperate need for Indian reform. Indeed, remarkably much of Morley's India Office policy has its earliest intimations in his thin "Historical Study" of Edmund Burke. There for the first time he came to grips with the moral dilemma of England's role in India. Perhaps, as he judged Burke did, Morley, too, retained "a silent conviction that it would have been better for us and for India if Clive had succeeded in his attempt to blow out his brains in the Madras counting house,"[25] but since instead he had founded an empire, the problem Clive's British heirs had to resolve was how best to govern it. Man's situation, in Burkian terms, was, after all, preceptor of his duty. Were Britain to abandon her control over India "from however exalted motives," the immediate result would be "disaster and confusion." She was left with no choice, therefore, but to rule as justly as possible, bearing in mind the "great lesson" of Warren Hastings' impeachment: "That Asiatics have rights, and that Europeans have obligations." Morley awarded Burke the laurel wreath of "lasting reverence" as "the first apostle and the great upholder of integrity, mercy and honour in the relations between his countrymen and their humble dependents."[26] His own scathing criticism of bureaucratic indifference and official arrogance is often reminiscent of Burke's trenchant forays against Hastings. Both men detested all that was imbecile or arbitrary, especially "folly and cruelty in high places."

Steeped as he was in Burke's diatribes of righteous indignation, Morley saw the stains of vice and greed splattered broadside across the early pages of British India's history. He recognized the continuing obstacles, moreover, to improving relations between Englishmen and Indians, not the least of which was geographical distance, while "the corrupting effects" of conquest and spurious superiority of race added still wider gulfs of human social distance to be bridged by Englishmen serving in India. Burke's insistence that the dominant power was obliged to "observe the highest current morality" in all its dealings with a subject people became the moral imperative underlying Morley's India Office policy. The only ultimate justification, moreover, for continuing British rule in India was seen by Morley, as by Burke, in that dominion's being "a trust for the benefit of the inhabitants of India."[27] The first installment of Morley's *Burke* appeared in the *Fortnightly Review* of February, 1867, the year in which Morley completed his literary apprenticeship by becoming editor of that important journal.[28] Founded in 1865 by Anthony Trollope, Frederic Chapman, and its first editor, George Henry Lewes, the *Fortnightly* grew during Morley's fifteen years of deft editorial supervision into the most influential radical journal of its time. The list of its regular contributors between 1867 and 1882 reads somewhat like an index of mid-Victorian intellectual history, including such luminaries as Thomas Henry Huxley, Herbert Spencer, Matthew Arnold, Leslie Stephen, Charles Swinburne, Walter Pater, Frederic Harrison, and, of course, Trollope, Mill, Meredith, and Morley himself. No one but an editor of Morley's own literary and political talents could have attracted so brilliant a constellation of artists and advanced thinkers. Much later in life Morley recollected how "audacious" he was accused of being in opening the *Fortnightly*'s pages to such radical new ideas as Huxley's popularization of Darwinian theory, and how Fitzjames Stephen said he was taking "great risks" by spelling *God* with a small g, "though whether he meant here or hereafter I don't know."[29]

Morley's own writing in the *Fortnightly* reflected the ambivalence of his interests—what was to remain for the rest of his years an unresolved internal tug-of-war between literature and politics. He tried his best to reconcile both passions either by writing about subjects of topical political interest or by tackling biographies of politicians and statesmen like Burke, Cobden, and Gladstone. In the May *Fortnightly* of 1868, he launched his series of biographical studies of French luminaries of the eighteenth century with, improbably enough, that champion of Catholic reaction, Joseph de Maistre. It was Morley's nascent interest in Ireland, however, which led him to investigate de Maistre's career as exemplifying ultramontanism's spirit and power. By the October issue de Maistre was finished, and Morley could turn to his true hero of eighteenth-century France, the moderate scholar-statesman, Turgot. Here again, as in his *Burke*, Morley affirmed his faith in political order, and showed his preference for evolutionary rather than revolutionary change. Though his *Voltaire* (1872) and *Rousseau* (1873) abound with sympathy for the egalitarian, democratic ideals of the revolution, both were acutely critical of their flamboyant subjects. Morley's affection for Voltaire at least was not unmixed, and years later, while writing his *Gladstone*, he noted a "parallel" between his younger terrier, Eileen, and Voltaire, especially with respect to "spitefulness."[30] The last of his great Frenchmen was Diderot, whose encyclopedia's massive tomes surrounded Morley from morning till night, "like being in a tunnel; or like making a tunnel,"[31] throughout most of 1875.

Diderot and the Encyclopædists (1878) does not, however, complete the list of John Morley's books published during this prolific literary interlude in his life. A volume of biographical sketches and reviews, *Critical Miscellanies*, appeared in 1871. *The Struggle for National Education*, published in 1873, was written in response to Forster's education bill as an ardent and persuasive argument in favor of complete separation of Church and state in matters of public education. Morley's radical criticism of that legislative measure, carried by Gladstone's first administration, brought him into initial conflict with the devout leader in whose last two ministries he was to hold honored positions. But in 1873 Morley considered it useless "trying to say smoothe things to the clergy. They are our foes," he wrote his radical comrade in arms, Joseph Chamberlain, "and one can't dissemble it."[32] Morley's ambition at this date was to use the *Fortnightly* to articulate a coherent platform for the still amorphous radical group represented below the gangway in Parliament by members like Chamberlain, Charles Dilke, and Henry Fawcett. He felt such an organ alone could show "the world" (by which he meant the "respectable middle class" who managed it) that there was "a group—a very small one—of men with a good many years of work before them who mean to press certain principles on the constituencies, irrespective of the old and worn out party grooves; men who know what they want, who believe they can in time bring the people over to them, and who intend intrepidly to go to work without more loss of time."[33] These principles were soon to emerge as the Liberal party's credo of peace, retrenchment, and reform. The *Fortnightly* under Morley was animated by what its editor termed a philosophy of "rationalism without chill." It clamored for freedom in school and church, as in field and factory, yet it called for social morality as well, especially in condemning rapacious employers who, under the fatuous guise of freedom, virtually enslaved their workmen. At such times Morley and his journal were denounced for radical "intemperance," to which charge he replied, "Intemperateness is only another name for being in earnest about some abuse which the upper classes want to keep."[34]

On Compromise, which appeared in 1874, went "through the young of those days like a flame,"[35] and elevated Morley's status in the world of letters from the debased coin of journalism to the pure gold of philosophy. He initially planned the book as a series of political papers designed to show "what a beggarly mood England is in just now, because she has no faith in Principles,"[36] but decided instead to "throw my notions on compromise into severe and philosophic shape." The result was a tone at times pontifical and a thesis perhaps belabored, though one well worth reiteration. Morley insisted that what "made all the difference" was whether truth was given first or second place in one's scale of values. The "principle" of clinging to truth and right was exalted from press and pulpit, he argued, yet "in practice" everyone compromised, "putting immediate social convenience in the first place, and respect for truth in the second."[37] He condemned the "slovenly willingness" with which most people hold "two directly contradictory propositions at one and the same time," and called for more integrity and honesty, and less "disingenuousness, self-illusion, dissimulation, indolence and pusillanimity."

By 1880 Morley's literary reputation was so exalted that he succeeded to the editorship of the *Pall Mall Gazette*, one of London's most prominent evening newspapers,[38] and was commissioned by Macmillan to write Richard Cobden's biography. Both of these tributes to Morley's writing talent, coming as they did the same year as his second defeat in campaigning for political office, might have sufficed to make a less ambitious man abandon his dreams of Westminster and rest content with his Fleet Street realm. But Morley's heart never truly belonged to the fourth estate. His three years at the throttle of the *Pall Mall Gazette* presses served more to enhance his reputation as a radical champion of Irish civil liberties and land reform, if not as yet home rule,[39] than to establish his name as a great editor. Morley's interest in Ireland seems to have stemmed from his first brief visit to the United States in the winter of 1867, where he was made rudely aware of how soiled an image of England the Irish revolt projected abroad. When Parliament passed the first of three Irish coercion acts in 1881, it was Morley's *Gazette* that most vigorously "fought against that mistake" evening after evening, predisposing such influential readers as Britain's future foreign secretary, Sir Edward Grey, to Irish home rule. In 1882 Morley paid his first visit to Ireland and continued to work vigorously against the coercion acts and in favor of land reform, though he could hardly have dreamed at the time that less than four years later he would be seated in the cabinet as Ireland's chief secretary.

As to Cobden, here again Morley's literary effort was inextricably bound up with politics, for if by 1880 his political creed could be defined in a word, the most accurate would have been "Cobdenism." Like Cobden's, his was an individualistic, laissez-faire, Little-Englander liberalism, with a healthy infusion of humanitarian concern and philanthropic generosity. If Burke taught him to doubt the wisdom of Britain's acquisition of India, Cobden led him to look with "a despairing eye" at the increasing drain of England's human and material resources required to maintain an empire from which there could be "no future but trouble and loss and disappointment."[40]

Early in 1883 Morley stood for the seat vacated by Ashton W. Dilke's death at Newcastle-on-Tyne, the then most populous constituency in Great Britain, a bustling mining, shipping, and industrial stronghold of the Liberal party. For at least ten years Morley had had his eye on Newcastle,[41] and his election as its second member in the spring of 1883 marked the beginning of his quarter of a century in the Commons, and was in many ways the most important turning point of his career. Though some half dozen of his books remained to be written, only one, his *Gladstone*, was a work of major importance, for after 1883 Morley gave the best of his days to political action. The high road of letters, along which he had started in 1880, had to be abandoned now for the rougher, more slippery climb toward the top of Westminster's greasy pole. The glamour of public life, after the Newcastle victory brought him inside its citadel, proved too tempting for Morley to resist at first, and later its obligations proved too compelling to elude. Yet he often cast a nostalgic eye at the road left untaken, confessing to one intimate in 1899 that he would "rather have been Victor Hugo" than "almost anyone."[42] and appearing "visibly disquieted"[43] near the very end of his life when he learned that Thomas Hardy said, "If only Morley had let politics alone he might have been the Gibbon of his age." He had chosen instead to try to become the Burke of his era.

From his maiden speech in the Commons, delivered with "quiet force" in a "fine, clear voice,"[44] Morley was accepted by the world's most discerning and critical club as a member whose statements mattered. He rarely enjoyed public speaking for his was too tense and self-conscious a personality, but when obliged to he spoke well, much the way he wrote, with eloquent simplicity and forthrightness of language, turning a phrase now and then for its own sake, yet never forsaking candor for rhetoric or truth for affectation. He came to be called "Honest John"[45] in this period by colleagues and constituents alike. When the general elections of 1885 brought home rule to the forefront of British politics, Gladstone brought Morley to the front bench of his party. Though technically subordinate to Ireland's lord lieutenant, the Earl of Aberdeen, Morley's cabinet seat as Irish chief secretary put him in actual control of his administration's key policy plank. Morley's new position was "at once generally regarded as decisive of Mr. Gladstone's ultimate intention"[46] to press for colonial government for Ireland. Thanks to the first home rule bill, however, the Liberal party became a house divided, and Gladstone's ministry was turned out by the Tories after a mere six months in power. But neither Morley nor his venerable leader abandoned the platform that was soon after to prove so disastrous to Liberal fortunes. "Ireland," as Morley put it, "is my polestar of honour, even if I were to know that I am driving straight on to failure."[47] He waited patiently for six years on the opposition front bench while Arthur Balfour fanned the flames of Irish passion for independence with a policy of unflinching coercion. Although ousted quickly from his office, Morley had proved himself so excellent an administrator that by the end of 1886 he was hailed by influential Liberal colleagues as "one of the foremost, most popular, most trusted leaders of the party."[48]

During the interlude between Gladstone's third and fourth ministries, Morley was probably the most articulate and popular member of the "shadow" cabinet, in the Commons as well as outside. His numerous speeches were trenchant, droll, and increasingly well received. By 1889 he could entertain after-dinner audiences by confessing that, though Tories called him a socialist,

[I am] a little at a loss sometimes to know what to call myself; because I have, I think, within the last 12 months seen myself styled by every possible political contradictory. I am sometimes a sluggish Whig. The next day a Nihilist. I am a grovelling Opportunist, then a doctrinaire with his head in the clouds. It is said that I am a Rousseauite without the passion of Rousseau; that I am a Burkite only without either the wisdom or the eloquence of Burke. I am a Jacobin and a Girondin; I am a Marlborough House man, and a St. Just. Such is the fate of an idealist who attempts to realize his ideal. Gentlemen, I do not call myself a Socialist. The name of Radical is good enough for me. (Loud cheers.)[49]

By ignoring all "millennial problems" he labored to prove that "practical idealism" was not an inherently contradictory goal. His motto became "Ago quod ago—I do what I am doing." "To each day its task"[50] had long been at the core of Morley's pragmatic response to life's many challenges, and was no philosophic expedient suddenly adopted after he moved into the India Office. "Let us achieve the task which is assigned to us," he told his confreres of the Eighty Club in 1889; "let us do what we have to do."

For Morley, among other things, that meant writing, and with the enforced leisure a Tory government provided he was able to undertake, for his old friend Macmillan, the editing of the popular series, "Twelve English Statesmen."[51] He himself wrote the biography of England's great eighteenth-century "peace minister," Horace Walpole, first published in 1889. Though never a doctrinaire pacifist,

Morley's abhorrence of war brought him into repeated conflict with the more aggressive wing of his party, led by the Earl of Rosebery in the 1890's, and later by Henry Asquith and Edward Grey. Gladstone himself leaned more toward Morley's pacifist predilections than to Rosebery's militancy, and was prepared to appoint Morley foreign secretary in 1892,[52] but neither Rosebery nor William Harcourt would have tolerated such supercession. Although ideologically he was closer to Harcourt than to Rosebery, Morley liked the latter but personally despised the former, considering Harcourt "coarse"[53] and "a windbag,"[54] and as late as 1891 doubtful that "he could ever serve with Harcourt"[55] on the same cabinet again. The June elections of the following year, however, returned some 355 Liberals and Irish nationalists to support Gladstone's last government, a coalition ministry with the precarious majority of forty votes in its favor. Once again "Honest John" was made Irish secretary, while Harcourt was moved to the Exchequer, and Rosebery to the Foreign Office.

Morley set about at once to revamp the business procedure of his department, putting himself into direct communication with all public bodies in Ireland rather than waiting for information to be filtered to him through his undersecretary.[56] He got to work immediately on the second home rule bill, which Gladstone presented to the Commons in April, 1893. The following year proved to be the most frustrating one of John Morley's life. The "Home Rule Parliament of 1893–94"[57] devoted no less than eighty-two full days of the labor and attention of the Commons to fierce debate over the momentous bill, which finally scraped through the lower house by a 34-vote majority, only to be ignominiously repudiated by the Lords, 419 to 41. It was the tragic finale to eight years of untiring effort and unflinching devotion to a single cause, which for Morley and Gladstone both had acquired as much the character of a personal obsession as of their political platform. Gladstone never recovered from the blow of this failure, retiring, defeated and dispirited, at the session's end, to be succeeded by Lord Rosebery who lacked the political acumen and stamina to keep the floundering Liberal party long above opposition waters. For Morley the bitter lesson of 1894 was not to be forgotten. He learned that to pilot a major bill through Parliament was not only the most arduous of ministerial responsibilities, but potentially the most treacherous. He saw years of his painstaking, patient labor negated by a single division in a single house. He learned never again to underestimate the obstructionist power of his reactionary adversaries, and though he now resolved "to mend them or end them" he knew that until the Lords could be stripped of their legislative veto they remained a constitutional factor with which he would have to reckon if ever he hoped to succeed in another major legislative effort. Now twice burned by reform bills, he became four times cautious, and much of Morley's anxiety in anticipation of Indian reforms can be understood only in the light of his still vivid memories of the Irish debacle. Had success crowned his campaign in 1894, Morley would have been undisputed heir to Gladstone's mantle of Liberal leadership. As it was, the rising star of his political career plummeted swiftly, for instead of inheriting the Grand Old Man's political fortune Morley's legacy became but a junior partner's debt in the now bankrupt cause.

Had Morley thrown his weight behind Harcourt instead of Rosebery during the Liberal succession struggle, it is more than probable that the reluctant peer of the 1890's would never have become Britain's premier. Morley was certainly justified, therefore, in expecting Rosebery to offer him a position more attractive than the Irish Office. Rosebery himself realized that Morley's hopes were pinned to the Foreign Ministry, but considered that "an impossible appointment, partly because his wife could not have received the Ambassadors' wives, she having a slight cloud on her, John having anticipated the ceremony of marriage."[58] Appointing Lord Kimberley foreign secretary instead, Rosebery offered Morley the now vacant India Office, simultaneously pressing him not to leave his Irish "post," and "by a self denying ordinance"[59] John agreed to "lock myself fast in the Irish backkitchen."[60] Knowing full well that home rule was dead for at least another session, Ireland was tantamount to a cabinet demotion, but worse shoals lay hidden in the troubled political seas ahead. In June, 1895, Rosebery grasped the opportunity offered by a vote of no confidence to resign, and the general election of the following month returned a thumping Unionist majority of 152 members to the Commons, ousting, among other Liberal leaders, John Morley, whose popularity had declined even in Newcastle.

He retired temporarily to the country, having fallen to the nadir of his political career, feeling himself a failure in every respect. "If your wanderings should bring you to Tomick, Beauly, N.B.," Morley wrote his good friend, Leonard Courtney, in July, 1895, "there you would find a peaceful hermit, ready to deliver to you any oracle which any occasion of public or private life may demand. Having made a mess of his own affairs, he is specially qualified to advise other people."[61]

But Morley did not long remain in the doldrums. Loath though he said he was "to go back to the parliamentary vomit at all,"[62] when pressed "hard" by Party whips, he ran in the February, 1896, by-election for the Liberal "pocket-borough" of Montrose Burghs. It seems historically appropriate that he was still a member for Scotland when he took command of Indian affairs just a decade later.

For the Liberal party it was a decade of headless floundering and fragmentation. Rosebery proved himself more of an imperialist than Salisbury, and, after passing his threadbare mantle of official leadership onto Harcourt's weary shoulders in 1897, did his best to destroy the party he had been incapable of commanding. With the aid of front benchers like Grey, Fowler, and Asquith, Lord Rosebery vied with Chamberlain and Milner for the statesman's share of popular plaudits won in battle by heroes like Kitchener and Jameson. The Liberal imperialists jumped noisily onto empire's bandwagon in Egypt and South Africa as the century rumbled to its militant finale for a Great Britain determined, wherever the pretext could be found, to grow ever greater. Unable to stem the tide of a party rushing so swiftly away from its primary principles, Harcourt resigned his leadership in December, 1898, and Morley joined him in this ultimate act of political protest. The party of Gladstone seemed as dead as its founder. Henry Campbell-Bannerman or "C. B.," as Morley called him, worthy millionaire of Dunfermline heritage, now presided over the opposition corpse in the Commons. Morley accepted him "as the lesser among evils," confidentially appraising his next prime minister in a note to his fellow radical, Charles Dilke, as "a Tory, perhaps, but so are they all, if in the pocket of R. [Rosebery]. He [Campbell-Bannerman] will hold his own (quietly) against R., if R. goes against Radicals in H. of C."[63] Tired now of the "heavy corvée" imposed on him by Montrose stumping, and of the "gush, buncombe and claptrap"[64] that filled the air of public life, Morley withdrew to the solace of writing.

He accepted Macmillan's commission to undertake the *Life of Gladstone* in the fall of 1898, moving with his wife and newly hired research assistant, the young Oxford Liberal, Francis W. Hirst, to Hawarden. For the next four years the small red house in the shadow of Gladstone's castle became John Morley's intermittent home. The job of sifting through the monumental mass of documentary material preserved at Hawarden proved almost too much for Morley, and he once observed to Hirst how fortunate Gibbon was to have written about a time for which so much of the primary source material had been destroyed. Asked what he should do "if all our material were burnt," Morley replied, "I should probably write a better book."[65] Many a faithful reader of all three copious volumes of the completed *Life*[66] might agree, though scholars have long been in Morley's debt for having reproduced so much valuable documentary evidence in this most significant of his historical biographies. Often, when he sat at Gladstone's desk, sifting through the overstuffed trunks and fading bundles of papers scattered around him, Morley must have felt misgivings about his fitness for the task he had embarked upon. As an agnostic, he knew he could never empathize with Gladstone's "all pervading pieties, though all through they were the key to him."[67] Moreover, although he had fought many a political battle at his leader's side, he had learned to doubt so much of late himself, that more than once he wondered if he truly understood how Gladstone felt about issues of crucial importance. Home rule, for example—had it been a mistake? "Mr. G." never *said* so, but had he thought it a mistake? The nagging doubts familiar to every historian became his constant companions in these years of literary travail. They were years of lonely labor. "The *solitude* of authorship on this scale and on such a theme," he confessed to Arthur Godley in mid-1902, "is, I assure you, formidable."

Had he begun perhaps to miss the political arena? Two years earlier, after calling the Khaki Election "the most hollow and insincere election since 1865," Morley expressed great relief at being "out of the hubbub."[68] Although he had risen fearlessly in the Commons in June, 1899, to denounce Kitchener's barbarous behavior at the Mahdi's tomb and had stood again to brave a national flood tide of jingoist passion that September in Manchester when he attacked the Boer War, Morley remained by and large aloof from public life between 1898 and 1904. Yet the formidable solitude of writing full time appears to have increased his tolerance for political strife. He was too old and experienced a hand at politics to remain very long in retirement once the fortunes of his party showed signs of revival in 1902. Balfour's budget that year raised the specter of protection, and the price of imperialism was recognized by his Unionist colleagues to be some scheme resembling "fair trade" rather than the Liberal gospel of free trade. Morley's warning to the Commons in 1901 that "it is idle for a militant Imperialist to say he is an ardent and unshakable free trader"[69] proved alarmingly prophetic. Yet in 1903 he still demurred at Campbell-Bannerman's overtures to return as a front-bench regular instead of remaining an inactive party reservist. He was not quite ready to put his "neck under the yoke again," anticipating that the "game of selfish intrigue" would continue, asking, "Why come near such a scene having once escaped?"[70] The virulence of Liberal League propaganda was too fresh a memory, moreover, to reconcile him to the idea of sitting "next to the bad fellows in your boat . . . if I can avoid their proximity." Finally, Morley argued, as much to convince himself perhaps as Sir Henry, that what he really wanted to do was "to *write*, which I can do, not to speak, which I cannot." He was in fact planning to write a biography of Cavour, and thanks to Carnegie's munificence now owned Acton's personal library, much of which he added to his own collection in the huge library room he had had constructed at his new Wimbledon Park home. At sixty-five, however, he would surely have been justified in retiring on the plea of age alone, had he been so inclined. But two years later he was back on public platforms, telling groups like the "Young Liberals" that "politics . . . are a great field of public duty," while books, unless they inspired and directed action were but "a very superficial form of self-indulgence—a kind of narcotic."[71] In the struggle for Morley's allegiance, life again emerged victorious over literature.

The fiscal controversy of 1904 lured him back to the battle front at Westminster, while the Unionist coalition collapsed as Liberals of every foreign policy complexion rallied to the clarion call of "Free Trade in danger!" Thinking perhaps of enhancing his qualifications for the Foreign Office, Morley visited America as Andrew Carnegie's guest late in 1904. He remained skeptical about the "not very promising experiment" of our political system, but greatly admired Theodore Roosevelt, whom he linked with Niagara as one of the "two wonders" he had seen in America. Shortly after returning in January from his "orgies of blue-point oysters, millionaires, the Atlantic Ocean, etc.," Morley made his way to Campbell-Bannerman's home to talk about "the political situation" and "offices." As in 1894, Morley's ambition was for foreign secretary, but Sir Henry proposed India. The idea of accepting the office he had turned down more than a decade ago was hardly flattering, and as late as November 25 Morley informed both Campbell-Bannerman and Grey: "I doubted if at the last moment I should not stand out." Until less than a week before the new ministry was formed, Grey persisted in refusing to accept the preferred Foreign Office unless Campbell-Bannerman agreed to move to the Lords, and leave Asquith, Grey's fellow Liberal Leaguer, to lead the Commons.

Sir Henry remained adamant in rejecting this "impossible" dictation from the imperialist wing of his divided household, and Morley thus persisted in the vain hope that he might still be offered the position for which he so long considered himself singularly well qualified.[72] If, however, Campbell-Bannerman capitulated to Grey, Morley decided to hold out for the Exchequer,[73] though if Grey backed down, taking the Foreign Office while leaving Sir Henry as premier leader of the Commons, he would "accept the India Office."

On December 2, 1905, Morley received "a message from Downing Street" and wired Campbell-Bannerman that "a certain personage," the conventional code designation for King Edward VII, desired that he keep himself "available Monday afternoon." Balfour's resignation was to be tendered before midday, December 4, and Campbell-Bannerman would then be called upon to form a new government. For the Liberal party a decade of wandering in the wilderness had come to an end. Grey surrendered at the eleventh hour to the new premier who proved he would not be "bullied," as Morley reported "the crisis" on the eve of receiving his seals from the Crown. "I would rather have stood outside," he added, with an almost audible sigh, "but they would not have it, so I am at the India Office."[74]

As the fog lifted, the ministerial carriage moved slowly along the Mall toward that imposing mass of marble beyond St. James Park, the bureaucratic beehive of Whitehall, standing as it did both geographically and symbolically between Downing Street and Westminster.

John Morley reached his office early that afternoon, appearing "older in manner"[75] than his private secretary, Frederic Hirtzel, had expected. But then he was old. His face was shrunken and wrinkled with innumerable scars of age and anxiety, his blue eyes so deeply sunken into "the delicate and finely moulded skull" that one visitor was soon to record he looked "like a mummied relic of the Gladstonian age."[76] Yet this "relic" wasted no time in getting to work. "The first question which he took up at once was the military administration question," Hirtzel noted in his diary that day, "and he worked through all the papers and saw every one he possibly could."

But unlike his Irish "backkitchen," India was virtually a world unknown to John Morley, as "vast as it is unfamiliar,"[77] he groaned after three months at his new office. It was a world more complex and strange than any his author's imagination might have contrived, yet he knew quite well that its thorny problems and desperate needs were all too urgently real. He drove himself harder than ever before, still he complained that the "day vanishes almost before it has dawned," despite the fact that for lunch "I usually munch a sandwich at my table here." At this time, moreover, he admitted in a letter to the viceroy that the "distance and the strangeness are terrible."[78]

Perhaps it was simply that India had become too big a problem even for the best-intentioned and wisest of strangers to resolve.

2

CURZON'S LEGACY

> When shall we learn . . . "that what attaches people to us is the spirit we are of, and not the machinery we employ"?
> Morley's *Recollections*, I, 129

By the dawn of 1906, even Englishmen of his own party put much of the blame for the "trouble in India" on the strained back of Baron George Nathaniel Curzon (later Earl and Marquess of Kedleston), who had served as governor-general and viceroy of India from 1899 through 1905. Balfour, who conceded having made only "two mistakes" during his premiership (1902–1905), confessed that one of them was "allowing Curzon to return to India"[1] after his visit back home in 1904. No British viceroy had in fact attempted so much on his own initiative as did Curzon, accepting so little advice or criticism either from his superior at Whitehall or subordinates in Calcutta, while for the most part contemptuously ignoring nonofficial opinion from Indian sources. Even Lord George Hamilton, Tory secretary of state from 1899 through 1903, and one of Curzon's most sympathetic supporters at home, eventually admitted that the egocentric viceroy with whom he had served had "led him a dog's life."[2] St. John Brodrick (later Viscount and Earl of Middleton), Hamilton's successor as Indian secretary from 1903 to 1905, was more blunt in comparing his former classmate's imperious posture, "whether in or out of India," with that "of Louis XIV—'L'état c'est moi.' "[3] Minto, the collapsing Tory government's choice as successor to Curzon in 1905, complained of "how intensely Curzon's egotism (I can call it nothing else) and ambitions have shed their influence over public life in India,"[4] reporting to Morley of "the bitter native feeling he has aroused against him by the Partition of Bengal and his speeches in connection with it." The Prince of Wales (who was crowned George V in 1910) reacted so strongly against Curzon's arrogance during his royal visit to India in 1905–06 that he "censured severely"[5] the departing viceroy, forming the negative impression at this time which, in 1923, became a key factor in keeping Curzon out of Number 10 Downing Street. Not the least of Curzon's adversaries, of course, was Lord Kitchener.

Though starting as a controversy over military administration, Curzon's vendetta with his famous commander in chief, the Earl of Khartoum and Broome, soon emerged as no less than a bitter struggle for control over the government of India waged "at daggers' drawn"[6] between Britain's foremost egoists of the hour. Kitchener's insistence, for reasons of "military efficiency,"[7] on the abolition of the military member of the viceroy's executive council (then General Elles) was attacked by Curzon as posing an unconstitutional military threat to civilian rule. The hero of Khartoum, however, pressed his ambitious scheme for army reorganization in India upon the cabinet's Committee for Imperial Defence, justifying his military policy by the cry of an ever-present "threat" of Russian invasion through Afghanistan.[8]

Curzon returned to India in December, 1904, determined to fight for retention of the system of dual military control, blissfully unaware, Brodrick noted, of "on what a precipice he stands with regard to Kitchener."[9] The Viceroy refused to accept arbitration by a royal commission under Lord George Hamilton, which Brodrick proposed to send to India in February. Thereafter, Simla swiftly became too small a place to support the openly conflicting titans. Curzon's "fatal" weakness, as perceived by Lord Esher, was his inability to "put aside *himself*."[10] Not that Kitchener could be accused of lacking vanity, though being far less brilliant than his adversary he was somewhat less arrogant, or at least more amenable to guidance, accepting the shrewd advice of much wiser men at home.[11] By March the antagonists were "radically divided, each accusing the other of imperiously setting aside all arguments which are not convenient, and each believing that the other frightens all his subordinates into compliance with his views."[12] Brodrick chaired a special committee of his council, including among its members outside military authorities like Lord Roberts, the former commander in chief for India, and Sir George White. The committee reported unanimously in Kitchener's favor, and after obtaining cabinet approval for his action, the Secretary of State personally drafted a strong dispatch on "Army Administration in India,"[13] which called for downgrading the Military Department, and reforms along lines suggested by the commander in chief. At that point "Curzon declared war," no longer corresponding privately with any one at the India Office in London, "thereby making the Government of India impossible."[14] Simla civilian officialdom "divided into hostile camps," as did the officer corps of the Indian Army. Tory leaders back home began to wonder if the cleverly ambitious young Viceroy was perhaps "thinking of establishing a party 'core' in opposition to Mr. Balfour!"[15] Balfour himself subsequently confessed that he did not "think George C. is (or ever has been) quite sane over this affair."[16] The end came in August. Curzon insisted that Brodrick had no right to refuse sanctioning the appointment of Sir Edmund Barrow, the Viceroy's nominee for the newly created post of military supply member. Brodrick, however, reported to King Edward the opinion of the cabinet that "unless the Secretary of State is to abrogate all his functions and look on while the military position in India is rendered impossible for Lord Kitchener the Viceroy must give way."[17] But George Curzon felt strongly enough about Barrow's appointment to "make a stand" for it against the weight not only of Kitchener now, but of the head of the India Office as well. On August 13, 1905, the Viceroy's resignation was laid before the King by Brodrick, and a week later, after Milner refused the offer to succeed Curzon, Minto's appointment was announced.

Ironically enough, the viceroy who had more often, and with greater success, asserted the government of India's independence of Whitehall than any of his predecessors was thus toppled from his Simla throne, less by the mighty soldier with whom he fought, than by the mild minister of state to whose "jealousy and vanity" he was later to ascribe "all the troubles."[18] In a pathetic letter to Kitchener shortly after her husband's resignation, Lady Curzon put in "a *human plea* for a peaceful *Finale* to this miserable experience," urging the commander in chief to "let the vital difference be with the *Secretary of State*," recalling that "just 3 years ago we were hassling with Brodrick [then secretary of war] to get him to send you to India. We little thought that in three years that same Brodrick as Secretary for India would be getting us out of Asia!"[19]

The six years of Curzon's viceroyalty, then, marked at once the peak and point of rapid decline in the power and prestige of the government of India vis-à-vis His Majesty's government at home. Minto never forgot the lesson of his predecessor's fall. If, however, he seemed to forget, Morley could remind him by mere mention of the word "Curzonian" (which hereafter became part of the Anglo-Indian lexicon) that even George Nathaniel Curzon, "that flaming figure of a man," who had tried to hold India as rigidly as the steel-lined corset held his own ailing spine, could not elude Whitehall's restraining rod. The resolution of Curzon's controversy with Kitchener, while superficially appearing simply to be a victory by the military over civilian government in India, actually was far more important as the first practical assertion of the constitutionally stipulated dominance of Whitehall's secretary of state over the government of India, an assertion which was to be irreversibly confirmed by Morley during his era.

While India's government was thus divided from top to bottom by so open and protracted a conflict between its two leading officials, a different sort of partition, of far greater significance to India, was perpetrated in the country itself. Bengal, the largest of British India's seven provinces, containing some 85 million people, more than a quarter of the subcontinent's total population, was divided on October 16, 1905, by the creation of the new province of Eastern Bengal and Assam. This partition, avowedly undertaken by government solely in the interests of administrative efficiency, evoked an unprecedented storm of popular (predominantly Hindu) protest when it was realized that the newly created province would have a Muslim majority of some 6 million. The scheme was then denounced by politically conscious Indian nationalists as the most naked and insidious example of the British government's "policy" of divide and rule. Popularly regarded at once as a reward to the predominantly politically passive and "loyal" Bengali Muslim community, partition was at the same time believed to be Britain's punishment of the vocal, politically self-assertive, if not actually "disloyal," Bengali Hindu intellectual community, whose leaders played so active a role in the National Congress. Whatever the actual merits of such arguments[20] may prove to be, the truth of their historic impact was no less real than that made by the "greased cartridge" complex among sepoy soldiers half a century earlier, or, to reverse the historic shoe, by the passion evoked with the phrase "black hole" among Englishmen a century and a half before. No amount of public disclaiming by the officials responsible for partition diminished the popular conviction that Curzon's imperial policy was based on Roman practice. Remarkably enough, Curzon himself went so far as to deny[21] all responsibility for the proposal, though partition remains the single most famous (or infamous) administrative act of his viceroyalty. As for Sir Andrew Fraser, lieutenant governor of Bengal from 1903 to 1908, he protested, perhaps too much, in a note subsequently written to Morley that the "policy of *'Divide et impera'* is one which, in my judgment, is entirely inconsistent with the principles of our policy in India ... it is utterly wrong to set one class against another, or to lean upon one class for the sake of repressing another."[22]

Shortly after taking over India's administration Minto found official opinion within his government "unanimous in approving" of partition as "the only possible solution of the undoubted difficulties of the position,"[23] yet he personally recognized that "local feeling" had been treated with "want of sympathy" in executing the matter, and that the actual line of partition might better have run "in another direction." He later admitted, moreover, in a singularly long-winded way of saying "divide and rule" that the scheme "may possibly be advantageous in a political sense in adjusting the balance of Bengali influence which might have become a preponderating factor difficult to deal with in questions affecting advanced Indian ideas, if the boundaries of Bengal had not been curtailed."[24]

Yet even if partition stemmed from no political motivation whatsoever, its political after-effects were monumental. Svadeshi and boycott, national education and svaraj, the major planks of India's independence movement, assumed nationwide significance for the first time in the scheme's wake. "The whole country," proclaimed Gopal Gokhale in his presidential address to Congress that December, "has been stirred to its deepest depths in sorrow and resentment, as had never been the case before." Although the mass demonstrations and boycott bonfires that raged from Calcutta to Poona in October had subsided considerably by December, 1905, antipartition agitation, especially in Eastern Bengal and Assam, was to remain a continuing source of harassment and embarrassment to administration throughout the next half decade. What Morley was wishfully to call in the Commons a "settled fact" restlessly refused to abide by his description.

The singular stimulus to political action and militant unrest provided by Bengal's partition proved to be the crowning irony of George

Curzon's viceroyalty, for he had early proclaimed "one of my greatest ambitions" to be that of assisting a "tottering" Congress to its "peaceful demise."[25] Ostrich-like, he believed that ignoring Indian aspirations for political power would make them disappear. His policy of paternalism led to the worst of actions for the best of reasons. In the name of efficiency he perpetuated racial discrimination, arrogantly and, as Indian history subsequently proved, erroneously proclaiming that "we do not employ more Natives in the very highest ranks of the Service . . . because they are not competent, and because it is our constant experience that, when placed in authority, if an emergency occurs, they lose their heads or abdicate altogether."[26] Not that Curzon confined his contempt, as already seen, to Indians alone. Nor did he particularly discriminate among classes of Indian society in unleashing that contempt, for he denounced princes as caustically as politicians: "I do not at all deprecate the remark that to a large extent we act as their schoolmasters," he wrote with reference to India's princes, insisting, "It is not only true, but it is inevitable. For what are they, for the most part, but a set of unruly and ignorant and rather undisciplined school-boys?"[27] As a good Tory, however, Curzon recognized the political value of even an inferior aristocracy. He sought, therefore, unsuccessfully but with characteristic vigor, to weld the princes into a political counterpoise to Congress by organizing a council, which he would, of course, as "Paramount" prince, have directed and guided himself. This scheme, originally Lord Lytton's idea, was picked up by Minto and his successors as well, but, unlike the National Congress, which flourished without government support, the princely council idea, being fundamentally an artificial attempt to create political aspirations among people who had none, failed despite the most powerful official sponsorship. When the Prince of Wales visited India at the end of Curzon's reign, what most appalled him was the lack of human "sympathy" he noted[28] everywhere, and the "stiffness and superiority" of manner with which government officials treated the people they ruled. Such was the legacy of George Curzon's hauteur, and of the contempt he lavished unsparingly upon his Indian wards, while so bravely bearing his white man's burden. He thought that by industry alone, by untiring dedication to his desk work, he could elevate an empire's debased standard all by himself, and win with efficiency the loyalty and devotion, the gratitude and affection, which neither Indians nor his own fellow countrymen ever bestowed upon him. Like Othello's tragedy, Curzon's failure was as much the result of excessive devotion as of misguided genius. Although he regularly labored from twelve to fourteen hours each day, he soon realized that the mere volume of work he attempted so conscientiously to tackle would have been divided among three or four men in England, for he was his own foreign minister and tried to rule Afghanistan and Tibet as well as India. "It cannot go on much longer,"[29] he complained at mid-tenure, yet, instead of devolving some of his responsibilities upon others, he continually took more work upon himself, hoarding power like an administrative miser until, by the end of his era, the government of India had reached a point of almost paralyzing centralization. Here again Curzon sought to justify himself by insisting his goal was that "of raising the standard of administration all round."[30] Yet, believing as he did that few men were intelligent enough to trust, Curzon thought this standard-raising goal could be reached only by personally directing every project himself.

Sir George Clarke, governor of Bombay from 1907 to 1913, summed up Curzon's administrative methods metaphorically in a letter to Morley, stating that "[Curzon's] whole conception of the Government of India was that of a stupendous organ with a multiplicity of stops and key-boards on which he could play at will, and from which he could produce any quality and quantity of sound that he desired. His colleagues might attend to the bellows, or standing at his elbow, might pull out any stops which he indicated, but no more."[31] India was too vast and varied a land for such solo performances, and though Curzon's intellect and stamina helped him play better perhaps than anyone else, "his thunderous fugues deafened and confused the whole administration." In many ways Curzon's obsession with efficiency led to grossly inefficient practice, and in terms at least of annual volume of official correspondence alone his viceroyalty proved to be the most ponderously bureaucratic in India's recent history. Once more, the result was the opposite of that which Curzon desired, for he inveighed against bureaucratic red tape as virulently as he did against Bengali *Babus*. Inevitably, however, as the viceroy's role became greater and more complex, the beehive secretariat world of Simla and its power expanded, while provincial officers devoted more and more time to drafting the detailed reports demanded by an insatiable viceroy.

Curzon refused even to consider the alternative of decentralization of authority, which was one of Morley's most important administrative innovations. He viewed his local governments much in the same negative manner as he did most Indians. "If you wait for their initiative or activity, the machine will remain unaltered and unreformed for a century," he complained to Hamilton during the fifth year of his reign. Then with typical Curzonian modesty he added that "all the great administrative reforms" of his time had "to spring from the Supreme Government—because there is no other fountain of initiative in India. . . . in nine cases out of ten it has had to spring exclusively from myself."[32] As Sir Alfred Lyall once trenchantly put it, Curzon's "real conception of decentralization is the concentration of authority in the hands of a very active and energetic Governor-General."[33]

Activity and energy were indeed the most conspicuous features of Curzonian diplomacy. Like the true disciple of Chamberlain's school of imperialism that he was, Curzon viewed most of Asia as British India's front line of defense against the rest of the world. He saw Tibet and Afghanistan at least as no more than protectorates of his suzerain government, and tried desperately to sell his "forward" frontier policy to a cabinet grown increasingly disillusioned by the price of imperialism in Africa. Balfour refused to buy any "permanent entanglements"[34] in Tibet, however, not for fear of fiscal strain (since the cost, unlike that in Somaliland, would come entirely from India's pocketbook), but to avoid possible conflict with China, and "because I think we have as much on our hands as we can look after." This sensible admission of the finite capacity of British imperial aggrandizement would doubtless have been branded treasonous by Curzon had it emanated from any less tainted a source than his own party's premier. Curzon himself, after all, seriously proposed the invasion of the United States of America through Canada at this time, compared with which idea the permanent occupation of Tibet was rather a timid matter. Colonel Younghusband's "mission," moreover, proved to be an eminently successful military invasion of the Chumbi Valley. The convention Younghusband concluded with the Lhasa administration in September, 1904, called for a seventy-five-year occupation of the Chumbi, throughout which period the government of India was to receive an annual "indemnity" from Tibet, thereby converting the latter into another subsidiary princely state under British Indian paramountcy. A separate trade agreement was concurrently concluded providing for a British "trade" agent to be permanently based at Gyantse, but with full access to Lhasa whenever desired. All of this was but a poorly veiled Curzonian variation on Wellesley's familiar old subsidiary treaty system. So shabby was the disguise, in fact, that His Majesty's home government[35] promptly intervened on Tibet's behalf to temper

Younghusband's convention, stipulating that no more than three years be spent in occupation of the Chumbi Valley, and proportionately reducing the indemnity. As for the trade agreement, there was "no alternative" but to disallow it as "inconsistent" with Britain's long-accepted policy "that Tibet should remain in that state of isolation from which till recently she has shown no intention to depart and which has hitherto caused her presence on our frontier to be a matter of indifference to us." Curzon's "whole attitude" in matters of diplomacy, whatever its effect may have been on Britain's supposed enemies, at least succeeded in frightening his own nation's cabinet "to death."[36] As viceroy with "Russia on the brain,"[37] he sought to secure India's western border by turning the amir of Afghanistan into "a British vassal," something that two Afghan wars had so painfully proved impossible. Yet Curzon was eager to recall Louis Dane from his Kabul mission in February, 1905, after some signs of self-assertiveness on the amir's part seemed to raise "questions not of form but of substance. If they are accepted," insisted the volatile viceroy, "we lose undisputed control of foreign relations . . . we thus forfeit all substantial returns for subsidizing, arming, and engaging to defend Afghanistan, and we surrender on every point to the Amir."[38]

But neither the cabinet, nor the India Office Council, nor authorities at home like Sir Alfred Lyall and Lord Roberts, agreed with Curzon's estimate of the situation. Again he was overruled. Dane was ordered to keep talking till he could negotiate a treaty, which Curzon considered cowardly capitulation, "grumbling" by March as much about Afghanistan as he did about Tibet "which he has never got over."[39] Little more than two months later, however, the keystone was blasted from the arch of Curzon's foreign policy when Russia's Balkan Fleet fought its way to the bottom of Japan's sea. The bogey Goliath, which for half a century had served as ultimate justification behind the aggressiveness of "forward minded" Anglo-Indians, was laid to rest by a mere upstart Asian power. Had he been in a position to do so, Morley could hardly have ordered a shift in the balance of international power more favorable to his own India Office policy of nonaggression.

By November 18, 1905, when George Curzon steamed away from Bombay's harbor, still flying the viceregal flag which he tenaciously kept aloft until Suez,[40] few people regretted his departure. In his Byculla Club swan song he acknowledged the "hostility" he had incurred from "the educated classes," wryly remarking that "when I remember how impartially it is bestowed on every Viceroy in the latter part of his term of office, I conclude that there must be something wrong about all of us which brings us under a common ban."[41] Few of Curzon's more serious conclusions about India were as true, for the very reason Gokhale gave when Prince George asked him, "Would the peoples of India be happier if you ran the country?" "No, Sir," Mahatma Gandhi's guru replied, "I do not say they would be happier, but they would have more self-respect."[42] Curzon's policy was too paternalistic to allow for anything so intangible as "native" self-respect. He comforted himself with the rationalization that whatever he did was done for "the Indian poor, the Indian peasant, the patient, humble, silent millions," who read "no newspapers" and have "no politics." Nor can it be denied that by encouraging irrigation and the creation of cooperative societies and by reducing the salt tax and opening new lands in the Punjab to "colonization," Curzon initiated several most significant reforms in Indian agriculture. None, however, took root in his own time, an era blighted with the horrors of rampaging plague and protracted famine. In the first six months of 1905 alone, an estimated 1 million Indians died of bubonic plague, while famine took its numberless toll of human and draft-animal life throughout the sorely afflicted Deccan. The exorbitant expenditure of peasant money and official energy lavished by Curzon on his pompous Delhi durbar in 1903, moreover, coming as it did in the midst of agricultural penury as harsh as any ever experienced by India's "humble, silent millions," adds a macabre note of disingenuousness to Curzon's proud apology. Perhaps it was simply a total lack of awareness, aristocratic inability to empathize with the plight of anyone less fortunate, which explains the gulf of self-contradiction between Curzon's personal professions and his official actions.

By the eve of his departure from India, George Curzon felt so embattled and embittered that he could not so much as bring himself to receive his viceregal successor graciously. Lord Minto reached Bombay after dark on November 17, and at Curzon's "orders"[43] was left to land "privately" without ceremonial welcome, rushed in a closed carriage to Government House. Instead of greeting his successor on the doorstep "according to the invariable custom and etiquette,"[44] Curzon received him in the drawing room "ten minutes after the arrival in a short coat and a pair of slippers," and "Lady Curzon did not curtsy to Lord Minto!!" It was precisely the sort of slight which Gilbert John, the fourth Earl of Minto, would find most offensive. "The whole performance was lamentable all through,"[45] Minto moaned, and thanks to this social slap he became as avid an anti-Curzonian as Kitchener himself. "I hope you won't think I am becoming childish in my suspicion of Curzonian influence," he wrote Arthur Godley, permanent undersecretary of state for India, in April, 1906, "but really I want no more of it here." Although a fellow Tory, Minto remained far more bitterly opposed to Curzon for this personal reason than Morley ever became.

"When I see Curzon's immense gifts," Morley wrote Minto less than a year after taking office, "—and they impress me more every time I see him—I cannot but be sorry that the gods poured some evil dose into the bowl and spoiled their whole brew."[46] It was hardly easy not to blame George Curzon, exaggerated as so much historical responsibility heaped onto any one man's shoulders was bound to be, for the general tone and policy of the government of India during the seven odd years prior to the dawn of 1906. But over the next half decade both tone and policy of British India's administration were to experience many significant changes. Not least important among these was the shift in focus of initiative, as well as power, from the government of India at Calcutta and Simla to His Majesty's government at Whitehall, a shift presaged by Curzon's dramatic fall, and virtually completed by John Morley between 1906–1910.

3

WHITEHALL VERSUS SIMLA

> It is a terribly cumbrous and artificial sort of system, and I am not certain that it will last forever, or even for many years to come.
>
> Morley to Minto, October 19, 1910

From its very inception, British rule over India was administratively schizophrenic. In the early days of John Company's raj the directors at Leadenhall Street wrestled interminably, and generally to little or no avail, with their "servants" at Bombay and Forts William and Saint George. Between 1785 and 1857 the Board of Control added Parliament's power to the "Honourable Company's" prestige in its continuing struggle with a vagrant and persistently irresponsible government of India abroad. By 1858, however, Britain decided that the only way to prevent its Indian tail from further precarious wagging of the home dog was for the Crown, that is, Parliament, to assume direct control over the East India Company's administrative affairs.

The transfer of power inaugurated by the Government of India Act of August 2, 1858, was in some respects revolutionary,[1] but the Englishmen who ruled India continued to be confounded by the strain of having to "make their watches keep time in two longitudes at once." Although the act fully empowered "one of Her Majesty's Principal Secretaries of State" to direct and control Indian affairs, the government of India remained in practice virtually autonomous. After 1870 the Suez Canal, steam transport, and electric cables simultaneously conspired to bring India's government within rapid reach of Whitehall's India Office arm. Periodic assertions of the "great principle" that the home government retained "final control and direction"[2] over Indian affairs then became fashionable. To the hour of Curzon's fall, Salisbury served perhaps as the one Indian secretary whose clear dominance over his viceroy, Lytton, may be cited as the exception to prove the rule of ever-increasing viceregal pretentions to independent action. Among the more obvious reasons for the continuing relative autonomy enjoyed by the government of India were its complete freedom from Treasury supervision and remoteness from the average Englishman's political consciousness. The retired civil servants and "India-returned" businessmen or soldiers of the Pukka Sahib caste provided Simla with a virtually unopposed Tory home lobby in the pre-Morley era, while Liberals like Gladstone, who were willing to sacrifice their political fortunes for Ireland, said and wrote almost nothing at all about India.

It was more than historical accident that the growth of liberal English consciousness of India coincided with the "Rule of Democracy"[3] at home, and the sudden acceleration after 1905 of Indian nationalist agitation. The great Liberal Parliament of 1906 numbered no less than 150[4] among its members of the Commons on the "Indian Committee" ready to support demands of India's National Congress. John Morley wasted no time in using the leverage of so impressive a popular mandate to pry an autocratic government of India from its Olympian isolation, determined as he was to bring it effectively within the responsible orbit of Her Majesty's Liberal government.

"The new Parliament, and the new Cabinet, will be in the highest degree jealous both of anything that looks like expansion, . . . and of anything with the savour of 'militarism' about it,"[5] Morley warned Lord Minto in one of his earliest letters. "There are at least five men in the House of Commons, who will be likely to raise Indian questions," he added the following week, reminding the Viceroy to "recognise that the centre of gravity is utterly changed . . . by this amazing election."[6]

So began a struggle that Morley himself considered of "cardinal" importance throughout the half decade he spent as secretary of state for India: his continuing effort "to depose the Government of India from their usurped position of an independent power."[7] This unabated struggle with Simla became no less than a pitched battle against Anglo-India's massive bureaucratic machine, for Morley early resolved not "to walk blindfold in the ways of bureaucracy, as the court in Peterhof and its precious Tchin [officials] had been walking blindfold in the ways of autocracy."[8] Most studies[9] of this era present either a grossly distorted appraisal of this conflict between Whitehall and Simla, perversely arguing that Morley was "high-handed," "despotic," and "autocratic" in his treatment of a misunderstood and long-suffering government of India, or else ignore the struggle entirely, diplomatically insisting that relations between Minto and Morley were little less than idyllic.[10]

Although by an irony of history Minto's name has been linked more intimately to Morley's than any other individual's, few men were more different, less basically in sympathy with one another, than the patrician viceroy and his radical secretary of state. Known to the sporting world as "Mr. Rolly," Lord Minto's first passion was horseriding, his second, hunting. He had won the Grand National at Auteuil in 1874 as sole "gentleman rider" in a field of seventeen jockeys, fought for the Turks against Russia and under Lord Roberts in the second Anglo-Afghan War, and served in the largely ceremonial role of governor-general of Canada (1898–1904) before becoming governor-general and viceroy of India on November 18, 1905. By the age of sixty, then, when the fourth Earl took up the reins of Indian administration, he was still enough the gentleman so that friends could wonder "how a man who has never done a real day's work in his life" would stand up to an existence as arduous and administratively demanding as that of India's viceroy. The appointment of Lord Minto was indeed considered by some informed sources an unprecedented error of choice. "We have had elderly men as Viceroy," commented Lord Ampthill gloomily, "but they were men of established reputation and conspicuous brilliancy; we have also had younger men but they were men who were capable of sufficient work to make up for the lack of brilliancy. We have never yet had an elderly man who was neither brilliant nor hard-working."[11] Yet, although no one ever accused Lord Minto of excessive intelligence or industry, there is some validity to the argument that his "negative qualities"[12] helped give India a much-needed rest after so strong a dose of Curzonian vitality. Laissez faire, or, more accurately perhaps, as Morley once put it, "Anything for a Quiet Life,"[13] would best define Minto's "political philosophy." Partisans of Curzon, like General Sir Edmund Barrow, who remained on active duty in India after their hero departed, obviously exaggerated when they reported that "'K' [Kitchener] and the Secretaries run the Government, Lady Minto runs the patronage and H.E. [His Excellency—Minto] runs the stables."[14] It is, however, true that, like many men reared on a military chain of command, Minto delegated far more responsibility than his predecessor had, and, whether from lack of interest, capacity, or inclination, looked into far fewer official matters of business himself.[15]

"My idea of good administration," wrote Minto in one of his rare, if somewhat jumbled, attempts to state his administrative philosophy, "is that the personnel of State machinery should be as efficient as possible and of selected ability in its important posts, whilst the Supreme authority should feel safe in leaving details to be dealt with by its trusted officers whilst keeping in its own hands the direction of all great questions of policy and consequent administration and exclusive action."[16]

Morley had met Minto briefly at Ottawa in 1904, and recognized, after several months of weekly correspondence with the Viceroy, that he was "not very clever."[17] Later he more openly expressed regret that he had not been blessed with a viceroy "less stupid"[18] than Minto, sensing that what the government of India lacked most was something no one in the world could give them—"common sense." One thing, at least, which years of dealing with Minto taught Morley was "the full truth of the saying that politics are an affair of the second best."[19] Time brought to light only further revelations of Minto's mediocrity and of the "mediocre or even a trifle below that"[20] caliber of his council.

But the struggle between Whitehall and Simla waged in this era was no mere conflict of personalities. Basically it was a battle between responsible and irresponsible rule, between some semblance of democracy and absolute despotism. Underlying all of Morley's "autocratic" orders, reprimands, and warnings to the government of India was the first principle and final article of the liberal political faith he shared with his great teacher, Mill: "No government can be trusted if it is not liable to be called before some jury or another, compose that jury how you will, and even if its majority should unluckily happen to be dunces."[21] The only democratic jury powerful enough in his day to impose judgment on an offensive government of India was the Commons, and Morley recognized that

however decorously veiled, pretentions to oust the House of Commons from part and lot in Indian affairs ... (and this is what the tone now in fashion on one side of the controversy really comes to)—must lead in logic, as in fact, to the surprising result of placing what is technically called the

Government of India in a position of absolute irresponsibility to the governed. Now this, whatever else it may be, is at daggers drawn with the barest rudiments of democratic principle.[22]

It was always as executor of Parliament's will, as trustee of Parliament's Indian affairs, as a representative member of the democratically elected responsible government of Great Britain, that Morley wrote to Minto, and acted officially during his era at Whitehall. As a servant of His Majesty's government he never forgot that he served the people first, reminding enfranchised audiences whenever the opportunity presented itself that "you and the democratic constituencies of this Kingdom are the rulers of India."[23] Indeed, if there was one principle which may be said to have guided Morley's relations with Simla, it was precisely that all members of the government of India were "servants and agents of Parliament in a free country."[24]

Every attempt[25] on Minto's part to adopt Curzon's style of referring to the "Government of India" as an entity aloof from "His Majesty's Government" brought immediate rebuttal from the head of Whitehall's India Office. Early in their association (February 9, 1906), Morley warned Minto that the "Cabinet would certainly take fright at any language or acts of ours pointing in the Curzonian direction, by seeming to set up the Government of India as a sort of great power on its own account." The "plain truth," he insisted soon after (July 6, 1906), was that India could not have "two foreign policies." No more than British India could be ruled by two administrations, by officials of the government of India as distinct from His Majesty's government. "They are all officials of His Majesty's Government," thundered Morley (April 4, 1907). "You and the Commander-in-Chief are appointed by His Majesty's Government; are responsible to His Majesty's Government; and can be recalled by His Majesty's Government." Possibly to be quite certain that Minto understood his message, Morley relayed it once (June 24, 1908) in racetrack jargon, reminding "Mr. Rolly" that "Curzon tried a fall with the Cabinet, and was spilled in the operation."

Not that Minto was ever truculent in attempting to dispute Morley's claim to overriding and complete authority. On the contrary, he was, if anything, disarmingly amenable, readily acquiescing that it would be "impossible" for the government of India to adopt "a policy . . . apart from that of His Majesty's Government."[26] Throughout his viceroyalty, Minto argued, he had "always endeavoured loyally to serve the Secretary of State and His Majesty's Government."[27] His major complaint, however, was that Parliament was too openly critical of the government of India, and that radical members of the Commons like Keir Hardie kept coming to India and embarrassing officialdom with their brashly outspoken public statements about Anglo-Indian despotism. "The modern House of Commons," Minto groaned in exasperation, "is absolutely incapable of understanding Indian humanity and the influences of many creeds and traditions, and is to my mind perhaps the greatest danger to the continuance of our rule in this country."[28] This was precisely the sort of complaint "Honest John" found least palatable. "Your tone about the H. of C. produces in me just the same *jar* that would be produced in you by disrespectful language about the King,"[29] he replied. Sardonically reminding Minto that he had sat long enough in the Commons when it was a "Tory or Unionist Assembly" to know full well its "weaknesses," Morley nonetheless insisted: "If ever there was a time when a ruling assembly deserved credit for its confidence in a Minister, and *the local agents* for whom he is answerable, it is this present House, radical though it be" (italics added). The distance between Simla and Whitehall was more than a matter of geography. The men presiding over each domain were as differently oriented as the very premises of Conservatism and Liberalism.

"You say that 'reforms may not save the Raj,'—they certainly will not," Lord Minto wrote smugly. "But when you say that 'if reforms do not save the Raj nothing else will,' I am afraid I must utterly disagree. The Raj will not disappear in India as long as the British race remains what it is, because we shall fight for the Raj as hard as we have ever fought . . . and we shall win as we have always won."[30] An accompanying flourish of bugles could almost be heard behind the pen scratch of the old Scottish laird-soldier. Morley's retort rang with the idiom of another *Weltanschauung*. "It is not you nor I who are responsible for 'unrest,' but the over-confident or over-worked Tchinovniks [bureaucrats] who have had India in their hands for fifty years past," he insisted, adding wryly, "I demur, in the uplifted spirit of the Trodden Worm, to the view said to be current at Simla, that the Home Government is always a d——d fool."[31]

Halfway through his tenure, Morley still labored to enlist Minto's services in his crusade against the "close corporation of bureaucrats, bureaucratic maxims, traditions, habits, and practices," telling the Viceroy, "I look to you to prevent the corporation from assuming that the Secretary of State in C. is nothing better nor worse than an inconvenient, but not alarming, phantom."³² Morley naturally preferred "parliamentary rule, with all its faults" to "Prussian bureaucracy" and was so heretical a Millite as to admit to Minto in 1908 that he was "less passionately in love than ever even with bureaucracy as model machinery for governing alien races!"³³

For some time Minto tried innocuously to continue his sniping at Parliament by relaying to Whitehall the complaints of exalted civil officers like Sir John Hewett, lieutenant governor of the United Provinces, but Morley was not easily fooled. "What a balloon these men [like Hewett] live in!" he replied. "A more truly silly thing than to quote Native Gentlemen as wondering why we allow questions [in Parliament] about Indian subjects, I cannot imagine. Please Heaven, Hewett himself will have to submit to questions before we have done with reforms."³⁴ Yet Minto never abandoned entirely his reactionary complaints about radicals in Parliament, until, more in utter amazement than in anger, Morley finally wrote: "You strongly deprecate public criticism and parliamentary discussion. I don't know if like King Canute and his courtiers at the seaside you have people who assure you that you can keep back the ocean. Discussion may be undesirable as you please, but then neither you nor anybody else can prevent it."³⁵

Morley himself recognized full well how the Indian tide was flowing. He perceived that the empire over which he briefly presided would not last "for ever, or even for many years to come."³⁶ The London Colonial Conference of 1907 made him suspect in fact "that old England is played out in all respects."³⁷ In one subsequent moment of depression he sardonically confessed to wishing "that Clive had been arrested in his exploitation of Bengal!!"³⁸ Most often, however, he philosophically accepted the irreversible process of time, and labored somehow to resolve "one of the most difficult experiments ever tried in human history,"³⁹ that of ruling an empire through the agency of democracy, of seeking to reconcile "personal government" with "free speech and free right of public meeting." He called it "the great riddle,"⁴⁰ and, unlike the Viceroy and others of his caste, was never deceived about "the impossibility of forecasting British rule in the Indian future."⁴¹ As a member of the Committee on Imperial Defense as well as the cabinet, Morley found himself "daily" confronted with the question of "whether we have good brains enough available to work with effective means the British Empire, and to meet all its incessant and exacting demands?"⁴² He had the foresight not to "envy" those "men who will have to keep the British empire on its feet five and twenty years hence."[43] He was sensitive, honest, and concerned enough with the problems that crowded his desk to confess, moreover, that "the longer one stares at India, the more grim and ugly it all is."[44]

Few of India's nationalist leaders of the day saw as lucidly as John Morley did "how intensely artificial and unnatural is our mighty raj."[45] This keen historical insight, debilitating though it might seem for the head of that raj, made him work all the harder at the "business" of assuring that "the next transition, whatever it may turn out to be," would be "something of an improvement."[46] For, like Mill, Morley was intellectually incapable of sanctioning even a temporary imperial despotism as "legitimate" unless he felt that the "Government by the dominant country" was such as "in the existing state of civilization of the subject people, most facilitates their transition to a higher state of civilization."[47] He thus labored to bring Anglo-Indian bureaucracy within the orbit of democratic control, and to prevent the bureaucratic machine from becoming either "mechanical and lifeless" or predominantly "Military."[48] He worked to clear the road that has led to independent and democratic India of autocratic barricades and reactionary rubble piled high by an alien, long-suffering, and increasingly unsympathetic regime at Simla. Growing "estrangement and lessening sympathy"[49] between British civil servants and the Indians they governed were clearly discernible aspects of British Indian society after 1857, Morley learned from the most astute of his English and Indian[50] advisers. Unwittingly, Minto admitted much the same thing himself when he wrote, "We all feel that we are mere sojourners in the land; that we are only camping and on the march. Everyone is looking forward to a well-earned rest at home at last."[51]

Morley sought to diminish the estrangement and increase the sympathy between India's rulers and those they ruled by initiating the reforms for which his era is best remembered. He tried to effect the same reversal in Anglo-Indian social relations, moreover, through his less publicized, though equally strenuous, struggle against Simla's *tchinovnik* raj, by conscientiously asserting his constitutional right to select and veto key members of the government of India hierarchy. Burke taught him that the "chief aim in any system for governing a people, so much behind ourselves as the natives of Hindustan, must certainly be to get the various administrative posts filled by men of trained skill and of the highest character that the governing people can produce,"[52] and Morley did his best to adhere to that formula. He never let his ministerial responsibility of "recommending" appointees to His Majesty for royal "approval" atrophy into a mere matter of rubber-stamping Minto's nominees.

On the eve of the first vacancy in Minto's Executive Council, Morley instructed the Viceroy, when suggesting some names to him, to send "not less than two to choose from, with your [Minto's] own arguments and preferences. Don't let seniority count for too much," he cautioned, adding, in a spirit that transcended his own age, "a strain of fresh blood will do no harm anywhere."[53] It was a theme to which Morley often reverted, the urgent need of transfusing a healthy potion of new ideas, new outlooks, new habits of mind, into the rigid body of British India's bureaucracy. "We ought to insist," he wrote Minto in May, 1908, "on going outside all rings, vested interests, and even personal partialities and prepossessions, in search of fresh and independent minds. If ever there was a moment when such ought to be our ruling thought, it is this very day."[54]

"Freshness of mind" was indeed the attribute Morley valued most highly when seeking councillors, either for Whitehall or Simla.[55] He vigorously advocated doing "away with all the arguments about Seniority and Juniority!!"[56] and had he been blessed with a viceroy of somewhat similar concern, disposition, and judgment, might well have effected a revolution in India by wholesale change of personnel alone. Lord Minto, however, lacked either the inclination or the ability to choose first-rate men, and reportedly had "not got a really good man about him."[57] Morley soon learned that he could place little or no faith in the Viceroy's recommendations of personnel, and much of his most contentious dialogue with Simla was over relative merits of individuals like General Sir Charles C. Egerton.[58] (Egerton was a member of Morley's Council of India from 1907 to 1909.) "I wish that you had not been an accomplice in planting Egerton upon me," Morley groaned to Minto. "He evidently is a fossil of the most tiresome species . . . an antediluvian. He wrote a note in defense of military flogging, which might be written by any Cossack."[59] With reference to Sir Harvey Adamson[60] (home member of Minto's Executive Council from October, 1906), whom Minto was proposing for lieutenant governor of Burma, Morley protested, "I fancy that he is the very opposite of an active-minded man, and that he is as obstinate as a dozen mules . . . a pig-headed mediocrity."[61]

The more Morley listened to the reports of "high Indian officials who come across my horizon," the more discouraged he became concerning the mental caliber of British India's bureaucracy. "All of them talk the same lingo," he complained, "and say exactly the same things about 'weakness being contemptible,' 'the Native mind not understanding anything but force,' etc., etc."[62] Even an official like Sir Andrew Fraser, who returned home after attaining the pinnacle of service power as lieutenant governor of Bengal, was a man without "grasp, or insight, or any breadth of vision."[63] As for Sir Denzil Ibbetson,[64] Curzon's foremost crony in the civil service, Morley concluded, after meeting him, that he had no "ideas, or shred of policy, beyond repression."[65] Sir Denzil inspired him to add in commiseration to Minto, "It is your hard lot to have to carry things forward by the agency of men whose feeling is backward."[66] It was the sort of reflection he would have been better justified in having about himself, although he was trying, of course, by every verbal artifice at his command to convert the "sow's ear" of Minto's administrative talent into a "silk purse." For the first half of his tenure in office Morley hoped to be able to win the Viceroy's active support in battling "inelastic bureaucrats" like Sir Lancelot Hare,[67] second lieutenant governor of East Bengal and Assam.

Hare was Minto's personal choice for the sensitive post at the helm of India's new province, focal point of unrest since partition. "He impresses me," recommended the Viceroy in August, 1906, "as a thoroughly sensible, cautious man. He is certainly not brilliant, and thinks several times before he speaks, but when he does, it all seems sound."[68] Such faint praise was enough to make Morley "somewhat anxious," but Minto confidently asserted "if you met him, you would think the same as I do. I am sure we could not have found a better man . . . the right man for the job."[69] In less than six months, however, Hare had shown himself inclined to panic in the face of agitation, and Minto had to overrule several of his repressive proposals, inviting his appointee to Calcutta for a dressing down. "The more you can infuse your own wise common sense (forgive compliments) into your tchinovniks," wrote Morley wishfully to the Viceroy, "the better for them and for us."[70] Whatever sense Minto managed to infuse into his lieutenant governor did not, however, last very long, for within a year he reported, "Hare, too, is knocked up. Work and anxiety have told on him heavily."[71] Nor did a rest cure help. By July, 1909, Morley called Hare's appointment the "worst thing that has been done in your reign,"[72] adding in exasperation, "Have you not power to oust Hare, *nolens volens*? Can we not find the power somewhere? It strikes me as simply disgusting (pronounced with immense emphasis) that form, etiquette, usage, claims, and all the bureaucrat paraphernalia, should block the way to energetic and yet sensible government (for energy is not the same thing as sense) in a situation like ours in India to-day, and still more tomorrow."

It was not the first time that Morley had tried to convince Minto that an "incompetent official in an important place is a curse, and a curse all around. Look at your Council," he wrote after receiving Minto's letter of January 15, 1908, stating that James Finlay, member for commerce and industry, had "utterly broken down." He went on:

I have never understood that you regard it [the governor-general's Executive Council] as other than extremely mediocre, and it is regarded by the public as containing nobody of real quality except K. [Kitchener] and Baker. Scott is a mere cypher, and now Finlay is no better. . . . fresh blood. That's the only cure in bureaucracy. . . . The presence of a broken-down head of a department . . . spreads a sense of executive slackness and easygoingness, which is about the most demoralizing thing that can befall a government, except perhaps corruption. . . . Depend upon it, our only chance of keeping clear of the mischiefs of Yankee abominatoins in public business, is to insist upon rigorous strictness about men doing the work for which they draw public pay.[73]

A month later he preached the same sermon, informing Minto that what

we ought to bend ourselves to break down is the bureaucratical and hierarchical notion of this man and that man having a claim that it is as much as your life is worth to disappoint. . . . If these great appointments are all to be made on the Roster principle, it will doubtless save you and me a vast deal of trouble, but I am perfectly certain that it is not the principle on which vigorous government is kept alive. . . . I won't enlarge further on this tiresome, but really very important, topic.[74]

Unfortunately, the man whose cooperation Morley thus sought to enlist in doing battle against mediocrity in office was himself the epitome of his council's character, which Morley once classified as belonging "to the great *Duffer* genus."[75] By the beginning of 1910, when Morley was "anxious to get rid of Minto,"[76] his own time in office had virtually expired as well. He had waited too long, deceived initially by the Viceroy's shrewdness in avowing agreement with everything he suggested, deterred moreover by his own staff at the India Office, where the "general principle is accepted that the Government of India should be overruled only for cogent reasons."[77] Morley's struggle with Simla and the Anglo-Indian bureaucracy was indeed made doubly difficult because of the bureaucratic "expert" advisers and ultraconservative Council of India, so firmly entrenched all around him in Whitehall itself.

The most influential of these Whitehall India experts were conservative career bureaucrats, who had never been to India and had little, if any, sympathy for Indian political aspirations. They served as innocuous, but singularly effective, buffers, not only between Morley and Minto, but between Morley and his nonofficial Indian advisers like Gokhale and Dutt as well. Their function, of course, was to provide continuity of administration despite any gyrations in political power, so that, although supposedly apolitical themselves, these civil servants were in fact as conservative as the very establishment they maintained. The bureaucrat who had run the India Office for no less than twenty-two years when Morley arrived there was Sir Arthur Godley.[78] He had survived ten shifts of administration as permanent undersecretary to seven different ministers and lingered on throughout most of Morley's tenure before retiring in October, 1909. Godley was, perhaps, the classic example of bureaucracy at its best and worst. Thoroughly competent at the routine work he performed, admired by his most able juniors as "the best man in the Civil Service,"[79] he was nonetheless as spiritless and disinterested as the machine he managed. Two years before Godley retired, Morley wanted "to get rid" of him, sensing that he was "getting old, lacking in initiative, and freshness of mind."[80] He felt, moreover, that Godley "was very conservative," and "had not been a good adviser" because his mind was "not fertile."[81] Godley himself later confirmed Morley's suspicions in his *Reminiscences*, admitting that for "my first twelve or thirteen years at the India Office my work was to me thoroughly interesting, though never absorbing: for the next two or three years it was an invaluable distraction," but "for the remainder of my time, about eleven years, it was, though not irksome or disagreeable, pure taskwork."[82] Yet more than two decades at his post had armed Godley with such command over the guild secrets of daily India Office routine that Morley, a relative novice to Whitehall's ritual, refrained from encouraging his unimaginative, unsympathetic assistant to retire until feeling confident that Richmond Thackeray Ritchie,[83] secretary to the office's

Political and Secret Department, was ready to take control of the India Office's large staff and expenditure. Although Morley was firm and active enough a minister to see to it that Godley in fact no longer "ruled India,"[84] the Permanent Undersecretary nonetheless served as Minto's foremost agent[85] in Whitehall for four-fifths of Morley's tenure. He often advised Morley to soften his tone of intended reproach in letters and telegrams to the government of India, and on at least one occasion prevented "a full dress eclaircissement with Minto" by dissuading Morley with warnings "of the perils of these full dress protests in public business."[86] Even after retiring, thanks to the influence he exerted over older members of Morley's council, Godley's conservatism helped counteract Morley's liberalizing influence. To Lee-Warner on August 5, 1910, Godley (by then Lord Kilbracken) wrote conspiratorially: "Things are not so bad as you think, and honest John will not be in office much longer. You must not think of resigning—stick to your guns; you are of the greatest use *quand meme*, and I don't think you would ever forgive yourself hereafter, if you were to retire now merely because you cannot effectively oppose what you disapprove."[87] That Godley was obviously anxious not to afford Morley the opportunity of replacing one of the Council of India's most reactionary members with a liberal appointee was made clear in another letter to Warner two days later, congratulating him on deciding not to resign. "You may not have much power to prevent mistakes where you are now," noted Godley, "but it is certain that you would have still less if you retired, and made way for a successor who might be selected possibly for his known subservience."[88]

Sir William Lee-Warner,[89] thus kept in harness until after Morley resigned three months later, was the senior member of Whitehall's Council of India in 1906, and served that year as its vice-chairman. A member of the council since 1902 with thirty-three years of experience in India to his credit, Sir William was considered an eminent authority on the princely states and western Indian attitudes, and his influence at the India Office was most powerfully anti-Congress and anti-Hindu. He tried his worst to poison Morley's mind against Gokhale[90] and generally denounced Indians as lacking any "sense of honour,"[91] specifically slandering Gokhale's saintly guru, Justice Mahadev Govind Ranade, to Morley as a petty pilferer. Curiously enough, Lee-Warner himself was twice involved in legal charges of assault by and against Indians; the first time was in Bombay, in 1875, after he tried to drive his "buggy" through a procession of Parsis "bound on some religious ceremony."[92] The Parsis, as an Anglo-Indian newspaper of the time quaintly reported, "chose to interpret Mr. Lee-Warner's hurry to get past them as an insult. The Undersecretary pluckily contended against overwhelming odds, seized one of his assailants, and stuck to him until the police came up." More than thirty years later, on January 11, 1909,[93] Sir William seized another Indian, a young Hindu student named Bhattacharyya, and deterred him from presenting a petition to Morley at the India Office. "I then left for the Athenaeum," Warner wrote in his letter of explanation the next day to Godley. "He kept hanging behind me. . . . I was suddenly assaulted from behind with both fists which were harmless but had the effect of propelling me along the road. . . . I told him I could not allow such behaviour. . . . He said I had called him names [Bhattacharyya wrote that Lee-Warner "called me 'Dirty Bengalee, niggar [sic]' etc."] . . . absolutely false . . . I had called him no names. I took him by the arm and gave him to the constable."

The Metropolitan Police constable involved in the incident reported that upon presenting the student to him "Sir William said 'he has followed me across the park and just now . . . deliberately pushed me, which really amounts to an assault.' I explained to Sir William that there was no power of arrest unless the assault was serious. . . . When he replied 'That will do—Sir Edward Henry will understand.'"

Sir Edward Richard Henry, commissioner of London's Metropolitan Police, was a former member of the Indian Civil Service[94] and an old friend of Sir William's, but even he found it difficult to accept Sir William's story of the "assault," writing Lee-Warner on January 18, 1909: "From what we have learned about K. Bhattacharyya . . . he is not a person from whom violence need be feared. Indeed I am more than astonished that he should have ventured on such action as he did take against you." A few days later, however, Sir William charged that another young Bhattacharyya "caned" him on the very steps of his club, the Athenaeum. On February 11 the case was tried and the *Morning Post* of the following day reported:

> Bhattacharyya was defended by L. W. Ritch, barrister, who asked—"Did you say to the defendant 'Get away, you dirty nigger'?"
> *The Witness* [L.-W.]—"no, it would be impossible for me to do so."
> *Ritch.* "Did you call your first assailant the 'son of a pig'?"
> "Certainly not."
> "What did you do after the defendant, as you say, had struck you?"
> "I watched my adversary—not without amusement."

"Had you any weapon?"
"I had my umbrella. No, there was no pushing."
"Did you strike back?"
"No, certainly not."

Bhattacharyya was found guilty, fined, and sent to prison for a month. Among those who found the charges of bigotry and bullying against Sir William credible enough to take seriously, however, was King Edward VII, who was reported to be "very indignant with Lee-Warner *re* the assault case: 'had he not behaved very badly,' 'had he not called the man a dirty nigger?' etc."[95]

After 1907 when Morley appointed two Indian members to his council, Lee-Warner's influence at Whitehall progressively diminished until, as noted, he came to feel thoroughly frustrated and ineffectual by the last year of Morley's era. His personal impact on the reform scheme, however, was, as will be seen, in some respects most deleterious.

The official at Whitehall who influenced Morley most[96] was, not surprisingly, his own private secretary. Frederic Arthur Hirtzel, who had been on the India Office staff for more than eleven years (the last two as private secretary to the secretary of state) when Morley arrived, was efficient, unobtrusive, unemotional, and highly intelligent. Hirtzel won Morley's complete confidence, thanks to his "ability and character."[97] Considered at first with Ritchie for Godley's post, Hirtzel was, however, so very much the latter's junior that he was assigned instead to replace Ritchie as secretary of the Political and Secret Department, later succeeding his as permanent undersecretary. Morley's "right hand man,"[98] Hirtzel had more opportunities than Godley, Ritchie, or any member of the Council of India to affect policy at moments of critical decision. Like Godley, he served as Simla's advocate whenever Morley appeared to become short-tempered or irate at the government of India's course of action. He, too, manipulated assiduously against Gokhale,[99] supporting Minto's position at every possible opportunity,[100] letting Morley "work off some of his feelings" on him if a particularly sharp conflict between Whitehall and Simla seemed about ready to explode, writing "private letters" to "J. M." more fully stating his arguments if verbal appeals failed. Taken separately, none of Hirtzel's "victories" was significant, but the incremental impact of his daily influence, exercised as it was over a period of more than four years, can hardly be overestimated. His diaries show that he never missed an opportunity. When an Indian press attack upon Minto happened to make Morley casually remark that he could understand now why people said "that the Viceroy is the man who must be supported," Hirtzel immediately "seized this admission, and rubbed the idea well in."[101] He pointed out, moreover, that "the same principle applied to the Lieutenant-Governors, and the district officers," moving from that new foothold to tell him "Edge's [member of Council of India] remark that it was almost as bad that it should be known that the Secretary of State was asking questions [of the government of India] as that he should actually overrule. He [Morley] said he saw the force of that. I said I thought we had asked too many questions last session. He quite agreed, and said that he was determined to make a stand against the Indian party [in Commons] next session." When a telegram arrived from Simla stating that some "emergency" made it imperative for Minto to dust off an ancient repressive ordinance and put it into effect tomorrow, Hirtzel

sat with J.M. while he read it. He was greatly perturbed. . . . He read it twice carefully, and then threw it down saying "No, I can't stand that. *I will not have that.*" I said I did not see how we here could measure the emergency. He said "Then it comes to this, that I am to have nothing to say, but am to let them do just what they like." I said yes, it did amount to that for the next week or so, at all events: he could give them general warning and advice but he must leave particular action to them. At least then, he said, he must have proper information, and I agreed, and left him to draft [a] telegram. This, when done, began "I cannot of course take responsibility of disallowing Ordinance." I demurred strongly to this. He said he had power to disallow it, why should he not remind them of it? I pressed on him that disallowance would be so extreme a measure that it was inadvisable even to allude to it, and at last he gave way. . . . It was a nasty little crisis while it lasted![102]

Hirtzel's influence only increased with time, and a month after the "nasty little crisis," Morley, in recommending Hirtzel for the king's honor list, wrote the Prime Minister: "To me Hirtzel is almost life and death: a more competent and zealous public servant does not exist."[103] Nonetheless, the private secretary did not win every argument with his boss, nor was Morley so poor a judge of character as not to recognize Hirtzel's limitations, once remarking of him to someone else that "[Hirtzel] 'ought to have been a soldier'!!!"[104] The impact, however, of the colorless and all too often anonymous personnel of the civil service on the course of India's recent history was extremely important, even in an era so powerfully dominated by a minister like

Morley. Hirtzel and his bureaucratic colleagues served the establishment well as potent deterrents to liberalizing change.

Morley used his own powers of patronage to appoint Indians to high administrative posts, including the executive councils, one of the most important and far-reaching aspects of his reforms (considered in a chapter of its own), and also planted several of his "men" in key Indian positions. The first of these Morley men infused into the bloodstream of the government of India's autocracy was Sir George Clarke [later Lord Sydenham], secretary to the cabinet's Committee of Imperial Defense, whom Morley appointed to succeed Lord Lamington as governor of Bombay on October 18, 1907. Although at fifty-nine Clarke found himself "almost too old"[105] for the "physical strain" of administering India's largest and most prosperous province, he was introduced by Morley to Minto as a man of "ceaseless mental activity . . . well worth consulting" and inclined to "what I will call the economic, pacific, anti-alarmist, anti-militarist school."[106] This appears to have been information enough to convince Minto that he had nothing in common with the new governor, who after more than a year in India, had still "not been invited"[107] to Simla's summit for direct consultation. Morley, however, kept up continuous correspondence with Clarke, whose letters "give me as much pleasure as any that reach me from India," he wrote in February, 1908, "first, because they come from a very active and observant mind, second, because they show that the owner of the mind is intensely interested in his work."[108] Morley's "only wish" was that "as much could be said of every other man in the huge official hierarchy around you." Congratulating Clarke for taking "exactly the line of sound policy," Morley, like a good headmaster, then pithily gave his own formula for attaining this rare yet most desirable of administrative goals: "as much personal contact, face answering to face, as possible; tact tempering authority; considerateness smoothing power, ceaseless and rightly directed industry dispersing the cobwebs of routine."

In May, 1909, Clarke was finally invited by Minto to visit Simla, the isolated Himalayan hill station that for some seven months of each year served as British India's administrative capital. Exclusively populated by British officials, their families, Indian servants, and soldier guards, Simla's Olympian atmosphere gave Clarke an "impression of unreality," for India seemed "a far away country from which only echoes reach us. . . . It is as if the political capital of Europe were established beyond the North Cape."[109] Thanks to Clarke's vivid reports, however, Morley received his first accurate account of how the government of India operated at its bureaucratic command post. Clarke wrote:

> I have not discovered the Government of India at Simla, where I find only Secretariats working on papers in water-tight compartments, and somewhat jealous of each other though occasionally uniting in jealousy of the Provincial Governments. There are no Councils, and I do not see how important questions of policy can be dealt with by Members of Council writing to each other. It is now most clear to me that no Civilian who cherishes further ambitions in India should ever become an M. C. [member of council], which should be the recognized crown of his career ... present arrangements are plainly demoralizing to the administration. Again, four continuous years with the Government of India should be the maximum for Secretaries and Under-Secretaries, who should go back to actualities after this period, so as to regain that touch with the life of India which is completely severed by being sojourners among these mountains.[110]

After conferring with "about 35 of the leading officials, civil and military,"[111] the astute Governor of Bombay wrote another letter to his friend in London, confirming the initial impression he had formed of the "dangerous ... utter lack of coordination" within the government of India.

Practically all business is now transacted between the Viceroy and the Department Secretaries [Clarke explained], except that I gather that the masterful Lord K [Kitchener, extraordinary member of council as commander in chief] has usually dealt direct. Secretaries here have powers which would never be conceded to their analogues in the Presidency Governments, and which ought unquestionably to be withdrawn. When, added to these powers, it must be remembered that Councils are not held and that Members of Council are debarred by regulation from consulting together without the Viceroy's permission, one can well understand why policy is nowhere and departmentalism is rampant. ... Below the Secretaries is an army of Deputy and Assistant Secretaries—far too numerous. The Home Department has now four. ...

I do not wish to seem to deal in "supercilious disparagement" of Secretariats generally. I am too old and now too sad [Clarke's wife had very recently died] to be supercilious; but I certainly do find, as you expected, something "quite different" from what "we conventionally suppose" the Government of India to be. ... Surely, in days gone by, Government was not as now, or we could not have established our Rule. Is the difference due to men, or to methods, or to methods for which men are responsible?

Or is it rather due to the vastly increasing complexity of Indian Government, in part at least arising from the monstrous over-centralization which has grown up unchecked? The burden must be lightened; the methods must be changed, if the Government of India is to be made into an effective instrument for promoting the progress of India. The machine is so cumbrous as to discourage all progress.[112]

Clarke's last report, a week later, was still more pessimistic, restating all that he had earlier noted about "want of unity" and "lack of necessary coordinating power," adding the warning that while "first class brains" alone were "now adequate vis a vis to the clever Indians who are becoming an influence," British "brain power here is not even second class."[113] Minto himself "has never consulted me on any matter —even about my own Presidency," Clarke complained, "and I have asked for an interview as I want to know his mind on some points." At that interview the Viceroy was "most kind," but Clarke judged that he "seemed to have very little grip or knowledge and to shun discussion with his Ministers for that reason."[114]

Another impression [wrote Sir George] which one cannot fail to derive here, is the great waste of money. There are large numbers of people who ought not to be at Simla and who are doing nothing of the least value to India. There is a Government of India architect, for example, of course with an Assistant.... There is a Government of India sculptor ... apparently engaged in carving effigies of horses on the Viceregal Stables, of course with great deliberation. I have had a good talk with the "Director General of Education" Mr. Orange, a very nice man who knows a great deal about Western Education but nothing about Education in India. I drew him out gently on his morning's work, which was to discover by wading through "files" whether some local government had spent some grant allocated by the Government of India. Of course this is not directing Education.... Then there is a Director General of Archeology, a very nice man, but his place is obviously not Simla. A "Director General of Commercial Intelligence" is employed in cutting extracts from newspapers which are made up into a journal. A Director General of Civil Veterinary Services with a considerable staff spends his seven months on these hills, divorced from any possibility of being of any practical use. These and many more such people play with papers, at great cost, and do nothing for India. Great capital expenditure is also visible everywhere in the huge overgrown Secretariats, and ... new costly carriage roads quite unjustifiable as only three persons are allowed to use carriages [viceroy, commander in chief, and lieutenant governor of the Punjab].[115]

But more devastating still than these formidable criticisms of inefficient administrative method and excessive expenditure was Clarke's condemnation of the very environment of Simla as an inherently debilitating seat for India's central government.

> The curious fallacy, that anybody attached to this Government of India becomes, ipso facto, an expert for all India, is evidently rampant [he wrote]. The fact is that, in this rarified atmosphere, a man loses much of what he may have acquired, because he is cut off from all connectoins with actualities.... Some officials here undoubtedly work hard, but largely upon small questions which should not come near them, and which leave them too little time to think of weighty affairs. The general standard of diligence is, however, not high, and the abundance of social frivolities cannot be good for the younger men.[116]

After reading these letters, Morley wrote back, "I feel like a man in a nightmare, intent on striking out, but powerless to lift his arm."[117] He found Simla's "manifest shortcomings" nothing less than "exasperating—no other word will do." From his desk six thousand miles away he noted in words bordering on despair, "The Machine may be a stupid Giant, but a Giant it is, and who is [to] amend the creature Heaven only knows. No S. S. can do it by himself." Then divesting himself momentarily of the burdens of office, he donned his mantle of historian-philosopher to conclude that the "great fault of all despotisms is not their violence or strength, but their weakness, due to *irresponsible* stupidity and clumsiness."[118] The more experience taught him of the malignant weakness of India's autocratic government, then, the more firmly John Morley adhered to the tenets of liberalism, especially the need for responsible civil rule and impartially administered law. What frustrated him most, however, was the lingering sense of strangeness about India itself, his remoteness from the roots of so many of the problems confronting him. Therefore, although he was seventy when Clarke invited him to "come out to Bombay"[119] to look around for himself, Morley welcomed the prospect eagerly.

It was a visit he had wanted to make from his very first months in office, and though he had mentioned "playing with the idea of a scamper to India" in several letters[120] to Minto, the Viceroy never took up the hint by responding with an invitation. Clarke's suggestion, however, spurred Morley to notify Minto that he had all but decided to make the trip east, but Minto replied with all the evasive rationalizations his inefficiently apprehensive mind could muster to keep the Secretary of State at home, arguing that it would be quite impossible for you to divest yourself of the Secretary of State—In normal times I am sure neither of us would need to think either of that or of the Viceroy's surroundings—but times are not normal—and it would be quite impossible for you to remain politically incognito. . . . Of course at no time would it do for you to visit Clarke and not me—one must remember the probable effects of things and the strange conclusions the public is always ready to jump at.[121]

The tortured message of anxiety came by wire as well as sea mail, and though Morley's initial reaction was contempt at how "small"[122] a man the Viceroy was and an inclination "to go at all events" to Bombay, he subsequently decided that a visit in the face of Minto's opposition might easily do more harm than good. "My India trip is over!!" he notified Clarke in October, 1909. "Lord Minto thinks that my appearance in India would be altogether inopportune, or worse. . . . Well, I have offered not a word of comment on all this to the G-G [Minto]."[123] Morley naturally saw through the pretense of Minto's argument, adding to his friend in Bombay, "If times are abnormal, that is all the more reason why we should take abnormal trouble to get full exchange of views among responsible people." Much indeed "would have been different," as Morley ruefully recognized in February, 1909, had Minto "been one of his own party."[124] "Everything," he went so far as to argue somewhat later, "depends upon the personal qualities of the Viceroy, his ideas [of] how to manage the bureaucrats."[125] This was why Morley, at least in choosing Minto's successor, adamantly resisted "very severe"[126] pressure from Windsor, Downing Street, and Simla, all urging the appointment of Lord Kitchener. To make Kitchener viceroy, Morley sensed, would be "to plant our Indian system on a military basis, and would be the signal to India that this is what we mean."[127] Morley's last great service to India was his single-handed resistance to any such appearance of reversion to a policy of jingoist imperialism. With Edward VII's death on May 6, 1910, Kitchener's strongest advocate disappeared from the scene, and at the royal funeral Morley was able to offer young Charles Hardinge, then undersecretary at the Foreign Office, the coveted position. Morley soon noted that his viceregal appointment was "uncommonly well taken both in India and at home," and considering how little known Hardinge was in either country, attributed such "general approval" to "relief that the Viceroy is not to be the great soldier."[128] Had Morley's own successor, Lord Crewe, been half as energetic and capable a secretary of state, the next half decade of Indian history might have been one not only of harmonious intercourse between Whitehall and Simla, but of significant Liberal achievement as well.

Thanks to Clarke in Bombay, Morley not only received a clearer picture of Simla's system, but was also able to recruit better men with Indian experience for the Whitehall council over which he presided. Created in 1858 as an administrative mausoleum for John Company's Court of Directors, the Council of India,[129] since the act of August 11, 1869, had come under the direct control of the secretary of state with regard to all appointments as well as business transactions. Less powerful a body than the viceroy's council, which technically shared with the governor-general executive responsibility for the government of India, Whitehall's council, though administratively subordinate to the secretary of state, retained considerable control over Indian finances. The value of new blood in so conservative a body could hardly be exaggerated, and among the more important of Morley's appointments to it was, at Clarke's recommendation, Sir Lawrence Jenkins of the Bombay court. "We want a man of good sense and a liberal mind," Morley wrote to Clarke. "Can you discover for me how Sir L. J. stands in these non-professional, or extra-professional aspects? Is he of the hardened bureaucrat species?"[130]

In reply Clarke, though not certain of Sir Lawrence's "politics," wrote: "He is most unlikely to have Tory proclivities being a rather fiery little Welshman, and he is as far as possible removed from 'the hardened bureaucrat species.' The Civilians here look with a shade of suspicion upon him on account of his strong sympathies with Natives."[131] Naturally, Morley appointed him at once, and within a few months referred to Jenkins as "a tower of strength to me."[132] In January, 1909, when Sir Francis W. Maclean, chief justice of Calcutta's High Court since 1896, at long last retired, Morley felt reluctantly obliged to send Jenkins back to India as chief justice. "His value to me is not to be told," he informed Minto, "his readiness, resource, clearness of mind, and unsparing industry. I shall miss him sorely."[133]

Now Jenkins started sending Morley letters from Calcutta which in their own way were as frank and depressing as Clarke's. Many Indians had apparently lost confidence, Sir Lawrence reported, "in the administration of justice."[134] It was generally assumed that judicial promotion was the reward of conviction in "political cases," and "at any rate it has gone out of fashion to give the prisoner the benefit of the doubt." If the average caliber of British civil servants in India was poor, the Englishmen shunted off into the judicial branch of the service were worse still. Since both executive and judicial branches recruited from a single Indian Civil Service pool, "and the prospects held out make the Executive branch far the more attractive . . . the best men go there, and the inferior men, in some cases the failures, come into the poor judicial."[135] Jenkins advised separate judicial recruitment "so that it would not be possible for a man to think, as I have heard it said by one recruited under our present system, that he was 'hauled howling into the judicial.'"

Commenting more broadly on relations between Englishmen and Indians, Sir Lawrence reported that "what confronts us here is not mere unrest: it is distrust [preceding word underlined by JM]. . . . And unhappily the distrust is not only of the rulers by the ruled; it is reciprocal and the White man (I of course only speak generally) appears to entertain a profound distrust of the Indian, and even of those who do not share and act up to this distrust."[136] The virulent racial hatred so euphemistically described by the word "distrust" was then illustrated by India's new chief justice, who related how his "colleague Fletcher, who is a most excellent judge, had the misfortune to decide a case with a political colour—it was Lajpat Rai's case—for the Indian and against the Englishman: for this he is an anathema to the White man, and he has even received a letter threatening his life, which cannot have come from an Indian source. . . . Similarly this small talk will have it that because I allow Indians to call on me 'I am in league with the agitators.'" On the bench as well as off, Jenkins' liberal judgments and egalitarian approach to mankind soon led, as he was "sorry to say" to Morley, to a "difference of opinion with Simla."[137] The India Office had been made painfully aware of that "difference" several months earlier when Minto refused to recommend Jenkins for a Star of India Knighthood (K.C.S.I.), despite Morley's very strong appeal that the honor be granted. One reason given by Minto for his refusal was Jenkins' "rumoured exaggerated Native proclivities on account of which it might be wise not to emphasize his appointment too markedly."[138] Morley felt so incensed that he confided to Godley that it "would make a permanent difference in his relations with the Viceroy."[139] To Minto he wrote acridly, "I care not a straw for the honour itself, no more, I am sure does Jenkins."[140] The battle between Whitehall and Simla was thus fought in the morass of personal vindictiveness as well as on the high plateaus of public policy.

Another Morley man sent to India to fill a truly important position was Guy Douglas Arthur Fleetwood Wilson, the economy-minded director general of army finance, whom Morley made finance member of Minto's council on November 9, 1908. Morley considered Finance "*the* department of Supreme Importance" to India at this time, and informed Minto: "You want a man—if you can ably chance to find one—possessed by a zealous spirit, not only of economy, but of financial management, contrivance, and grasp."[141] He had flatly refused to accept Minto's recommendation of Sir Herbert Hope Risley,[142] secretary to the government of India's Home Department, associated as Risley was "with the Partition of Bengal, and . . . generally *persona ingratissima* not only to Bengali agitators, but to most other people."[143] Fleetwood Wilson had impressed Morley as an extremely capable guardian of the public purse when, in championing the army's claims against the India Office on the Cromer Committee, he proved so persuasive that India's contribution to home military expenditure was actually increased. Unable to beat him, therefore, Morley decided to try luring Fleetwood Wilson away from Haldane's War Office, and convinced him to take "the risks of going to India for the first time at fifty-seven."[144]

Shortly after reaching India, Fleetwood Wilson sent home (not directly to Morley but to T. R. Buchanan, parliamentary undersecretary of state at the India Office, who showed the letters to JM) such scathing reports of the "deplorable" state of India's administration that Morley was "shocked"[145] and soon realized that, thanks to Minto's misleading letters, he had been "kept in the dark all the time."[146] Like Clarke and Jenkins, Wilson swiftly found himself "at daggers-drawn" with most of Simla's bureaucracy. Jenkins indeed became one of his few friends in India, outsiders that they were immersed in an often hostile enemy camp.[147] Writing to Sir Lawrence (High Court judges remained in Calcutta all year) from Simla, Wilson "confidentially" reported in July, 1909:

> Here we are likely to have a recrudescence of the *old* Adamsonian [Sir Harvey Adamson, home member of council] regime of panic legislation and drastic police methods. . . . if the present system of acting solely on the advice of Adamson and Risley is to continue no self-respecting man can remain here. . . . —I don't so much mind being ignored. What I will not stand is being pledged without my opinion being recorded. . . . I rarely see Lord Minto. . . . The last Council was put off owing to his not being equal to it. The whole Government is in the hands of the Secretaries. They see him once a week and it seems to me that they do just what they like with him. Which is bad for India. . . .[148]

Wilson's complaint of being "pledged" without consultation was the very criticism of Simla's uncoordinated administrative bureaucracy to which Clarke had referred in his earlier reports. The situation was seen by Wilson as essentially unconstitutional, for, "subject to the orders of the Secretary of State," India was "governed by 'the Governor General in Council,' not by the Governor-General, who, except for certain strictly defined and limited purposes, cannot act independently of his Council."[149] Wilson specifically protested that though on May 3, 1909, a telegram was sent from Simla which conveyed "to the Secretary of State the opinion of the Government of India . . . upon a subject of much gravity, *viz.*, the conditions under which the rights of citizenship should be denied to equal subjects of H.M., who have suffered deportation," he "had only heard of it in the street on the 27th of May."[150] He detected "a growing tendency" at Simla "to assume that a Member of Council's responsibility is limited to the work of the Department of which he is the head," yet added quite accurately and logically that "a Member of Council must accept his full share of responsibility for what is done in the name of the Government of India," and, therefore, "has the right to know what is done."[151] Minto's private secretary, Colonel J. R. Dunlop Smith, replied for the viceroy in a palpably offended tone, writing that "your note really amounts to a reflection upon the System under which the business of the Government of India is conducted."[152] The matter was then dismissed in classic bureaucratic fashion with advice to the "Honourable Member" that he submit "any proposal" he might wish to make for changing the "Rules of Business" to the Home Department. Fleetwood Wilson carried his struggle, however, to the point of appending notes of "dissent" to important government of India dispatches with which he could not agree. His picture of the "Simla System" was even more dismal than Clarke's:

> I do not join in the chorus of condemnation of Risley [he wrote in 1909], but I do think that Risley as the mouthpiece of Lady Minto [renowned as "the real Viceroy"[153]] *is* a source of danger. I am irresistibly reminded of the Holy Trinity. Lord M. is the long suffering Holy Ghost. But at any rate Risley has brains. Adamson has only got grey matter. . . . I have twice had to pull up Lady Minto for absolutely unauthorized and in my opinion "illegal" expenditure the result being that she cordially hates me. . . . Harvey [member of Council for Commerce and Industry since July, 1908] holds out but he is the only one who does and his influence and voice are negatived by his *very* regrettable indolence. He will

agree to anything to save himself trouble or work. . . . nothing can be worse than an entire lack of policy and that is our condition. . . . No one can say that Lord Minto is a clever man. I do not think he would claim to be so; but up to now the Scotch common sense of which he is undoubtedly possessed, has pulled him through very fairly well. I cannot help feeling, however, that he has changed much of late. I am inclined to attribute it to the Pasteur treatment,[154] followed by a severe and obstinate attack of diarrhoea. He looks better than he did and *is* better but the change in him becomes very apparent if he has to deal with any work. He seems to me to have become worn and listless. He seems supremely bored. The result is most unfortunate. The administration has drifted entirely into the hands of Secretaries to Government who are all powerful . . . policy has fallen completely into the hands of the Home Department which means that a purely policeman's view and the C. S. [civil service] detestation of the High Court marks indelibly our approach towards any case of "unrest" or sedition or foolish conduct. We all feel the lack of a directing hand and clear head. Mercifully we have both at the India Office and may they last there till there is a change here![155]

Always within sight and sound of his Simla colleagues, Fleetwood Wilson's personal plight was more difficult than that of either Clarke or Jenkins. Aware of the resentment of his colleagues, he wrote: "I am disliked because I preach the gospel of economy and try to avoid prejudice. 'They' look on me as an English nuisance who tampers with their time honoured 'perks,' [perquisites] for that is what it comes to."[156] Lord Minto himself by now considered Fleetwood Wilson his "chief trouble," branding him, among other things, as "absolutely disloyal" and "a dangerous intriguer." There was a story "going the rounds" about Wilson, "which is characteristic," Minto reported, adding with unconsciously ironic ambiguity, "and I believe true. On coming out of Council lately, he met a lady friend, who asked him what he had been doing. 'Listening,' he said, 'to the attempts of six stupid men to overrule me'!"[157]

Morley's "grand support" alone induced Wilson to remain at his job, resolving that "if I can start a train of thought inclining to Economy, Courtesy to Indians and sobriety in politics I shall die satisfied."[158] Morley himself was most pleased with Fleetwood Wilson's performance. He clearly proved his satisfaction with his London appointee by once again "passing over the entire Indian Civil Service,"[159] as the *Times* complained editorially, in naming W. H. Clarke, of the British Board of Trade, who had never been to India, as commerce and industry member of Minto's council in July, 1910.

Prior to Morley's era, appointments to lieutenant-governorships, the choicest patronage plums at the top of the Indian Civil Service ladder, were left exclusively to the viceroy's discretion. This policy had indeed become so firmly established through practice that Morley himself acknowledged, during his first year in office, at the "obdurate" advice of his permanent staff, that "the Governor-General is technically and constitutionally the sole authority over Lieutenant-Governors."[160] As his confidence in Minto diminished, however, he significantly augmented the Secretary of State's direct influence over Indian administration by bringing lieutenant-governorships within close range of Whitehall's scrutiny.

"From some expressions in your telegrams about Dane [candidate for lieutenant governor of Punjab]," he wrote Minto in January, 1908, "I rather gather that you regard the consultation of the Secretary of State about a Lieutenant-Governor as exceptional ... for my own part I could not consent to take the responsibility of recommending a Lieutenant-Governor to the King, unless my own judgment, so far as I had material for a judgment, went with the Governor-General's proposal."[161] By 1908 Morley had in fact so little faith in Minto's judgment that he was loath to appoint a good man to the Lieutenant-governorship of Bengal "partly because he *won't* take the G. G.'s [Governor-General's] recommendation."[162] Sufficient other testimony concerning the Liberal predilections of Sir Edward Norman Baker, finance member of the viceroy's council, subsequently convinced Morley, however, to approve his promotion to West Bengal's Belvedere House on December 1, 1908. But Minto's attempts to assert that the viceroy must always be left a free hand to select lieutenant-governors met with immediate rebuttal from Morley, who armed himself "with the *legalities*" and sent back a formal constitutional verdict to serve his successors as well as himself. "To put it plainly and in a single sentence," he concluded, "the responsibility of recommending a Lieutenant-Governor to the Sovereign is a compound thing, to which both the Governor-General and the Secretary of State contribute, but the Secretary of State cannot help having the last word."[163] Minto continued to disagree, however, arguing that he felt "very strongly that the Viceroy is entitled to choose his own chief officers," submitting "the names of those he wishes to appoint to the King, through the Secretary of State [last five words underlined in the original by Morley]."[164] Morley's answer was unequivocal. "The Viceroy can no more 'submit' anything to the King," he replied, "than Godley can. Any Whig ghost, or living lawyer, will convince you of this."[165]

But selection of officers was only a first step in the assertion by Whitehall of its control over the government of India. For that control to remain effective, direct correspondence between the India Office and all members of the administrative service abroad would have to be established and maintained at the secretary of state's discretion. This was precisely what Morley wanted to do. Minto, however, refused to allow Dunlop Smith to correspond directly with Hirtzel,[166] and "took exception" to Morley's attempt to establish an independent line of communication with Kitchener.

"I am entirely opposed to the principle of approving a channel of correspondence on state affairs between an official serving under me and a Member of His Majesty's Government [last five words underlined by JM],"[167] wrote the Viceroy. He argued that if such correspondence "became a recognized thing" the position might prove "awkward" for the Viceroy. Morley on the other hand was determined to "assert (tho' not necessarily to use) his right"[168] to correspond with whomever he pleased in the government of India. In his letter of April 4, 1907, he told Minto as much, explaining that as "Indian Secretary" he was "not a fortuitous member of government, but the head of the Indian department, responsible to parliament for all that is done or left undone in the whole sphere of Indian administration."[169] Though a principle was thus vigorously asserted and defended by Morley, in practice Minto won his point. With the exception of Clarke, with whom Morley exchanged weekly letters for several years, his only regular correspondent in India was Lord Minto himself, indeed a "dark" window as Wilson's and Clarke's letters from Simla both revealed.

In some respects the struggle between Whitehall and Simla was a cold war of nerves, of threats pushed to the brink of action, verbal barrages hurled intercontinentally. Many of Morley's "victories," like that following the battle of the letters, actually changed nothing. Some, as will be seen in the chapters dealing with reforms, proved purely pyrrhic. Despite an overworked "hot line" cable between London and India, and a personal staff of six secretaries and aides assigned to the Viceroy, Morley complained throughout his era[170] that Minto kept him insufficiently informed. Minto, on the other hand, often gasped[171] that he was obliged to spend so much of his time writing and wiring England that he had none left to devote to India. To its own author's mind each complaint was equally justified, for Morley and Minto governed according to totally different rule books. Morley wanted to run India by techniques he had learned over a quarter of a century in the Commons. Minto could no more appreciate the reasons for such responsible rule than Morley could enjoy a horse race or a tiger hunt.

Perhaps the ultimate failure of Morley's attempt to harness an autocratic government of India to the Commons' traces may best be seen in the battles over repression. These are considered in detail in another chapter, yet, as already noted, Hirtzel, or somebody else at the India Office, stood ever ready to caution Morley that "emergencies" could be judged only by "the man on the spot." There was just enough truth in that argument to leave the government of India with as broad a margin of autocracy as it liked for much longer than Morley or his party would have acquiesced at home. Once or twice only did the "liberal Conscience" of his time emphatically refuse to swallow that "stand behind the man on the spot" line. When Kitchener insisted upon the need for a special press law, for example, to keep his soldiers free of ideological contamination, Morley's reply was, "He [Kitchener] is no fit judge whether writing is likely to promote sedition. That is for the civil power."[172] Then, too, when Sir Arthur Lawley, governor of Madras, threatened to initiate action against Bepin Chandra Pal for sedition, Morley exercised his power of prior veto, having "as little confidence as possible" in Lawley's "fitness to judge a delicate and critical situation."[173] Minto he only "beseeched,"[174] cajoled, eventually threatened. Often wasting both sarcasm and historical allusions, he tried by long-distance letter to beat autocratic swords into responsible ploughshares. "I have often thought that Strafford was an ideal type, both for governor of Ireland in the Seventeenth century, and governor of India in the Twentieth century,"[175] he wrote Minto, "But then, they cut off poor Strafford's head, and that idea of Government has been in mighty disfavour ever since,—not in Russia, however, nor apparently in the Punjab or the United Provinces. . . . Let Sir Denzil [Ibbetson] go for an honest guillotine, and be done with it."

On rare occasions, Morley's eye was drawn to some act of official brutality or callous disregard for human suffering, but his strong, spontaneous reactions served less to ameliorate the Indian system than to highlight the gulf in human values yawning between Whitehall and Simla. "I beg your attention to the enclosed flogging case," Morley directed Minto, referring to a sentence of thirty stripes, reduced through judicial compassion to six strokes, and then carried out. "It fills me with disgust. Now I have told the House of Commons that I am considering flogging, with the Government of India—and I must be able to make a full statement.... Will you kindly press the authorities concerned to put the steam on?"[176]

A year later the overburdened secretary in charge of a department of state embracing no less than 300 million people had to take the time to send another note to his ever-vigilant viceroy. Morley now acted as advocate for a "criminal" sentenced to eight years of rigorous imprisonment for stealing a water jar "or some such thing." "I don't want to bring down the sledge-hammer of the Crown," he wearily warned Minto. "I only bespeak your personal interest in the case. When you have leisure, peruse the Beatitudes—chapter V of St. Matthew—I refer from memory. But the Governor always knows the Bible. Pray, let him out, will you."[177]

Minto used what leisure he had for his horses and hunt, although, even if he had had the time, it is highly improbable that the Viceroy would have spent it in trying to implement Morley's mere wishes concerning matters so trivial. With reference to a prisoner of the fame and popularity of Lala Lajpat Rai, for example, about whom Morley wrote at least half a dozen times to Minto appealing for rapid release, and concerning whom at least a dozen questions were asked in Parliament, indifference to Whitehall's Liberal leader, amounting to official insubordination, was the bureaucratic rule.

Studying Lajpat's "file" several months after his release, Morley was shocked:

It seems clear from the papers that the Lieutenant-Governor of Burma refused Lajpat's request to see his solicitor. This is in itself a hateful thing to do, only worthy of Russia, or, say Austria, in her Italian days. But worse still, I was allowed to tell the H. of C. that access to a solicitor would of course be allowed. In this, nobody in your government set me right.... More than that, I was permitted to say that he was allowed to receive letters from his family. It now seems that some 50 such letters were stopped, and I was never told. Now, even the officials responsible in India, must surely know that in this country, which after all, is and means to be their master, for a Minister to mislead Parliament in matters of fact, is as heinous an offence as he can commit.[178]

It was not the heated opposition, but rather "the cool indifference of your officers and ministers to what is said or done in Parliament,"[179] which frustrated Morley most, and succeeded in effectively stalemating his efforts to liberalize the administration. Open defiance on Simla's part would have meant inevitable defeat; unflappable inertia brought the easiest of victories. By his final year in office, Morley learned that the only language Minto understood was that of blunt and direct warning. After more than a year of appealing to the Viceroy to release political suspects who had been deported without trial and kept in "preventive detention," Morley wrote *"the clock has struck . . . let me know whether you accede to my private request, or whether I shall be forced to official instruction. I should like a telegram, if you please."*[180] A week later he shouted, "Your mention of Martial Law in your last private letter, makes my hair stand on end. . . . Martial Law, which is only a fine name for the suspension of all law, would not snuff out murder-clubs in India, any more than the same sort of thing snuffed them out in Italy, Russia, or Ireland. . . . It would be neither more nor less than a gigantic advertisement of national failure."[181] Yet the increasingly strident and short-tempered tone of Morley's letters, whenever dealing with matters of repression, may be taken as a gauge measuring his failure as long-distance liberal missionary to Simla. Minto himself and the bureaucratic machine he managed remained unconverted, unregenerate autocrats.

In its report of April 2, 1909, the Royal Commission upon Decentralization, appointed by Morley, affirmed that the secretary of state "has the power of giving orders to every officer in India, including the Governor-General,"[182] but failed to explain how he could compel any officer to carry out those orders in a manner even vaguely approaching the spirit in which they were issued. Morley's friends[183] as well as his political enemies[184] accused him of the "very great mistake" of trying to govern India "too much from Whitehall." His real error, however, was trying to govern with too few agents inclined to pay more than lip service to his policy. Toward the end of his era the mere threat of administrative delay in introducing reforms sufficed to make him abandon all detailed criticism of reform regulations, and even appeal to Clarke not to "fight too hard over every disputable point." "The Government of India must almost necessarily win with the last word," he sighed, since the "Government of India threaten me with delay 'for another year,' if we here intervene too actively with machinery, electoral rolls, etc. . . . 'Another year'! The announcement of any further long delay would discourage all our Moderates. . . . The miscarriage of delay would be a huge disaster, and nothing less."[185]

Ironically enough, Simla fought Whitehall by methods of "non-cooperation" long before Gandhi made that technique the *credo* of India's National Congress.

In summing up the accomplishments of Morley's half decade in office, his last parliamentary undersecretary, young Edwin Montagu,[186] frankly informed the Commons that although "responsibility" for the government of India "rests ultimately on the people of Great Britain, and is exercised through the Secretary of State in his Council,"[187] that "Secretary of State is separated from this task by the sea, hampered by the delays of communication, often checkmated by the lapse of time. . . . the most liberal-minded, hard-working Secretary of State is helpless without a loyal, conscientious and statesmanlike Viceroy."[188] It was at once a proclamation of Whitehall's theoretical omnipotence over Simla, and a confession of its often practical impotence. Yet this remarkably revelatory portion of Montagu's budget message was eclipsed entirely by the sensation-stirring statement that "Lord Morley and his Council, working through the agency of and with the help of Lord Minto, have accomplished much."[189] The *Times* immediately protested that "the Viceroy and the Government of India, though possibly exceedingly unobtrusive, still exist," and that it was not "quite a healthy procedure for the Home Government to claim leadership in every new measure designed for the better welfare of India."[190] Old Indian correspondents in London like Lovat Fraser were anxious to jump into print with attacks against "Lord Morley's growing tendency to usurp the functions of the Government of India."[191] Fraser considered this tendency "most mischievous and dangerous," as he noted in a "private" letter to Lee-Warner, asking the disaffected councillor "if you can suggest any lines of research bearing upon the point, or can recall past instances of conflict." Lee-Warner was obviously tempted, but in his official position merely wrote on the top margin of Fraser's letter, "Is this a trap? Anyway I declined to help." In Simla itself Minto and his council manned their barricades, and vigorously penned minutes "regarding the powers of the Secretary of State and of the Government of India."[192] Everyone present but Fleetwood Wilson agreed that Montagu had gone too far, yet all concluded that pitched battle with Whitehall over this issue would be dangerous. Minto wrote:

> I am sure no one is more strongly tempted than I am to take immediate official exception to the attitude assumed by Mr. Montagu, but after much consideration I entirely agree . . . that such action on our part would

afford an opportunity to the Secretary of State for a definite pronouncement as to his interpretation of his constitutional authority and the powers of the Government of India. There would be grave risk . . . of the conversion of his "pretensions" into "usage."

As usual, Simla chose to conquer by silence if not by actual stooping, yet had Minto paused to "consider" Montagu's reference to himself as the "agent" of Whitehall a moment longer he might have remembered that this phrase was already well established constitutionally, thanks to Morley's "usage."[193] Two days after Montagu's famous speech, however, Morley wrote to inform Minto that "the title of Viceroy, etc., etc., confers on the Governor-General no special powers. Canning's despatch of the 24th December 1859, endorsed by Sir Charles Wood, justifies the Governor-General in regarding himself as vested with authority to confer native titles, but his powers in this respect, as in all other respects whatever, are subject to the control of the Secretary of State."[194] For the public record, shortly after resigning his office, Morley took great pains in writing a most significant essay called "British Democracy and Indian Government," in which he insisted:

Nobody will dispute that the Cabinet are just as much masters of the Governor-General, as they are over any other servants of the Crown. The Cabinet, through a Secretary of State, have an inexpugnable right, subject to law, to dictate policy, to initiate instructions, to reject proposals, to have the last word in every question that arises, and the first word in every question that in their view ought to arise. On no other terms could our Indian system come within the sphere of parliamentary government.[195]

The victory of Whitehall was thus proclaimed for all who could read to admire, and many of Morley's most vigorous political opponents were first to concede his claims. "You ask me whether the complete obliteration of the Government of India is realized in India, and if it is deplored," wrote Sir John Hewett,[196] lieutenant governor of the United Provinces, to Lord Curzon in February, 1910. "I think that there is no doubt that the answer to both these questions is in the affirmative. Lord Morley is not altogether blamed for this, though every one regards him . . . as grasping of power. But the main blame is put on the Viceroy for allowing the Government of India to be dominated as it is. He has a wretchedly weak Council, but he has never been in the habit of consulting it. . . . I regard the position as hopeless."[197]

An unsigned article entitled "India under Lord Minto," printed in the influential *Quarterly Review* of January, 1911, took much the same line, arguing that Minto was induced "to break away from the custom of all his predecessors"[198] by abandoning weekly meetings of the Executive Council, thereby destroying the "cohesion and force" of India's government. The "system" introduced in its place was described as

> a most convenient one for the Secretary of State, who could always meet Parliamentary critics with some communication from the man on the spot upholding his own views.... The two-man Government thus set up inevitably becomes one-man Government, the Government of him who has the last word. As between Lord Morley and Lord Minto, unsuspicious, unambitious, unassertive, the result was never doubtful. Too late in the day, the Viceroy realized the position into which his easiness had led him. ... As the time for his departure drew nigh, Lord Minto must have become conscious that he was not leaving behind him a measure that could be called his own.... The loss of reputation thus incurred by the Viceroy is a blow to our prestige and therefore to our security in India hardly less serious than that dealt by the defeat of Lord Curzon in his dispute with the Commander-in-Chief.[199]

Yet, after five years at the India Office, the Old Philosopher knew better than his most pessimistic enemies how much of his struggle with Simla and the bureaucratic machine that governed India remained unwon. He gauged fully the bitter distance between assertion of a principle and its practical implementation. He was seasoned veteran enough in "the art of the possible" to understand that any battle waged against a machine as massive as the government of India's bureaucracy could not be won simply in half a decade. But with that optimistic outlook concerning the future, often reserved as a special gift for the very aged, Morley realized that if he started a worthy struggle others would follow to help achieve his goals. As long as he remained in office, he was determined not to lie down supinely like the dying Tsar Nicholas, who, as Morley put it, complained that "Russia was governed by ten thousand tchinovicks. Autocrat as he was, they were his master. That was bureaucracy with a vengeance, and it ended ill."[200] Though Morley could not destroy British India's *tchinovick* raj, therefore, he could and did bring it within firing range of the one adversary powerful enough to control it—responsible democratic government.

4

THE ARMY AND FOREIGN AFFAIRS

> If I were Lord Chesterfield writing to a son whom I meant to be a statesman, I should say to him, "Remember that in the great high latitudes of policy, all is fluid, elastic, mutable; the friend today, the foe tomorrow; the ally and confederate against your enemy, suddenly *his* confederate against you . . ."
>
> Morley to Minto, February 28, 1907

As an old-fashioned Gladstonian, Morley believed in the enduring virtues of peace, retrenchment, and reform. His India Office policy may indeed be said basically to have consisted of these three strands of Liberal aspiration, and his era may be analyzed by considering how each of these goals was pursued, and with what degree of success.

Like his Liberal forebears Morley made the pursuit of peace the preeminent part of his policy, recognizing that its attainment was in fact a prerequisite to retrenchment and reform. In the recent history of British India, of course, the maintenance of internal order was often more difficult and challenging a task than securing peace beyond the borders. Problems of internal pacification are considered in the next chapter.

Kitchener's victory[1] over Curzon and the latter's replacement by a soldier-viceroy in 1905 made the possibility of a military autocracy fastening its grip upon India seem all too imminent. Conscious as he was of this threat, Morley lost no time in directing his attention to the scheme of military reorganization which had led to Curzon's resignation. Military administration was indeed "the first question which he took up"[2] as India secretary, for Morley was determined to be sure that "the civil power must be unquestionably supreme, not only on paper, but *practically*."[3]

Brodrick's military reorganization scheme, inaugurated on November 18, 1905, had abolished the old Military Department of the government of India, distributing its work between the newly created Army and Military Supply departments. The commander in chief was no longer a mere "extraordinary member" of the viceroy's Executive Council, appointed at the secretary of state's discretion, but became hereafter the regular member in charge of the Army Department, which inherited control over most important facets of military policy. From its inception[4] the Military Supply Department was meant to be little more than a device for relieving the commander in chief of relatively minor but burdensome administrative matters concerning matériel. When Curzon failed in his attempt to enhance the status of the Military Supply Department by making its member a general of independent mind (Barrow), Kitchener's man (General Scott) was appointed instead, and the commander in chief became in fact sole arbiter of military matters, on the Executive Council as well as at army headquarters. Morley "never thought much of the scheme on its merits,"[5] yet knew he could not revert to the old system of dual military control so soon after Curzon's resignation without "almost compelling" Kitchener and "quite possibly inducing" Minto "to retire."[6] Although he personally never admired Kitchener's military or mental prowess,[7] Morley was responsible enough to warn his cabinet colleagues in February, 1906, that the effect of the commander in chief's resignation "upon Indian respect for British government, would be an extremely undesirable sequel to the performances of last August." What Morley hoped to do was to keep Kitchener content enough to stay in India, while holding him under civilian control.

The problem was compounded by the fact that Minto was also a soldier, and readily fell into step with his commander in chief, who was reputed to be "a very clever humbug."[8] The "rumour spreading through India" by January, 1906, was "that Kitchener has completely 'nobbled' Lord Minto."[9] Minto's early letters to the India Office certainly show that the Viceroy had at least developed profound respect and admiration for his hero-colleague. "I believe that the country possesses in Kitchener," Minto wrote, "a most able administrator, possessed of great financial talent and, what is rare amongst soldiers, a strict regard for economy."[10] The Viceroy insisted that Kitchener, far from aiming at "military autocracy, fully recognizes his constitutional questions."[11] "The unreasonableness of Kitchener," Minto reported, "is a perfect myth. In all the conversations I have had with him he has been absolutely fair and broadminded."[12] There were indeed few subjects on which Minto lavished as much literary attention as he paid to the character and personality of his commander in chief, calling him "one of the few broadminded soldiers I have met, very pleasant in conversation with a taste for gardening and art—rather more I should say inclined towards administration than active service—or perhaps it would be fairer to say, in time of peace inclined to look to large administration, and leave military details to subordinates he can rely upon," adding, however, that "in a great war he would no doubt look for his chance."[13] Clearly Minto was convinced of Kitchener's universal genius, although Morley remained more than skeptical. His doubts about the great soldier and the new army scheme flowed in red ink along the margins of Minto's laudatory letters, lingering as lines drawn by Morley's questioning hand under many of Minto's words.

"It appears to me that in selecting a Commander-in-Chief we ought to be prepared to *accept him distinctly as the adviser* of the Government of India on military matters," wrote Minto, "provided always the supremacy of the Civil authority is absolutely *guaranteed*."[14] Morley did the underscoring and asked in the adjacent margin, "But how?" On the lower margin he noted, "You are to accept him as the adviser, distinctly. But as single adviser? How are you to test and check his advice? Is his advice to come to you direct or thru' Sec. of War Department?" Minto's letter concluded reassuringly: "In doubtful questions I should not hesitate to consult leading soldiers in India other than the Commander-in-Chief." Morley, however, again underscored the ambiguous word "doubtful" and explained his qualms in the margin, writing "Yes—but a civilian G.G. [governor-general] will not always know *when* a military question is doubtful." What Clarke termed the "bogy of military domination" remained vividly "present to Morley's imagination."[15]

Morley's military policy was first formally articulated in his dispatch to the government of India of February 9, 1906,[16] in which he overruled both Minto and Kitchener on what he told the King was "one very important matter, affecting the subordination of the military to the civil authority."[17] That matter dealt with the rules of business proposed by the government of India for the new Army Department. Kitchener wanted to short-circuit the Army Department's secretariat by permitting members of his headquarters staff to propose administrative and financial matters directly to him as member in charge of the department, rather than through the usual channel of submission to the department secretary, who reported to the viceroy, who could, in turn, consult other council members at his discretion. Ironically enough, Kitchener's usurpation of the Military Department's administrative burdens as commander in chief removed the latter office from active field control over wartime operations, and thus contributed to the tragic debacle in Mesopotamia in the First World War, as the Mesopotamia Commission was to report in 1917.[18] Morley's subsequent abolition of the Military Supply Department ultimately contributed further to the creation of a grossly inefficient system of Indian military administration, but Morley did not plan for war, and indeed believed so strongly that England could and should have stayed out of the First World War that he resigned[19] from the cabinet when its majority decided to the contrary. What concerned Morley most about military administration in India was keeping a civil check upon Simla's headquarters staff. In paragraph 7 of his dispatch of February 9, he wrote:

> I consider that, if the supremacy of civil government is to be real and effective, and if the Viceroy is to be in a position to fulfill the duty cast upon him by the Statute of 1833, of "supervising, directing, and controlling" military affairs in India, then it is necessary that the Secretary to the Government of India should have status, powers, duties, and responsibilities precisely similar to those of the Secretaries to the Government of India in the other Departments.

Morley made the governor-general in council's dominance over the commander in chief the "Cardinal object" (par. 5) of his India military policy, and protested: "In so far as the proposed Rules do not keep the Army Department distinct from the Headquarters Staff" (par. 8), they failed to adhere to that policy. Minto, although not in agreement with Morley, readily acquiesced to his demanded changes in the rules. "Personally, as you know," wrote the Viceroy, "I do not think it necessary to draw a distinct line between the Army Head-Quarters and the Secretariat."[20]

Morley was as determined to prevent India's bureaucracy from becoming predominantly "military" as he was to keep it from being "mechanical and lifeless."[21] He kept close watch over Kitchener's attempted encroachments into realms of civil responsibility,[22] and encouraged Minto to remove Major General C. H. Scott, "Kitchener's mumbling shadow,"[23] from the Executive Council. Morley was, in fact, anxious to abolish Scott's Military Supply Department entirely, since by Minto's own admission it was "good neither for administration nor for economy."[24] It was only Minto's repeated apprehension that the department's abolition would revive smoldering embers of the Curzon-Kitchener controversy which kept Morley from acting more promptly than he did in removing the "cypher" of Scott from India's supreme council. When, in 1910, he finally abolished the Department of Military Supply, its place was appropriately filled by the new Department of Education.

By defending the viceroy's supreme authority over the commander in chief, Morley was naturally indirectly protecting his own claim to control military policy through Minto's "agency." When Minto seemed loath to accept Whitehall's lead in fighting Kitchener, Morley was quick to complain of "military autocracy with a vengeance,"[25] or insist, "It is very well to argue that Lord K. should know best; only to admit this without conditions, is to acquiesce in that 'military autocracy' so bitterly predicted by Curzon and his partisans three years ago."[26] In no other realm was Morley's assertion of Whitehall's dominance over Simla more emphatically and persistently made than in this overlapping zone of military and foreign affairs. "We have hitherto been far too parochial, separate, isolated, and divisive, in dealing with military and naval organization; only moved now and then by the temporary whim of this or that autocratic proconsul, like Curzon,"[27] Morley told Minto in March, 1906. In the future, he insisted, Indian military questions could no longer be divorced from overall British foreign policy. Significant "new factors" in the field of foreign affairs had appeared, including Russia's dramatic fall in status, Japan's sudden emergence as a world power, the Anglo-French entente, and Germany's ubiquitous challenge to English interests. Among these, Russia's defeat by Japan was by far the most important factor for India, and Morley was determined to take full diplomatic advantage of it.

Since the 1860's Anglo-Indian foreign policy had been dominated by the specter of Russian expansion across Central Asia. The fear that Russia's manifest destiny lay beyond the Oxus and over the Hindu Khush remained very real in Simla until at least mid-1905.[28] Kitchener's master plan for army reorganization[29] was in fact predicated upon the assumption that a Russian invasion was imminent. "What is the main danger which threatens our position in India?" he asked in his "secret" note on "Military Policy" penned at Simla on July 19, 1905. "To this there can be but one answer—it is the menacing advance of Russia." In order to counter this menace, Kitchener proposed reducing the "obligatory garrison" stationed throughout India for suppressing revolt so as to more than double the number of divisions (from four to nine) held ready to "be released for frontier war" in the northwest, erecting cantonments along the northwest border to garrison these troops "in peace under command of war officers," augmenting the total size of Britain's army in India to a strength of 128,844 officers and men and 434 heavy guns, and extending strategic railway lines from Peshawar over the Khyber and from Thal up the Kurram Valley to Parachinar. All of this was to have been accomplished in five years (beginning in March, 1904) at a cost of approximately £20 million plus an annual charge of another £1.5 million. "A great deal of money," Morley noted as his first reflection upon the Kitchener scheme, "especially for a country where a good many people are miserably poor."[30] The best way to reduce that expenditure, he perceived, would be to remove the primary rationalization for having introduced the scheme in the first place by reaching a rapprochement with Russia over Central Asian affairs. Morley made the conclusion of just such an agreement the keynote of his India Office foreign policy. Not that he originated the idea of Anglo-Russian entente, for that was born in the Foreign Office. It was, in fact, part of Grey's legacy from Lord Lansdowne, who had proposed, in 1904, much the same[31] Central Asian convention that the Russians accepted three years later. Credit for the change of heart in Petersburg, moreover, which predisposed the Tsar's government in March, 1906, to "reopen negotiations,"[32] belongs with Japan, while Sir Arthur Nicolson's astuteness, Sir Henry Hardinge's diligence, and Sir Edward Grey's shrewdness each deserve their own laurels in helping conclude the convention of 1907. But, as Grey himself put it, "Without Morley we should have made no progress at all, for the Government of India would have blocked every point, and Morley has removed mountains in the way of negotiations."[33] Morley's overriding concern for peace and military retrenchment indeed motivated him to become Grey's "most active" cabinet colleague in pursuing the policy of Anglo-Russian entente. "It is hard to believe," Morley early insisted to Minto, "that there is no alternative to the stupid and ignoble rivalries that now constitute what is called our Central Asian system."[34]

From Morley's first mention of the possibility of reaching agreement with Russia, Minto reacted with moralistic skepticism. "I have always been very doubtful as to the reliability of the professions of Russian diplomatists," argued the Viceroy. Then he added, as though he were the Liberal in the dialogue, "I cannot help saying that Russian rule to my mind conveys much that is corrupt and horrible and that I do not like the feeling of making friends with the Mammon of unrighteousness!"[35] Slightly later Minto self-righteously "confessed" that "it goes against the grain with me, even in view of future advantages, to appear in any way to support the most infamous tyranny in modern times in the shape of the Russian government. Personally I would much rather that we stood aloof."[36] Minto's foreign policy, in sharp contrast with Whitehall's, would have been (had Morley permitted him to pursue it) to attempt negotiating an Indo-Afghan-Persian alliance against Russia. "The Amir [King of Afghanistan, Habibullah Khan] is a more dangerous neighbour to us than Russia, and therefore in respect to India a more necessary friend," argued the Viceroy. "If we are to enter upon an 'entente' with Russia, let us bargain with her elsewhere than in Central Asia."[37] Morley responded that "the policy of *entente* with Russia" was not "an open question," explaining that "H.M.'s Government have determined on their course, and it is for their agents and officers all over the world to accept it."[38] Minto nonetheless hoped, by personal diplomacy, to effect closer ties with Afghanistan at least, taking it upon himself to invite Habibullah to visit India. When, in September, 1906, the Amir "accepted our invitation," Minto wrote Morley that as regards "the political aspect of the Amir's visit, there is a great deal to be said. Personally I ascribe immense value to it ... from a big point of view the Amir's visit is full of future possibilities."[39] Little did he anticipate what these were in fact to be, for at the time Minto added, "What I feel is that as regards the Amir we are dealing with what they call in the New World a 'live man.' Russia at the present moment is not a 'live man.' "

Morley disagreed. As he explained to Lamington, "I am no Russian, heaven knows, but I won't put on great blinkers, to prevent me from seeing anything else but Russian intrigues, mendacity, etc., etc., in the whole field of international policy."[40] His perspective from London was, of course, much broader than Minto's, encompassing especially the challenge of German diplomacy in the wake of her expanding commerce. "To weaken England," Morley tried to explain to Minto, Germany was prepared to "use the Russian and the Turk wherever she can. She increases her fleet, in order to give courage to her merchants."[41] By the logic of diplomacy then, "for the same reasons that make Germany seek coldness or a quarrel between us and Russia, we ought to do what we can to baulk her." Friendly Russian overtures early in 1907 to England's Asian ally, Japan, moreover, were recognized by Morley as "pointing to an Anglo-Russo-Japanese understanding that expansion of territory in Central Asia or the Far East, is to come (for the time at least) definitely to an end. This will be indeed a blessed consummation, if the immortal gods will only allow sensible men to bring it about."[42] Morley had, on the other hand, no faith in the prospects of Minto's personal diplomacy, and actually instructed the Viceroy "on no account to open any political questions"[43] in his discussions with Habibullah. The entire visit of the Amir, starting as it did in January, 1907, and lasting for three critical months during the delicate negotiations with Russia, was considered ill-timed and ill-advised by Morley. He cautioned King Edward against personally wiring the Amir at the visit's conclusion, fearing that "any exaggeration of our triumph with the Amir will be likely to place a weapon in the hands of the Military and anti-English party at St. Petersburg."[44] Even so, coincidental with the visit, Minto reported "a good deal of Russian activity on our Central Asian Frontier," ingenuously explaining, "The Amir has also heard rumours of this activity which may perhaps be intended as an indication that our relations with him have not passed unnoticed."[45] In almost palpably futile frustration Morley scrawled in the margin as he read this letter, "Just what was certain to follow Amir's visit." To Minto he wrote presciently of another "future possibility" of the visit which had never occurred to the viceroy:

> I find myself wondering now and then how the Mullahs and the anti-English Sirdars, etc., will like it all. If the Afghans are really the furious fanatics of whom we have always heard, won't they be scandalized by this close hob-nobbing with unbelievers? Heaven forbid that I should deprive myself of an argument against excessive military expenditure—and a friendly Amir is an argument in that direction—but still I don't feel quite sure that one of these days we may not find Habibullah a broken reed, surrounded by revolters, just as the French have found the Sultan of Morocco.[46]

That was precisely what happened to the "fat little man"[47] who liked wearing European clothes, developed a penchant for "talking to English ladies,"[48] and prefaced his "witty" remarks with the phrase

"Now I make joke," soon after he returned to the perilous fastness of his hermit kingdom. Within a fortnight the Amir was "having a hot time with his Mullahs," Morley noted from telegraphic reports of an attempted assassination by several of Habibullah's "devout" subjects as he passed through Lughman between Jellalabad and Kabul. "I always thought this most likely," added Morley "and it was one of the reasons for the policy of holding as much aloof as possible from all bargains, cooperations, and the like, with a community made up of elements so unstable and incalculable. The Mullah denouncing Habibullah is like John Knox denouncing Mary Stuart for her consorting with French idolaters."[49] In a year Habibullah, whose "wives dress like English ladies,"[50] was reported to be losing strength at Kabul to his austere anti-British brother Nasrulla. After another year the Amir's enemies, led by the mother of his imbecile half brother Umar Jan, hatched an abortive plot to murder Habibullah.[51]

Minto's "live man" had turned into a "light weight,"[52] and, although Habibullah Khan lingered on his throne for another decade before being assassinated, Nasrulla Khan, who retained the respect of the Mullahs, became the more powerful brother at Kabul. By personal diplomacy, Minto had succeeded in doing little more than to wean Habibullah from his own countrymen.

Resolved not to give the Amir an exaggerated sense of his own importance, Morley ignored Minto's proposals that Habibullah be consulted fully "as to matters appertaining to his own kingdom during the negotiations with Russia."[53] Instead, Grey was able to tell Nicolson he "need not fear delay on our side about Afghanistan. I spoke to Morley about it, and when a satisfactory Asiatic Agreement is in shape, I think he will be prepared to agree and to settle with the Amir afterwards, without hanging the whole thing up."[54] That agreement came on August 31, 1907, when Nicolson and Isvolsky signed the Anglo-Russian Convention in St. Petersburg.

Divided into three parts, the convention[55] served to define Russian and British "interests" and spheres of influence in Persia, Afghanistan, and Tibet. As such, it was a frank admission of imperialistic encroachment in Central Asia. Morley was well aware that "critics will say that we have sold the popular party in Persia, and the Amir in Afghanistan, and it will not surprise me," he admitted to Minto, "if the Government had to face a sort of compound attack from the regular opposition, *plus* the ultra-Radicals, who will resent an entente with a 'despotic bureaucracy' like Russia. We shall not get any thanks at the best.

That's the way of the world to its benefactors."[56] He understood, however, that in Russia, as in Britain at that time, there were factions whose foremost interest was peace, and others who yearned for military expansion. By patient diplomacy the latter had been thwarted, especially with regard to Afghanistan, where the danger of war was most acute. Article I of the Afghan portion of the convention engaged Britain "to exercise their influence in Afghanistan only in a pacific sense," while Russia accepted the fact that Afghanistan lay "outside the sphere of Russian influence," and promised to conduct all political relations with the Amir "through the intermediary of His Britannic Majesty's Government."

The threat of a Russian attack against Afghanistan and India was thus "ruled out of practical politics during the period of the agreement at least."[57] Morley knew better than most men just how important the practical elimination of such a threat was to the "military requirements" of the British Empire, for he, "a notorious lover of peace,"[58] had only recently been "pressed"[59] into chairing a subcommittee of the Committee on Imperial Defense (CID) appointed to consider that very problem. India was "the key governing the normal size of our army in peace,"[60] since the largest call likely to be made for reinforcements in the event of an Indian war would more than amply cover all other imperial needs. Morley's subcommittee reported to the full CID in May, 1907, "We accept the view that the gates of India are in Afghanistan," concluding that "the frontiers of India and Afghanistan are, from the point of view of Anglo-Russian relations and resistance to designs of aggression, identical."[61] On the basis of these conclusions, the policy recommendation made to and accepted by the CID was that "Russian aggression into Afghanistan should be followed by a declaration of war"; the Indian Army should advance to occupy Afghan strong points; strategic railways in the northwest should "simultaneously" be "prolonged"; and the "military organization of Great Britain should be such as to enable 100,000 men to be despatched to India during the first year of war."[62] No sooner was his report accepted than Morley sent a copy to Minto, informing him that it showed "what a tremendous load of military charge and responsibility you have to carry, if you won't come to terms diplomatically with Russia."[63] That was precisely why Morley worked so hard to affect a Central Asian *rapprochement* with Tsarist despotism. He knew his own battle plan alternative. So did Minto, of course, yet he no more welcomed the concluded convention than did Kitchener. "It grieves me to the quick,"

Morley wrote the Viceroy, "that you should attach 'no value at all to the Convention,' as a contribution to the cause of peace; and that you should insist on predicating incessant Russian intrigue . . . because all depends on the spirit in which (on both sides) the Convention is worked, and undoubtedly if the agents of the British Government approach the working of it with counsels of suspicion, anger, and despair, the prospect is not cheerful."[64] Morley's true statesmanship was never more evident than in his patient and wise advice to Minto on foreign affairs. "I am for cool heads, civil tongues, and keeping our powder dry,"[65] he cautioned early in 1906 when Minto was writing of the imminence of a "Russian smash." Now, more than a year later, with a convention of peace duly signed, Minto spoke pessimistically of Russia's "phantom friendship." "A good phrase," commented Morley, "but so is phantom *enmity* a good phrase, and a fact besides."[66]

Kitchener's reported anxiety that the convention would lead to reduced military expenditure and changes in policy filled Morley "with considerable disgust."[67] He had vacillated[68] almost a year before extending the Commander in Chief's appointment in March, 1907, finally agreeing to do so only because "if by perverse fate the tide should rise high about your reform proposals and the Europeans should lose their heads in fear of a Native knife at their throats, they might be comforted by the continued presence of K. among them."[69] Personally Morley grew to dislike Kitchener more and more, considering him "a fox,"[70] suspecting, in time, that he was as unscrupulous at his work as he was reputed to be dishonest at play.[71] Kitchener heartily reciprocated such feelings, calling Morley, among other things, "pig-headed and dangerous," "sandpaperish," and "a man who positively hates military efficiency."[72] He hated military dominance, at any rate.

Just a few days before the Anglo-Russian Convention was signed, Morley received word through the Archbishop of Canterbury that Kitchener "dominated" the Indian scene, with a "bad, wicked race dominance"[73] which was also referred to by the missionary informant as "tyranny." Morley wrote Minto:

> I hope it is all exaggerated, but I hear a good deal of the same sort of thing. They say that in the European regiments both officers and men are full of contempt for Natives, servants, et cetera; and then, when the officers are placed over Native troops, they take no trouble to conceal the same spirit there. One thing, at any rate, is certain, that the sore feeling engendered by this hateful arrogance won't be healed by any amount of political reform, any more than by drastic press acts. . . . This overbear-

ing arrogance is really as shameful, as it will in the long run prove to be dangerous.[74]

He did not inform the Viceroy that this missionary's letter to the Archbishop also reported that Kitchener's influence at Simla was "now supreme, and Lord Minto a mere figurehead."[75]

With the "threat" of Russian invasion diplomatically removed, Morley was "determined to overhaul military policy."[76] Soon after taking office, Morley warned Kitchener that he would be "most reluctant to sanction any increase in military expenditure,"[77] explaining, "I am not at all satisfied with the degree of supervision and control that has been exercised in this Office over the military details. . . . This curtain must be thrown open." In November, 1906, he appointed a committee, under the chairmanship of Sir F. Mowatt, to report to him on "the measures involving special military expenditure."[78] The Mowatt Committee concluded (par. 22) that "if the possibility of hostile action by Russia could be disregarded, and it could be assumed that the greatest military danger to be provided against is either a tribal rising or a hostile combination of the tribes and the Afghans, the strength of the army in India could be reduced." It recommended (page 36) then that Kitchener's five-year plan of military reoganization could be extended, with safety, to ten years, the effect of such prolongation being "to allow of an immediate reduction of at least £500,000 a year in the charges to be met from the revenues of India." Yet, even after the convention was ratified in September, 1907, Kitchener and Minto insisted[79] that military expenditure could not be reduced without risking the security of British India. Morley protested:

> It cannot really be argued that the Russian Convention is to make no difference whatever in India's military needs. . . . military policy has been framed, and the size, distribution, and organization of Indian military force settled on the principle of resisting, or being ready to resist, Russian aggression. If you insist that all must go on absolutely as before, though danger from Russia has ceased . . . then you are landed in the curiously awkward position, that we must have been carrying on government all this time with forces that were entirely inadequate. Not a flattering conclusion for those who have held the post of Commander-in-Chief, down to last August.[80]

In his official military dispatch a week later, Morley wrote that the "time has now arrived when Indian military expenditure should be reviewed. If it may safely be reduced, Your Excellency will be first to admit that it is your duty to effect reduction without delay."[81] Morley wanted not only to cut the size of British divisions in India, but also to curtail Kitchener's cantonment building scheme and to "stop strategical railways."[82] On March 1, 1908, he had ordered Simla to suspend all military building connected with Kitchener's redistribution projects unless prior sanction from Whitehall was granted.[83] Kitchener was "very much upset" and Simla's Military Finance Department was "shocked" at this bold new India Office policy which, exclaimed Minto, "would seem to imply an immediate stoppage in the continuance of the redistribution scheme."[84] The Viceroy now closed ranks beside his Commander in Chief, arguing, "We cannot afford to reduce our British strength here," particularly after "the [seditious] warnings of last summer. Our eyes have been opened to dangers of which we had no suspicion when Kitchener's Army schemes were set on foot."[85] The threat of internal unrest thus emerged at a most convenient time to replace the danger of a Russian invasion.

"Whatever else the Bombs may do," lamented Morley to Clarke, "they have at any rate made a considerable hole in the chances of any policy of mine. I hoped for instance to get some military reduction. Of course, the answer will be that to reduce now will be dangerous in itself; and, what is more, will look like weakness, and that also is a danger. Nor can I deny a certain force in such an answer."[86] The reduction in expenditure on Kitchener's scheme recommended by the Mowatt Committee was, however, made in 1907, when a decrease of £500,000 in military spending was announced by Morley in his budget address. Yet, despite his very real desire to further reduce military spending, in 1908 Morley sanctioned the not inconsiderable increase of £300,000 annually to be paid by India to England's War Office for the training of reserves at home for the British imperial army. This remarkable departure from principle on Morley's part was, however, a product of overriding national economic self-interest, rather than military policy, and may therefore be considered more appropriately in the chapter on imperial economy.

In addition to unrest, there was the ever-present possibility of frontier war to help keep up the "premium on the insurance of the country,"[87] Minto's euphemism for military expenditure. Although the land frontier of British India extended in a half-circle arc over 1,500 miles, the only segment of frontier along which war had become virtually endemic lay to the northwest. The treacherous territory of the northwest frontier had indeed from the dawn of Indian history harbored nomadic tribes who posed a potential challenge to the ordered world of India's sedentary agriculturists. In the employ of enemy invaders, moreover, or at the instigation of a hostile Afghanistan or Central Asian power, the rugged tribesmen along the traditional land gateway to India could prove a serious threat to India's paramount power, or at least a continuing source of local irritation. To reduce that threat and to relieve the irritation, viceroys like Lytton and Curzon, and generals like Roberts and Kitchener, advocated the "forward" policy of expansion beyond India's northwest passes. "There is nothing on which Liberals ought to set their hearts more firmly," John Morley insisted long before coming to Whitehall, "than resistance—strong resistance—to what is called the forward policy in India."[88]

Morley's frontier policy, of the Lawrence-Ripon nonexpansionist school, was indeed based on the strongest resistance to territorial aggrandizement, and though two successful frontier campaigns were waged in his era, neither served to add an acre to British India's dominion. While conceding that there are "real difficulties in the nature of the case, with a wild and unruly frontier like ours," Morley early warned Minto: "Worse difficulties still are due to the spirit of restlessness, and energy misplaced and out of season, that was kindled throughout your service by your terrible predecessor. . . . Our present line is to take in sail and to go as slow as we can."[89] Interestingly enough, that "terrible predecessor" himself, trying however possible to discredit his bête noire, had already warned Morley "that one of the main reasons for which Kitchener desired my departure and for which his predominance in India may be such a source of danger is that he desires to substitute for my cautious frontier policy a policy of vigorous and aggressive initiative against the tribes. This I need hardly say can have no other end than frontier war and disaster."[90] According to Minto, however, Kitchener was virtually a pacifist. "Unless one attributes to him the most Machiavellian methods of procedure," wrote the Viceroy, "I can only say he [K.] is as much opposed to fighting as the most ardent lover of peace could desire."[91]

As for Minto's own frontier tastes, he told Morley in April, 1906, "I am very anxious that you should not think I am afflicted with land hunger," but then went on to explain that "the Mahsud territory [in Waziristan to the northwest] is one which I can imagine our being forced someday to take over," adding slyly, "I am told that the chief men of the country would not much object to this."[92] Less than a year later the Viceroy reported raids into British India by the Zakka Khels,

Afridi tribesmen of that very same border region, and pleaded with Morley "if an expedition is necessary" to "allow us to keep the posts in question."[93] After another five months a Zakka rising appeared imminent to Minto, who argued, "I can only repeat what I have so often said, that I hope, if we are obliged to enter Waziristan, you will allow us to stay there for good and all."[94] Time seemed so intensely to whet Minto's appetite for land that in September, 1907, Morley had to warn him, "I am convinced that we shall have no business to hold on after the thrashing has been administered; and that it will be my duty to ask H.M.'s Government to forbid it."[95] In January, 1908, he reiterated, "I do not believe the time has come for absorption, incorporation, or by whatever other name the Deanes and Crumps[96] choose to call a process that would inevitably mean fresh responsibility and increased expenditure."[97] Minto now felt obliged to appeal to history in defense of his "forward" predilections, writing, ingenuously enough,

But after all the whole history of India has been acquisition after acquisition of territory. . . . That is how the Empire has grown to be what it is. . . . And now the state of affairs on our frontier is becoming simply disreputable. We shall have to fight and of course we are sure to win. But in doing so are we to spend lives and money to throw aside what we may gain?[98]

Morley himself wanted to spend neither lives nor money on the frontier, yet was determined, if the price of order was both, to grab no land in the bargain, and offer no campaign decorations[99] as added attractions to frontier "firebrands." His instructions to Minto and Kitchener were to send the army on a purely punitive expedition, if that was deemed absolutely necessary, ordering the troops to "advance without tents," then, after inflicting "punishment," to "come out again."[100] Two brigades moved into the Bazar Valley of Waziristan in the second week of February, 1908, and the campaign against the Zakka Khel Afridis was concluded by March 2. "The success of the expedition is most gratifying," Morley then wrote to King Edward, "and not least so to myself who insisted that we should not talk of remaining in occupation of an inch of their territory. But for those firm instructions from here, we might very easily have had a *blaze*, instead of having the general body of Afridi strongly on our side."[101] In writing to Clarke, Morley termed the Zakka expedition a "triumph of sensible policy," despite the fact that, "as you may easily guess, there were certain high people in India, who would fain have made the thing the first move in 'rolling the tribes up to the Durrand line.' "[102] "Your decision against the policy which Lord K. has laid down caused much dismay at Calcutta," replied Bombay's governor, "and I imagine that if you had left a loophole we should now be in for another '97 [the year the Tirah Campaign followed the Maizar Outrage]."[103]

Minto and Kitchener felt as depressed after the campaign's conclusion as Morley and Clarke were elated. "I hear from home re the Zakkas," wrote the Viceroy to his Commander in Chief, "that neither you, nor I . . . are ever mentioned, but that everyone talks of John Morley's expedition, and John Morley's troops!!"[104] Just a month later, however, a second campaign was embarked upon, this time against the Mohmands. "I had hoped it would have been unnecessary," Minto reported, "but there were insulting replies from some of the tribal sections which . . . we could not ignore."[105] Like the Zakka Khel expedition, the raid upon the Mohmand tribes was purely punitive, lasting in all less than one month. By June 30, 1908, Morley could, with obvious satisfaction, report to Parliament that "we have had two large or considerable frontier enterprises. Both have been conducted with extraordinary military skill and efficiency and have been entirely successful mainly because we adhered closely to the policy . . . that we would not annex or occupy or plant posts or make roads in any portion of tribal territory."[106]

Morley's frontier policy of nonannexation and nonaggression was as deep-rooted a part of his Liberal faith as his belief in the ameliorative powers of reform. When the Amir of Afghanistan proved unexpectedly dilatory in responding to British requests that he accept the Anglo-Russian Convention, Minto wrote pessimistically, "We may be forced into an Afghan war, whether we like it or not," to which Morley angrily replied:

> The only people who could think of such a war without abhorrence and disgust are the soldiers. Now I hear stories (more than gossip) of important soldiers near you, writing to important, or at least very exalted, personages here, that an Afghan war, or short of that, a grand frontier blaze, would be the very best thing in the world for keeping the Native Army right. There is some plausibility in a view of that sort, I daresay, but you will agree that to act upon it would be to damn beyond redemption or excuse our whole system and our presence in India.[107]

Indeed, Morley felt so strongly about the need for "cool heads, and civil tongues" in handling India's neighbors that he once informed Hirtzel that "an insuperable objection to K. as Viceroy would be his frontier policy! So he must be struck off the list."[108]

The same principles that governed Morley's policy concerning the volatile northwest frontier were applied to the then less troublesome northern and northeastern border regions. The Manchu dynasty on the eve of expiration could not serve even as a bogey threat to British India, while Lamaist Tibet, though as much a hermit as Afghanistan, was not nearly so militant. Morley could, therefore, with less contentious opposition from Simla's military experts, insist upon the government of India's adhering to his policy of nonintervention and nonaggression. Within a fortnight of assuming office, he wired the warning to Minto that "His Majesty's Government would certainly be altogether opposed to any proposal extending our authority and responsibility in Tibet."[109] This urgent cautioning was occasioned by an official visit of the Tashi Lama to Calcutta, after an invitation had been extended to him "without any notification to His Majesty's Government."[110] An outspoken critic[111] of the Younghusband "mission," Morley was extremely suspicious of anything that seemed to smack of an attempt to revive Curzon's policy of intervention and aggression in Tibet. The Tashi Lama, potential temporal as well as spiritual rival to the Dalai Lama, had "entered into very friendly relations"[112] with Captain W. F. O'Connor, India's "Trade Agent" at Shigatse, and the loyal friend and disciple of George Curzon. O'Connor had taken it upon himself "to hold out to the Tashi Lama the possibility of his deriving greater advantages from his visit to India than the Government of India ever intended."[113] Lord Minto, too inept[114] initially to perceive that O'Connor was trying to use the Tashi Lama to expand from his Shigatse beachhead into Lhasa, was soon recommending the wisdom of his "agent's" policy of imperialistic adventure to Whitehall. On February 2, 1907, the Viceroy wired the Secretary of State:

I have private information from O'Connor that unless Tashi Lama is put in position to defend himself there is good reason to fear Chinese and Lhasa Government may compass his destruction and that Chinese have not forgiven his visit to India. . . . If violence is done to Tashi Lama we shall be in awkward position. To avoid this it seems to me very necessary to show our teeth at once to Chang and to give all possible indication of friendship to Tashi Lama . . . [who] possesses very few arms. O'Connor suggests sending him three or four hundred rifles. This could easily be done quietly if you authorize me to do so.[115]

Morley replied he was "wholly adverse both to O'Connor's visit to Tashi Lama, and to any despatch of rifles."[116] In a follow-up letter to Minto he conceded that the Tashi's murder would indeed be an "awkward business," adding, however, "But so it will be an awkward business if we identify ourselves with him, are drawn into another *mission* (following our 400 rifles), and have endless complications with China, to say nothing of gratuitous troubles between Nicolson and Isvolski. . . . This is *my* notion of an 'awkward position.' "[117]

As a comprehensive settlement of mutual Central Asian interests, the Anglo-Russian Convention contained an "arrangement"[118] concerning Tibet. Recognizing "the suzerain rights of China in Thibet," Britain and Russia agreed essentially to abstain from any intervention, political, industrial, or financial, in this most remote region. By an "annex" appended to the arrangement, Britain, moreover, reaffirmed her promise to end the occupation of the Chumbi Valley immediately after the third annual installment of the Tibetan indemnity was paid. Morley's Tibetan policy of strict nonintervention, predicated on recognition of Chinese suzerainty and already affirmed by the Sino-British Convention of April 27, 1906,[119] was thus solemnly reiterated. In 1908 Minto tried to make Chinese quibbling over revision of the Tibet trade regulations of 1893 reason for extending India's occupation of the Chumbi. Morley would have no part of such jingoist tactics, however, replying:

> It is suggested that we may use our occupation of Chumbi as a weapon to be brandished in the face of China, to make her give way in the questions arising out of the Revised Regulations. . . . But we shall surely be in a completely false position if we break our engagement to come out of the Chumbi. . . . A row about these Regulations, carrying with it an evasion (for so it will be deemed, and so in fact it will be) of our undertaking to clear out, will stultify our Asiatic policy at the beginning. . . . We have bound ourselves not to interfere in the internal administration of Thibet; and for my own part I have a suspicion that some of your proposals come perilously near internal administration.[120]

On January 29, 1908, when the final indemnity installment was paid, British Indian troops were ordered to withdraw from Tibetan soil. China was so obviously impressed by this proof of Britain's integrity that she proposed an "offensive and defensive alliance." Morley was "much amused" and remarked that such a treaty would not really be of "much use now, but in 30 years?"[121] Captain O'Connor was crushed and transferred to Quetta from where he wrote gloomily to inform Curzon that the "present regime at Simla as you know does not take a very firm line vis-à-vis the Secretary of State and concerns itself little with Frontier facilities."[122]

Throughout this era Morley did in fact keep India's Foreign Department on a tight leash. In 1910, when the Dalai Lama started feuding with China, Morley reminded Minto that "all the business of the Dalai Lama is to be in effect conducted and decided by the F.O. and the I.O. *here*. It involves Russia and China, and other people too, and so long as I am responsible, I can be no party to any risk of a repetition of the Curzon-Brodrick policy of 1904. . . . So there must be no sort nor shadow of committal by your foreign department."[123] Morley was as suspicious of Nepalese warnings of Chinese aggression as he was loath to rush to the Dalai Lama's assistance. "Nepal is important, no doubt," he concluded, "but the Prime Minister is not without craft [he had been to visit Morley at the India Office in July, 1908], and it won't be the first time that he tries to use the fears of the Indian F.O. for a game of his own."[124] As to the Dalai Lama, he warned that "we must not take his story for gospel; still less must we allow him to set England and China at loggerheads, for the sake of his *beaux yeux*."[125] Morley felt "convinced" it would be "a disastrous error" to place China in Russia's former position "as the standing bogie"[126] of British India.

"China is awakening," he cautioned Minto, "and is beginning to have increased knowledge of, and interest in, the geography and conditions of her dependencies. So we have no right to be surprised if China seeks to render more effective that shadowy control that she always possessed in Tibet, and which we vehemently blamed her for not exercising more effectually in practice."[127] Morley worried less about Chinese military power at this time than about provoking "a Chinese boycott of British goods" by "showing our teeth too ferociously,"[128] as Minto kept urging him to do in the face of growing Chinese truculence along the northern tier. "Of course," Morley added ruefully with a most modern-sounding sigh of complaint, "if China were a decent place, we should settle the boundary by arbitration, joint commissions, and the other resources of civilisation; only these devices are not well suited to people who speak disdainfully of latitude and longitude, and work their oracle by forged maps."[129]

Morley's policy toward Persia, like his policy toward Tibet and Afghanistan, was based, first of all, upon concluding a peaceful settlement with Russia in order to reduce the threat of war and undermine

Anglo-Indian military pleas for increased frontier expeditions. He hoped, through the Russian convention, to remove permanently the threat of war in Seistan and thus to allow India "to end her Persian engagements."[130] So far as the government of India was concerned, his Persian policy was one of nonintervention. Morley was in fact "determined to put a stop to"[131] direct relations established between Simla and Teheran, instead of working, as Minto urged, "for a consolidation of British friendship with Persia off our own bat, distinct from any combination with Russia."[132] Verbally sweetening the bitter pill of informing Minto he was for "cutting down the intervention of the Government of India in Persian affairs to a minimum," Morley whimsically informed the Viceroy: "You may hold up your hands with horror if you like; and cry out that you have got a Secretary of State who is not only that dismal creature the Little Englander, but that even more dismal being, the Little Indian. This is what the Imperial Curzon would say!!"[133]

Kitchener opposed, as "very inopportune," Whitehall's attempts at Petersburg to negotiate "a general settlement of affairs in Persia."[134] But Morley gave no weight to his commander in chief's judgment of foreign affairs, informing Minto that, merely by offering gratuitous advice, Kitchener was "going beyond the soldier's province altogether. Does he know more of the present state of Russia than we do?"[135] Minto meekly protested to Godley that "with the traditional distrust here in Russian diplomacy, it is only natural that the views of the Government of India should be strong, and as such they would be wrong not to express them, and that is an entirely different thing from their assuming that there is a policy for the Government of India apart from that of His Majesty's Government. This is, of course, impossible, though I believe it has not always been considered so here."[136]

The agreement concerning Persia, part one of the Anglo-Russian Convention, sliced the Persian melon in three, vouchsafing to the Russians their northern sphere, to Britain the Persian Gulf ports and east, while between the two was a portion reserved for mutual exploitation. This commercial partition of his country was accepted by the Shah of Persia in return for a promised loan[137] of 4 million pounds sterling, half to be paid by Russia, half by Great Britain. The British half of the loan was, in turn, to be shared between the India Office and His Majesty's Exchequer. Once again, as in the matter of reapportioning military expenditure, Morley's economic loyalties were sharply divided, although in the case of the Persian loan (as will be seen in the chapter on imperial economics) he fought more vigorously to guard Indian interests than he did in his disputation with the War Office.

The interdependence of Morley's pacific military and nonforward frontier policies was perhaps most clearly revealed by his handling of the Aden protectorate and its hinterland. He warned Lamington (then still governor of Bombay) in March, 1906, to avoid "like fire, any intervention that we can possibly with decent self-respect, stave off, in the rows and quarrels of the gentry of the unruly hinterland"[138] of Aden. A month later he wrote again, with his "hair standing on end," to protest about the "little short of *maniacal*"[139] language employed by the British officer in command at Dthali when addressing Arab sheikhs. With regard to Arabia, Morley was "absolute for non-intervention" and "decidedly against a forward policy."[140] He early resolved, moreover, that the surest way to prevent blundering into both was to reduce the size of Britain's military garrison at Aden and Dthali, where, much to his amazed chagrin, Morley learned that "we have as many as 1200 men in garrison ... we—who are at our wits' end for troops!!"[141]

The one other nation with which India was diplomatically and militarily involved was Japan. When the CID met[142] in 1906 to consider questions emerging from the Anglo-Japanese Agreement of 1905 (extending the original alliance of 1902), the "expediency" of mutual Indo-Japanese military aid in wartime was discussed. Morley had "the gravest objections"[143] to sending an Indian contingent anywhere in Asia in order to assist Japan, whereas Minto and Kitchener did not consider it at any time "advisable to employ Japanese troops in or through India."[144] The resulting agreement was singularly opportunistic. "In case of an Indian quarrel with Russia," Morley reported following the Anglo-Japanese Conference of May, 1907, "Japan would do nothing for us on the Persian side, nor on the Kandahar line [Afghanistan], nor in truth anywhere else except Siberia and Manchuria. That is to say, under the plea of rendering us aid under the treaty, they would help themselves to another slice in the Far East. The Japs, like our American friends, are essentially a *practical* people."[145]

Morley's careful attention to foreign affairs and his salubrious suspicion of military machinations helped make his era a predominantly peaceful one for India, indeed for all Asia. Nor was the least of his contributions to India's continuing pacification his success in keeping Kitchener from grabbing by law the viceregal throne, which so many people said he had usurped in fact. With seemingly unconscious irony, Minto himself wrote in September, 1909, that "Lord K. left for good on Monday. . . . 'Le Roi est mort, vive le Roi,' has to me a sad ring about it."[146] But for Morley's presence at Whitehall, Kitchener would have been India's king indeed, not only from 1906 to 1910, but for the next half decade as well. He returned to London in order personally to lobby for the coveted appointment, making it clear to all his powerful friends that unless he was "sent to India as Viceroy, he will leave this country."[147]

"I advised him [Kitchener]," Esher noted in his journal on May 12, 1910, "not to threaten John Morley, as he is a stubborn, proud and obstinate man. He [K.] talked volubly, and although his strength looms big, especially when he sets his jaw, and shows his overlot of teeth, he is not the silent strong man, but the talkative headstrong man." Morley, of course, had long since decided to rid India of Kitchener's arrogant bluster, appointing Charles Hardinge as Minto's successor in June, 1910. In writing to Minto about Sir Charles, then permanent undersecretary at the Foreign Office, Morley noted that "no G.G. [governor-general] has ever known so much as he knows at first hand, either of the immediately outlying States, e.g., Persia, Russia, or, may I add, of the European forces of today," but, what was still more important, he "is a firm Free Trader, and he is an enemy of the Forward Policy—two vital points with me."[148]

Kitchener, who had been so confident of the appointment that he actually named his viceregal staff, found the blow so galling that he "disappeared entirely for ten days to hide his disappointment."[149] As to Kitchener's grand scheme of military reorganization, Morley left that in the hands of his India Office adviser, General O'Moore Creagh, whom he had appointed commander in chief in 1909, and who "turned out to be far more anti-K. [Kitchener] and all his works than Barrow [the only other contender for the job] would have been."[150] Until Morley mentioned Creagh as a possible nominee, none of the military men at Simla's headquarters staff took him "seriously . . . and consequently have considered him out of the running," Minto reported in "amazement," adding that "K. declares emphatically that its [his new Indian Army's] complicated command could not be placed in O'Moore Creagh's hands even in peace time without apprehension."[151] Less than half a year after Creagh had taken command, the rumor in India was, "If K. comes out as Viceroy, it will be a case of '*No more Creagh*'!"[152]

By replacing Minto with "an enemy of the Forward Policy," and Kitchener with a general who might find his army too "complicated" to command, Morley hoped that his peaceful policy would survive his own tenure in office. He labored to convert the government of India from a military-minded to a peace-loving administration, once in fact feeling so exasperated by Minto's repeated references to the "Fortress India" and its "Glacis ramparts" that he wrote:

> All this military analogy from Fortress and Glacis strikes me as essentially misleading, or at any rate narrow and partial; and the result of it is to make the Government of India, as it always is, and always will be, (except when by the mercy of Heaven there is an accidental Secretary of State of the opposite persuasion in power) virtually and by the natural drawbacks of the position what I will call for short, and without offence, *jingo*. I think this mischievous for several reasons, and among others because this sort of absorption in military apprehensions, forecasts, and the like, withdraws the best and most capable minds in government from the vast problems lying outside the master idea of a Fortress. You are so much more than a Fortress. . . . In a poor country like India, Economy is as much an element of defence as guns and forts, and to concentrate your vigour and vigilance upon guns and forts, and upon a host of outlying matters in Tibet, Persia, the Gulf, etc., which only secondarily and indirectly concern you even as garrison, seems to me a highly injurious dispersion from the other and more important work of an Indian government.[153]

To wean India's government from the military mentality of eternal preparation for war, so that more time and money might be spent on helping to develop the latent resources of so impoverished a country, was one of Morley's fondest ambitions. He was hardly oversanguine about his chances of success, yet the ambition itself might be noted as the ultimate justification of his foreign policy of nonintervention, much as for the same reason independent India was subsequently to make nonalignment the central theme of its policy.

5

PILLS FOR THE EARTHQUAKE

>What people call their principles are really their pretexts for acting in the obviously convenient way.
>
>   Morley's *Recollections*, I, 122
>
>So little evidence goes such a long way once your mind is made up.... Mr. Gladstone and Chamberlain ... both of them often astounded me by the tenacity with which they held to dubiously supported opinions.
>
>   Morley's *Recollections*, II, 190
>
>Cromwell, in an interview he had with a certain band of Presbyterian ministers, said to them, "My brethren, I beseech you in the name of Christ to think it possible that you may be mistaken."
>
>   Morley to the Imperial Press Conference, June 11, 1909

During this era keeping the peace beyond India's frontiers seemed at times a relatively minor problem, compared with the task of maintaining internal order. In November, 1905, when Minto mounted his viceregal throne, the "political horizon" was already "clouded by dissatisfaction and unrest."[1] Half a year later, in his first budget address, Morley noted that everyone complained of a "new spirit abroad in India," but asked, "How could you expect anything else? You have now been educating the peoples for years with Western ideas and literature."[2] He knew that his own speeches and writings were partly responsible for this "new spirit," alternatively called "unrest." Gokhale, for one, had admitted in his 1905 presidential address to India's National Congress:

Large numbers of educated men in this country feel towards Mr. Morley as towards a Master.... He, the reverent student of Burke, the disciple of Mill, the friend and biographer of Gladstone, will he courageously apply their principles and his own to the Government of this country or will he too succumb to the influences of the India Office around him, and thus cast a cruel blight on hopes, which his own writings have done so much to foster?[3]

It was an embarrassingly forthright question, and focused upon what was to become the most difficult dilemma of Morley's India Office career. In trying to fashion a policy to cope with the challenge of unrest, Morley was compelled to test his noblest principles in the acid of everyday application.

The new provinces of West Bengal and Eastern Bengal and Assam, "smouldering" with agitation from the inauguration of partition, "burst into flame"[4] early in 1906. The svadeshi bonfires of Calcutta and arrests at Barisal sent sparks of unrest across India's subcontinent. "We did not come quite into a haven of serenity and peace," Morley reminded his critics in Parliament. "When we came into power, our policy was necessarily guided by the conditions under which the case had been left."[5] As to partition, Minto reported, "Opinion is decidedly that there has been a want of consideration for local sentiment, that people have not been consulted who ought to have been consulted, and that the over-bearing tone of Curzon's speeches on several occasions has tended seriously to increase the bitter feeling which exists.... we have been committed to a somewhat unfortunate piece of legislation."[6] Morley himself felt "great anxiety"[7] about partition from his first days in office until the end of his tenure. Although he publicly admitted it was "undoubtedly an administrative operation which went wholly and decisively against the wishes of most of the people concerned," he nonetheless insisted in his first statement on partition in February, 1906, that the "redistribution of Bengal is now a settled fact."[8] Morley's reasons for adopting this formula at the time were, first of all, that antipartition agitation had recently subsided; second, that fresh reconsideration of the scheme would involve an exorbitant new outlay of taxation; and, finally, that after Curzon's era of energetic activity India should now be allowed to take breath. Clearly of two minds in this matter, Morley was hardly able to disguise the fact that his natural sympathies were with the antipartition agitators. His Irish experience had taught him that at least "half the mischief" in conflicts of this kind was "done by the fuss and bullying of police."[9] He urged Minto to "let a hint be given" to keep the law enforcement officers "as quiet as they can." The Viceroy reassured him that "the Partition agitation is settling down."[10] It was to be one of the slowest settling processes in recent Indian history.

In April, 1906, partition's fire blazed more fiercely than ever as the Bengal Provincial Conference of Congress, convened at Barisal, was violently dispersed by Sir Bampfylde Fuller's police. Fuller, Curzon's appointee as first lieutenant governor of Eastern Bengal and Assam, was not a man to waste any sympathy on Bengali politicians. Surendra Nath Banerjea, conference president and "uncrowned King of Bengal," was summarily arrested, and more than 300 students were suspended from college and sentenced to "absolute exclusion from government service" because they had dared to shout "Bande Mataram" in public. Morley was shocked by Fuller's "excess or folly,"[11] considered the proceedings against Banerjea highhanded, and wrote in shame to Minto, "The British Raj must be a poor sorry affair, if it trembles before a pack of unruly collegians."[12] Calling partition "a disagreeable pill," Morley argued that the wisest policy would surely be to "take any chance of gilding it."[13] Not with "wormwood," however, as "Fuller and his like" had done, but by acts of "justice and Clemency—two words that the rulers of men, especially if irresponsible, like the Government of India, are slow to learn."[14] He advised Minto to order immediate reinstatement of all the suspended students, and expressed doubts as to the legality of Fuller's other highhanded repressive measures, but added that, even if they were perfectly legal, questions of so distinctly a political nature "must be settled not by law alone, but by prudence, policy, and common sense."[15] Minto agreed and immediately advised Fuller accordingly. By the end of that month the schoolboys had "all been unconditionally pardoned."[16] Again, the Viceroy reported that "things are settling down."[17] But Morley made up his mind that "Fuller must be got rid of,"[18] for he considered Barisal "a thoroughly impolitic blunder"[19] and went so far as to admit to Lamington that, instead of agreeing with the arrest of the agitators, he was "altogether on their side." "Don't forget," cautioned the historian-philosopher at the India Office, "that 'law and order,' without common sense and sense of proportion, are responsible for most of the worst villainies in history."[20] He continued to urge Minto to find a less sensitive post for Fuller, asking irately if the Viceroy knew of "any reason why we should at every turn back up all executive authority through thick and thin, wise or silly, right or wrong?"[21] Such unthinking administrative practice, Morley insisted, merely helped "play the agitator's game" and "sets up his case for him." Yet, knowing all of this, and feeling personally as he did, Morley persisted doggedly to the end of his term with the inflexible policy of the settled fact. Why?

It was partly Minto's insistence that "any hope held out of a change" in Bengal's status "would be most mischievous, not only in Bengal, but throughout India";[22] and that "the real question at issue is whether the Bengali agitator or the Government of India is to rule here, and I believe status of our Government of India in the future is seriously involved in the decision."[23] But that was only part of it, for Morley had by now begun talking "disparagingly of Minto, who had had no political experience."[24] Nor was he ever quick to succumb to arguments about prestige and status, the same line taken in defense of Fuller. Ironically enough, Fuller unwittingly came to Minto's aid and helped fasten the settled-fact status over Bengal by flamboyantly offering to "resign"[25] in mid-July, 1906, unless the government of India would more fully support his proposal to press for disaffiliation of several colleges. Sir Bampfyllde never expected to be taken seriously,[26] of course, but Minto was overjoyed[27] at the opportunity of doing precisely what Morley had asked of him for more than a month without incurring any of the odium of actually dismissing a subordinate. He promptly accepted Fuller's resignation, appointing Sir Lancelot Hare, as already noted, to the Dacca *gadi*. Now it was the embattled Anglo-Indian community's turn to agitate and profess anxiety. In England as well as in India, letters[28] poured into the press in Fuller's defense, and Sir Bampfyllde became and remained[29] something of a symbol to rank-and-file Anglo-Indian bureaucrats, and the Tory party at home, of the Liberal regime's "surrender" to Congress agitation.

Morley knew very well that Fuller's resignation would come as "a serious blow" to "officials of all classes."[30] He hoped indeed that it would help chasten the more arrogant among them, like Sir Denzil Ibbetson, of whom he wrote Minto in August, 1906:

These men, even the best of them, seem to think much more of their own dignity, and convenience, and personal friendship, and advancement than they think of the Supreme government. Well, the only way of meeting this spirit is by resolutely overruling them. . . . Their sense of the dignity of their office, of the necessity of always backing them up, and all the rest of it, is the regular cant of all bureaucracies. The Fuller case ought, I hope, to give them a hint.[31]

At the same time, however, he realized that Fuller's resignation might well tempt Indians to step up the tempo of agitation in the hope of gaining still further concessions, and so agreed that "we should have to be very firm now."[32] Nonetheless, if the new lieutenant governor had been willing to "propose a different line of partition," Morley would have been only too glad to "re-open"[33] the question. A week after Fuller resigned, in fact, Morley "threw out"[34] for Minto's consideration the idea of starting "a departmental inquiry" into the success of the partition operation on the anniversary of its first year. He was convinced, by August, that "we were under entirely mistaken impressions as to the public feeling against partition subsiding,"[35] which, since that had been his primary reason for proclaiming the policy of the settled fact, was tantamount to saying he was prepared to abandon it. Morley's next letter to Minto was filled with commiseration for the Viceroy over the harsh treatment he had been receiving from the Anglo-Indian press, but concluded: "Partition was a sad mistake; it came to us by inheritance. . . . Whether in time, after the row has abated, we should modify the particular line of partition, we can judge some months hence."[36]

Minto, however, stormed at from press and pulpit, could now expound his arguments with the zeal of a beseiged warrior on the battle line. "All India is looking on now," warned the Viceroy in response to Morley's many hints that it was time for a change, "and whether Partition was right or wrong, the faintest sign of withdrawal on our part would be construed as weakness—it would poison our whole rule here. There is only one answer to the suggestion of a reconsideration of Partition. It is dead, dead, dead. We shall have no peace till there is certainty as to that."[37]

Yet it is more than probable that even so passionate an appeal, given its source, would not in itself have convinced Morley to abandon all thought of partition revision. What finally appears to have done so, however, was his independent conclusion that partisans on both sides of this volatile issue were testing *his* resolution, not that of the government of India, nor of Fuller, Hare, or Minto—but of John Morley alone, Little Englander, radical, Liberal. He was made joltingly aware of this test by a "most secret" intelligence report from the Governor of Eastern Bengal and Assam, which was transmitted to him as an enclosure with Minto's letter of September 10, 1906.[38] The report contained a long statement from Hare concerning the "representative" character of the impending Muslim delegation to Minto, and a "private and confidential" letter which Surendra Nath Banerjea had circulated to his leading lieutenants in the new province. Dated March 20, 1906, this letter from Banerjea, written on the eve of his Barisal arrest, quoted in turn from a letter sent to him by the Honourable C. J. O'Donnell, former commissioner of Bengal and now M.P., second only to the Honourable Sir Henry Cotton in outspoken parliamentary attacks against partition. "Dear Mr. Banerjea," wrote O'Donnell, "Keep on agitating and do so effectively . . . *mass meetings* by the *dozen* in *every* district. . . . Morley will yet yield."[39] Banerjea added, "I beg you will follow Mr. O'Donnell's advice which is in harmony with what Sir Henry Cotton wrote to say a few weeks ago. . . . Mr. Morley's attitude is one in which his convictions are apparently at variance with his conclusion; and under the circumstances it is our clear duty to continue the agitation so that he may be persuaded to act in accordance with his convictions." Had Fuller himself been Machiavellian enough to attempt composing two letters, which, once they reached Morley's eyes, could prove more damaging to the antipartition cause than those of O'Donnell and Banerjea, he could hardly have succeeded in doing so. For Morley was a singularly sensitive and stubborn man, not without some vestige of that vice so often associated with greatness—pride. He liked, moreover, to believe that, should he do something for which he was bound to incur almost universal opposition from official colleagues at home and abroad, he would be doing it for real, rather than artificially provoked, reasons. Naturally, O'Donnell never learned that Morley had seen his letter, but almost a year later when that "impudent fellow" (as Morley called him) came to Morley's room at Westminster, "J.M. would not shake hands with him, and when O'D. said it would help if he sometimes consulted them [Morley] replied that he had never had a word of sensible advice from any of them [Cotton, O'Donnell & Co.] yet."[40]

From September, 1906, onward, at any rate, Morley's attitude toward partition became perceptibly stiffer, and far more cynical. When Godley informed him that "public opinion" in India believed that the secretary of state was "in the charge of the Congressmen," Morley replied, with a touch of bravado, "Why have they not compelled the said Secretary of State to revise Partition? And what is their leverage on that dummy of a man?"[41] More than a year later, Morley admitted in debate with Curzon that though he never regarded partition as sacrosanct, "for me it is so because it has *become a test*, and by that test I mean to abide."⁴² (Italics added.)

Morley thus fell victim to the very folly of executive rigidity against which he had so wisely cautioned both Minto and Lamington, and because of which he had predisposed Minto to accept Fuller's resignation. After learning that his administrative stamina was being tested by agitators in the Commons and Calcutta, while officials waited eager to shout "we told you so!" he locked his mind and stubbornly decided to pass the test at all costs. It was one of the worst decisions of his India Office career, a product of personal pride more than of rational policy. The settled fact became his badge of imperial merit, which he wore to keep restive officials in line if they dared allude to "wire-pullers in Parliament" making a "puppet" secretary of state dance. "If politicians at home are such low caste beings," he complained to Minto concerning some remarks by Risley [Sir Herbert Hope Risley, secretary to the government of India, Home Department], "how comes it that the immortal partition of Bengal is still 'a settled fact,' when I had only to lift my finger, and the H. of C. would instantly have passed a resolution that would have overthrown the 'settled fact' in a trice."⁴³ While readily boasting his "firmness" in this matter when communicating with propartitioners, Morley most uncharacteristically came to shun any discussion of partition with its opponents. He refused absolutely ⁴⁴ to "waste" any words on the subject when Indians, including Gokhale and Banerjea, came to call. He was "very irate"⁴⁵ when one of his own official advisers sought an interview to "press him" about partition. He "refused absolutely" to reconsider the settled fact, though Leonard Courtney, one of his oldest radical comrades, spent more than an hour "pleading" the case on its merits.⁴⁶ He heaved a sigh of relief because Parliament's opportune adjournment "allowed me an escape from the threatened discussion of the lively question of the Partition of Bengal."⁴⁷ None of this was like Morley. Such closed-door, close-minded tactics had never found favor in his pen or heart before, and indeed on no other Indian issue was he so singularly sensitive, so peremptory, so positive—or was it rather so obviously conscience-stricken and guilt-ridden?

Although the fact of partition remained settled, Bengali agitation did not. In October, 1906, Romesh Dutt,⁴⁸ whom Morley respected most highly among his Indian advisers, wrote to report that "moderate leaders are losing their hold on the people" in Bengal; men were "getting disheartened" and "extremists are having their chance."⁴⁹ But

Minto again thought that "partition agitation" was "dying down."[50] Then in May, 1907, as a result of "disturbances" in the Punjab as well as Eastern Bengal and Assam, an emergency ordinance[51] was proclaimed by the government of India empowering district officers to suspend all public meetings and call for punitive police to be quartered in specially disturbed areas. Morley, in one of the least lucid (perhaps because it was among the most embarrassed) passages he ever penned, "explained" to the Commons in his June, 1907, budget address:

> The course of events in Eastern Bengal appears to have been mainly this —first, attempts to impose the boycott on Mahomedans by force; secondly, complaints by Hindus if the local officials stop them, and by Mahomedans if they do not try to stop them; thirdly, retaliation by Mahomedans; fourthly, complaints by Hindus that the local officials do not protect them from this retaliation; fifthly, general lawlessness of the lower classes on both sides, encouraged by the spectacle of the fighting among the higher classes; sixthly, more complaints against the officials.[52]

Meanwhile, West Bengal began a long series of prosecutions for sedition against the editors of Indian-owned newspapers.[53] Shortly after that there were complaints in the Commons against the employment of punitive police in Eastern Bengal and Assam, and suspiciously enough the mere request from Whitehall for information led to Hare's withdrawal of the burdensome forces.[54] Dutt repeatedly warned Morley that partition was "a real and permanent source of discontent,"[55] insisting that it "continues to rankle in the hearts of the people" and that "they will never be reconciled to it within this generation."[56] Less than a week later Khudiram Bose's bomb killed two innocent women who happened to be riding in a carriage behind that of an English district judge, marked for assassination, in Muzaffarpur. Was it mere coincidence that the terrorist's ultimate weapon of desperation made its lethal debut in Indian History in the partitioned province of Bengal, thrown by a hate-crazed young Hindu who admitted to have been "inflamed by the writings in the *Sandhya, Yugantar, Hitabadi* and other vernacular papers"?[57] On November 6, 1908, the Lieutenant Governor of West Bengal himself was fired at by a would-be assassin. Morley felt "rather perturbed by the rise of feeling ... in Calcutta."[58] The following month the governments of West and Eastern Bengal moved for the arrest and deportation of nine persons under Regulation III of 1818, thanks to which it was neither necessary to formulate charges against the individuals involved, nor to bring them to trial. This infamous act of "Preventive Detention" eliminated habeus corpus by empowering government for "Reasons of State" to "place under personal restraint individuals against whom there may not be sufficient ground to institute any judicial proceeding, or when such proceedings might not be adapted to the nature of the case, or may for other reasons be inadvisable or improper."[59] Once again Morley nodded mutely and closed his liberal eyes. Had he guessed how high a price in conscience and principles sacrificed he would have to pay for his decision to "pass the test"?

When challenged by Sir Valentine Chirol of the *Times* with a "persistent rumour" that he was in fact intending soon to "undo partition," Morley replied in March, 1909, "that so long as he was S. of S. it was a settled fact," then added, revealingly enough, "There might come another S. of S. who would be wiser!"[60] From Calcutta, Sir Lawrence Jenkins, once established on his High Court bench, reported how he was struck by the "unanimity" with which his "old Bengali friends" attributed "this unrest and the anarchism and violence which have accompanied it to two causes," the first of which was partition.[61] At Oxford a fortnight later, when speaking to the Indian Civil Service "Probationers," Morley admitted, concerning Partition, "I don't think well of the operation," yet added in the classically mind-effacing bureaucratic tradition he most despised, "but that does not matter."[62] His partition policy was a tragic blunder, for not only did Morley act contrary to his best instincts in stubbornly adhering to the least popular of Curzon's acts, but, barely more than a year after he left Whitehall, the "settled fact" he defended was undone by George V's royal proclamation at the Imperial Durbar in Delhi.[63] What, then, had Morley accomplished by this policy? He petulantly proved to O'Donnell and Banerjea that he could resist their pressure. Had he been less of an agnostic, we might almost read irony rather than sarcasm in his weary confession to Clarke in 1910 that "if I go to heaven, one reason will be that in spite of much pressure here, long and loudly continued, I stood firm by the Settled Fact."[64]

By early 1907 the sparks from Bengal appeared to have blown north and west across the Gangetic Plain. The "influence of seditious machinery is undoubtedly spreading," reported Minto in March, "and I am afraid has, to a considerable extent, captured the Punjab."[65] Just a few weeks earlier the editor and the proprietor of Lahore's most popular newspaper, *Punjabee*, had been tried and found guilty of sedition. The sentences, two years and six months of rigorous imprisonment, were considered "too severe"[66] by Morley, but Minto assured him, "The strong hand carries more respect in India than even the recognition of British justice."[67] That was no doubt what the Viceroy's senior councillors, Kitchener and Ibbetson, had taught him about India. In March, 1907, to enforce this policy of "the strong hand," Minto appointed Sir Denzil Ibbetson lieutenant governor of the Punjab. Within a month of Sir Denzil's assumption of personal command over the Punjab administration rioting rocked Lahore. The province whose staunch loyalty had saved the raj in 1857, and which had proved India's prime recruiting ground for the native army ever since, suddenly echoed with strident cries of unrest, virtually on the eve of the fiftieth anniversary of the mutiny at Meerut. On learning of these new outbursts Morley ruefully remarked that "if I had a son I don't know that I should wish to think of him as either Secretary of State or Governor-General."[68]

The trouble in the Punjab was a composite product of natural, political, and economic disorder. Bubonic plague, which had ravaged western India since 1896, was peculiarly virulent in northern India early in 1907, claiming more than half a million lives throughout the country in that year's first four months alone. Unscrupulous politicians, some belonging to the now politically oriented Arya Samaj, used the plague to arouse superstitious peasants against the British raj by telling them that "Europeans stayed healthy during Plague and were really the ones who spread it by poisoning wells and streams in villages."[69] Many peasants, already suffering economic hardship from the newly enhanced revenue settlement at Rawalpindi, increased water rates, and more stringent *begar* (forced labor) requirements, and anticipating depreciation in the market value of their property because of Ibbetson's Punjab Colonisation Bill, were singularly susceptible to inflammatory arguments. Most Hindu cultivators and landowners felt specially aggrieved, at least since Curzon's regime had passed what Romesh Dutt called "the grandmotherly"[70] Punjab Alienation of Land Act (Act XIII of 1900). By empowering local government to determine which "bodies of persons in each district" were "agricultural tribes" and making all sales of land to nonagriculturists illegal, the act was viewed by the many Hindus thus debarred from landownership as part of the government's pro-Muslim policy. The Punjab Colonisation Bill, until disallowed by the Governor-General, was seen in the same lurid light as yet another example of British mendacity and recourse to tactics of divide and rule. Then too, as Minto himself reported to Morley shortly after the rioting at Rawalpindi subsided, the new colony lands opened to Punjab peasants through government irrigation schemes were made lucrative sources of extorted profit by petty officialdom. "I am told on excellent authority," wrote the Viceroy in August, 1907, "that the amount collected in fines during the last four years was 11 lakhs, and that in all probability reckoning in addition to the fines bribes paid by the colonists to subordinate officials, the whole amount would equal about a crore and a half [15 million rupees]. It is perfectly monstrous. It really makes my blood boil. No wonder there was discontent."[71]

In his budget message that June, Morley informed the Commons that twenty-eight "meetings" were "known to have been held by the leading agitators in the Punjab" between March 1 and May 1, 1907. The best attended of these was at Rawalpindi on April 21, when Ajit Singh, pleader and sometime "employee" of the "Russian spy Lasseff,"[72] was reported to have told his mass audience of Jat and Khatri peasants that "people of Punjab must be prepared to sacrifice their lives for sake of mother-land, those who were afraid of bloodshed better go home; petitions to the British King were useless. Punjabis had helped to put down Mutiny, they were now ill-treated, and were suffering for their past treachery to their own countrymen. Now was the time to resist and not to be afraid of Martinis and Howitzers. People should . . . withhold payment of increased land revenue."[73] There were several such speeches, thanks to which Deputy Commissioner Patrick Agnew invited Ajit and two other pleaders to attend his court at Rawalpindi on May 2, 1907, for public inquiry as to whether or not they should be prosecuted for sedition. As the hour of inquiry approached, crowds of students and peasants assembled outside Agnew's office, threatening, it appears, to have made the hearing so truly a public one that Ibbetson wired[74] his deputy and ordered Agnew to cancel proceedings. When the crowd was told no inquiry would in fact be held, rioting began; it "subsided" only after Sir Denzil called in the 10th Hussars. On May 5, Minto wired to notify Morley that Ajit Singh and his pleader cohorts were arrested "presumably for abbetting recent disturbances." The Punjab Chief Court considered their crime so heinous that it denied the pleaders bail, though a few months later when Mr. Stirling, joint editor of the *Civil and Military Gazette*, murdered his "Native servant,"[75] bail was granted at once. The entire Punjab regime would thus appear to have become a brilliantly monolithic reflection of its new lieutenant governor's image.

Sir Denzil, who (as Curzon once reported to Hamilton) "never spares himself,"[76] went on personal tour of his province in the wake of the riots, "consulting district officers of 27 out of 29 districts and leading loyal Hindus and Mohammedans," then sending the Governor-General what Minto inimitably termed a "most weighty and emergent minute."[77] The political picture, Ibbetson felt, gave cause for the "gravest apprehensions." Sedition was everywhere openly preached, and the longer government permitted it to "flourish unrebuked," the worse the situation would become. It was time for action. A "secret committee" of the Arya Samaj was already at work on the native army. If their propaganda infected the Sikhs all might be lost!

On May 6 Morley had wired to caution Minto, "Steps, if any, about seditious speeches, meetings or writings, should only be taken after reference to Home Government," but then he left the regrettable loophole, "unless, of course, sudden emergency."[78] Ibbetson saw precisely such an "emergency" in wiring Minto the same day for permission to arrest and deport Ajit Singh and Lala Lajpat Rai, moderate congressman, teacher, and respected leader of the Arya Samaj. Without bothering to consult Morley, Minto[79] approved the issue of warrants on May 6 for the deportation of both men to Mandalay prison, Burma. The Lala (teacher) was arrested at once, but Ajit could not be found until June 3. On May 10, Minto brought the Punjab under the emergency repressive ordinance of the Police Act of 1861. Morley shouted to Hirtzel, "No, I can't stand that; I *will not have that*,"[80] but was soon "reconciled" to Simla's position. Next day he brought the subject of "unrest" before the cabinet, but they refused to relieve him of his burden, not wishing "to interfere with his discretion."[81] After having given Sir Denzil a free hand with his stick, however, Morley got Minto to add a mollifying dose of sugar to Punjab policy by urging the Viceroy "to withhold assent"[82] from Ibbetson's unpopular Land Colonisation Bill. It was just the sort of "play to the gallery"[83] which tempted Minto, who had begun feeling a bit nervous, reporting in the same letter that Kitchener himself said in council: "My officers tell me it is all right, but they said the same thing in the Mutiny days till they were shot by their own men." There was "always that native purdah behind which it is so difficult to see."[84] By May 21, however, Minto notified Morley that "the arrest of Lajpat Rai and the proclamation of the Ordinance have done endless good in restoring public confidence."[85] But his approval of severe repressive measures only left Morley feeling "depressed and tired," for he found it "very difficult to formulate what he would have to say [to the Commons] in explanation of Lajpat Rai's deportation."[86]

In his budget statement on June 6, 1907, Morley was again obliged to speak with two voices at once in vainly trying to reconcile by the power of words alone two systems of government as basically antipathetical as the Punjab's military autocracy and Westminster's liberal democracy. "See the emergency and the risk," he explained to his fellow members of the Commons.

Suppose a single native regiment had sided with the rioters. It would have been absurd for us, knowing we had got a weapon there [Regulation III of 1818] at our hands by law—not an exceptional law, but a standing law—and in the face of the risk of a conflagration, not to use that weapon; and I for one have no apology whatever to offer for using it. Nobody appreciates more intensely than I do the danger, the mischief, and a thousand times in history the iniquity of what is called "reason of State." I know all about that. It is full of mischief and full of danger; but so is sedition, and we should have incurred criminal responsibility if we had opposed the resort to this law.[87]

The *Times* was delighted to find that "in a matter of such immense importance as the maintenance of the internal tranquility of India," John Morley was "not going to be fettered by shibboleths or to be misled by abstract theories."[88] Thanks to his assent to the deportation of Lajpat Rai alone, moreover, Morley wrote, "Curzon magnanimously receives me into the bosom of the Imperialistic Church."[89]

Morley himself was less pleased with his Janus-like performance. He hardly needed Henry Cotton's letter[90] to the editor of the *Times* to remind him that in April, 1902, a Liberal M.P. named Morley had led the fight in the Commons against Balfour's government for the arbitrary detention of one Mr. Cartwright in Cape Town. Almost a week before that letter appeared, Morley warned Minto not to allow Indian officials to "fall into the delusion that this country will turn a blind eye towards acts of repression."[91] Quite the contrary, he insisted, calling for "a fullish and exact account" of Lajpat Rai's treatment, adding, "And of course there must be no *over-free* resort to 1818 however great the temptation." He had just seen Ibbetson, returned to London for stomach surgery, and found him devoid of "ideas" or any "policy" other than "repression." Morley's opinion of Ibbetson hereafter continued to drop precipitously. In another interview with the Lieutenant Governor after his operation, Morley was appalled to learn that Sir Denzil intended to keep Lajpat and Ajit "under lock and key" for a minimum of two years. Reporting the conversation to Minto, Morley wrote: " 'That's impossible,' I replied, 'a long *punitive* detention without charge or trial could not be defended. The measure is *preventive*, and in England can only be enjoined on that ground. The moment you think the immediate peril is at an end, then you must either haul him into a law-court, or you must turn him out.' 'Very well,' he answered, 'at any rate, he should not be released under six months.' "[92]

Such cynical bargaining with human freedom served to highlight the totally irrational and arbitrary character of preventive detention, and made Morley urge upon Minto the earliest possible release of all deportees. Meanwhile, he cautioned Lamington against resort to the Regulation of 1818 as "too violent a measure, and too much out of harmony with the political spirit of the time," telling Bombay's Governor to remember "that an insurrectionary movement is one thing, and a street row, even a bad street row, is quite another thing."[93] More than a month passed, and Minto failed to respond. "I beseech you not to lose sight of the indisputable fact that—provided things are pretty quiet in India,—it will be impossible for me to face the H. of C. in January," Morley wrote, "if the two men are still under lock and key. . . . So, pray, give the matter a front place in your thoughts."[94] Minto, however, complained of the "howl" of protest he anticipated from Calcutta society if he let his culprits out too soon. Morley pressed on,[95] noting he could not be answerable for "indefinite detention," advising that if Ibbetson "threatens to resign, let him," reporting how *"very unhappy"* Lord Ripon felt, repeating his advice to "let Lajpat and Ajit go!" By October 26, 1907, he had had enough arguing and ordered immediate release in his draft of a telegram to Minto, but Hirtzel "eventually"[96] managed to get him to cut that part. Two days later he felt "sorry he had not sent the part of Saturday's telegram about Lajpat's release, which he is quite determined must be before Parliament meets."[97] By October 30 Morley could "contain himself no longer!"[98] He wired his order of release to Minto, deciding, if the Viceroy demurred, to refer their conflict to the cabinet at its next meeting.

Minto, however, could not have been meeker. He suddenly discovered that "there is nothing whatever that I know of to justify his [Ibbetson's] assertion that one of Lajpat's main objects is to tamper with the loyalty of the Indian Army." Remarkably enough, he now added, "I have never seen any evidence in support of this."[99] Lajpat Rai and Ajit Singh left Rangoon on November 12, 1907, arriving back in India the night of the 14th. Ibbetson "of course opposed their release," Minto informed Godley, "but his arguments against it were very weak and contradictory."[100]

No Punjab uprising followed the return of Lajpat Rai to Lahore. Gokhale, who had vouched for his moderate comrade as "a patriot and a self-sacrificing man of high character and pure life,"[101] was fully vindicated in his faith. When at long last Ibbetson revealed all the nebulous evidence he had used in recommending the deportations, moreover, Morley shamefacedly told Minto: "Nothing could be *thinner* than what they called evidence. But all that is a State secret, which we will keep to ourselves (I think I must send you a lecture I once delivered at Oxford on Machiavelli, only I hardly dare to read it once again myself!). What remains, and what we should be foolish to forget, is that Ibbetson has been weighed in the balance, and found utterly wanting.... That comes of bureaucracy."[102] The more carefully he examined the "Lajpat file," the more irate Morley[103] became at realizing that, like all of India, he and his colleagues in Westminster had been treated contemptuously by the roughriding government of India, either lied to or ignored with respect to specific questions and instructions concerning Lajpat's prison treatment. "I shall not be in a hurry to sanction Deportation any more, that is very certain," Morley promised; "and if it all comes out, I should not be surprised if the Regulation of 1818 has to disappear."[104] Unfortunately, however, nothing "came out," for, instead of accompanying Gokhale to England in order to press libel charges against a London newspaper, Lajpat Rai decided to remain home and soon after went off to America. Sympathetic members of the Commons quickly forgot about his case and, as a loyal minister of the Crown, Morley kept his "State secret." Regulation III of 1818 thus lingered on as a respectable statute not only for the remaining years of the British raj, but continues to this day as part of the "legal" artillery used by independent India.

Lajpat Rai's loss of resolve and change of itinerary in 1908 may have proved, therefore, a more important negative influence upon recent Indian history than had all his positive agitation. Morley's personal views on "preventive detention" and its manifest drawbacks, however plausible the imagined emergency, remained unaltered. As he warned Minto: "Russian methods, or an approach to them, are a political blunder in India, from every point of view. Among other things there is that wonderful entity to which Mr. Gladstone was so fond of appealing, 'the Civilised World.' I am slowly beginning to think that a tide of strong opinion may one day swell in U.S.A. about our rule in India, of the same kind as has prevailed here about Austria, Russia, the Turk, etc. . . . To cut the moral short—while sitting tight, it is our business to keep our system fair, legal, constitutional, and all the other good things that make one sing 'Rule Britannia' with a clear conscience as well as lusty lungs."[105]

Hardly a month later the Bishop of Lahore came to tell Morley his impressions of India, painting a picture far different, more vivid, fresh, and bright, than that drawn by any of the service bureaucrats. The stirring of new life, which officialdom called "unrest," explained the Bishop, was for the most part attributable to ideas brought to India by British rule. "It is we who are on our trial, not India,"[106] concluded the good man whom Morley found so refreshingly wise that he wished he "could have made him Lieutenant-Governor of the Punjab."[107]

Morley knew that the most senseless part about employing cruel or arbitrary repressive measures, found so strangely appealing "in the perverse imagination of headstrong men,"[108] was that instead of restoring order and calm they served as "suggestions for provoking lawless and criminal reprisals." He preferred forbearance to force, adhering to the time-honored dictum that "to know how much of an evil is to be tolerated is a master-key of statesmanship."[109] After the tragic bomb murders at Muzafferpur on April 30, 1908, the British community in Calcutta became, as Minto described it, "hysterical." Asserting that he was "as much for vigour as they are," Morley cautioned, "but I am not going to admit that vigour is the same thing as *Pogroms*. On the contrary, I believe that just as you approach Russian methods of repression, so in precisely the same proportion do you bring down Russian ferocious methods of reprisal."[110] He personally suspected, in fact, that the bomb thrown at Magistrate Douglas Kingsford's[111] carriage (which killed the two women riding in the carriage behind) was meant as "revenge on Kingsford for having ordered seditious persons to be flogged."[112] Two years earlier Morley had by astute "management"[113] convinced his council to pass an antiflogging dispatch, which after much "vexatious delay"[114] at Simla was converted into a whipping bill,[115] designed to amend India's criminal law so as to preclude "political and quasi-political offenses" from such obnoxious punishment. Yet Morley's instructions, and what had virtually become the government of India's own law, were flaunted with cool indifference. Writing to Minto shortly after the Muzafferpur tragedy, Morley noted:

> Kingsford is said to have sentenced some political offenders (so-called) to be flogged. That, as I am advised, is not authorized either by the law as it should, or as it will stand under flogging provisions as amended. Here also I have called for the papers and we shall see. About Lajpat again, the notion of refusing him access to a lawyer is utterly abhorrent to me, and to you also, I should think. Sir L. Jenkins said to me on that matter this morning, "You see, the great executive officers never like or trust lawyers." "I'll tell you why," I said, "tis because they don't like or trust law: they in their hearts believe in nothing but the virtues of will and arbitrary power."[116]

The cycle of harsh repression and violent retaliation, once set in motion, was not easy to stop. "It is the oil that is coming out of the mustard seeds," wrote one Indian journalist, explaining an attempted assassination in Eastern Bengal. "The more the *Feringhi* (foreigners) will press, the more oil they will get."[117] yet for every Englishman like Morley, who recognized that cruel punishments often provoked outrages, there were ten to insist that disorder was invariably the product of an excess of official weakness rather than of harshness. Anarchy was seen as a direct result of agitation, not repression; the cure prescribed was more stringent control over all sources of agitation, especially the vernacular press. It is, moreover, true that since the birth in 1907 of Tilak's[118] "New Party," organized to accelerate boycott, stimulate svadeshi industry, and preach the gospel of svaraj, nationalist agitation had reached a new fever pitch of intensity. No evidence of any direct link between "extremists" like Tilak and practicing terrorists could be discovered, yet Clarke warned that there were "plenty of irresponsible young fanatics who are capable of translating the seditious propaganda into action, and the bomb is the weapon of unarmed people.... I shall be interested to see what Tilak's papers have to say next week."[119] In June, 1907, local governments had been reempowered[120] to initiate "sedition" proceedings (under Sec. 124A of the Indian Penal Code) against newspaper editors on grounds that "delay involved in referring every case to us [Simla] would defeat the paramount object of repressing dissemination of sedition amongst army and civil population."[121] Though Clarke insisted, "I hate Press prosecutions, and I am not sure that in the long run they do much good," by May, 1908, he nonetheless "found it necessary to institute proceedings" against several Bombay papers which had recently "passed all bounds."[122] Such prosecutions were of purely provincial significance, however, while Tilak's second trial in June became a focal point of national and international interest.

Recognized throughout India as the foremost leader of the New or Nationalist party, in Bombay Tilak was "hailed as Maharaja and is also supposed to be a late incarnation[123] of Vishnu," Clarke reported. "We could not arrest him without a chance of disturbance in Poona and some other Deccan towns."[124] Of all Anglo-Indian officials, Clarke was perhaps the last who might have been expected to initiate the trial, destined to become India's classic example of an editor's struggle for freedom of the press, as not merely his civil right but his sacred responsibility, or occupational *dharma*. Hardly half a year earlier Bombay's Liberal governor had, after all, played host to Tilak and some seventy other local editors of the vernacular press, and when the Government House party was over, "to my astonishment Tilak got up and thanked me very nicely in the name of the assembly."[125] Clarke then "shook hands with them all—including Tilak—and we parted with great cordiality, they cheering me most heartily." Reporting his own impressions of the *Lokamanya* (Tilak) to Morley, Clarke most perceptively noted, "I can't help thinking that long ago he might have been taken in hand; but a high caste Brahmin—I am told—never forgives imprisonment."[126] Morley congratulated his protégé "on such a proceeding, all the more, because it is rather a surprise to me that you should have thrown a successful fly over Tilak, of all people in the world. I mark your picture of him . . . I like this high-caste Brahmin of a man, never forgiving the stain of imprisonment, as you say. Quite a man worth trying to get hold of, and I dare say you are right in thinking it might have been possible at an earlier stage. Alas!"[127] Two months later Morley again found cause for congratulating Clarke, telling him of a letter from Gokhale "to an English friend [probably Sir William Wedderburn], in which he says that 'the Governor of Bombay has been winning golden opinions all round since his arrival . . . a wonderful man—picking up things as I have seen very few men do; and he has the power of imagination to enable him to realize what we feel.' You may believe how intensely satisfactory all this is to me,"[128] Morley added. A week later, obviously encouraged by Clarke's approachability and cordiality, Tilak himself wrote to request an interview with the Governor "to beg me to allow the picketing of liquor shops in Poona."[129] Might there still have been time for "trying to get hold of" the "Father of Indian Unrest"?

Ironically enough, Clarke confessed to Morley just a month before ordering Tilak's arrest that it "must, I think, be admitted that no educated Indian outside the public service is at heart favourable to the existing regime. Aspirations assume different forms, ranging from a wish for gradual changes to the preaching of violence. There is, however, unanimity in the desire for a closer association with Government."[130] Then, in response to Morley's own request of him for "any remedy or palliative" to the growing unrest, Sir George most sensibly advised "three main lines" of policy:

"1. More consultation and especially more public and formal consultation of Native opinion. (This question will I hope soon be before you.)

"2. More Natives in administrative posts under Government. (I have referred to this question in some previous letter.)

"3. Prompt redress of real grievances which are often small and local: but are turned into political capital. (This I try to do here as much as possible.)"[131]

Yet on June 24, 1908, ignoring all of his own wise preaching, and never once seeking Morley's advice, Clarke suddenly decided to order Tilak's arrest and prosecution for sedition. This decisoin was clearly a product of Anglo-Indian "hysteria" evoked by the appearance of the bomb, which led in Bombay as well as in Calcutta to the strident demand that something strong must be done or the raj would lose face. The increasingly frenetic impact of this atmosphere on Clarke's thinking concerning Tilak may be seen in his letters to Morley from May through July, 1908. On May 22 Clarke reported, "we are quiet here," yet explained calmly that "organized agitation goes on steadily and is conducted with great cleverness." On May 27, he did "not think that the organization of murder goes deep, but the mischief which leads to murder is certainly tending to spread." By June 9 the pressure had begun making itself felt, for Sir George reported: "I have had a little tussle with my Council over the 'Kesari' [Tilak's Marathi-language paper]. Both members are *particularly* anxious to catch Tilak, and clearly if he could be retired from public life for a time it would be a great advantage, not to this Presidency alone."

Clarke was, however, still reluctant to proceed because of Tilak's great popularity, and the danger of further enhancing his power if government failed to get a conviction. "Our legal Remembrancer and Acting Judge Advocate think we should succeed," explained the Governor. "Probably because I have been differently trained, I felt somewhat doubtful. All opinion being against me, I compromised by agreeing to abide by the judgment of Inverarity who is perhaps the greatest barrister in India. If, therefore, you hear that Tilak is arrested, you will know that all the best legal advice available has been taken."[132] On June 24 Inverarity pronounced his verdict of "guilty" against two *Kesari* editorials commenting on the Muzafferpur murders, and Clarke capitulated to the will of Bombay's Anglo-Indian majority. The past few weeks had left him an isolated, embattled, and exhausted figure incapable of further resistance to the clamoring call for revenge. "The question has caused me sleepless nights," Clarke admitted to Morley, pathetically adding, "but I hope you will feel that I have acted for the best in the light of all the knowledge at my disposal."[133] The rationale was, familiarly enough, that "it is not right that he [Tilak] should defy the Government; nor is it desirable that it should be said that Government is afraid of him, and dares only to prosecute the small fry."

Morley did not "count among welcome things" Tilak's arrest, and upon reading one of the editorials for which Tilak was charged with sedition added, in "secret" surprise, "I confess that at the first glance, I feel as if it might have been passed over."[134] Committed as he was, however, Clarke now insisted: "Policy, in the larger sense, demanded the prosecution of Tilak as the head of the Extremist party in Western India and a powerful influence for evil. I could not strike at the smaller men and allow it to be said that we were afraid of Tilak."[135] Morley was not impressed. That very day he wrote Minto:

I have read the two articles. Bad enough to warrant a prosecution, if you wanted one on general political grounds; but not at all so bad as to make a prosecution inevitable.... Of course Clarke might easily have convinced me that the proceedings were wise, if he had shown that the state of his Presidency made a severe lesson and stern example necessary. But I gather from his letters that he thinks nothing so ill of his people, and he plainly has not weighed all the ulterior consequences of every sort. If his people are in an inflammable state, the trial will inflame them still further. If they are not, he could afford to let Tilak's shuffling stuff, with all its vicious innuendos and mischievous plausibilities, go bye.[136]

Unlike Clarke, Morley felt not the slightest apprehension about getting a conviction "because the jury is most obviously a packed jury; it is evidently not the Goddess of Chance that has brought about the singular result of 7 Europeans and 2 Parsees, and *not one Hindu*." The next day he wrote sardonically to Bombay's governor: "The jury seems to have not one Hindu on it, which is a curious result of pure *Chance*. I became familiar with Chance's caprices of that kind, when I was Irish Secretary."[137] The jury behaved as was expected of them, and Tilak was sentenced to six years in Mandalay prison, the same jail in which Lajpat Rai had been confined. Minto was jubilant at the news, on which he commented to Morley in his letter of July 23; but Morley, who felt "all along" that the prosecution was "a grievous error," shook his head sadly and remarked that "Clarke would have done better to invite him [Tilak] to his garden party!"[138]

"The conviction of Tilak fills me with anything but exultation,"[139] wrote Morley, who understood that it was "as inevitable as anything in the laws of political parties and factions can be, that the moderates will be bound, by the necessity of things, to take his side against us." Clarke naïvely expected a much different response from the moderate Congress leaders who had blamed Tilak for the split at Surat; indeed the Governor hoped "Indians of all classes" who "have assured me privately that we were absolutely right and that it was dangerous to let Tilak go free"[140] would volunteer similar public support. After the trial ended, however, Clarke reported:

I have had a very harassing time. I have learned much and shed many illusions. I began by calling a meeting of what are called "leading citizens" whom I addressed and chided mildly for their apathy and inaction. . . . I gathered that every Hindu sympathized in his heart with Tilak and had not the slightest idea why. I should say that these rich Bombay Indians, who are clever in business, have no political instincts of any kind. . . . Of Tilak's proceedings and aims they had not the faintest knowledge. They had glanced at his defence in the papers, and they thought it a dreadful thing that so clever a man should have a six years sentence. Here then was an exact parallel to the mental attitude of the mill-hands, who say "you have taken away our guru," although they have not the faintest idea who or what Tilak is.[141]

A few days after Tilak's conviction protest strikes paralyzed Bombay's cotton mills and soon spread to the markets as well, turning India's richest city into a barricaded battleground. Troops were called in to support Bombay's police, road blocks were erected to protect the fort, street riots raged daily. Within two weeks of Tilak's conviction the official death toll from rioting alone was fifteen, and the number of wounded in the hospital was thirty-eight, of whom two would "probably die."[142]

"If you had done me the honour to seek my advice as well as that of your lawyers," Morley reprimanded Clarke a week earlier, "I am clear that I shall have been for leaving him alone. And I find no reason to believe that any mischief that Tilak could have done, would have been as dangerous as the mischief that will be done by his sentence. Of course the milk is now spilled."[143] Conceding that "we must keep order," Morley added, "but excess of severity is not the path of order; on the contrary it is the path to the Bomb." Then he asked plaintively, "Why should I say all this to *you*? Of all the ruling men in India, there is not one of whom I am more sure that he shares right views about these things." Nothing Clarke wrote in self-vindication succeeded in shaking Morley, who admitted that Tilak's trial was "morally and legally justifiable," even that "the result may bring certain advantages at the moment." Yet, as Burke's faithful student to the end, Morley insisted that "the only political test" of true value was "the balance of gain and loss, when the whole ultimate consequences are counted up."[144] By that test Tilak's trial proved to be a blunder of monumental proportions, the worst of Clarke's Bombay career. Morley sympathized "to the full" with his friend's anxieties in finding Indian opinion unanimously hostile, and tried to ease the shock of the unexpected by explaining, as he did in his letter of August 19, 1908:

> The situation is of course a revolutionary situation (of a peculiar and limited sort). Now I've known three revolutionary leaders—Mazzini, Gambetta, Parnell. I knew them well, and studied their operations and temper from the inside. Fierce and eloquent denunciation of them and their policy by Austria and the Pope, by Napoleon III, by Mr. Gladstone, was mere waste of breath. Appeals of moderate and rational men to throw off their yoke, and to cooperate with reforming power, were wholly thrown away; and such appeals will always in these great conflicts be thrown away, even if they do not further exacerbate a crisis. The greatest statesman was Cavour. The Mazzinians made huge and provoking difficulties for him at every turn. But for a long time (and indeed all through) he held his peace about them, knowing that *events, not words*, are the real teachers, guides, and masters. So in India. Mere denunciation from us won't touch people, and won't move them. And no words of yours or mine have the slightest chance of inducing a Moderate to denounce an Extremist; he won't do it; he has nothing to gain by it; it would, as he is perfectly aware, have no sort of effect on the Extremists; and it could therefore, while damaging himself, do no service to the Government. We shall be wise to abstain from the luxury of invective. . . . For my part, I mean to look our enemies in the face with a cool and stern and steady gaze, but I won't foam in the mouth.[145]

Minto, on the other hand, assured King Edward that "the Tilak sentence" and other prosecutions and punishments "had the most marked effect in reassuring the loyal population as to the determination of the Government of India to maintain order and put down the preaching of anarchy and murder."[146] The Viceroy's major anxiety was the failure "at home" to appreciate the "position of the European population in India." There was, he explained, "a feeling of personal danger" and the knowledge of course that "British women and children" were especially vulnerable. Morley was sent an even more "vivid picture of the electric atmosphere of the daily life around" by the Governor-General but knew that all the outrages were not initiated by Indians. "I wish you would in your next letter tell me the end of the story of the young corporal who in a fit of excitement shot the first Native he met," Morley requested. "What happened to the corporal? I should really like to know that. Was he put on his trial? Was he hanged? ... If we are not strong enough to prevent Murder, then our pharisaic glorification of the stern justice of the British Raj is windy nonsense."[147] By the next mail, of course, the case of one hate-crazed corporal and his anonymous victim reverted to historical oblivion, yet the *event* (and how many more like it?) left its ugly mark on India's history. Violence fed on itself. The cycle of hatred, fear, repression, more hatred, once set in motion, picked up momentum daily in every corner of the country. At Tinnevelly in Madras, Chidambaram Pillay, among others, had been tried for "seditious" speeches and sentenced to transportation for life. Morley found "remarkable" the learned judge's summing-up statement: "In England political speeches were common. But political speeches in this country laboured under a difficulty. *There was no lawful occasion, so far as he could see, for any man in this country to make a political speech.*" "And so far, in good Russian Pogrom style!" Morley added. "This explains Bombs."[148] (Italicized words underlined in original.)

Again, as Indian secretary, Morley was obliged publicly to defend a policy he found personally repulsive and knew to be virtually useless, for the government of India tried desperately to outlaw unrest and legislate loyalty. On June 8, 1908, the Explosive Substances Act was passed, followed directly by the Newspapers (Incitements to Offences) Act. Both measures were rushed through Minto's legislative council under the vigorous guidance of the Home member, Sir Harvey Adamson, who argued that there were "two factors in this emergency ... the actual making and using of bombs ... (and) the public incitement to murder and acts of violence carried on through the medium of an infamous section of the Press."[149] Under the new act, presses could be seized by a local magistrate if he judged anything printed by them an incitement to murder or any other offense under the Explosive Substances Act. Morley managed, however, to introduce into the act an element of judicial restraint, insisting that the magistrate's order of forfeiture be appealable to the High Court. "Apart from general principles of a Free Press," he argued in explaining to Minto why he considered High Court appeal indispensable, "it will tend to reconcile Liberal opinion (not in a party sense) here, and ... will make it easier for the Moderates to resist the Extremist attack."[150] Minto acquiesced, but announced in council on enacting the measure that he was not concerned about "exaggerated respect for principles of English freedom," since they were "totally unadapted to Indian surroundings."[151] Morley found himself a "regular Janus, with one face regarding the heavy responsibilities of the Government of India, with the other regarding public opinion in England."[152] In public he defended the introduction of "executive action into what would normally be a judicial process," beginning with his usual disclaimer, "I do not believe that there is a man in England who is more jealous of the freedom of the Press than I am. But ..."[153] Conveniently forgetting Cavour's advice he eloquently argued that "an incendiary article is part and parcel of the murderous act. You may put picric acid in the ink and pen, just as much as in any steel bomb."[154]

After each new repressive action Indian officials wrote home to report how much "better"[155] the Indian situation seemed. On the eve of his departure from West Bengal, Lieutenant Governor Sir Andrew Fraser[156] sent Morley a "rose colour" picture about "the cooling of the feeling in regard to partition" and of "the lesson that all moderate men have received of the dangers of violence."[157] The next morning an attempt was made on Fraser's own life as he started home. That very month, November, 1908, violence flared with a vengeance in the "settling down" provinces of divided Bengal. An inspector of Calcutta's police was murdered on the 9th; the principal witness in a trial against a leader of Dacca's *Anusilan Samiti* was murdered and decapitated on the 13th.[158] The government of India, unable to collect evidence since it was incapable of protecting its witnesses, decided that the only solution was deportation of "conspirators." By the month's end Minto pressed Morley to grant him permission to deport suspects "without previous sanction" from Whitehall. But after his experience with

Lajpat Rai, Morley was "not prepared to leave them a free hand."[159] On November 30 he wrestled all day with his staff at the India Office, his conscience, and his sense of duty. He was finally convinced that "if he insisted on previous reference Ld. M. would resign, and would not be fit to be G.G. if he did not resign." The full repercussions of so sudden an upheaval on the eve of the reforms were unpredictable. What if anarchy increased instead of subsiding? The risks were too grave for Morley, who changed his mind, sent for Godley, Jenkins, and Hirtzel, "and said he had decided to allow the immediate deportation of the instigators, but thereafter to require previous reference." A few hours later, however, this surrender still tormented him; Morley confessed to his secretary that "sooner or later we should 'smart for it.' How he hates the whole business, poor man!"[160]

On December 14, 1908, nine Hindus of Bengal were spirited from their homes under Regulation III of 1818, and deported to solitary confinement in various jails throughout the Punjab, the United Provinces, and Burma. Minto "earnestly urged that no suggestion as to the possibility of their early release may be made," and that "personal interviews with legal advisers should for the present not be permitted, as we must absolutely shut off the dangerous influence of these men."[161] Morley, who could not surrender quite so abjectly, wired back: "Refusal of all personal access to legal advisers . . . cannot be defended in Parliament."[162] Bracing himself for the parliamentary storm, he asked furthermore to be "fully-promptly supplied" with information about the deportees' condition. Cotton asked the first question as to "what charges" had been made against the deportees, to which the answer was that under Regulation III of 1818 "it is not necessary to formulate charges," but that the "Government of India are satisfied that their seclusion under the Regulation is necessary for the security of the British dominions in India."[163] The original draft of this answer, written by a member of the India Office staff, had concluded with the sentence, "Their action has the entire support of the Secretary of State," but Morley's red-ink line deleted that with an angry scrawl.

Once begun, the questions in the Commons concerning Bengali deportees continued with harassing persistence. Within a year no less than eighty-two direct questions were asked by some twenty-six members, most active among whom were Cotton, Mackarness, Rutherford, Keir Hardie, Lupton, O'Grady, Greenwood, Collins, and Ramsay MacDonald. By May, 1909, the tide of protest reached flood level when 150 M.P.'s signed a letter[164] to Prime Minister Asquith, denouncing the deportations. Morley became "very anxious about the deportees," and though he anticipated that "we may be able to get through session," he did "not see how we can meet Parliament next session if the men are still locked up."[165] Minto was undisturbed by parliamentary criticism, arguing that "one cannot rule this country by namby-pamby sentimentalism."[166] Naturally, thanks to the deportations, he found the "political outlook . . . wonderfully reassuring,"[167] but cautioned against any lowering of government's guard. Presumably the isolated detention of nine men, who were never brought before any court of law, was essential to prevent further anarchical outrage. In mid-February, 1909, however, Ashutosh Biswas, public prosecutor of Bengal, was murdered, and Minto explained that "we must not expect to get rid at once of this anarchical disease."[168] Every effort was made to keep the germ spreaders under foolproof quarantine. The prisoners were guarded with the greatest of caution and held in isolation cells. "They lock me up from dusk to daybreak and poor me! I am deprived of the privilege of enjoying the cool breeze and the charming moonlight of this season," wrote A. K. Dutt to his nephew. "How much I envy the lot of even those convicts who have been imprisoned in this ward! They walk about in the compound."[169] Smarting sorely for his failure to extend to such a man the basic legal rights of British citizenship, Morley noted on the jacket holding this letter, "Not pleasant reading." Yet instead of ordering Minto to brings charges or release his deportees at once, he tepidly advised in June, 1909, "if I were Governor-General to-day, I would make up my mind to have an Amnesty on the day when the new Councils Act comes into force."[170] For there were by now many political prisoners, and on June 11, 1909, the name Ganesh Damodar (Veer) Savarkar was added to the growing list with a sentence of transportation for life on the charge of "waging war against the King."[171] Born in Nasik, a student leader of the boycott movement in Poona, sent to London on Tilak's recommendation for a Shyama Krishnavarma "scholarship," where he received considerable training in revolutionary activity, Savarkar was believed by Clarke to be one of the leaders of the "wide spread" Deccan "conspiracy," the adherents to which "have a rudimentary organization and of course a bomb section."[172] Ever since Tilak's arrest, after which Clarke received "threatening letters one of which states that we are all to be killed on the 15th inst." (of July, 1908), Bombay's governor warned of "groups of conspirators aiming at violence in many parts of India."[173] On March 31, 1909, he told Morley: "I should never be surprised to hear of an attempted assassination."[174]

Then, on the night of July 1, 1909, with all the deportees still safely behind bars and Savarkar sentenced to life in the Andamans, a twenty-five-year-old Punjabi student, Madan Lal Dhingra, murdered Morley's political aide-de-camp, Lieutenant Colonel Sir William H. Curzon-Wyllie,[175] at the Imperial Institute in London. It happened as Wyllie had started leaving the annual summer "At Home" of the National Indian Association, attended by some 200 of the estimated 1,000 Indian students then residing in England. Dr. Lalcaca, a Parsi physician standing nearby, bravely tried to disarm Dhingra after the fatal shot had been fired, and was fatally wounded himself. "I don't know if you were acquainted with poor Wyllie?" Morley wrote Clarke a week later. "A more kind, genial, unselfish, and helpful creature never existed; nor could a more blind and purposeless piece of bloodshed be imagined."[176] Much the same lament was uttered by Sir Lawrence Jenkins in a letter to Morley: "Why he of all men with his large store of kindly sympathy for all things Indian should have been singled out for this tragic end I can't conceive: there is a cruel irony in it all. And poor India: she too, I suppose, must pay the penalty for this wicked madness; how poorly is she justified of her children!"[177] A terrorist captured some eight months later reported[178] that Dhingra thought he was aiming at Lord Curzon, who appears to have been marked for assassination, and was at any rate anxious enough "about his own safety" to "put himself under police protection"[179] at this time. By macabre coincidence Curzon-Wyllie, who had befriended more Indian students than any other British official at Whitehall, had "heard" more than half a year earlier that a "student has been chosen by lot to assassinate, and also a victim, but he did not find out anything more."[180] Ever since May, 1907, there were rumors of an "Indian plot to assassinate J.M.,"[181] which grew so alarming after October, 1908, that he was secretly "shadowed."[182] Morley found such undivided attention "a nuisance" or "bore,"[183] and managed for a while to persuade Scotland Yard to leave him alone. Two weeks after Curzon-Wyllie's murder, however, there were "3 men watching J.M."[184]

Morley's official reaction to his aide's assassination was to keep cool and try to engender a spirit of calm sanity among those around him. Maintaining that "the crime was an isolated act," he was "inclined to pooh-pooh any suggestion for facilitating inquiry into what is going on in London. He declares now that he has never seen a particle of evidence during the last 2 yrs. pointing to a conspiracy."[185] Lee-Warner, Hirtzel, and the Attorney General, nonetheless, pressed upon his attention inflammatory articles in Shyama Krishnavarma's *Indian Sociologist*, against which it seemed possible to "get a conviction both for seditious libel and for incitement to murder."[186] Morley judged it best for the India Office to "keep out" of such prosecutions, however, even should the French government be induced to extradite Krishnavarma from his new residence in Paris, of which Morley correctly assumed there would be no chance. He was fully conscious of Krishnavarma's revolutionary propaganda, from as early as July, 1907, when J. D. Rees,[187] Liberal member of the Commons, asked him about an *Indian Sociologist* editorial that hailed "rebellion" and the "school of Indian patriots whose ideal is not only to have independence in Government in India by ousting the English from that country, but also to recover untold millions of money of which the Indian people have been unjustly deprived."[188] The question went on at some length, recounting Krishnavarma's ideas, then asked if government would not consider proceeding against him "in view to his ultimate expulsion as an undesirable alien." Morley's answer was in the best spirit of Cavour's philosophy of forbearance: "I do not think that the language that my hon. friend quotes is worth either the advertisement that he has given it himself, or that which he wishes me to give it." After Curzon-Wyllie's murder, however, the Home Office initiated an action against the *Indian Sociologist*'s printer, young Guy Aldred, who was sentenced to one year for "printing seditious libel."[189] Krishnavarma remained safe in Paris. Dhingra was sentenced to death on July 23.

From India the clamor for more stringent press legislation was now revived. Even Clarke added his voice to the din of Anglo-Indian apprehension. "The appearance of further repression the very day, as it were, before the launch of Reforms, would have a paradoxical, or even an absurb look," protested Morley to his friend. "I thought you expected that the conviction of Tilak would do your business for you. I never took that view myself. And I am most doubtful about a new press law.... If you cannot govern India without this, you won't be better able to govern with it."[190] To Minto he continued urging release of the deportees as an act of good faith to help bolster the spirit of Congress moderates. In October, after quoting Gokhale, who noted "the feeling is general throughout the country" that most of the deportees, if not all, were innocent men, Morley insisted that "the time has come for release."[191] But Minto still felt it was "too soon" to remove the quarantine. Then, in November, 1909, some coconut bombs were thrown at the Viceroy's carriage while he was on tour at Ahmedabad. The bombs failed to explode, and Minto reacted calmly to the attempted assassination, but now argued that there was in India "a fraternity (I don't know what else to call it) of anarchists such as exists in some European countries, which no legislation affecting the people as a whole is the least likely to demolish."[192] On November 25, 1909, Bombay's High Court confirmed Savakar's life sentence and less than a month later the retiring collector of Nasik, "Pandit" Arthur Mason T. Jackson, was shot down by a young Brahman in the Deccan's most sacred city. With the unerring irony of such murders, Jackson happened to be "one of the best friends of Indians"[193] in the British service.

Insisting that "our first duty is to give confidence to the public,"[194] Minto ordered by "Gazette Extraordinary" (January 4, 1910) the extension of Criminal Law (Amendment) Act XIV of 1908 to the Bombay presidency. This most recent legislative weapon of repression in the government of India's arsenal had been enacted on December 7, 1908,[195] to speed up trials in cases of anarchical offense by eliminating legal stumbling blocks to efficiency such as juries, bail, cross-examination, and right of appeal. The act was most aptly described by Fleetwood Wilson as a twentieth-century model of Judge Jeffrey's criminal procedure.[196] But the murder at Nasik, coming so soon after the attempt on Minto's life, led to an outcry for more repression and extraordinary law, which Morley was unable to resist. He cautioned Clarke, however, "not to dream of starting a fresh repressive panacea on the recurrence of every new act of terrorism."[197] He refused, moreover, to be deterred by terrorists from securing the release of deportees, and on January 27, 1910, wrote peremptorily to Minto:

> You have nine men, locked up a year by *lettre de cachet*, because you believed them to be criminally connected with criminal plots, and because you expected their arrest to check these plots . . . [but] being locked up, they can have had no share in these new abominations; but . . . [you say] their continued detention will frighten evil-doers generally. That's the Russian argument:—by packing off train-loads of suspects to Siberia, we'll terrify the anarchists out of their wits, and all will come out right.
>
> This is the last letter that I shall inflict upon you in this matter, but I cannot budge from my case, and *the clock has struck*.[198]

On February 9, 1910, the deportees were set free. The Home member of India finally felt obliged to admit to his council colleagues that "the policy of deportations had failed."[199] The policy of repression, however, was by no means abandoned. One day before the deportees' release, a new press act was passed. "I don't object to it," sighed Morley in the wake of Jackson's murder; "only to suppose that it will touch the root of the many mischiefs around us, is surely an idle dream. A pill for an earthquake! Not much more than that, is it?"[200] For he well understood that "the forces with which we are contending are far too subtle, deep, and diversified, to be abated by making seditious leading articles expensive,"[201] which was really all the new act would do, except to help placate British India's mercantile associations,[202] of course, and, it was hoped, strengthen Indian securities in the London market, which because of unrest had altered for the worse.[203] But to India as a whole no press act would "bring the millennium," for, as Chief Justice Jenkins put it: "Fresh outlets must be found for the energies of our young men and I somehow feel that instead of giving them an education which fits them only for clerkships and minor posts in the government service we should train them for productive occupations and pursue towards India a policy that will enable industries to come into existence; this I fear is heresy, for is it not swadeshi?"[204]

Morley himself had approved of harsh measures only in the hope that as temporary expedients they might serve to keep order and quell violence, which he recognized as prerequisities to progress.[205] He was not so blind to history, however, as to accept the extremist Tory policy, "Martial law and no damned nonsense."[206] He saw not merely the froth of unrest, but the deep-rolling sea that churned it. "Much of this movement arises from the fact that there is now a considerable, a large, body of educated Indians who have been fed at our instigation, by our means, upon the great teachers and masters of this country—Milton and Burke, and Macauley, and John Stuart Mill," he explained to his fellow Englishmen. "I am not surprised at all, are you, that these educated Indians who read these great masters and teachers of ours are intoxicated with the ideas of freedom and nationality and self-government which those great writers promulgate? I entirely agree. . . . Who of us can forget, shall I call it the intoxication and rapture with which we made friends with these truths?"[207]

Personally, Morley believed the problem went deeper than education, sensing that the "root of the unrest, discontent, and sedition, so far as I can make out," was "racial and not political. Now, that being so, it is of a kind that is the hardest to reach. . . . it is a dislike not of political domination, but of our racial domination."[208] This nagging suspicion of the ultimate untenability of the British raj made Morley feel at times as though, no matter what was done for India under his aegis, it would be no more "than drawing our hands through water. Will your reform policy, Natives on my Council, Decentralisation, Economising of Taxation, and the rest of our virtuous deeds," he inquired rhetorically of Minto in August, 1907, "really make a pin of difference in their feelings about British rule?"[209] Certainly he knew enough about human nature and nationalist struggles to understand that "if one were to speak with tongues as of men and angels, I suppose it would not quench the perversity of people who do not want and do not mean to be pacified."[210] Yet Morley added, as his imperative of action, "One can only go steadily forward on what one takes to be the best line." That line was for him a middle path between harshness and conciliation, a road of policy designed to run between the extremes of total repression and complete reform.

"The first duty of any Government is to keep order," Morley admitted, but his own ideal was "Order *plus* Progress."[211] In India, he argued, there was a "living movement . . . for objects which we ourselves have all taught them to think desirable objects. And unless we somehow or other can reconcile order with satisfaction of these ideas and aspirations, gentlemen, the fault will not be theirs. It will be ours."[212] Order was to be enforced, then, until reforms could do the more effective, enduring job of maintaining it, not through tyranny, but by weeding out the roots of disorder, raising instead a system of government designed to develop self-imposed rules of restraint. Fashioning such reforms was the job to which Morley devoted the best of his energy and talent.

6

AN ACT OF REFORM

> I wish I could have a solid fortnight all by myself to work it out coolly. But that is not to be had, and one has to be content with second best, and as I have said a million times, all politics are an affair of second best.
> Morley to Minto, April 17, 1907

> Both contemporaries and historians, more often than they suppose, miss a vital point because they do not know the intuitive instinct that often goes farther in the statesman's mind than deliberate analysis or argument.
> Morley, *Politics and History*, page 45

The reforms for which this half decade deserves to be best remembered were constitutional innovations of fundamental and far-reaching significance.[1] Hailed in India just after their parliamentary debut as a "great step forward" toward "the grant of representative government,"[2] they were welcomed with equal enthusiasm by enlightened English opinion as "seeds the fruit of which is Parliamentary government."[3] Morley himself credited his Indian Councils Bill with "the opening of a very important chapter in the history of the relations of Great Britain and India,"[4] yet at the same time insisted that he wanted neither to establish a parliamentary system in India nor to introduce reforms that might lead "directly or necessarily"[5] to the creation of such a system. There is, however, good reason to believe that this disclaimer of great potential for his legislative progeny was a matter of political exigency on Morley's part, rather than naïve self-deception concerning the implications of his own policy. Before attempting to answer the challenging question of just how much Morley hoped his reforms bill would accomplish, however, the almost equally murky matters of the bill's paternity and preparliamentary evolution should be clarified.

Curiously enough, Minto claimed the reforms as his very own, proudly announcing at the first meeting of the expanded imperial legislative council, in 1910, that the scheme was "based entirely on the views I had myself formed of the position of affairs in India" and was "due to no suggestions from home," and that "whether it was good or bad, I am entirely responsible."[6] Few contemporaries were fooled, however; as one astute analyst put it: "As the time for his departure drew nigh, Lord Minto must have become conscious that he was not leaving behind him a measure that could be called his own. The more earnestly he asserted himself the father of the constitutional reform scheme, the more convincedly the British Press ascribed the paternity to Lord Morley."[7] Lady Minto loyally labored to create for posterity an image of her husband's achievement as viceroy of India which bears little resemblance to reality. Among other remarkable claims staked out by the Countess for her husband was the title "Minto, Originator of Reforms."[8] Buchan's[9] "official" biography of Minto, whose "India" portion is based primarily on Lady Minto's diaries and interpretation, tried much the same sort of historical image inflation, and numerous scholars[10] have since been found ready to credit Minto with varying degrees of reforming initiative and zeal. By now, the phrase "Morley-Minto Reforms" has become as much a cliché of Indian history and as misleading a misnomer as the "Mutiny" or the "Black Hole Massacre." Indian students have read this hyphenated rubric so often in examination primers and textbooks that many imagine Morley-Minto to be the compound surname of a single Englishman!

The Morley-Minto correspondence shows clearly, however, that the impetus for and the direction given to Indian political reforms came from the Secretary of State rather than from the Viceroy. Left to his own devices, Minto might have added an Indian version of the Privy Council to his viceregal administrative machine, but nothing more radical. "I have been thinking a good deal lately of a possible counterpoise to Congress aims," he confessed to Morley in May, 1906. "I think we may find a solution in the Council of Princes; or on an elaboration of that idea, a Privy Council not only of native rulers, but a few other big men to meet, say once a year."[11] He mostly feared that the House of Commons and Morley would forget that "We are here a small British garrison surrounded by millions composed of factors of an inflamability unknown to the Western world, unsuited to Western forms of government, and we must be physically strong or go to the wall."[12] Such was Minto's instinctive response to the challenge of Indian political unrest, a response by no means surprising for a patrician lord who had been trained as a soldier. It was, however, hardly the vision of the man to be credited with initiating the act that brought the hitherto autocratic government of India at least "to the threshold of representative government."[13] Thanks only to Morley's suggestions, repeated prodding, astute urging, and deft management was Minto induced to recognize and accept the need for real reforms. Like many converts, it is true that he became at times a more zealous believer than his preceptor, yet his faith remained superficial and was easily shaken. In good measure, moreover, Minto's attitude toward reforms, as to most other aspects of his work in India, was guided by an overriding desire to follow the path of least resistance and mental strain. He delegated most of the responsibility for hammering out the reform scheme to a committee of his council and then to its secretary, H. H. Risley. Unlike Morley, he paid scant attention to the scheme's details and, as will be seen, failed to grasp the bill's basic policy after having spent almost two years in helping to fashion it.

How then is Minto's remarkable reputation as liberal innovator[14] to be accounted for? Much of the blame for this flagrant example of historical distortion belongs with John Morley. Far less concerned with future self-aggrandizement than he was with bequeathing to India's government a real measure of reforms, Morley used every trick in his storehouse of political experience to assure the successful passage of his last great bill. Twice he had given himself, head, heart, and soul, to the task of trying to help pilot Irish home rule through parliamentary rapids too treacherous to traverse after the winds of the opposition's intransigence began to blow. He was now too old to risk a spill with his cargo for India. At times he did not really expect to be vouchsafed the strength or the tenure for even one attempt. He had to plan carefully, therefore, and chart his course well. First of all he worked to win Minto's support, and if possible, to induce Balfour's own appointee as governor-general to sponsor a bill that the Tory majority in the Lords would then find it singularly embarrassing to oppose.

"Not one whit more than you do I think it desirable or possible, or even conceivable, to adapt English political institutions to the nations who inhabit India," wrote Morley in his inimitably disarming style to the none too subtle viceroy on June 6, 1906. "Assuredly not in your day or mine. But the *spirit* of English institutions is a different thing, and it is a thing that we cannot escape even if we wished, which I hope we don't."[15] A week later, however, Morley abandoned this spiritual approach and pressed on in what sounded more like his positivist self, writing: "I wonder whether we could not now make a good start in the way of reform in the popular direction.... Why should we not now consider as practical and immediate things—the extension of the Native element in your Legislative Council; ditto in local councils; full time for discussing Budget in your Legislative Council instead of four or five skimpy hours; right of moving amendments."[16]

He had been primed with these suggestions by Gopal Krishna Gokhale, then president of India's National Congress, who had come to London during the spring of 1906 especially in order to brief Morley on India's problems and Congress demands. By mid-June Morley had sat through four lengthy sessions with Gokhale, who rightly viewed his task as no less than a monumental "tug-of-war" against "the officials of the India Council as to who should capture Mr. Morley's mind."[17] Hirtzel, Lee-Warner, Godley, Dunlop Smith, and others[18] labored assiduously to discredit Gokhale in Morley's eyes, succeeding all too often in sowing seeds of suspicion, doubt, and mistrust, where there should have been nothing but good faith. For Gokhale's integrity was as unblemished as that of his guru, Justice Ranade, his devotion to truth no less religious than that of his foremost disciple, Mahatma Gandhi. Despite recurring doubts, Morley remained attentive to Gokhale's advice[19] throughout his era, early admitting to Minto how much "more vividly" Gokhale presented Indian problems "before me—a great advantage to a Minister groping his way in dark places."[20]

In concluding his letter of June 15, Morley offered Minto the option that has led to such confusion as to the question of reform initiative. "Either do you write me a despatch, or I'll write you one by way of opening the ball," he suggested shrewdly. "It need be no long or high-flown affair," he added, offering as a final suggestion, "I suppose the notion of a Native in your Executive Council would not do at all. Is that certain?" Here then were the major ingredients of the reforms introduced in 1910, foreshadowed in a single paragraph written by

Morley to Minto just half a year after "Honest John" took command of the India Office. Appointment of Indians to the executive councils of Whitehall and Simla was accomplished without legislation (the subject is considered in chap. vii), whereas the reforms noted earlier (increased Indian representation on the imperial and provincial legislative councils, more lengthy budget debates, and permission for non-officials to move amendments) were all to be incorporated into the Indian Councils Act of 1909. If anyone deserves to share credit with Morley for initiating the reform scheme, it is Gokhale rather than Minto, although Gokhale's role was, of course, advisory. From its inception in 1885, after all, the National Congress had been passing resolutions[21] calling for legislative council reforms by addition of elected members, and for two decades these solemn recommendations had been noted and politely or impatiently ignored by governor-generals and secretaries of state alike. Even within Campbell-Bannerman's cabinet, had members like Elgin or Fowler[22] been appointed to the India Office instead of Morley, Gokhale's eloquence and sweet reasonableness in argument would probably have been of no avail whatever.

Morley's next letter to Minto contained the urgent reminder: "I should much like to open one or two of the points I named to you in my last letter. . . . You will, I think, receive this letter that I am now writing, early enough to send me a telegram, indicating your inclinations and intentions in this matter. If I were in a position to state that a move of this kind would be made when your next Budget comes forward, it would be an effective answer to Cotton and Co. You understand, I hope, that I would wish the move to be directly and closely associated with yourself?"[23] Thus the option of taking credit for initiating proposals of political reform was again extended to Minto, although Morley had decided "to make an announcement in his budget speech,"[24] scheduled for July 20, whether or not the Viceroy agreed by then to join him in advocating reforms. He hoped Minto would voluntarily agree to initiate the proposals (as he did) since the Lords with its Tory majority of three to one still stood as an often insurmountable wall of reaction between the Commons and legislative enactment. Morley revealed his rationale for launching the council bill campaign by this clever tactical maneuver as early as 1889 when he informed the Liberal Eighty Club:

The Tory Party, we are told, are as capable as we are of undertaking the solution of the problems of social reform. I wish they would . . . because they have special advantages for dealing with them. I have observed within the last two or three years as to proposals when made by Mr. Parnell, or when made by some of us on the front Opposition Bench, were denounced by the Chief Secretary as mad and foolish, and were denounced by the Prime Minister as dishonest; yet the moment they were taken up by these gentlemen themselves, they became consummate statesmanship. They can pass measures with ease, which, if proposed by us, they would be sure to resist with might and main.[25]

Long after Minto had taken his bait, moreover, Morley spelled out his strategy to the man who had unwittingly become his accomplice in outmaneuvering the peers of his own party. Commenting on the Viceroy's budget message in March, 1907, Morley wrote:

I think you were wholly right in disowning pressure from home. That will stop in advance what would otherwise have been the first parrot-cry of Anglo-Indian criticism and resistance, official and otherwise, and your public, Native and European, will have to judge the proposals on their merits. On the other hand, it leaves me free from responsibility up to this stage. That will help to take the proposals out of the party lines, and Balfour and Lansdowne[26] will be bound to treat respectfully a policy emanating from a Governor-General appointed by them, and a member (as I believe) of their own party.[27]

As urged by Morley in his letter of June 22, Minto cabled his reply on July 14, 1906: "Am thoroughly in agreement with you as to necessity of meeting indications of popular movement."[28] He expressed his willingness to explore the possibilities of extending the budget debate and expanding the imperial legislative council, although cautioning that "popular representation, as understood at home, is, of course, out of the question." He seems to have realized that Morley was determined to move ahead without him if necessary, and decided to make a virtue of necessity by taking credit for starting what he lacked the power to stop. "I consider it of the greatest importance that any official initiative as to reforms in Indian administration should emanate from here," Minto's wire continued. "It would be most unfortunate for present and future if Government of India should appear to act in this matter only on pressure from home." His pretense to independent initiative was never abandoned by Minto, who now most jealously guarded his adopted brainchild, particularly against any claim or threat of repossession by the legitimate father. "I am rather puzzled," wrote Minto to Morley in September, 1908, "as to your exact meaning when you advise that our despatch should 'wind up with some sentences inviting whatever expansion may be thought worthy of consideration by His Majesty's Government and promising your earnest and faithful co-operation.' I have always laid great stress on the immense political importance from an Indian point of view of the *initiation of our reforms emanating from the Government of India*, and ... I cannot think it would be right for the Government of India to give a blank cheque, so to speak, to be filled in for us at home."[29] (The italicized words were underlined with Morley's red ink.) Morley must have been struck by the irony of Minto's paternalistic anxiety. As for himself, Morley had earlier informed the Viceroy, "I have no ambition whatever to have my name associated with a new departure. If you and I stand together, 'we can do something,' as Cavour used to say."[30]

The problem of deciding just what, of course, was a formidable one, yet from the start Morley stressed the overriding importance of increasing "the representative element"[31] within India's legislative councils, and broadening the powers of those councils. Was he influenced by the priority[32] Gokhale gave to this particular aspect of reform, or was it simply his own high regard for the Commons as the heartbeat of British democracy which naturally predisposed Morley to seek a solution to India's political problem in the direction of more representative assemblies? Whatever the reasons, it is significant to note that, while Minto stressed the role of princely cooperation and later that of executive council reform, and while some members of Whitehall's Council of India wanted to "divert the entire attention of the Indian Opposition from an enlargement of the Legislative Councils"[33] by creating a powerful "Council of Notables," Morley consistently singled out the enlargement of the legislative councils as "by far the widest, most deep-reaching, and most substantial department"[34] of the reform scheme. If indeed he did not anticipate the evolution of reformed legislative councils of his day into India's *lok sabha* and state assemblies, he was, at any rate, quick to appreciate the cardinal importance of popularizing and strengthening those councils.

Inaugurated in 1853 with the addition of six officials to the governor-general's council when it assembled to make laws and regulations, the imperial "legislative council"[35] was enlarged in 1861, at which time provincial legislative councils were created for Bombay and Madras. The act of 1892[36] increased maximum additional membership on the imperial council from twelve to sixteen, only ten of whom could be nonofficials. Although all members would continue to be nominated by the viceroy, an important innovation was introduced, since five of the additional appointees would, as a rule, hereafter be selected upon the recommendations of electorates, consisting of Calcutta's chamber of commerce and nonofficial members on each of the four provincial legislative councils.[37] Within the more dramatically expanded[38] provincial councils, moreover, the new elective element included members chosen by such broadly representative bodies as municipalities and district boards, as well as special interest groups like landholders' associations, university senates, and chambers of commerce. As recommended by the Aitchison committee in 1888,[39] "class or interest" rather than territorial representation was thus saddled to the elective principle indirectly introduced into India's council chambers in 1893. By the act of 1892, nonofficial members were granted the right to give written notice of questions to government, although no supplementary questions were permitted. Finally, one day was allotted at the end of each legislative council session for general discussion and criticism of the budget. Nonofficial members, privileged to speak only once, if they wished to, were denied permission to submit resolutions. The act of 1892 has been generally recognized as a "small measure"[40] of grudging concession to popular demand designed primarily to avert pressure in favor of the more liberal bill that Charles Bradlaugh had drawn up for India in 1890. Yet neither the liberal secretary of state, Henry Fowler (1894–1895),[41] nor his Tory successors, George Hamilton (1895–1903)[42] and St. John Brodrick (1903–1905),[43] not to mention their viceregal colleagues, Lord Elgin (1894–1899)[44] and Lord Curzon (1899–1905),[45] had ever considered it necessary to broaden the representative base of these legislative councils. Nor did any of them or Lord Minto believe it possible to introduce the elective principle directly.

Within a month of Morley's promise to the Commons that political change was in the offing in India, Minto appointed his reform committee, under the chairmanship of Sir Arundel Arundel, Home member of the executive council. "The political atmosphere is full of change, questions are before us which we cannot afford to ignore," Minto informed his newly appointed committee. "And to me it would appear all-important that the initiative should emanate from us, that the Government of India should not be put in the position of appearing to have its hands forced by agitation in this country or by pressure from home."[46] The Viceroy noted four points on which the committee was to report: (1) a council of princes, "and if this is not possible might they be represented on Viceroy's Legislative Council?";[47] (2) a native member of the Executive Council; (3) increased representation on the legislative council of the viceroy and of the local governments; and (4) prolonged budget debate and the power of moving amendments. In less than two months, somewhat to Minto's "surprise"[48] at their swiftness, his committee submitted its report.[49] On most points of reference they agreed to disagree, for their political philosophies spanned the spectrum of England's party system. Arundel, whose subsequent briefing[50] made Morley feel much at home with his committee, described Denzil Ibbetson as "a sound Tory or official Whig," Edward Norman Baker as the committee "Radical," Earle Richards (legal member) as "a lawyer of no pronounced political leaning," and himself as "a Liberal Unionist." On the question of the native member, the committee was deadlocked with Arundel and Baker in favor, Ibbetson and Richards opposed. (Their reasons are considered in chap. vii.) As to the other three points of reference, there was greater consensus.

Arundel, Baker, and Richards concluded (par. 11) that a council of princes was desirable, as a purely informal group of selected chiefs to be summoned intermittently by the viceroy for consultation concerning such matters as imperial service troops and military questions. Ibbetson dissented (pars. 12–16) primarily for fear that, should the princes and chiefs be made conscious of their united strength, they might pose a serious political challenge to British paramountcy. Regarding the expansion of the imperial legislative council, all were agreed in recommending (par. 50) that maximum membership be doubled to forty-nine, the majority of twenty-five to remain officials. Members appointed on the basis of the elective principle introduced in 1893 would continue to be chosen by the Calcutta chamber of commerce and the nonofficial cadres of provincial councils (now increased to seven), but would also include one representative of the nobles and great landowners of each province, and two Muslims. The Muslim members were to be selected by a separate Muslim electorate (par. 59), thus introducing religion as well as class and interest as a basis of enfranchisement in British India. This departure has proved so significant a factor in South Asia's subsequent history that its genesis and development during this era are traced in a separate chapter.

As to the budget, Arundel's committee suggested two major reforms: creation of a special budget committee (par. 65), including nonofficial Indian members, whose criticism or advice on financial matters could thus be offered "at a stage when effect can if necessary be given to them" (par. 70); and additional time for the annual budget discussion. Baker alone, noting his need to "dissociate myself altogether from the 'sop to Cerberus' theory" (par. 74), advocated empowering nonofficial members to move budgetary amendments. Arundel, Ibbetson, and Richards, however, sensed in such a proposal "the first step towards an Appropriation Bill" (par. 89).

Using the committee's report as the point of departure, the government of India tackled the job of preparing an official reforms dispatch for submission to the secretary of state. More than two months later, however, Minto reported[51] that this dispatch would not be ready before February, 1907. But in January he found preparing the dispatch "such a very serious affair"[52] that he doubted if his government could manage it within a month. On February 17 he cabled[53] Morley it would be "quite impossible" to send the dispatch before May. As far as Minto was concerned, many matters took priority over reforms. "All Departments," he wired, were "full of work" until after the budget. Morley, however, refused to tolerate so long a delay. "Time is one thing," he gasped "and eternity is another."[54] Accustomed to the pressure of cabinet work, he considered the government of India's total preoccupation with its budget an indication of gross ineptitude. "Do you think the fact that Asquith is busy with his coming budget, and Haldane and Tweedmouth with their huge estimates, prevents the Cabinet as a whole from considering every other of the host of big questions, home and foreign, that come surging in upon us?" he asked wryly, scolding, "You may think it a trifle arrogant, but I make bold to say that, when His Majesty's Government propounds questions for your deliberation, those questions should come first, after the immediate claims of the administrative business of the hour."[55] The ultimate weapon used to prod Minto along was the repeated threat of inaugurating a full-scale parliamentary inquiry into the administrative methods of the government of India. Morley was to appoint the Royal Commission on Decentralization instead (whose work is considered elsewhere), but the mere threat of sending "a capable committee of experienced and cool-headed men" from the Commons to "examine the centralised organization of Indian government on the spot,"[56] did wonders to help Minto find time for work he never believed possible. On March 9 he wired that the dispatch was being drafted and would be shipped off by the mail boat of March 21, as it was. Although dated more than five months after the Arundel committee's report, the government of India's reform dispatch[57] arrived at the same conclusions as those reached by the majority of its select committee. What the dispatch contained, however, which the report did not include, was a statement of the broader implications and the political philosophy behind these proposals. No doubt it was a statement to which Minto himself devoted much time and earnest thought, and may perhaps help explain why the dispatch took so long in coming. The proposals were described in paragraph 6:

> An attempt to give to India something that may be called a constitution framed on sufficiently liberal lines to satisfy the legitimate aspirations of all but the most advanced Indians, whilst at the same time enlisting the support of the conservative elements of native society . . . not an experimental makeshift, but a working machine representing all interests that are capable of being represented and providing for an adequate expression of the sentiments and requirements of the masses of the people. . . . We are not without hope that in the course of a few years the constitution which we propose to establish will come to be regarded as a precious possession round which conservative sentiment will crystalise and will offer substantial opposition to any further change. We anticipate that the aristocratic elements in society and the moderate men, for whom at present there is no place in Indian politics, will range themselves on the side of the Government and will oppose any further shifting of the balance of power and any attempt to democratise Indian institutions.

This "new system" was called "a constitutional autocracy," concerning which the dispatch insisted: "There is all the difference in the world between the arbitrary autocracy of an Asiatic despotism, and the constitutional autocracy which binds itself to govern by rule, which admits and invites to its counsels [sic] representatives of all interests which are capable of being represented, and which merely reserves to itself, in the form of a narrow majority, the predominant and absolute power which it can only abdicate at the risk of bringing back the chaos to which our rule put an end." Here, then, was Minto's "Liberal" motivation for reform, and as clear a statement of the philosophy underlying his government's scheme as was ever really attempted. By enlisting princely aid and rallying the aristocracy, Minto and his council hoped to silence the cry for colonial self-government. Explaining the value of the proposed "Council of Nobles" (no longer confined solely to princes), the dispatch stated (par. 11) that its members would "furnish the heads of local Government with a useful counterpoise against the body of advanced opinion which tends to obtain undue prominence in the Provincial Legislative Councils." By directly introducing representatives chosen from the nobility and great landholding families of British India into council chambers, moreover, it was hoped that the undeserved "prominence" which the elective system of 1892 had unwittingly afforded to Indians of the legal profession would, in the future, be vitiated. A healthy infusion of "the more stable elements of the community" into legislative councils was to be guaranteed by making it mandatory for landholding magnates to elect one of "their own number" as their representative (pars. 43–44). Finally, the dispatch insisted on maintaining official majorities in all councils, provincial as well as imperial. Among other reasons given was the argument that had been one of Curzon's favorite self-justifications for ignoring Congress demands, that is, "The officials would represent the cultivators, the artisans, and the petty traders, forming together 85–90 per cent of the population who are incapable of taking an effective part in any kind of elections" (par. 58).

Morley at once appointed a select committee of his council to tackle the dispatch, although he hardly expected its members' advice to be "very helpful" since, as he put it, "certainly with one or two exceptions, they are not exactly of the noble tribe of born reformers."[58] Nor did they fail to live up to his expectations. All liked the idea of a council of notables, by and large sharing the opinion of Lieutenant Colonel Sir David W. K. Barr, who noted that "the principle of recognizing the aristocracy of India as the class most worthy of the confidence of the Government of India is one that commends itself entirely to my judgment."[59] Theodore Morison,[60] who, thanks to his long tenure at Aligarh and close identification with Indian Muslims and their causes, came to be known as the first "Muslim Member" of the Council of India, was even more enthusiastic. "In pursuance of my idea of diverting the entire attention of the Indian opposition from an enlargement of the Legislative Councils," wrote Morison, "I desire to make the Council of Notables an institution capable of exercising a real influence upon Indian politics."[61] Economically speaking, he argued, India was at that stage of historical development which, in England's history, coincided with the political rule of "country gentlemen." If political institutions were to "be a reality," he insisted, they must accurately reflect socioeconomic forces. For India "this would mean conferring a privilege upon a somewhat narrow oligarchy, but the justification of such a political regime is that Indian society at the present day is oligarchic and aristocratic."

The committee was much less happy about legislative council expansion, although it grudgingly resolved: "Having regard to the whole position . . . they must assume it to be practically settled that there is to be a considerable increase in the number of Members."[62] "Maintenance of an official majority in each council," however, was deemed "absolutely indispensable" (resolution 10). Least happy among the members was Sir Hugh S. Barnes, who regretfully conceded, "Our fondness for a system of election is, I suppose, ineradicable," but went on to warn "we won't get the best men by adopting it. The System is incompatible with the Indian conception of personal dignity."[63] Barnes would have been content to leave the councils unchanged, indeed, to forget reforms entirely. What India more urgently needed, he argued, was "a cold douche" administered "to the aspirations of the Nationalist party" and "an immediate and considerable increase to the White garrison."[64] Sir John Edge felt the legislative council proposals were "not yet ripe for discussion here."[65] Lee-Warner and Morison argued that inadequate provision was being made to assure separate representation of "the more important races, classes and interests," by which they meant the Muslims. They proposed the creation throughout India of electoral colleges based on "race, caste, or religion."[66]

As for the government of India's recommendations concerning the budget, Morley's committee "unanimously agreed"[67] to oppose the creation of a legislative council budget committee. Here the Council of India was defending its own fortress, empowered as it was by statute to have the final say concerning India's budget, insisting that "there should be no disclosure of the Budget outside of the Governor-General's Executive Council until it has been sanctioned by the Secretary of State in Council, and has been published." After that, however, "fullest discussion on the different heads of the Budget" (resolution 18), meaning in fact an expanded debate, was approved. Morison dissented from even the latter concession, arguing that "financial control . . . is a cardinal function of Government, and it is therefore the last with regard to which the Government of India can afford to surrender to non-official members its absolute discretion."[68] Baker's minority recommendation advocating permission for nonofficials to move budgetary amendments received no support whatever.

Morley was hardly surprised by his council's reactions. "As was to be expected, considering who they are and what are their antecedents, my Council show no enthusiasm," he reported to Minto. "They are, almost without exception, conservative and skeptical about reform."[69]

Yet, although critics often accused Morley of doctrinaire disregard for his counselors' advice, he was most sensitive to their criticism and opinions, trying always to sway them by reason to his position (as he tried when in disagreement with the government of India as well), rather than attempting to ride roughshod over the constitutional hurdle of their dissent. He knew that the role of any political administrator who hoped to inaugurate some measure of meaningful reform was as weighty an educational as it was a legislative job. He challenged his council to think intelligently about India, much in the same way as he did his constituents and colleagues in Parliament. "The truer all you say is—about 'inflamed minds, sedition-mongers,' etc.," he informed those around him who grimaced pessimistically at reforms, "—the more incumbent it is upon you to tell us how you hope and intend to abate the mischief."[70]

The one retired official to whom Morley turned consistently for advice, a man he knew and respected for almost forty years, and whom he considered "the most instructive and luminous of the writers that Indian experience has produced,"[71] was Sir Alfred Comyn Lyall.[72] With the possible exception of Hirtzel, no individual in England exerted so strong an influence upon Morley's mind at critical moments of decision making as did Lyall. Unobtrusive to the point of timidity, the key to Sir Alfred's power at the India Office was his long-standing personal friendship with the Secretary of State, and almost half a century of experience, both in India and on Whitehall's council. Retired since 1903, Lyall had no professional or political ambitions, and seemed to Morley's eyes "to mount to the high summits of policy"[73] each time he voiced an opinion. Lyall's written "observations," preserved among the Morley papers, offer only some indication of how much Morley was influenced by his friend's judgment, for, during the time when he was most actively engaged with the problems of reform, Morley discussed[74] them privately with Sir Alfred at least once every fortnight.

Lyall's reaction to the government of India's dispatch differed most significantly from the committee's with respect to the council of notables. He expressed "little or no faith in advising councils—believing that advice without direct responsibility is of small value."[75] He also reported from his personal experience that Indians "*very rarely hold their tongues*, except where their own interests are intimately concerned. . . . Nor do I think that individual consultation *by letter* is advisable. . . . They *very seldom write even their ordinary letters*"

(Emphasis added by Morley).[76] Finally, Lyall warned that so large and influential a body might eventually unite in "some kind of political opposition to the British Government." As to the legislative councils, he agreed that the measure of reform proposed was politic and necessary, but suggested representation of Indian commercial interests as well as landholding interests. "As a class," he noted, "the leading bankers and merchants of India are particularly sagacious and shrewd men; they have a wide and close acquaintance with the conditions of the people, and the economical affairs of the country." A painstaking critic and adviser, Lyall also pointed out the fallacy of the government of India's assumption that peasants "can *only* be represented by the official members," explaining to Morley, "The main, perhaps the only, grievance of the cultivators relates to heavy assessments of land revenue, and it is to be remembered that in assessing the revenue the officials often fix the rents; while in Madras and Bombay the rents are directly assessed on the ryot by the officials. I am not convinced that the cultivators will regard the officials as their best representatives."[77]

Gathering together the Arundel committee report, the government of India dispatch, the special committee resolutions with assorted notes, and Lyall's letters, Morley went to work on his reform dispatch. It was, as he confessed when finished, "a wretched sort of affair, and though I have written a thousand pieces in my ill-spent days in which I took but little pride, I never felt so little proud of anything as this."[78] What troubled Morley most about his dispatch was its inconsistency, for it spoke, as he put it, "with two voices,"[79] expressing viewpoints as incompatible and irreconcilable as liberty and autocracy. Not surprisingly, the dilemma at the root of so much of the conflict between Whitehall and Simla extended into the matter of reforms. Just when Morley was writing his dispatch, in fact, the rioting broke out in Rawalpindi (see chap. v), which, he lamented to Minto, "will make it much harder to carry out the bold line of reform that you and I have marked out. It is an old and painful story. Shortcomings in government lead to outbreaks; outbreaks have to be put down; reformers have to bear the blame, and their reforms are scotched; reaction triumphs; and mischief goes on as before, only worse."[80] As for "the Future," he added, "Tis like the Czar and the Duma." Merely a historical analogy, of course, but one to indicate perhaps that Morley, at that time, thought his reforms might create an Indian duma (parliament), or at least pave the path to one. At its last annual session in Calcutta a few months earlier, the Indian National Congress had officially proclaimed "self-government" (svaraj) its ultimate political goal. Dadabhai Naoroji's famous presidential address, delivered for the ailing grand old man of Indian politics by Gokhale, contained the sacred word "svaraj" itself, and the ninth resolution of the 1906 Congress called for extension to India of "the system of Government obtaining in the self-governing British Colonies." Minto and his advisers considered such a platform dangerously "extreme," but Morley was prepared to accept it as a "moderate" demand. Indeed, in the original draft of his dispatch, which he sent to Lyall for criticism, he had observed that a "moderate party demands the system of a self-governing colony."[81] Lyall, more conservative politically than his friend, was shocked. Self-government was "not a very moderate request," he argued, and Morley, ever alert to the danger of putting up conservative backs against his forthcoming bill, obliged by substituting for the word "moderate" the phrase "less extreme."[82] It may be noted, on the other hand, that as a rule Minto used the word "moderate" only with reference to the most conservative forces in Indian society, the aristocracy and landed gentry. Were an understanding of Morley's true intentions concerning the nature and goals of Indian reforms less crucial to a proper appreciation of the cooperative and inspiring role played by British Liberals (in office as well as out) in helping to fashion India's parliamentary democracy, such minute analysis might not be necessary. It is, however, essential to leave no altered phrase unappraised if it may help recapture Morley's real meaning on this vital point, for, as is shown later, historians generally have come to interpret his stand on parliamentary government for India as precisely the opposite of what it actually was.

While fashioning his reform dispatch and planning strategy for guiding through Parliament the bill that was to emerge from it, Morley did not neglect the need of trying to resolve the dilemma of having not merely to "keep time," but also "good faith," in two political latitudes at once. "I wish one could think of some sort of machinery for acquainting the Indian public—so far as there is what is to be called an Indian public—with the real motives and intentions of Government in what they do," he wrote on the eve of signing his dispatch. "As it is we are all in a cleft stick: we don't know the minds of the Natives, and the Natives don't know what is in our minds. How to find some sort of bridge? That's the question."[83] He was tormented by the paradox of "Liberal" imperialism. He knew how strongly politically conscious India relied upon him *personally*. Romesh Dutt had written Morley in September, 1906, that the "people of India will not believe that England will be ungenerous, suspicious, and unjust, towards India at the present juncture. They firmly believe that, from the present Government, and from your hands—pardon me mentioning this—they will receive some extension of popular rights and influence in the administration of the country.... They *will not* believe that in these days of political progress all over the world, the most Liberal Government which England has seen within 30 years will leave India in discontent and despair."[84]

The dispatch of May 17, 1907, reflected Morley's acute consciousness of his liberal responsibility and sense of divided allegiance. "The foundation of our case for paramount British power in India is that it is good for the vast population there committed to it," he argued, striving for moral self-vindication in a way that would never have occurred to the government of India, insisting:

When the East India Company was some half century ago deposed, and all its old dominion transferred to the Crown, its champions protested that they had always regarded it as the most honourable characteristic of the Government of India by England, that it had acknowledged no such distinction as that of a dominant and a subject race, but had held that its first duty was to the people of India.... They claimed, moreover, that for at least two generations theirs had been in all departments one of the most rapidly improving governments in the world. Such was the language, such the principles, such the claims of the Company; and rule under the Imperial Crown to-day justifies itself, and can only be justified, by firmly standing in the same beneficent ways [par. 4].

By thus insisting that right rather than might was the foundation stone of British power in India, John Morley accepted the position of Indian liberals like Gokhale, who argued that harsh methods of repression and callous indifference to public welfare by officials were in fact aspects of un-British rule, and should, like the House of Lords, either be mended or ended. In his other political voice, however, the Secretary of State for India noted, "Your Excellency's disclaimer for your Government of being 'advocates of representative government for India in the Western sense of the term,' is not any more than was to be expected," and went on to offer his "cordial concurrence" in the government of India's professed goal of simply seeking "to improve existing machinery" (par. 5).

Actually, of course, the Viceroy's favorite proposal was to add a glittering new princely council to the existing machinery. Morley was never attracted by this idea of reviving the brainchild of Lytton with which Curzon had toyed "as a device for countering the Congress."[85] Morley suggested in his dispatch that, instead of an imperial council of princes, it might prove "fruitful in good results" to have provincial councils for collecting the "opinion of the natural leaders of Indian society within the British dominion [pars. 8–13]." Minto persisted, however, with his original idea that the notables be mostly princes, and their council "primarily Imperial."[86] The Viceroy talked this matter over "a good deal"[87] with princely comrades of the hunt like Scindia (Maharaja of Gwalior). Although provincial governments were divided in their appraisal of the scheme, the government of India officially recommended[88] the creation of an imperial council composed solely of "Ruling Chiefs" appointed by the viceroy. After more than two years of thought, discussion, and criticism, Minto had reverted to his earliest scheme of surrounding himself with a privy council of "purely advising" princes. Morley considered the idea "nonsense," and finally decided[89] to reject it outright, instead of laboring to devise an alternative patchwork quilt. Although he was by that time a member of the House of Lords himself, Morley had changed neither his name nor his republican predilections with the shift in venue of his parliamentary seat. Thanks to his rejection of Minto's pet plan for rallying Indian royalty around the British raj, the scheme, although later resuscitated, never lived long enough to bear historic fruit. Divided as they remained vis-à-vis British India, the more than 500 princely states were integrated with relative ease into the self-governing dominions of India and Pakistan in 1947. Thus, even if Morley had never dreamed of bequeathing a duma to India, he may at least be credited with having helped depose her many czars.

His May, 1907, dispatch, however, stressed the predominant importance of legislative council expansion, foreshadowing what was to become one of Morley's most important reform innovations, the overthrow of official majority legislative bodies in the provinces. Noting that insistence upon maintaining an official majority "implies the necessity of limiting the number of non-official members" (since only a small number of officials could ordinarily be spared from their regular duties during the busy winter season to attend meetings of the legislative councils), Morley urged the government of India to face up to the question of "how to provide for the due representation, within the narrow limits thus imposed, of the vast diversity of classes, races, and interests in the Indian Empire" (par. 22). Here again he proved himself a singularly shrewd and subtle advocate of representative rule, for, instead of proposing immediately a radical new departure, he based what became the thin edge of a wedge of revolutionary change upon a long-accepted and conservative-sounding formula. Representation by "classes, races, and interests," after all, was the old Aitchison committee slogan reaffirmed by Lansdowne and Cross in 1892 and accepted as axiomatic by Minto and his council in their first dispatch. By now the most conservative members of the House of Lords would hardly flinch at it. Morley's change in this formula, moreover, was the insertion of only one small word—"due." Yet the argument favoring "due representation" of India's diversity was to succeed in deposing official majorities from all provincial legislative councils after 1910. The government of India's spurious claim that officials "represented" the inarticulate 85 to 90 percent of India's population and had, therefore, a moral right to remain in the majority was implicitly repudiated. Morley, of course, understood the radical implications of the change he contemplated. Steeped as he was in his country's history, he fully appreciated the power of precedent and the evolutionary character of English constitutional law. He moved cautiously, alluding only by implication to his own negative predilection in his 1907 budget statement to the Commons. At that time, after reporting "acceptance of the general principle of a substantial enlargement of Legislative Councils," Morley remarked that *"so far it is thought best in India* that an official majority must be maintained" (italics added).[90]

In the government of India's Home Department circular of August, 1907, presenting the reforms scheme to local administrations for comment, the official majority was termed "an entirely legitimate and necessary consequence of the nature of the paramount power in India. ... That is not an open question."[91] Here again, provincial governments were notified that "the widest [not "due"] representation should be given to classes, races, and interests, subject to the condition that an official majority must be maintained" (par. 20). Clarke alone demurred, and although unable to "get my colleagues to go as far as I wished," wrote personally to inform Morley, "I believe it might be an advantage to give up the official majority in the Legislative Council.... I do not believe it will ever be necessary or desirable for a Provincial Government to force any measure opposed by *all* the representatives of Native opinion."[92]

By 1908, Risley, a most astute, vigorous, and extremely ambitious young secretary to the government of India's Home Department, had taken charge of fashioning the reforms scheme in India. Lord Minto was preoccupied with too many other "anxieties,"[93] and "had not had time to read the local governments' reports," Risley notified Morley, "and I therefore went over the whole ground with him and afterwards wrote to Dunlop Smith [Minto's private secretary] a rough sketch of possible conclusions under the different heads."[94] That "rough sketch" became the finished form of the government of India's scheme as officially dispatched five months later on October 1, 1908.[95] Writing informally to Morley, Risley defended the retention of official majorities on what he shrewdly assumed to be ground Morley would find "far more important" than any other. "If a subordinate government, such as the Government of Bombay, divests itself of its official majority," Risley explained, "it thereby makes itself independent not only of the Government of India but also of the Secretary of State and of Parliament."[96] Morley was unimpressed, however, for what Risley failed to realize was that "that man in Whitehall" jealously defended the prerogatives of Parliament against bureaucratic despotism, not representative rule. Coincidentally enough, on the very day Risley wrote the above, Morley was writing Minto, "I'd rather have parliamentary rule with all its faults than Prussian bureaucracy. As you guess by this time, I am less passionately in love than ever even with bureaucracy as model machinery for governing alien races!"[97] A week later Morley reported Field Marshal Lord Roberts'[98] opinion that "we are not there [in India] with the will of the people, and nothing that we can do for them will ever make them wish us to remain." While personally prone to agree with Roberts, Morley concluded by advising Minto that "we must persevere with liberal and substantial reforms, perhaps wider than those in your original sketch."[99] Minto, however, was "really becoming unhappy at having no time to think over the Councils question."[100] He complained bitterly by mid-1908 that it "requires so much thought and one has so little time here to digest matters." After July he no longer bothered even to pretend looking for the time, but reported "Risley is now nearly through his analysis of material, and I have appointed a Committee of Council to consider our final recommendations to you."[101]

Morley, who had in May been "impatient to get to work on 'Reforms,' as soon as ever your draft reaches me,"[102] groaned by August, "To do great things, Napoleon said, a man must suppose that he will never die. And to tackle such a business as Indian Reforms, a man must

AN ACT OF REFORM

suppose that he will live forever, and never be kicked out of office."[103] Wearily watching how "the Indian machine toils and travails," he began to "wonder whether we shall not be laughed out of court, for producing a mouse from the labouring mountain."[104] Risley sent him the report of Minto's council committee, dated July 18, 1908, "winding up with some story about further reference to the Foreign Department for their observations! After that, the thing has still to be discussed in your Council!!! So it will reach me a day or two before the Day of Judgment. . . . *India can't wait*,"[105] thundered Morley. More than two years had passed since his first promise to the Commons that reforms were on their way. At seventy, Morley's acute sense of urgency about wanting to see finished the job he had begun was hardly surprising. He had left Minto and Risley to "gang their own gait" long enough. His hints about speed and the possibility of abandoning official majorities had been smugly ignored at Simla. "The scheme does not, so far as I can make out, really *admit in any effective sense the Indians to a greater share in their own affairs*," Morley finally wrote in his letter of August 10, 1908. "It will have to be extended immensely. . . . We shall have to go both wider and lower" (italics added). By advocating the italicized part of this letter, Morley was in fact demanding no less than Gokhale, as official Congress spokesman, had been calling for since 1905.[106]

By September, 1908, with as yet no official dispatch from the government of India in sight, Morley exclaimed to Clark: "The delay in the matter of reforms at Simla is like nothing but the old Vatican at its worst."[107] Even before seeing the dispatch, moreover, he told Minto that he expected to throw overboard the "sacred doctrine" of the official majority at the provincial level, believing that "much will follow, if we increase the size of these bodies, and give them substantial powers, as I think we shall have to do."[108] Those who accuse Morley of ignorance of the implications of his achievement have underestimated the breadth of his historical perspective. He knew precisely what sort of constitutional chain reaction he was starting. Nor did he ever forget his role of parliamentary pilot for the bill. In selecting his second council committee to deliberate upon the long-promised dispatch, he informed Minto, "I have invited Lord MacDonnell [who had been secretary to the Aitchison committee in 1888] to join us . . . in considering 'Reforms,' he may have his uses, and at the worst it may prevent him from raging in the House of Lords against us."[109] Actually it did not, much to Morley's chagrin, for MacDonnell rebelled and became his bête noire in the Lords after the bill was read. But, if this particular tactic failed, it nonetheless indicates how painstaking and even devious Morley could be in pursuing his overall strategy to the victory ultimately won. In May, 1908, Gokhale returned to London to lobby again for more liberal reforms, and Morley saw him regularly;[110] despite earlier misgivings, he retained a high opinion of Gokhale's integrity, "the world being a scene, no doubt, of many imperfections."[111]

Morley was ready now to go farther along the road to self-government than Gokhale had requested as recently as 1906. Writing to Lord Lamington in June, 1907, Morley had tried, in a singularly self-revealing letter, to explain to the Governor of Bombay the psychology behind the actions and statements of a political leader like Gokhale, who

> has a hard game to play, for if he cuts himself off from the Extremists, he breaks up his Forward and Nationalist party, and his leverage for pressing Reforms upon the Government. He then inevitably sinks into impotence and is good for nothing to anybody either in our camp or his own. If so, then there is nobody to whom we can look for Native co-operation in the work of government. It is true that he has used language about National Autonomy, Self-Governing Colony, and so forth.—But I regard all this as merely words and phrases for marking time or keeping his head above water. I had several talks with him last year, and he knows as well as you and I know, that to turn India into a self-governing colony to-day is absurd and will not be attempted. He fully assented to the necessity of Government having an *official majority* on Legislative Councils. Like all politicians, in more advanced as in backward countries, he has to talk a certain amount of Moonshine. That is—if I do not scandalize you too much—an unlucky necessity of most Party Leaders.[112]

Morley might as accurately have been writing of himself and of the "hard game" he was obliged to play with the Lords and conservative Britain rather than of Gokhale's struggle against extremist India. Significantly enough, he singled out and stressed Gokhale's willingness to accept official majorities as evidence of his insincerity in demanding "National Autonomy, Self-Governing Colony," and such politically expedient "Moonshine." Might not Morley's own readiness to abolish official majorities, therefore, barely more than a year later, signify his intention of launching India toward the rugged sea of self-government, despite all the moonshine he, as secretary of state for India, felt obliged to spin to the contrary in the House of Lords?

The government of India's dispatch of October 1, 1908, proposed,[113] as expected, retention of all official majorities. But, in charging his select committee of council, Morley directed them to consider the question of "whether the principle of an official majority on Legislative Councils, other than the Legislative Council of the Governor-General, is indispensable, and not to be parted with."[114] The committee of eight, with one exception,[115] agreed it was dispensable. Lee-Warner, whom Morley had this time kept off the select committee, protested, in a separate note, against abandoning official majorities: "Whatever plan we adopt, Government must be able to pass its Bills, modified of course by discussion. This power of legislation must rest with the provincial as well as the Supreme Governments."[116]

Morley worried about questions of an entirely different character. "What are we in India for?" he challenged Minto on October 7, 1908. "Surely in order to implant—slowly, prudently, judiciously—those ideas of justice, law, humanity, which are the foundation of our own civilisation? It makes me sick when I am told that the Nizam or the Amir would make short work of seditious writers and spouters."[117] What most interested Morley about British rule in India was, in fact, the parallel he saw between British Indian and European historical process, of "progress from the medieval reign of physical force to liberty, which had worked itself out in Europe also."[118] He was anxious to do whatever he could to make that progression—was it not along the high road to self-government?—as smooth and successful as possible. He resolved not to let another year slip by without presenting his program to Parliament. In his council's discussions of reforms he found Lee-Warner's opposition "very tiresome," and Morison's "hardly less so."[119] They alone among his advisory opponents understood that several "great revolutions"[120] in the constitution of British India were being sanctioned by the Council of India with unprecedented speed, thanks to Morley's deft management. By October 29 Lee-Warner felt so "very agitated"[121] about the way these council meetings on reforms progressed that he let it be generally known he wanted a colonial governorship. On November 3, 1908, the Council of India completed its reforms deliberations. The day before that, Minto delivered the "Royal Proclamation" commemorating the fiftieth anniversary (which actually came on November 1, a Sunday in 1908) of the Crown's direct assumption of control over India. Ghostwritten[122] for Edward VII by Morley and warmly welcomed throughout India (it was published and given wide distribution as a special gazette), the proclamation promised that measures were "being diligently framed" which would give "politic satisfaction" to the claim of "equality of citizenship, and a greater share in legislation and government" called for by "important classes among you [the princes and peoples of India]." These reforms would, it was promised, be made known speedily, and were to "mark a notable stage in the beneficent progress of your affairs."

With all his data assembled[123] and his audience alerted, Morley withdrew to his "Etruscan Villa" at Wimbledon to draft the final dispatch, which he finished on November 16, and signed in its polished form on November 27, 1908. The two most conservative members of his council, Lee-Warner and James Thomson,[124] dissented, but Morley felt "well satisfied" at having completed his strenuous labors, for what he was most immediately anxious to do was to announce his scheme in Parliament before the last week of December, when the Indian National Congress was scheduled to meet in Madras. Unlike Minto, who had gloated over the Congress split in 1907 at Surat[125] as "a great triumph for us,"[126] Morley read in that violent rupture a "victory of Extremists over Moderates inside the Congress in force and determination if not in numbers,—and pointing to the ultimate conversion of the Congress itself, at some future day, not over-remote, into a definitely Extremist organization."[127] Concerned less with retention of power than the transmission of independent responsibility, he was most eager to bolster the position of moderate leaders like Gokhale by giving them the opportunity of rallying Indian support with tangible evidence of a reforms scheme set upon the parliamentary anvil. Before his departure for India, Gokhale, in bidding farewell to Morley on December 2, "rather stirred him"[128] by saying that, while for twenty-five years "nothing had been done for India" by the British, when "J. M. had come they [the Indians] had thought at last something would be done: but they were disappointed—he took the official view, like his predecessors: but they did not despair of him yet." Nor had they reason to.

Concluding in his dispatch that provincial official majorities "may be dispensed with," Morley argued that should all nonofficial members combine in opposition to a government bill, that would "be a very good reason for thinking that the proposed measure was really open to objection, and should not be proceeded with."[129] On December 17, 1908, he tabled his dispatch, together with that of the government of India's Home Department (of October 1), in the Lords, and announced "the opening of a very important chapter in the history of the relations of Great Britain and India . . . a chapter of constitutional reform."[130] During the remainder of his speech, however, Morley gave no further intimation that he so much as considered the scheme anything like a new or radical departure. He called it instead "a well-guarded expansion of principles that were recognised in 1861 and 1892." He stressed the retention of an official majority on the viceroy's council as proof that he was not trying to introduce parliamentary rule in India. In his most famous and frequently quoted disclaimer, he protested:

> If I were attempting to set up a Parliamentary system in India, or if it could be said that this chapter of reforms led directly or necessarily up to the establishment of a Parliamentary system in India, I, for one, would have nothing at all to do with it. . . . it is no ambition of mine, at all events, to have any share in beginning that operation in India. If my existence, either officially or corporeally, were prolonged twenty times longer than either of them is likely to be, a Parliamentary System in India is not at all the goal to which I would for one moment aspire.[131]

Lord Lansdowne found nothing "more reassuring" than this "frank statement" by Morley "that nothing is further from his intention than to introduce anything that can be described as corresponding with Parliamentary institutions."[132] Indian politicians, on the other hand, unconcerned by what Morley disclaimed any intention of attempting, were jubilant to note how much he was in fact ready to concede to them. Congress President Rash Behari Ghose welcomed the scheme as a "great step forward . . . in the grant of representative government for which the Congress had been crying for years."[133] He hailed the reforms as marking a transition from "autocratic and irresponsible administration" to "constitutional government." Ignoring the distinction Morley took pains to make between his viceregal official majority and provincial nonofficial majority councils, Dr. Ghose expressed "no doubt" but that the result of the experiment in provincial councils, if it proved satisfactory, would soon be expanded to the imperial level. This did indeed happen in 1919. On Christmas Eve of 1908, Minto was overwhelmed by the arrival of a deputation consisting of practically all the Indian members of the legislative councils of both Bengals, ranging from "ultra-loyalists to extremists," who came to present "a congratulatory Address on the Reforms!"[134] Congressmen felt "more than justified" in having urged people "to be patient and trust in honest John Morley,"[135] as one prominent Bombay leader put it.

Morley himself was pleased at how "extremely well . . . Gokhale and Co. had behaved."[136] He interpreted the "wonderfully good" reception given his dispatch as "not only a demonstration that the Moderates are now committed to constitutional courses, but a clear sign that Indians are as capable as other people of sound political judgment and wise political or party tactics"[137]—a truism today, no doubt, although a singularly radical position for an imperial official of Britain's Edwardian administration, and a notable advance beyond Mill's thesis on the political acumen of colonial populations.[138] Always conscious of his Irish experience, however, Morley hedged expressions of satisfaction with cautious words about "how rapidly gusts and squalls get up, when people have had time to worry about details."[139] He remembered too well that "you never can be certain that the Devil won't insinuate himself into the best men's hearts, until you have got to the Third Reading."[140]

Morley arranged to have his bill introduced for its first reading to the Lords shortly after the debate on the King's address ended in February, 1909. He had noted with alarm before the bill itself was presented that "a gale of wind" had already arisen in London over the question of appointing an Indian to the viceroy's Executive Council, and felt certain that, had such an appointment been made "compulsory by a clause in our Bill,"[141] the Lords would have drowned the scheme entirely. Here, too, he proved himself a master of parliamentary maneuvering. He was able to make the appointment that desegregated the government of India's last official sanctum of white supremacy without jeopardizing his bill, by simply waiting until it was through the Lords before announcing his selection of an Indian member. At that time, of course, the bill had yet to pass the Commons, but, given the Liberal complexion of the latter, Morley knew that "the vast majority there will cordially approve."[142] He felt no qualms of conscience in resorting to such tactics. He was hardly a novice, after all, in practicing the "art of the possible." Astute Indian liberals like Krishnaswamy Iyer recognized that "Lord Morley has achieved a signal triumph of statesmanship" and confessed that "our only prayer is that the Gods may favour the success of his enterprise."[143]

The bill[144] Morley introduced was confined, innocuously enough, to amending the Indian Councils acts of 1861 and 1892, and the Government of India Act of 1833, with respect to selection of members for legislative councils, maximum council sizes, business rules, and creation of new executive councils for lieutenant governor's provinces.

By clause 1, the principle of election to legislative councils was to be introduced for the first time into British India's constitution. Minto was so shocked to learn that he had hitherto entirely misunderstood Morley's intentions on this point that on February 8, 1909, a week before the bill was introduced to Parliament, he cabled in italicized anxiety: "*It has hitherto been assumed by us that you intended to maintain the existing system under which head of Government nominates all members, and elected candidates have to be recommended for nomination, their seat on the Council depending on the acceptance of the recommendation.*"[145] Morley replied, "I regard it as wholly impossible to act on your suggestion," considering it "essential that elected Members should, as such, be entitled to their seats."[146] Superficially it might appear that the conflict was almost a semantic one, since in practice no recommendation for council membership had ever been refused by government. General awareness of the very real possibility of viceregal rejection, however, had until now intensified self-censorship among nonofficial electorates, leading to the withdrawal of "undesirable" candidates. Yet more important even than so significant a screening factor was the psychological difference between paternalistically granting permission to nominate representatives by the grace of government, and arming an electorate, however small in the first instance, with the right to choose its own candidates. The mere process of holding a "national election" for the first time, of creating electoral machinery, which, as Minto moaned, "does not now exist,"[147] would be a long step toward education in self-government. Even the Viceroy was learning. "About election," he admitted to Morley, "we may perhaps have been at cross purposes with you as to the meaning of the word. In India it has not hitherto been interpreted in the same sense as at home."[148] Perhaps most important of all, Morley used the introduction of the elective principle in choosing legislative councils as justification for abolishing official provincial majorities.

In the House of Lords, when Curzon led the pack against direct elections and nonofficial provincial majorities, Morley refused to yield an inch. Frankly confessing himself "at a loss to understand why, holding the views he had expressed, he [Curzon] had voted for the second reading of the Bill," Morley argued, "By assent to the second reading the policy of extending the elective principle was accepted with all its consequences. What would be the advantage, what the sense, of adopting the elective principle for the councils if at the same time there was retained the old method of an official majority which would reduce the power of elected members to a farce? It would be a mockery to invite the people to take a larger share in administration if the official majority were to be maintained."[149] This argument was hardly logical, of course, and Curzon countered with a pertinent query as to why, then, the imperial legislative council remained predominantly official. But Morley understood perfectly well that most Tory lords were still too angry with, or afraid of, the jingoist ideas of George Curzon to pay much attention to anything he said. Lansdowne held the whip hand, and Lansdowne, though somewhat uneasy about the bill, was willing to go along with most anything Minto sponsored. They were more than old friends. Their clans had been united less than a year before when Lansdowne's son was married to Minto's daughter in Calcutta. What worried Lansdowne was the sudden expansion in the size of councils, which seemed "in effect little Parliaments with a great many of the attributes of Parliament."[150]

Indeed, the second section of the bill's first clause was to legalize expansion of the legislative council sizes to the greatly increased maximum membership listed in the first schedule: sixty for the imperial council; fifty for Madras (still officially called Fort St. George), Bombay, Bengal, the United Provinces of Agra and Oudh, and Eastern Bengal and Assam; and thirty for the Punjab, Burma, and any provincial council created in the future under this legislation. Clause 5, moreover, authorized discussions "at any meeting" of any legislative council "of the annual financial statement . . . and of any matter of general public interest, and the asking of questions, under such conditions and restrictions as may be prescribed in the rules." This meant that the budget would not only be criticized in one formal day of debate, but could be discussed at length by nonofficial Indian critics, who were empowered, not merely to pose questions in writing, but also to ask supplementary questions of responding officials. Nonofficial members would also be permitted to introduce subjects for legislation, and, under the new system, one of Gokhale's first official acts was to propose legislation for making elementary education free and compulsory throughout India. Although his elementary education bill twice failed to pass the imperial council, Gokhale used the council's forum, much as Morley had used the platform of the Commons, as a national classroom in helping to educate his own countrymen in the methods of responsible government and parliamentary agitation. Morley had, however, assured his peers in the Lords that the creation of a parliament was no part of his ambition for India, and Lansdowne's thunder was thus robbed of what might otherwise have been its fearsome power.

On March 11, 1909, in fact, less than a month after its introduction on February 17, the bill passed its third reading in the Lords, suffering the deletion of only one of its clauses, the third, which was later restored in amended form by the Commons. Clause 3 would have generally empowered the government of India to create executive councils in provinces that, unlike Bombay and Madras, were still ruled dictatorially by lieutenant governors alone. The proposal was in keeping with Morley's general philosophy of broadening the representative base of Indian government and decentralizing administrative authority. Curzon, appreciating its full, and to his mind awful, implications, argued in self-justification for voting against the clause that it would "take away from the I.C.S. the main prizes hitherto open to it" and "substitute over large parts of India a form of government never hitherto asked for by any responsible body of persons, unsupported by the Government of India, and subversive of the practice and experience of a century."[151] Most of the Lords agreed with him, reflecting their narrow and outmoded approach to Indian affairs. Nevertheless, telegrams flowed in to Morley's office from Indian associations as responsible as the Madras Mahajana Sabha (Public Society)[152] and from individuals as responsible as Motilal Nehru[153] and Pherozeshah Mehta,[154] expressing widespread disappointment at the rejection of clause 3, and urging its reinstatement into the bill. Morley pressed Minto for official expression of his support as well, and received it[155] within days of the Lords' adverse action. The Commons promptly amended clause 3, limiting the immediate extension of the executive council system to Bengal, whose lieutenant governor, Edward Norman Baker, had as yet alone requested the assistance of such a council, but providing for council rule in other provinces also, when desired, by proclamation of the governor-general in council, if a two-month interlude of nonobjection indicated approval of Parliament. Here again the pace of reforms was slowed down, but a vital principle of change was effectively introduced.

Morley was hardly fazed by the Lords' rejection of one section of his bill, for he felt confident that it would be restored in some form or other, and confessed to Minto with Machiavellian glee: "If we had satisfied the Lords at every turn, we should certainly have been laying up trouble for ourselves in the Commons. You laugh at me as a horrible double-faced Janus, for having in one House had to show how moderate we are, and now in the other, we must pose as the most ultra reformers that ever were known. Such are what we call tactical exigencies!!"[156]

Once in the Commons, the bill's fate was a foregone conclusion. By April 2, 1909, it passed "safe and sound" through its second reading before an almost empty house. Most perceptive among the Commons Tories concerned with India, however, was Earl Percy, who argued: "When they gave to these legislative councils the power of initiating legislation themselves, of passing resolutions which, nominally a recommendation of advice to the Government, would in fact be regarded as tantamount to votes of censure, and when, lastly, they gave to the unofficial members of these councils an actual majority, it was idle to suggest that they were merely developing and extending the principles of 1892; they were in fact transforming and revolutionizing the whole character of those bodies."[157] The leader of His Majesty's opposition, Arthur Balfour, was equally suspicious of the bill, and expressed thorough bewilderment, since, after all, "Lord Morley has stated as clearly and effectively and strongly as any man could state that, in his opinion, not only is India not fit for representative government (opposition cheers) but, unless I am misrepresenting him, it is difficult to conceive how it ever can be fit. . . . Therefore, there is no question of this being a representative government."[158] Yet what then was it? If not at least preparing India's political soil for representative government, cogently argued the former prime minister, "why you should have a majority, why you should encourage this style of supplementary questions, why you should do everything to make assemblies, which are not representative, and which you do not intend to make representative, mimics of all the worst and most laborious parts of our procedure—that, I admit, absolutely passes my comprehension." Fearing that government was making "a mistake in initiating the policy they had," Balfour disclaimed "any responsibility" concerning Morley's bill both for himself personally and for his party.

Radical leaders among friends of India's National Congress in the Commons found themselves for once in agreement with the Tories, at least insofar as interpretation of the bill's policy and promise was concerned. Sir Henry Cotton considered it undeniable that "the effect of this Bill was to extend the principle of representation"[159] in Indian government, agreeing with Percy that there was "no analogy between the importance of the present Bill and the Bill of 1892." Dr. Rutherford congratulated Morley "on reversing the Tory policy pur-

AN ACT OF REFORM 159

sued during the last ten years," and hailed the bill as an "instalment, though a modest one, of self-government."[160]

How did Morley himself view the measure? For one thing, he considered it "a good and sure start" toward "co-operation between Foreigners and Alien Subjects,"[161] but beyond that he recognized its didactic value for training Indians "in habits of political responsibility." British officials were usually most liberal in their condemnation of Indian political capacity, yet, as Morley cautioned Clarke at this time,

> I note what you say about the failure of Indians in constructive criticism. But it neither amazes nor much disquiets me. You cannot expect constructive faculty from people who have never had anything worth calling responsibility. There is not overmuch constructive faculty anywhere in the world, and what there is may most naturally be looked for among the men officially and actually engaged in administration. . . . My view has all along been that the Councils would still for many a long day to come need the guidance of their European chiefs. Only the difference will be that the chiefs will have to pay more attention to the people they are ruling.[162]

He certainly never imagined then that the transition from imperial autocracy to responsible self-government would be achieved overnight. What he called the "immortal Bill,"[163] enacted after receiving royal assent on May 25, 1909, was, however, a realistic first step up the road that led India to dominion status in 1947. Morley, moreover, knew it. No sooner was his law enacted than he used a new idiom in addressing British I.C.S. probationers, cautioning them, "While you are in India, and among Indians, and *responsible to Indians, because you are as responsible to them as you are to us here*, while you are in that position, gentlemen, do not live in Europe all the time" (italics added).[164] The educational ground had to be well laid in both countries for so momentous a change. Morley men in India like Sir Lawrence Jenkins struggled against English officials who tried to whittle away at the act by narrowing its code of regulations. Discouraged by the "grudging" interpretation the act received in some quarters of Simla and the growing racial distrust he noted in Calcutta, Sir Lawrence wrote Morley:

> As I read your reform scheme its purpose was not a fruitless endeavour to stem the tide of the world's progress, but to remove, or help to remove, the baneful causes of this distrust, by inviting the cooperation of the ruled

in the work of administration and creating fresh and increased opportunities of contact between them and the rulers in the hope that a better understanding might result. . . . This, as it seems to me, your opponents, and among them the Times, have signally failed to grasp: their imagination has never soared higher than the policy of keeping something up their sleeve. It was the essence of your policy to give largely, and not, as your critics desired, grudgingly or of necessity; at least so it seemed to me.[165]

Jenkins, who had worked more closely with Morley in the drafting[166] of his 1908 reform dispatch than any other member of the Council of India, was, of course, quite right. Like Alfred Lyall, he and Morley understood that the "aspiration of all Asia is toward a Renaissance, to be accomplished by throwing off the burden of European dominance and protectorate."[167] Morley had never been so naïve as to believe in the permanence of the British raj. His pleasure was undisguised when he read a Reuter cablegram reporting from Calcutta in early December, *"The elections are in full swing."*[168]

Perhaps Morley came closest to written admission of what he truly hoped to see proved by the reforms experiment he had launched, when, on December 8, 1909, he wrote Clarke: "I am in great hope that the elections will go on reasonably well. Difficulties are sure to arise, small or great, and people will say that they were all due to this or that mistake. Which the said peope had foretold. That's all nonsense. They would in some shape or another have arisen anyhow. . . . politics are ever a Second Best. If the experiment breaks down, it will only show that those were not wrong who told us that Indians are not yet up to self Government, or fit for it."[169] Although expressed in negative terms, the positive implication was clearly that Morley himself considered Indians capable of self-government, and trusted that the opportunities for its limited introduction afforded by his reforms would prove that fact to the world at large. Few politically conscious Indians ever doubted that such were his intentions. As Fleetwood Wilson correctly noted in January, 1910, "Lord Morley laid down that the reformed Councils were not the forerunners of a parliament, but does any reasonable man suppose for one moment that the Indian people interpret the reforms as anything but the beginning of representative government?"[170]

Minto labored to erase this general impression by informing the first meeting of the reformed imperial legislative council on January

25, 1910, "We have distinctly maintained that representative Government in its Western sense is totally inapplicable to the Indian Empire and would be uncongenial to the traditions of Eastern populations."[171] This denial sounded no more credible, however, than the Viceroy's insistence in the same speech that the scheme was "based entirely on views I had myself formed" and "due to no suggestions from home." For almost a year conservatives had been writing letters to the *Times* like that of C. H. T. Crosthwaite, complaining of "Lord Morley's Indian Reforms"[172] by arguing, "It is curious that a reform begun with eminently moderate and conservative intentions should have ended in a scheme which hands the better classes and the vast multitude of the people into the hands of a few thousands of men whose heads have been turned by an education which they have not assimilated"—gross exaggeration, no doubt, yet indicative of how radical the 1909 constitution sounded to many contemporary British ears.

Morley's philosophic position on the overriding virtues of representative and responsible government, while well known, was perhaps never so forcefully put as in his essay, "British Democracy," written in February, 1911: "No Government can be trusted if it is not liable to be called before some jury or another, compose that jury how you will, and even if its majority should unluckily happen to be dunces."[173] The essay, however, was more than a general defense of political democracy, written rather in specific justification of Morley's own policy toward India, and providing therefore an important key to the nature of that policy. In this work Morley described his act of 1909 as a "prudently guarded expansion of popular government in India."[174] He then went on to explain:

Self-government in India itself means two things. In one sense, it touches the relations of the indigenous population to European authority, whether central and paramount, or provincial and local. In another sense, it concerns the relations between both people and the organs of European authority on the one side, and the organs of home government on the other. The distinction is in the highest degree important. The popular claim under the first head, though not easy to adjust, is easy to understand; it founds itself on democratic principles borrowed from ourselves both at home and in the self-governing dominions. The second is different. It has not yet taken formidable shape, but it soon may. The ruling authority in India is sure to find itself fortified by pressure from the new Councils in forcing Indian interests, and, what is more, the Indian view of such interests, against any tendency here to postpone them to home interests.[175]

Perhaps no further evidence is required to prove that what Morley hoped to accomplish through his reforms was the expansion of popular government in India, leading gradually to parliamentary self-government along British lines, yet in 1928 the *Times* published several letters from Sir Richard Burn[176] emphatically stating that such was Morley's intention all along. Burn, who had just retired after thirty-five years in the Indian Civil Service, wrote in his first letter to the editor:

> Early in 1927 I had the privilege of spending several days at Benares with the late Lord Sinha. We had worked together in 1909 at drafting the rules and regulations to be made under the Act of 1909, and he talked freely of the discussions of 1917 and 1918, in which he had a large share. ... When the Montagu-Chelmsford scheme was taking shape he [Morley] told Lord Sinha he would like to see him. Discussing the proposals, Lord Morley said he thought they would do very well. Lord Sinha expressed surprise at this, in view of what Lord Morley had said about his own scheme and the clear advance which was now to be made in Parliamentary procedure. Lord Morley smiled and replied that he had not meant what he said. The position in which he found himself was a difficult one. While he set up Mr. Montagu [Morley's last parliamentary undersecretary of state for India] in the House of Commons to persuade it that their plan was momentous and far-reaching, he was trying to convince the House of Lords that it was purely experimental and not likely to lead to much.[177]

Burn then pointed out that this admission to Sinha was confirmed by Morley's letter to Minto of March 12, 1909 (see n. 156), concluding wryly, "It is not surprising that men like Lord Curzon and Lord Ronaldshay [Curzon's biographer] were unable to see that the statement of December 17, 1908 [see n. 131], was to be taken merely as a 'tactical exigency.'"

Theodore Morison, then principal of Armstrong College of the University of Durham, publicly responded to Burn's letter with "a flat contradiction to the charge of disingenuousness brought against the late Lord Morley,"[178] insisting that "Lord Sinha must have misheard him or put a wrong construction on his words." Morison based his attempted refutation of Burn's testimony on the self-contradictory arguments that, first of all, "I saw a great deal of Lord Morley while the Reforms were under discussion, and in private he always maintained the opinions which he proclaimed in 1908 in the House of Lords," and, second, Sinha could hardly have been told what Burn claimed since "Lord Morley was the last person in the world to give himself away in conversation." Morison's letter, moreover, was as emotional and self-righteous as it was illogical, claiming that "Morley was incapable of the meanness which Sir Richard Burn suggests," that "he had no interest in proclaiming himself a fool or a knave," and that he would never "have made an admission so damaging to his own good name." In a prompt and brief rejoinder,[179] Burn noted that Morison most effectively refuted himself, explaining, appropriately enough, that "Lord Morley was not the first politician to rejoice after a suitable interval at having 'dished' his opponents." Finally, he insisted, "My object was not to throw mud but to make plain what Lord Morley really had in mind." It is high time that Burn's scholarly ambition is rewarded by giving his testimony the full credence it deserves.

In his policy of sponsoring political reforms, as in that of mitigating official repression, however, Morley's aspirations for India were in many ways thwarted by the cumbersome and reactionary bureaucratic machine through which he was obliged to implement his ideas. The success of his reform act in Parliament, although a victory of singular significance, transforming the constitution of British India and bringing Indian ambitions for responsible government within range of practical realization by peaceful rather than revolutionary action, was now threatened by the government of India itself in the process of translating parliamentary legislation into rules and regulations. Clause 7 of the act specified that all regulations for its implementation were to be drafted by the government of India, subject to the approval of the secretary of state, and once again Minto's most formidable ally in sabotaging Morley's policy proved to be the tactics of delay rather than open opposition. The government of India's most corrosive impact on the progressive character of Morley's reforms—substitution of separate communal electorates for Muslims instead of the proposed general electoral college scheme—is considered in a later chapter, as are Minto's objections to the additions of Indians to enlarged provincial executive councils. With respect to recruitment for the new legislative councils, moreover, Minto labored to win by stringent disqualifying regulations the battle he lost over the substitution of direct elections for viceregal nominations.

Morley was adamant in refusing to permit any political disqualification clause from being written into the regulations, insisting as early as February, 1909, that even "Tilak, if elected, must sit."[180] Minto and his advisers were, however, extremely nervous about the prospect of finding themselves obliged to defend their positions against Indian members who were not only trained legal logicians but astute political agitators as well. "Indian officials are trained as dictators rather than debaters,"[181] wrote the Viceroy in pathetic apprehension about the future that awaited the government of India under the new liberal constitution. Minto pressed for blanket disqualification of any person deported under Regulation III of 1818, but Morley insisted it was "impossible to defend the attachment of any political disqualification to deportation after the deported man was once free."[182] Despite Minto's appeal to the contrary, Morley pledged His Majesty's government accordingly to the House of Commons. Pressure for veto power over elected membership to councils mounted, however, both from within the India Office and from the government of India. Morley's council committee to consider reforms proposed[183] sweeping powers of disqualification. Minto reported that in India local governments were "practically unanimous" in favor of disqualifying deportees, and in a "Private" telegram noted that "Sinha, who is on my Councils Reform Committee, has taken very strong line, insisting that disqualification is absolutely necessary in the case of deportees."[184] Hirtzel implored his chief to accept some disqualifying formula that, while not specifically political, might protect the government of India from political embarrassment. Morley, who was neither so doctrinaire nor so dictatorial as most of his critics insisted, finally agreed to a regulation disallowing the candidacy of anyone "whose character and antecedents the Government of India consider to be such that his election would be contrary to the public interest."[185] There was, however, to be no mention of "deportation" in the regulations, he added, since that would serve only to strengthen Regulation III and make it appear to be an ordinary, rather than exceptional, repressive measure. The telegraphic attention alone devoted to this one detail concerning regulations proved so expensive a drain of time and energy that Morley was obliged to surrender the substance of Minto's demand, while preserving only the principle of keeping political beliefs outside the realm of disqualification for public office. Minto's delaying tactic was surely apparent to Morley by the time he capitulated on this point in mid-May, though the Viceroy did not reveal his hand until October, when he warned that drafting regulation details might oblige the government of India to postpone introduction of reforms for another year. "Your telegram about Regulations," wrote Morley on October 14, 1909. "The last words of it positively make my hair stand on end—'postponement for another year'!!! If that catastrophe happens, we had better throw up the sponge.... 'another year' will in any case see you out, and possibly may see the present Cabinet out, and a Cabinet installed who thoroughly dislike and distrust the whole scheme of policy. I cannot imagine an outcome more pregnant with disaster and danger. So I won't allow myself to contemplate such things."[186]

It was Morley's overriding sense of urgency about the need for introducing reforms which induced him to yield as he had done, but now he reasserted the ultimate power of Parliament as a check upon the government of India's arbitrary use of its powers of disallowance, reminding Minto that such powers "will have to be very charily used, and you will have to bear in mind your full responsibility to parliamentary opinion."[187] On November 15, 1909, the regulations[188] for giving effect to the Indian Councils Act were officially issued by the Home Department of the government of India. Between then and the first meeting of the new legislative councils on January 25, 1910, India's first nationwide elections were held, returning some 141 additional members to legislative councils, which had hitherto included only 39 members nominated after recommendation to the viceroy and governors by their constituents. The enlarged councils now included a total of 346 members, compared with the earlier maximum strength of 126. Members were permitted to discuss the budget under separate heads, to challenge officials with formal questions as well as supplementaries, and to move resolutions. In the nonofficial provincial-majority councils, budget committees were created consisting of twelve members, half of whom were to be elected by the nonofficial block.

At its twenty-fourth session at Lahore in December, 1909, Congress, while "gratefully appreciating the earnest and arduous endeavours of Lord Morley and Lord Minto in extending to the people of this country a fairly liberal measure of constitutional reforms," nonetheless resolved "its strong sense of disapproval of the creation of separate electorates on the basis of religion and regrets that the Regulations framed under the Act have not been framed in the same liberal spirit in which Lord Morley's despatch of last year was conceived."[189] Specifically, the Congress objected to the "unfairly preponderant share of representation" given to Muslims, and the "wide, arbitrary and unreasonable disqualification and restrictions for candidates seeking election to the Councils." Practically, it called for revision of the regulations to "bring them into harmony with the spirit" of Morley's earlier recommendations. Obviously the final chapter on Indian reforms had hardly been written. Bureaucratic reaction had retaken some of the ground it seemed in danger of losing, but the Secretary of State had personally set an example for Indian politicians to follow, and clearly indicated the lines of legitimate agitation along which they could hope to attain future victories. For the present, moreover, Morley's spokesman in the Commons, Edwin Montagu, parliamentary undersecretary of state for India, was able to assert in his budget address of 1910:

> I think I may claim for the Indian Councils Act that it has been a great success . . . the right hon. Gentleman the Leader of the Opposition [Balfour] deliberately disclaimed on behalf of his party any responsibility for the consequences. . . . We are quite content to accept sole responsibility. . . .
> In effect, the Councils Act has resulted in producing excellent debates, creating opportunities for the ventilation of grievances and of public views, creating public opinion, permitting the Governors to explain themselves, giving to those interested in politics a better and more productive field for their persuasive powers than the rather sterile and discursive debates in Congress.[190]

Thus the foundation was laid for a new political structure to rise over India, one based on debate, the ventilation of grievances through informed public opinion, public explanation of official actions, and the productive development of politics as an institutional force in society, or, in summation, parliamentary rule in the British Liberal tradition. Less than a decade after summarizing the reform achievements of his mentor, moreover, Montagu himself was at the helm of the India Office establishment, and personally saw to it that India advanced to partly responsible provincial government under the dyarchy scheme of his reform constitution enacted in 1919. Thereafter, India's progress toward dominion status was clearly visible, and, though the precise timetable was arranged by the contingencies of unforeseeable historical forces, the end point of transition to full independence was seldom in doubt. Most contemporaries in 1910, however, believed quite the contrary, and most students of Morley's era have to date assumed that the majority was right in including John Morley among those myopic Englishmen and Indians who saw the British raj as an indestructible entity destined to stand as a breakwater against the tide of political change for centuries to come. Instead, Morley was a leading architect of India's political future, whose reforming zeal and political shrewdness blazed the constitutional trail Montagu fearlessly followed, and without whose preliminary labors and victories in principle, the long strides to responsible rule taken in 1919 and 1935 would hardly have been possible.

7

RACIAL RELATIONS

> The root of the unrest, discontent, and sedition, so far as I can make out ... is a dislike not of political domination, but of our racial domination.
> Morley at Arbroath, October 21, 1907

> To make races mix is about the most desperate task that fate can set a statesman.
> Morley to Minto, November 9, 1906

> The Indian member ... When I opened it to the Cabinet, I said, 'No more important topic has ever been brought before a Cabinet.'
> Morley to Minto, March 12, 1909

After 1857 perhaps the most volatile and intractable problem to confront British rule in India was that of racial antipathy between an elite minority of Europeans, self-righteously endowed for the most part with a "white man's burden" mentality, and the predominantly darker-skinned "native" population it governed. Racial hatred and distrust, generated in the wake of the Indian revolt[1] of 1857–58, reverberated throughout the half century that followed as a central, although generally unstated, factor guiding the formulation of British policy toward India, and motivating indigenous responses to British rule. Despite solemnly reiterated promises of equality of racial opportunity in recruitment for government services, and of equal justice for all in India, embodied in the Company's Charter Act of 1833 and the Crown's royal proclamation of 1858,[2] white supremacy and racial discrimination remained the actual policy of the raj, at Whitehall as well as in India, until the dawn of this Liberal era. The one abortive attempt, undertaken during Lord Ripon's viceroyalty, to implement the policy of professed racial equality with the Ilbert Bill[3] of 1883 proved how remarkably virulent a force Anglo-Indian racism had become.

The blow Morley struck against British white supremacy over India was of shattering significance. Morley's appointment of two Indian members to his own council, and of another to the viceroy's Executive Council, provided the capstone to an overall antiracist policy which emerges as a major motif of reform during this era. Here too, as with respect to legislative council reforms, Morley appears to have been influenced strongly by the arguments and advice of Gokhale, who, as spokesman for Congress in 1905, stated that India's entire future was "bound up with this question of the relative position of the two races in this country."[4] British racial domination, Gokhale insisted, had led to the moral dwarfing and material impoverishment of India's people. India's best interests, he argued, "no less than the honour of England, demand that the policy of equality for the two races promised by the Sovereign and by Parliament should be faithfully and courageously carried out."[5] Gokhale and the National Congress were most immediately concerned, of course, with the practical political implementation of racial equality of opportunity, and called for the election of at least two members of every Indian province to the House of Commons and the appointment of not less than three "Indian gentlemen of proved ability and experience"[6] to the Council of India, two Indians to the viceroy's Executive Council, and one Indian to each of the executive councils of Bombay and Madras. Another resolution on the "Public Services" asked for generally wider employment of Indians in all branches of government service, and restated one of the frequently reiterated demands of Congress—the holding of civil service examinations in India simultaneously with those in England.

Politically attuned as he was, Morley proved keenly receptive to such demands. Indeed, his policy against racial discrimination seems to have been motivated more by political than humanitarian considerations. Actually Morley recognized no dichotomy between the two motives, for, by giving talented Indians a real opportunity to administer their own affairs, he hoped to attract future generations of Indian leaders to constructive political labor rather than what he considered destructive revolutionary agitation or the final desperate outlet of violence. He personally came to believe, as he told his Arbroath constituents in 1907, that the root of Indian "unrest, discontent, and sedition" was, in fact, "racial and not political."[7] He early encouraged Minto to adopt Cromer's Egyptian policy of giving employment to "a Native whenever it was at all possible,"[8] rather than to a European, despite the fact that the latter might be far more efficient. He soon found a formidable ally for his policy of alleviating racial tensions in the Prince of Wales, who returned from a tour of India to complain of "the ungracious bearing of Europeans to Natives,"[9] which Morley promptly called to Minto's attention, advising him to "let it be known somehow that you thought such things both caddish and mischievous."[10] He had read enough history, he cautioned the Viceroy, to understand the harm caused by "bad manners." Once again he initiated a policy of fundamental change by trying, first of all, to convert Minto himself, appealing to his code of patrician honor by making racial discrimination sound like a mere breach of manners.

As already noted, Morley, when initially suggesting his comprehensive scheme of reforms to Minto in June, 1906, alluded to "the notion of a Native in your Executive Council," soliciting Minto's reaction. The Viceroy's initial response to this important Congress demand, which Curzon had dismissed as "out of the question," was equivocal. Minto, with the typical insecurity of a mentally mediocre subordinate anxious never to be caught napping by his chief, insisted that he had "very nearly, on several occasions,"[11] thought of suggesting such an appointment. He was, however, worried about exposing state secrets to such a colleague, and also warned of the need to find a man generally respected throughout India "with a stake in the country," and not simply to promote a political leader of the type personified by Gokhale. Yet the more he thought about it, the more Minto liked the idea of an Indian member on his council, and soon he admitted that perhaps his doubts stemmed from "inherent prejudice against another race."[12] Whatever other faults he possessed, Minto was fortunately no bigot like Kitchener, whose example of "bad, wicked race dominance"[13] became notorious in India, nor like Lawley, governor of Madras, who regarded "any attempt to bridge over the unfathomable chasm ... between the brown man and the white ... as hopeless."[14]

After starting the Viceroy thinking about an Indian member at

Simla, Morley set about preparing the ground for the same sort of revolution in Whitehall. In July, 1906, he informed Hirtzel[15] and wrote Godley[16] about his idea of appointing an Indian to the hitherto all-white Council of India. He was strongly tempted to act without delay, wiring Minto on July 13 for his opinion, but the Viceroy's response the next day urged caution. Morley hesitated, giving senior members of his council like Lee-Warner time to poison his mind against Indians as a race devoid of all "sense of honour."[17] Although temporarily deterred by Lee-Warner's story of having caught Justice Ranade in an act of petty pilfering, Morley by no means abandoned his idea of bringing an Indian member to Whitehall, and went so far as to mention Romesh Dutt in his letter of July 27, 1906, to Minto as a man he considered qualified for appointment to his own council. He continued to press Minto on this matter of Executive Council reform in India as well, urging him to "talk about the great subject with sensible and liberal-minded men of all conditions."[18] Throughout the summer of 1906, then, Morley took the lead in advocating the appointment of Indians to the two highest executive bodies of British Indian administration, although confronted by deeply entrenched opposition both at home and abroad. His policy of official integration was by no means limited, moreover, to rarified executive councils, for he took pains to notify Minto as early as 1906 that the presence of only fourteen Indians among the forty-two members of the enrolled branch of the Finance Department was "hardly in conformity with our policy."[19] Morley was asked at this time to fill two vacancies in the department, and offered instead to transfer his right of patronage to Minto on the understanding that the Viceroy would select Indians for the jobs. He appealed personally for Minto's aid in taking this "different line," as he called it, and they agreed to nominate one Indian at once, leaving the second post temporarily open.

In its report[20] of October 12, 1906, Arundel's committee was equally divided on the question of whether or not to appoint a "Native Member" to the viceregal council. The more liberal members, Arundel and Baker, advocated parliamentary legislation to enlarge the Executive Council by adding one seat, which would "always be filled by a Native of India" (par. 19). "A Member of Indian race," they argued, would be in closer touch with Indian thought and sentiment than the most sympathetic foreigner, and his presence "in the innermost circle of the administration will afford a permanent and visible guarantee that no great question affecting the interest of the people can ever be decided without responsible examination" (par. 24). Furthermore, appointment of such a member would serve only to strengthen the confidence and "enhance the loyalty of his fellow countrymen" (par. 27) in the raj. The committee's more reactionary members, Ibbetson and Richards, fearing that an Indian would "at once become the focus of intrigue" (par. 32), warned that any such appointment would prove to be but "the top of the slope at the foot of which lie representative government, constitution mongering, chaos, and the as yet unfathomed abyss" (par. 35). Morley assumed that Minto and the majority of his council were inclined to accept the Ibbetson-Richards line on this matter, and in November wrote to persuade the Viceroy that "the admission of a Native, whether to your Council or to mine or to both, would be the *cheapest* concession that we can make."[21] Alluding again to European bad manners, he added, in the same letter, "This arrogance would be perhaps a little, if it were only a little, softened by the presence of a Native in the seats of the Mighty." But he was, by this time, preaching to the converted.

Before the end of 1906, Minto personally came to believe that "the best reply that can be made to the unrest that is in the air would be the appointment of a Native Member to the Viceroy's Council."[22] Yet officially he remained indecisive, expressing in the same letter his concern about the possibility of such an appointment raising an unroar similar to that started among Europeans protesting the Ilbert Bill. Two months later Minto again warned that, should the appointment be resisted bitterly in India, "racial feeling would be more accentuated than it is at present."[23] This argument, weighing heavily on Morley's mind, contributed toward his decision to postpone the appointment, although he knew full well that in such delicate affairs "to stand stock still will be a serious venture too."[24] Paradoxically enough, then, just when Minto, after many doubts, finally decided to recommend the appointment of an Indian to his council, Morley reluctantly concluded that perhaps it was wiser to wait. Morley's turnabout, however, was only a temporary one, and his decision to drop from his reform scheme the proposal of adding a "Native Member" to the viceroy's Executive Council was based essentially on two major sources of apprehension.

First, Morley feared that strident reaction among Europeans in India might in fact start another Ilbert Bill controversy. The government of India's dispatch[25] of March 21, 1907, reflected the conflicting opinions of Arundel's committee, with Minto and Baker alone (Arundel had by then retired) favoring the appointment, the majority of the council being opposed. Minto and Baker argued that this particular reform was feasible, expedient, and necessary, especially in view of the gulf that had of late widened between Europeans and natives. "A generation ago the best Englishmen and the best Indians were working cordially together for the good of the country," the minority argued. "Now both are subject to influences which tend to force them into an attitude of mutual antagonism" (par. 15). The most obvious means of relieving such antagonism, they felt, was the appointment of a native member. This appointment alone would "tend to transform and tranquilise the whole tone of public life in India" (par. 16), since foresighted and talented Indians would be quick to realize that cooperative conduct promised to lead them to real power. If "an orthodox Hindu of moderate views and acknowledged talent" (par. 19) were appointed, insisted Minto and Baker, he would be accepted by all Hindus as representative of the community, whose members comprised some two-thirds of the Indian population. Finally, they argued now, there was "no sort of analogy" (par. 22) between this measure and the Ilbert Bill, and no grounds for fear that the making of this single appointment would lead to an outburst of racial feeling. Six members[26] of the government of India's Executive Council disagreed entirely with the minority's proposal, raising the usual arguments about concern for "security" (par. 26), fear of the appointment of a "political Native" (par. 28), and the setting of precedents for councils in Madras and Bombay, as well as the specious contention that the proposal "involves a complete departure from our attitude of neutrality as between races and sects" (par. 27). The most forceful argument, however, was a thinly veiled threat of violence by the European inhabitants of India, who, the majority contended, would view the appointment "with intense and active dislike," leading to "a conflict of race feeling of a serious character" which "would take a dangerous form" (par. 31).

Remote as he was from the Indian scene, confronted by this threat of reviving Ilbert Bill passions, and having little confidence in the soundness of Minto's judgment, Morley felt "*very* nervous about the Native Member of Council question."[27] He consulted with Lyall, who expressed himself, "as I have said before to you, against it,"[28] and argued that "the objections stated by the majority in this despatch should prevail. I may remark, by the way, that the selection of a man 'who has stood aloof from politics' (par. 17) would hardly provide a sufficient guarantee for his competency to deal with important political affairs."[29] In personal conversation with Lady Minto, who had returned for a London visit at this time, Morley said: "Here is the Viceroy and one Member of his Council advocating a measure which the rest of his Council and the whole of my Council are against: all old Anglo-Indians such as Lord Lansdowne, Sir Alfred Lyall, etc., are antagonistic. The question is, will it raise too great a storm? Will the racial feeling be too strong to stand it? Is the Viceroy too sanguine in thinking the opposition will not be as violent as in the case of Ilbert Bill?"[30] Morley lacked the courage to ignore such fears and bring his own brainchild to life, now that the decision confronted him alone, for the cabinet would have accepted his judgment on this as it did in all other matters of Indian policy. "The fear of reawakening the uproar of the Ilbert Bill days, and so reviving racial antipathy, will be a powerful fact in most minds," he wrote Minto, reporting the London climate on this issue, "as I know it has been in yours, and is in mine."[31]

Yet a second, more formidable, fear than that of raising the specter of the Ilbert Bill also deterred Morley. He believed that the Lords, with Lansdowne in control of their majority, would use the native member proposal as their excuse for throwing out his entire reform bill. Lansdowne's aversion to the idea of admitting "a Native to the Holy of Holies"[32] carried all the religious power of confirmed bigotry, added to the prestigious weight of his long experience as India's viceroy and present Tory leader of the Lords. Morley, on the other hand, was still unsure of his grasp of India's intricate problems, and did not dare in 1907, as he would a year later, to "confront Lansdowne as boldly as I please."[33] In April, 1907, therefore, he decided to accept his council's unanimous advice of rejecting Minto's proposal. In his very telegram[34] to the Viceroy intimating this decision, however, Morley proved that he was not abandoning his policy of council integration, but was temporarily shifting the field of battle, for he asked Minto to suggest the names of several Indians suitable for Whitehall's Council of India. At the same time he indicated how conscience-stricken he must have felt about his own retreat, however brief and expedient it would prove to be, for he asked Minto whether it would be possible "to keep secret that proposal was ever made and that you yourself supported it."[35] Minto's reply was negative, and Morley appeared to Indian eyes, as well as to many of his radical friends in the Commons, as more conservative than the Viceroy, whose official proposal of a native member he had officially rejected. As in other respects, however, such popular impressions were grossly deceptive. Just as Morley's early advocacy had initially converted Minto to the idea of adding an Indian member to his council, Morley's abiding faith in the importance of reducing racial conflicts and abolishing white supremacy later overcame the reluctant Viceroy's backsliding and brought the policy of council racial integration to fruition. But during the spring of 1907 Minto played the role of liberal in his dialogue with Morley, boldly proclaiming: "For myself I see nothing for it but to stand the shot. If Indian member is rejected and it becomes known, we shall be accused of giving in to bureaucracy and shall have serious fight before us. My opinion is that it is time to overrule bureaucracy."[36] With the next breath, however, he added fuel to Morley's fears and divested himself, as he could afford to do, of final responsibility, noting, "Am more apprehensive of opposition at home and in House of Lords than here, but you will know as to that."[37] Finding himself even without Ripon's support and faced by Elgin's and Fowler's hostility toward the proposal in his own cabinet, Morley surrendered with the impotent sigh uttered sooner or later by every idealist determined to retain a position of political power, "Cabinets and ministers have to take the world as they find it."[38]

No sooner did Morley drop the native member from his reforms bill, however, by rejecting the proposal in his dispatch of May 17, 1907, than Minto conceded: "Under the circumstances it was the only sound position to take up. It would have been impossible at the moment to overrule the hosts of opposing opinion."[39] Like a sleepwalker suddenly awakened, the Viceroy seemed shocked at the contemplation of his own position, and thereafter cautiously drew away from the advanced post he had taken and held for almost three months. Morley, on the other hand, moved to fashion another bill, which, innocuously enough, would call merely for raising the statutory limit of membership on the Council of India from twelve to fourteen.[40] He was determined to add at least one Indian member to the Council of India, as he notified the Commons in his annual budget statement on India of June 6, 1907, and felt it would be wisest to do so by increasing the statutory limit rather than removing a long-standing perquisite from the reach of retired members of the I.C.S. Yet his fear of the Lords was again reflected in his decision to avoid public debate of the racial issue by keeping his Indian choices for the new openings quite secret until after the Council of India Act passed its third reading in the Lords on August 26, 1907. Actually, Morley appointed two Indian members by July 25, the day his bill was first read in the Commons, but kept the fact highly confidential, since he considered it tactically "essential that my hands should seem free"[41] until the measure was clear of the Lords.

In soliciting Minto's recommendations for possible Indian members to Whitehall's council, Morley frankly admitted that "their colour is more important than their brains,"[42] underscoring his political motivation for these appointments. His choice of one Hindu, K. G. Gupta,[43] and one Muslim, S. H. Bilgrami,[44] moreover, clearly showed that Morley's gesture was designed to assuage the feelings of racial discrimination prevalent in each of India's major religious communities. As a leading member of the I.C.S., however, Gupta was hardly considered a representative of Congress opinion, while Bilgrami, one of the founding fathers of the Muslim League, was viewed by most Congress leaders as positively hostile to Indian aspirations for greater political freedom. Indeed, Romesh Dutt, whom Morley had at first been inclined to support[45] for Gupta's seat, considered the new members "the two most wrong and unpopular men (though able and competent) that I could possibly have found."[46]

By bringing Indians for the first time into his own council chamber, Morley once again set a most important historical precedent, dramatically asserting the idea of full racial equality of opportunity in the administration of India. "My object in making that great and conspicuous change in the constitution of the Council of India," as he explained it to his constituents in Scotland, was "to teach all in India, from the youngest Competition Wallah who arrives there that in the eyes of the Government of India the Indian is perfectly worthy —we do not say it is so in words only, we have now shown it in act— by giving a share in the Council of the paramount Power."[47] In November, 1907, Bilgrami took his seat at Whitehall; when Gupta arrived the following March, Morley escorted him into council and then wrote Minto, "Tis not Vanity that makes me say that I felt I was doing a historic sort of thing, such as I hope that *you* may do in your Council one of these days!"[48]

No public protest in London or India followed the Council of India appointments, and Morley was now ready to appoint an Indian to Minto's council at the earliest possible date. "Remember, that we do not need an Act of Parliament to give you a Native," he wrote the Viceroy in March, 1908, "if and when there is a vacancy to fill."[49] Morley felt strong enough in public confidence by this time to face any popular outcry, either in India or from the Tory Opposition at home. He had worked hard, and knew his job well. He could act with the conviction of sound knowledge, and would no longer be intimidated by the prejudiced arguments of old India hands like Ibbetson and Lee-Warner, whose experience had hitherto disguised their racial bias behind the specious cloak of dispassionate judgment. "Is not the time coming when we could put an Indian on your Council?" Morley inquired of Minto again in May. "What say you? Rashbehary Ghose? I wish you could have a man like Dutt at your ear. It is absurd that you cannot have."[50] But Minto, who grew more lethargic and cautious with the passage of time, now feared there was no suitable candidate for the job in all India. Morley pressed on, however, extolling "the usefulness of hearing the voice of Indian feeling,"[51] as he could at Whitehall, thanks to Gupta and Bilgrami. On July 1 Minto swung round again, and decided there were, in fact, several good Indian barristers who might be capable of directing the legislative department of the government of India. He recommended Satyendra P. Sinha,[52] advocate general of India at the time, and Dr. Asutosh Mukherji, vice-chancellor of Calcutta University, whom he had initially suggested for the post. Sinha was a member of Congress, Mukherji its outspoken critic. This difference predisposed Morley to Sinha. Minto, on the other hand, personally favored Mukherji, but recognized that Sinha was by training better qualified to fill the post of legal member.

Morley intimated his decision publicly when proposing his legislative council reforms to the Lords in December, 1908; he announced that the "absence of an Indian member from the Viceroy's Executive Council can no longer, I think, be defended. . . . The Secretary of State can, tomorrow, if he likes, if there be a vacancy on the Viceroy's Council recommend His Majesty to appoint an Indian member. All I want to say is that, if, during my tenure of office, there should be a vacancy, . . . I should feel it a duty to tender my advice to the King that an Indian member should be appointed."[53] His own council was still mostly opposed to the idea, with Bilgrami joining the majority of those on the reforms committee to vote against it. In London generally the proposal elicited highly critical responses from many influential persons, particularly King Edward VII, who promptly called Morley to a personal audience in order to press his objections against the Indian member.[54] The virulence of Tory reaction confirmed Morley's earlier fears that, had he pressed for parliamentary approval of the appointment, his bill would have been rejected outright by the Lords.[55] By the end of January Morley reported to Minto that the "bitter cry against the Indian Member grows more and more shrill,—reinforced of course by our Moslems. . . . not a single newspaper for us!!"[56] In India itself, however, unrest stimulated by racial conflict had reached so precarious a point by now that Minto wrote, "if the appointment *is not* sanctioned we shall have trouble!"[57]

Sir Earle Richards, legal member of Minto's council, was scheduled to retire in April, 1909, and on March 10 Morley proposed Sinha's name to the King for that vacancy. In supporting his recommendation, Morley wrote of the Indian appointment as "an act of high policy,"[58] insisting upon its expediency, amounting almost to necessity, for the contentment and stability of British India. From Biarritz came royal regrets that King Edward could not change his views on the subject, although he accepted the constitutional imperative of having "no other alternative but to give way much against his will."[59] Morley used the opportunity of replying to assert that his nomination of Sinha was made in fulfillment of Queen Victoria's historic promise of 1858 that "race and colour should constitute no bar."[60] The talismanic seal of formal approval was granted on March 20, and Sinha's appointment was made public on March 24, 1909. On April 18 the first Indian member took his seat on the viceroy's Executive Council, inheriting the portfolio initially held by Thomas Babington Macaulay. Sinha thus became an integral part of the ruling administrative body of the government of India, which, by statute, was constituted under the collective title of "Governor-General in Council." The policy of racial integration thus initiated at the highest level of British Indian executive responsibility remained unbroken until the last British governor-general and viceroy, Lord Louis Mountbatten, left the Dominion of India on June 21, 1948, more than ten months after India's attainment of full independence. Morley himself was fully conscious of the import of his precedent-making appointment. "A great thing, and a right thing, has been done,"[61] he affirmed with assurance. Throughout India, the news was acclaimed enthusiastically by leaders of all communities.

The appointments of Sinha, Gupta, and Bilgrami, while the most dramatic and symbolically important measures taken by Morley to alleviate racial tensions in India, were in themselves hardly a solution to British India's complex racial problem, nor were they the entire policy pursued in seeking its resolution during this era. Morley personally urged the employment of more Indians in every branch of official service throughout his tenure. He attached, for example, "great importance to keeping not less than three permanent Native Judges"[62] on the Calcutta High Court, wiring his policy in this matter to Minto. He urged presidency governors to promote Indians to their own high courts whenever a vacancy appeared, even if Englishmen of more seniority were available. As he cabled Lord Lamington, then governor of Bombay, "The question of disregard of seniority being justifiable depends on policy. Seniority not the only element."[63] Morley's policy was to appoint an inefficient Indian in preference to the more efficient Englishman whenever the former was technically qualified for a government job. He believed in the ancient adage that office tested the man, and knew that responsibility helped make men more responsible. The need for increased employment of Indians in the higher ranks of all government services had been one of the most pressing and long-standing demands made by Congress since its inception in 1885. Morley, anxious to revise the entire system of service recruitment so as to bring more Indians into government office at higher salaries, suggested the appointment of "a strong Commission to inquire into the question of the employment of Natives"[64] to Minto early in 1907. He even went so far as to recommend that six Indians should be named to such a commission of fifteen, and specifically included Gokhale and the Aga Khan on the list sent to Minto. But the Viceroy, as usual overwhelmed by the work already confronting him, pleaded for deferment of action along such lines. The greater priority given by Morley to his reforms bill and to the commission on decentralization appointed during his era, coupled with Minto's unwillingness to cooperate, led to the postponement of this royal review of service recruitment policies until 1912. The Islington Commission on the Public Services in India[65] appointed by Morley's successor, however, was the direct result of his earlier recommendation, and included both Gokhale and the Aga Khan among its members. The commission was chartered to study existing limitations on the employment of non-Europeans in India, and to recommend necessary changes. Morley's personal interest in this subject is attested by the file he kept on "Employment of Natives,"[66] which included a note penned by Gupta for him in October, 1908. The most shocking aspect of Gupta's note included statistics for 1907 showing, for example, that not a single post out of 278 paying £800 or more per year was held by an Indian in the forest, police, post office, telegraph, salt, survey, or political services of British India, while only 1 out of 49 in the Education Department and 2 out of 87 in the state railways were held by Indians.

Among the more than 1,200 members of the I.C.S. receiving salaries over £800 annually, some 10 percent, 123 of them, were Indians.

For all his personal concern and consciousness of the gravity of this *de facto* racist recruitment policy at higher levels of all services, however, Morley lacked the time and energy to introduce sweeping changes in procedure, and his policy in this area was thus limited to personal entreaty, private initiative, and deferred official suggestions. Annual examinations for the I.C.S. continued to be held in England alone, the maximum age of candidacy remaining only twenty-one, thus preventing most Indians from preparing themselves adequately for the tests even if they could afford the heavy expense of the passage to England and prior educational preparation. In 1909, out of fifty-two successful candidates for the coveted service, one alone was Indian, Benegal N. Rau (1887–1953), who attained the unique distinction of becoming independent India's first member elected to the International Court of Justice at The Hague; he passed his examinations with the highest grade in mathematics and was the only candidate to compete in Sanskrit.[67]

Expressions of racial prejudice were manifest at every level of British Indian administration and society by this time, and Morley's struggle against them, like his introduction of representative political institutions, was only the start of a long and arduous historic battle. From railroad carriages marked "Europeans Only"[68] and urinals labeled "European Gentlemen," as contrasted with humbler structures tagged "Men," to the open confession by the lieutenant governor who ruled Eastern Bengal and Assam, "Everybody hates Bengalis,"[69] the spirit of white supremacy ruled the raj. In the army, prejudice and segregation were even worse than those dividing civilian society. Morley was shocked to learn, as he reported to Minto, that "they say that in the European regiments both officers and men are full of contempt for Natives, servants, etc.; and then, when the officers are placed over Native troops, they take no trouble to conceal the same spirit there. One thing, at any rate, is certain, that the sore feeling engendered by this hateful arrogance won't be healed by any amount of political reform, any more than by drastic press acts. . . . This overbearing arrogance is really as shameful, as it will in the long run prove to be dangerous."[70] Minto, himself a soldier, drew the line of personal tolerance at the military ranks, arguing against Morley's suggestion that Indians be freely admitted to compete for commissions: "All our experience points to that want of judgment and decision in a Native which has made it impossible for him to command white men in action."⁷¹ Minto would go no further than Curzon in this regard, advocating the commissioning of Indians to command a *corps d'élite* consisting entirely of Indians. By selecting General Sir Garrett O'Moore Creagh (1848–1923) to succeed Kitchener as India's commander in chief in 1909, Morley replaced India's most powerful bigot with Whitehall's leading military advocate of officer integration. English ladies residing in India were often worse than their husbands in perpetuating the color line, Morley heard. He described the conversation of a group of "Anglo-Indian ladies" reported to him by an informant as "silly, arrogant, odious, whenever a Native was mentioned," concluding, "Such things give me a rather friendly feeling for Ajit Singh."⁷²

The one section of Morley's reform bill initially rejected by the Lords was clause 3, implicitly designed to bring Indians into positions of executive responsibility on all provincial governments of India. Until this time the only provinces with executive councils to assist and advise their governors were Madras and Bombay. All other provinces, including Bengal, were administered by lieutenant governors, generally appointed to their autocratic posts as the final reward of a lifetime spent in the I.C.S. No Indian had ever been appointed to this exalted position, though Gupta briefly served as acting lieutenant governor in Bengal, quickly replaced by an Englishman, as Minto explained, because of his color rather than his ability. "We may wish to believe that a Native and one of our own race are equally entitled to appointment to the highest posts, but as a matter of fact this can not be," wrote Minto in September, 1906. "It would be quite impossible under the social conditions still existing in India. To put it briefly, the British population simply would not stand it. . . . We can not, if we would, ignore the fact that we are the ruling race, and that there is a limit beyond which that race will not put up with the predominance of Native power."⁷³ Tacitly, Morley accepted this limit himself, yet, if he was not quite ready to appoint an Indian to administrative command of a province, he was, at any rate, determined to place at least one Indian councillor at the side of every such British ruler. In proposing council reforms to his special Whitehall committee⁷⁴ in October, 1908, Morley asked whether it would be politic to add "two (or one) members who should be Natives of India"⁷⁵ to the executive councils of Madras and Bombay, and, furthermore, whether there was any feasible plan for associating an Indian member on an executive council for lieutenant governors. The committee majority responded in favor of both changes, and Morley's reforms dispatch proposed adding two members to the governors' councils, "of whom one at least should always by usage be an Indian, though this need not be provided by statute."[76] The governors of Bombay and Madras, as well as Minto himself, unanimously opposed any appointment to provincial executive councils "on racial grounds alone,"[77] insisting that individual fitness be the sole criterion. Morley agreed, for, once the councils were expanded, he knew that qualified Indians would indeed be found to help man them. In Bengal, lieutenant governor Norman Baker strongly favored placing an Indian on the executive council he requested, and, as noted, when clause 3 of the Indian Councils Bill was restored by the Commons, it called for the immediate creation of such a council in Bengal alone, stipulating procedure for the creation in future of similar councils in other provinces.

Morley's attempts to make races mix, which once he described as "about the most desperate task that fate can set a statesman,"[78] suffered severe setbacks from Indian as well as British quarters. Barely one year after Bilgrami had joined the Council of India he took leave for home, and Morley suspected "that he is not likely to come back. It must be a horrid exile."[79] Within six months the first Muslim member of Whitehall's council informed his secretary of state that "he dares not face the English climate for another winter."[80] Worse problems soon beset Sinha in the rarefied atmosphere of Simla, where, as Clarke early perceived he would be, that brilliant and sophisticated Brahman soon became "very seriously disillusioned . . . now that he sees the Government of India from the inside."[81] Fleetwood Wilson, who became Sinha's only friend on Minto's council, reported less than three months after the historic appointment how "Poor Sinha . . . intended telling Lord Minto that he wished to give up his appointment," finding "Like myself . . . that no self-respecting man can remain here. The other men have Lieutenant Governorships dangled like a bunch of carrots before their noses but Sinha and I want nothing."[82] Wilson urged Sinha to stay, if for no other reason than from a sense of loyalty to Morley, who, when he learned of the news, expressed his dismay in italics, writing Wilson:

Our appointment of him [Sinha] to a seat on the Council was the most marked step taken since I took charge of this office, demanding as much courage and perseverance as anything ever done by an Indian Secretary.

... The edge of hostility to the appointment of any Indian member at all lost nearly all its sharpness from the personal qualities of Mr. Sinha, and we all regard it as a piece of providential favour for the policy that a man of such character and popularity happened to be available. His retirement will both discredit the policy at its outset, and prejudice a new choice.... its effect upon India would be disastrous.[83]

Sinha agreed to remain at his job, although only a few weeks later Wilson again noted that he had been badly handled, and that "Kitchener has been rude to him in Council."[84] It was generally known in India that Sinha, one of his country's leading barristers, had taken a cut in salary of more than £10,000 annually to serve at the post in which he was so rudely rewarded. Chief Justice Jenkins shed more light on the restraints imposed upon Sinha because of his place of birth as well as his appointment as legal member, rather than a general member, of Minto's council, explaining to Morley:

It is impossible to get away from the fact that his [Sinha's] position is complicated by his being an Indian, and thus in a sense a representative and exponent of the Indian outlook on affairs. One can well understand therefore that he should view with some anxiety a procedure which deprives him of the opportunity of expressing his views, and perhaps influencing the Governor General and his Council in matters on which there may be a strong public opinion among educated Indians. ... Let me illustrate my meaning: assume that you receive a telegraphic communication as to the true test of eligibility under the new Reform Scheme, or as to whether A B & C should be deported, you do not, I understand, get the opinion of the whole Council, but of the eminent statesman [Adamson] who may happen to rule the fortunes of the Home Department of the Government of India and yet those would seem to be matters on which Sinha's opinion would be eminently useful by virtue of his legal training and his knowledge of the Indian view, while at the same time his non-official training would incline him towards the more liberal opinion. ... Then how would he interpret the failure to consult him? Would it be unreasonable if he put it down to distrust? If he did so diagnose it, then I fear he would not have been very wide of the mark. In recent times the legal member has not exercised the influence that once was the fashion. I think this is much to be regretted, and I cannot help feeling that in most matters with which the Home Department of the Government of India deals a little leaven of law and non-officialdom would be an uncommonly good thing, and a little more infusion of Sinhaism there would bring the administration and policy of the Government much more into line with popular sentiment.[85]

Jenkins managed to convince Sinha to hold his resignation in abeyance, at least until they had a chance to discuss the matter personally at Calcutta during the winter, when government descended from the hills to the plain. Then, in November, 1909, Minto appointed Sinha chairman of his council's committee on fashioning reform regulations, but by February Sinha was again ready to resign. Among other things, he could not agree to the new Press Act, and had actually submitted his resignation to Minto a few days before the inauguration of the new legislative council. The assassination of Calcutta's police inspector, Shams ul-Alam, however, led Sinha to withdraw the resignation and eloquently to introduce the Press Act to the legislature. Sinha reluctantly remained in Executive Council harness only until an Indian replacement could be found for him in the person of Syed Ali Imam,[86] who became the second Indian legal member on November 21, 1910.

Despite all the discouragement and difficulties involved, Morley retained firm faith in the policy he had launched. "It is not obstinacy with me, it is conviction," he wrote Minto in April, 1910, when the Viceroy was pessimistic about the prospects of being able to replace Sinha with another Indian. "I must use up the very last atom of private energy and official power that remain to me," insisted Morley, "in preventing the principle of Indian member on the Governor General's executive council being smothered."[87] Minto had by now entirely abandoned his earlier bold stand, arguing that "it would be a mistake as regards the Executive Council to appoint an Indian qua Indian," although graciously conceding "*race* should *not debar* a suitable man."[88] His definition of suitable, however, was a far cry from Morley's, for ultimately he recommended Bombay's High Court justice, D. D. Davar, the man who sentenced Tilak to six years in Mandalay prison for sedition in 1908. Morley rejected Davar on purely political grounds, writing, "What the Indians think of our nominee is as important an element in deciding, as the qualifications of the nominee himself. And the record of Davar in the case of Tilak has not tended to make him popular with our Indian friends."[89] Not only did Morley save the principle of Indian participation in the executive affairs of Indian government, therefore, but he firmly established the political character of this appointment as well, making his policy one of integration in both the racial and the political sense of that word. Never again was the government of India's "holy of holies" to meet in white European isolation, pretending to be administratively aloof from the vital currents of India's turbulent political scene. The same applied to

Whitehall's Council of India, on which Mirza Abbas Ali Baig[90] was to replace Bilgrami in July, 1910. "He wears a peculiar headgear," wrote Morley of Baig, "which may bring home to the visual eye the realities of our new policy.... My hopes of him, however, were considerably dashed by the fears he expressed lest he should find the winter climate of this island too much for him. Let us trust the stars may give us good weather."[91]

Morley had no false illusions about the deep-rooted complexity of the prejudice he worked to dispel. His trusted lieutenants in India, like Sir Lawrence Jenkins, did not fail to inform him of the all-pervasive impact of racism on Anglo-Indian life. "What confornts us here is not mere unrest: it is *distrust*," wrote Jenkins in mid-1909 (emphasis added by Morley in pencil). "If what one hears is anywhere near the truth, the state of tension and distrust is really serious. And unhappily the distrust is not only of the rulers by the ruled; it is reciprocal and the white man (I of course only speak generally) appears to entertain a profound distrust of the Indian."[92] By way of illustration, Jenkins mentioned his High Court colleague, Justice Fletcher, who, after deciding in favor of an Indian in a case against an Englishman, was threatened with assassination in a letter that "cannot have come from an Indian source."[93] As for himself, Jenkins added that, because he allowed Indian friends to call on him at home, Calcutta gossip labeled him in league with the agitators. But India's racial problem, serious as it was, Morley knew, was hardly unique. Thanks to his annual vacation with his dear friend, Andrew Carnegie, Morley was never remote from the realities of American life, and, shortly before retiring from Whitehall, he met Booker T. Washington at Carnegie's Skibo castle. "The future of the Negro in the U.S.A. has always profoundly interested and excited me, as well it might," he then reflected. "What will the numbers amount to, twenty or fifty years hence? Terrible to think of!! Talk of India and other 'insoluble problems' of great States —I declare the American Negro often strikes me as the hardest of them all."[94] Yet, although he may have found some personal consolation in this consciousness of international company for India's plight, Morley was no more lulled by false pride than despair into abandoning his policy of Anglo-Indian racial integration.

8

SEPARATE AND UNEQUAL

> The crucial defect even in a superior kind of politician is lack of fibre. . . . We have all known men in public life almost deserving to be called great, who for want of fibre, fortitude, and sap proved broken reeds in a dark hour—the only real test of a man in earnest. Faintheartedness Mr. Gladstone called the master vice.
>
> Morley's *Recollections*, I, 196–197

> Ah, well, as I say to you once a month, and to myself once a day, "If we would love mankind, we must not expect too much from them!"
>
> Morley to Minto, March 26, 1908

Hindu-Muslim communal conflict[1] has been the thorniest, most deep-rooted social problem of recent Indian history. Despite nine centuries of coexistence on Indian soil, Islam and Hinduism never resolved their intrinsic tensions. By the dawn of the twentieth century, India remained a pluralistic society, fundamentally divided along religous lines. Because of the pervasive character of both religions, the division was broadly cultural as well, including matters as diverse as diet, music, law, and language. Prior to 1906, however, there had been no political communalism as such. Congress, although overwhelmingly Hindu in membership from its inception, excluded all divisive socio-religious questions from its annual deliberations. The Muslim League, on the other hand, was started in direct response to the prospect of legislative reform promised by Morley in his budget message of 1906. Thus, while helping pave the way for independent India's parliamentary government, the reforms of this era served also as the major stimulus to inauguration of the party that brought Pakistan to birth.

Few questions of recent Indian history have evoked such passionate historical partisanship[2] as those dealing with the genesis and aftermath of the creation of separate Muslim electorates under the Indian Councils Act of 1909. The policy of communal electorates has alternately been viewed as emanating from a consciously inspired British plot of "divide and rule"[3] which resulted in "the greatest victory for the British empire in the twentieth century";[4] or, contrarily, as "solely the work of the Muslim leaders"[5] which received impartial British support in the hope that "separate representation would eliminate the causes of irritation between various classes."[6] Let us first of all consider the question of the policy's origin: was it inspired by British duplicity or Muslim anxiety?

Within a month of Morley's announcement in the Commons of his intention to introduce legislative council reforms for India, Mohsin-ul-Mulk,[7] manager of the Muslim Anglo-Oriental College at Aligarh, wrote his principal, W. A. J. Archbold, who was then visiting Simla:

> If the new rules now to be drawn up introduce "election" on a more extended scale, the Mohammedans will hardly get a seat, while Hindus will carry off the palm by dint of their majority, and no Mohammedan will get into the Councils by election. . . . *It has also been proposed* that a memorial be submitted to His Excellency the Viceroy to draw the attention of Government to a consideration of the rights of Mohammedans. . . . Will you therefore inform me if it would be advisable to submit a memorial. . . . *You have, there, an opportunity of knowing the opinion of Government officials on the matter, and you can thus give me valuable advice in this connection* [italics added].[8]

As seen from the emphasized clause above, Mohsin-ul-Mulk's idea of submitting a Muslim memorial to Minto was not entirely his own, yet there is no clear evidence as to whether his initial advisers in this matter were Muslim Indians or Englishmen. Immediately after receiving Mohsin-ul-Mulk's letter, however, Archbold passed it on to Dunlop Smith, who promptly showed it to Minto, so that, within four days of its drafting, a copy could be enclosed with Minto's letter of August 8 to Morley. The Viceroy commented on this enclosure by warning Morley that "there is no doubt a natural fear in many quarters lest perpetual Bengalee demands should lead to the neglect of other claims to representation throughout India; so that we must be very careful in taking up these questions to give full value to the importance of other interests besides those so largely represented by the Congress."[9] Morley's initial reaction to the idea of a Muslim deputation was receptive, since he considered it an *"excellent occasion for vindicating our entire and resolute impartiality between races and creeds*, and deprecating any other construction of either language used by Government or action taken. We view all these questions in genuine good faith."[10] Minto disarmingly replied that "the line I shall try to take will be exactly as you say."[11] His response to the Muslim deputation on October 1 proved, however, to have quite the opposite effect; its tone, as well as the promises it carried, was clearly partial to Muslim aspirations. Thus the question of British policy in this matter hardly lends itself to any simple resolution, for here, as elsewhere, the policy of Simla was far different from that of Whitehall.

Minto's extraordinary departure from his usually cautious and noncommittal approach to official problems in the matter of Muslim representation seems indeed to lend credence to the claim of British duplicity, although, paradoxically enough, the "divide and rule" formula, if applied by Simla, was probably aimed more at weaning divided Indian opinion from dependence on Whitehall, thus enhancing the prestige of Simla, than at pitting Muslims against Hindus. Mohsin-ul-Mulk was even more outspoken in his criticism of Morley and British Liberal policy than he was of the Hindu majority, as seen from his letter of August 18 to Archbold (promptly submitted to Minto's private secretary), in which the conservative Muslim leader wrote:

> Nobody can say that the present state of Mohammedan feeling is without its justification. The Liberal Government is at the bottom of it and is responsible for it. I consider it a wrong policy arising out of the ignorance of the real conditions in India. Mr. John Morley is a philosopher and might well have been contented to give lessons in philosophy; and one cannot but feel sorry that the destiny of India has been placed in his hands. His policy has done a lot of injury to India and may do much more.... I only hope that the Government of India will do something to subside the growing Mohammedan feeling and remedy their hopelessness.[12]

This appeal was precisely the sort that Minto would find most flattering and congenial, echoing the familiar chant of Simla's bureaucracy, bolstering the Viceroy's Tory prejudices as well as his official vanity. Gokhale and the moderate-Liberal leadership of Congress had clearly turned to Morley and Britain's Liberal Parliament as the fountainhead of Indian policy. Minto now found, however, that at least one portion of articulate Indian society looked to himself and the government of India for protection and support. His reply to the Muslim deputation appears to have been the product more of wounded pride than of political treachery, rather a bid by Simla for independence from Whitehall's leading strings than any unified British scheme aimed at increasing Hindu-Muslim strife. In sponsoring Muslim demands, Minto was neither as altruistic as his laudators claim, nor as presciently nefarious as his detractors would have us believe.

The famous deputation of some thirty-five[13] Muslims, led by His Highness, the Aga Khan,[14] presented its address to the Viceroy at Simla on October 1, 1906. Since members of this deputation convened the first session of the Muslim League at Dacca two months later, the document[15] submitted by them to Minto must be recognized as the first major statement of Muslim political consciousness and aspirations in recent Indian history. The address, while loyalist and supplicating in tone, clearly asserted the separatist communal consciousness of its authors and their political astuteness. Specifically, the deputation requested "a fair share" of any extended representation on councils for the Muslim community. By this they meant, however, more than the mere fraction of the Muslim population of India reflected in the census (in 1901 there were 62 million Muslims in a total population of 310 million). Minto was urged that Muslim representative "status and influence should be commensurate not merely with their numerical strength but also with their political importance and the value of the contribution which they make to the defence of the Empire." The loyal and martial attributes of the minority community were stressed as bargaining points by implicit comparison with predominant Hindu "unrest" and pacifism. The demand for Pakistan first articulated so much later was, moreover, in some measure foreshadowed by references in this document to the Muslims of India as "a community in itself more numerous than the entire population of any first class European Power, except Russia," and "a distinct community, with additional interests of our own which are not shared by other communities." Further emphasis was added by use of the phrase "our national welfare." Thus fortified by their sense of unique identity, the Muslims appealed for permission to return their own representatives to all levels of administration, from local boards through the central legislative council. Without separate electorates, they argued, no Muslim truly representative of his community's interests would ever be elected by the Hindu majority.

Minto's reply[16] was cordial and generously conciliatory, but provided no dramatic new departure from the government of India's policy toward minority representation on legislative councils, since, from at least 1888,[17] that policy had promised Muslims representation in "numerical proportion approaching as nearly as may be thought desirable"[18] the community's proportion to the total population. The Viceroy, moreover, as has earlier been noted (see chap. vi), never imagined that a direct electoral system would become the key principle of Morley's reforms, assuming only that the number of representative "nominees" on all legislative councils would be increased. He was no more prepared to enfranchise the Muslim minority than the Hindu majority, nor did the deputation addressing him expect so radical a reform. "The Aga Khan," Minto reported to Morley three days later, "agrees with all the natives with whom I have talked who are worth mentioning that India is quite unfit for popular representation in our sense of the word."[19] Yet, because of Minto's overriding desire to win his suppliants' support and assert his official power, he assured the deputation, "I am entirely with you." He then publicly proclaimed:

> I am as firmly convinced as I believe you to be, that any electoral representation in India would be doomed to mischievous failure which aimed at granting a personal enfranchisement, regardless of the beliefs and traditions of the communities composing the population of this continent. . . . the Mohammedan community may rest assured that their political rights and interests as a community will be safeguarded by any administrative re-organization with which I am concerned.[20]

The latter part of this statement reveals with startling clarity the paternalistic pride of Minto's motivation, and indicates the contempt in which Simla's government held all democratically controlled constitutional processes. For, by his emphatic promise, the Viceroy at once proclaimed himself the personal champion of Muslim interests, and committed the government of India to inflexible agreement with the political demands of one Indian community concerning a reforms scheme that was still being fashioned in camera by the viceregal executive committee, after which it would first require reshaping by the secretary of state and his council, before submission for consideration to Parliament. Such action was hardly the vindication of British creedal "impartiality," which Morley had enjoined.

Morley's reaction to Minto's sweeping promise to the Muslims was ambivalent. As a politician he recognized the distinct advantage of being able to counter radical opposition to his India policy in the Commons with the rejoinder that, for all the unrest in Bengal, there was such as thing as a Muslim minority in British India which looked to the raj for protection against the Hindu majority. "I hope that even my stoutest radical friends will see that the problem is not quite so simple," he wrote Minto, in commenting on the "good effects" of his Muslim deputation, "as the ordinary case of a bureaucracy *versus* the people."[21] Nor did he ignore the importance of Muslim opinion in selecting his own councillors, as his oppointment of Theodore Morison,[22] former principal of Aligarh, to his Council of India in December, 1906, proved. He was well aware that Morison would be viewed in India as the "Muslim Member" at Whitehall, noting, in informing Minto of his choice, "I should expect it to give pleasure to people whom it is our interest to conciliate in India."[23] Not that his appointment of Morison was made primarily for this reason, but rather because Morley hoped that Morison, the son of his Oxford tutor, would add a "whiff of fresh air"[24] to an oppressively stuffy council, an expectation soon[25] abandoned because of Morison's conservative pro-Muslim bias. Yet, despite his recognition of the pluralistic character of Indian society, Morley himself was no more partial to Muslim demands and political expectations than he was to the pretentions of India's princes. He was shocked,[26] for one thing, to note how backward in educational preparation and progressive leadership the Muslim community was by comparison with the Hindu community. He was anxious, moreover, to provide Congress with equal official encouragement, and wrote to convince Minto that he should receive a Congress deputation as soon as possible, "having received the Mohometans."[27] No such deputation, however, materialized.

Thanks to the public (actually ex cathedra) nature of Minto's promise to the Muslims, his reforms committee (the Arundel committee) had no recourse other than to quote from the Viceroy's statement and promptly translate it into the official proposal that "a special Mahommedan electorate must be be constituted"[28] for the purpose of filling a fixed number of seats "exclusively" reserved for Muslims on each expanded legislative council. With Minto's council thus seconding his pledge, the government of India presented Morley with a united front on the matter of communal representation in its dispatch of March 21, 1907.[29] Faced with this weight of official opinion, Morley accepted the principle that "the Mohammedan community is entitled to a special representation on the Governor-General's and Local Legislative Councils commensurate with its numbers and political and historical importance."[30] Lacking firsthand knowledge of the Indian scene and still somewhat uncertain of his own support in Parliament, Morley was unwilling to repudiate what had become an unchallenged axiom of British analysis of Indian Society—"the broad principle that Indian society lives, thinks, and acts according to castes, races and religions."[31] The real problem confronting British officials, as they saw it, was not how to divide and rule India, but rather how to rule a divided India. Long before Jinnah articulated his "two-nation theory" or the idea of Pakistan acquired its name, officials like Lee-Warner argued that "we have to deal not with one nationality but with an Imperial federation of various groups. The Congress has tried for years to assimilate them . . . [but] the Mahomedans . . . have formally stood aloof . . . In short, the national division of Indian society is not territorial but sectional."[32] Although the accuracy of this interpretation may be challenged, the conviction with which it was held can hardly be doubted. If British policy exacerbated Indian disharmony, it did so more out of ignorance (or innocence) than malice.

Minto himself was most elated, for example, in reporting his interview with a mixed deputation of Hindus and Muslims from Bengal in March, 1907: "They are most anxious to put an end to unrest and bad-feeling. . . . it was simply marvellous . . . to see the 'King of Bengal' [Banerjea] sitting on my sofa with his Mohammedan opponents, asking for my assistance to moderate the evil passions of the Bengali, and inveighing against the extravagances of Bepin Chandra Pal."[33] Patrician that he was, Minto found the appeal for *"my* assistance," emanating from *"my* sofa," most attractively flattering, even though voiced by so dangerous a leader of discontent as Banerjea. He was, in fact, ready to follow Morley's suggestion and receive an all-Congress deputation, but on the eve of the Surat split Congress was a party divided against itself,[34] and Tilak's revolutionary wing would never have countenanced so demeaning a gesture as joining a deputation to "plead" the nationalist cause in the viceregal palace. Boycott was a far more popular Congress tactic at this time than petition, and, ironically enough, just when the Muslims had stopped sulking in their tents, emerging into political light along the very trail blazed by Congress, the latter (but for individuals like Gokhale, Dutt, and Sinha) began burning its bridges of contact with the raj. Perhaps it was inevitable, in view of official repression and the continued partition of Bengal, for Congress as an organization to stay aloof from Simla. In any event, within a year of the Muslim deputation, "Hindus all over India"[35] were convinced that government was "obsessed" with pro-Muslim, anti-Hindu prejudice. Even the official dispatch of the government of India admitted that the proposals for special Muslim representation were generally regarded by Hindus "as an attempt to set one religion against the other, and thus to create a counterpoise to the influence of the educated middle class."[36]

On December 30, 1906, the Muslims established their first national political association, the All-India Muslim League, which resolved, at its Dacca meeting, "to protect and advance the political rights and interests of the Mussalmans of India, and to respectfully represent their needs and aspirations to the Government."[37] The demand for separate electorates had brought this communal party to life, and it was hardly surprising therefore to find it hailing "the timely recognition by the Supreme Government of the sound principle of separate racial representation on the Councils of the Indian Empire"[38] at its 1908 Aligarh session, where the Aga Khan was chosen "permanent" president. League agitation on behalf of the separate electorate policy thus served indeed as a counterpoise to Congress' criticism of it, but Hindu charges that government synthetically "created" that agitation were no more realistic than the bureaucracy's charges that all the "unrest" in Bengal was artificially stirred up by Calcutta "troublemakers." Muslim politicians had in fact begun to recognize the value of united action, and, goaded by a zealous sense of minority grievance, tempted by the prospect of acquiring positions of real influence and power, they hardly needed British duplicity to spur them on. Actually, Congress itself served as their model and organizational mentor, for by 1908 a London branch of the League had been established under the direction of Amir Ali,[39] who followed the example of Gokhale and Dutt in appealing directly to Morley and agitating in London for support of Muslim demands.

By the end of 1908 Morley's ambivalence concerning Muslim representation increased considerably, for he was now faced with the immediate prospect of working out a formula of enfranchisement which would at once satisfy Muslim expectations, roused by Minto's promises, without violating his own Liberal revulsion against making religious affiliations the primary criteria for election. The 1892 formula of representation by "classes and interests," including landholders, chambers of commerce, and university senates, should, according to the government of India's recommendations, be expanded to encompass the Muslim religious minority as well. Municipal corporations and district boards, on the other hand, would elect members on the basis of territorial franchise, and Morley's own predilection was to strengthen this democratic side of the Indian constitution by assuring Muslim representation through a territorial rather than a religious franchise. The dilemma he faced, of course, was to find such a plan, which would nonetheless be "in conformity with the language used by His Excellency to the Mahometans in October 1906."[40] Morley posed this problem to a select committee of his council which emerged with a recommendation of proportional representation through electoral colleges chosen by territorial franchise, the college membership reflecting the percentage of Hindus and Muslims in the population as a whole. He found this scheme most attractive and recommended[41] it to Minto for the following reasons: it would reflect the "freely exercised" choice of the "electorate at large," rather than any "artificial" special electorate; it would meet the objections of Hindus; it would establish "a principle which could be applied to further claims for representation by special classes"; and, finally, it would provide a "healthy stimulus to local self-government." Here again Morley revealed the true purpose of his policy, which was to introduce a liberal and representative system of rule in India based on the gradual growth of local and provincial institutions of self-government. In proposing his electoral college scheme of proportional representation to Minto, he elaborated how it would work by using a hypothetical illustration, specifying the figures involved for any given province.[42]

Minto's reaction to Morley's scheme was negative. Warning that it "would certainly give Hindus power to elect Muhammedans representing Hindu views," he insisted, "We must safeguard communities,"[43] that is, the Muslims. The League's opposition to the proposal was unequivocal, moreover, and Amir Ali led a protesting deputation to Whitehall on January 27, 1909. Two days before the deputation arrived, Ibni Ahmad, secretary to the League, sent a written protest stating that "the entire Muhamedan people view His Lordship's suggestions with grave misgiving as calculated to subject Mussulman representation to the good will of a rival community—and place Mussulman interests in their hands."[44]

Conscious of the impending opposition to his reform bill in the Lords, Morley became "very anxious"[45] at the prospect of incensing Muslim opinion. The *Times* and other influential organs of opinion in London were notoriously pro-Muslim in this era, and might easily have stirred British sentiment against the entire scheme of council reform if they felt that Muslim interests were to be ignored by the India Office, especially after the "pledges" made by the government of India. Morley tried to assuage the feelings of Amir Ali and his deputation with a conciliatory statement,[46] but feared, in view of the deputation's obvious "disappointment," that "we are in very deep water"[47] regarding Muslim opinion. He then turned to Alfred Lyall for advice and was urged "to make any concession"[48] possible to Muslim demands. Lyall added the weight of his India experience to the argument based on social pluralism as the principle justification for granting Muslims separate representation. At this point Minto wired to reiterate the government of India's disagreement with the electoral college scheme, adding that local governments throughout the country were "unanimous in their condemnation of the system."[49] Clarke, who as recently as October, 1908, had written Morley to urge that Muslim electorates should "not be permitted" since the "Mahomedans are certainly moving in the matter of Education, and . . . the grant of special and peculiar privileges at this juncture might check a natural and wholesome process,"[50] unexpectedly decided now against Morley's scheme as well. Perhaps he was still smarting from Morley's caustic condemnation of the Bombay government's unjudicious judicial proceedings against Tilak. Minto reminded Morley, moreover, of his explicit promises of separate electorates to the Muslims in October, 1906, warning that "withdrawal of this concession would be regarded as a breach of faith."[51] British honor was thus added to the tide of Anglo-Indian and Muslim pressure against the electoral college scheme. Finally, and in view of Morley's own sensitivity this may have been a more important factor than it would superficially seem, the rumor had reached Morley's ear that in India "They" were saying that "the S.S. [Secretary of State] like all English Radicals hates Islam."[52] Morley took the trouble to repeat that charge in a private letter to Clarke, after which he protested, "What English Radicals think of quarrels between Crescent and Cross, I don't know, but Mahomet is one of the great saints of the

Positivist Calendar." A few days later Morley reported to Minto an interview with the Aga Khan: "I begged him to dismiss from his mind what I had seen stated, that 'like all other English Radicals, I had a hatred of Islam.' "[53] Was his conscience troubled by a "rumor" that struck too close to the truth? Was this the final straw that made him lean backward to prove that in matters of public policy he would never be swayed by private prejudice? At any rate, on February 16, 1909, just after learning of this rumor, Morley capitulated. He suddenly wired his approval of the Viceroy's formula, calling for a separate Muslim electorate to elect only Muslim representatives.

In announcing his about-face to the Lords, Morley most clearly expressed the dilemma of conscience and intellect which had all but driven him to distraction on this point, noting that, "as Calvin said of another study, 'excessive study either finds a man mad or makes him so.' "[54] He restated his own faith in the plan, but, explaining how much opposition had been voiced against it in India, conceded that "it is no use, if you are making an earnest attempt in good faith at a general pacification, out of parental fondness for a clause interrupting that good process by sitting too tight." He frankly confessed that "some may be shocked at the idea of a religious register at all," adding, "We may wish, we do wish—certainly I do—that it were otherwise. We hope that time, with careful and impartial statesmanship, will make things otherwise."[55] Time, however, served only to intensify the socioreligious division hereafter confirmed in political life by the seal of official recognition.

Muslim pressure increased immediately after Morley's announcement. League leaders like the Nawab of Dacca, whose vast estates had been saved from bankruptcy to Hindu creditors by the munificence of Curzon,[56] urged their benefactors in the Lords "to defend our rights and interests in the bill Lord Morley has introduced."[57] Provincial League branches wired Whitehall to demand that separate Muslim representation be "fully commensurate with their numbers and political importance."[58] Now that government had capitulated to its legislative council demands, the League started agitating for a Muslim member on the viceroy's Executive Council. Amir Ali and Bilgrami clamored once again about government's "violation of pledges."[59] Heady with success, the new party seemed to assume that any and all demands it would make were bound to be fulfilled. Amir Ali went for another interview with Morley, who came to consider him "nothing more than a windbag."[60] Even Minto was revolted by so blatant a show of Muslim political greed, and admitted he found Bilgrami "stupid" and had "doubts about Amir Ali too."[61]

Hindu agitation against the promise of separate electorates for Muslims reached Whitehall as a barrage of cablegrams.[62] From Bengal to the Punjab, from Fyzabad to Madras, Hindu organizations held public meetings, denouncing the promised "Partition" along "racial or creedal" lines as worse than any provincial partition, warning that the grant of "excessive representation" to Muslims would "nullify" the value of reforms as a whole. Congress leaders like Lajpat Rai wrote to protest: "That the present reforms are not based on the democratic ideal of the West may be true; but the reason for their enthusiastic reception in India is that they are believed to be a step towards an actual democratic form of government, with no distinction of Hindu, Mahomedan, Parsi, and the rest. That is the goal of the Hindu politician; he does not seek a Hindu majority crushing Mahomedan or other minorities. Aiming then to obliterate all religious distinctions for national political purposes, he objects to communal representation or communal voting which would accentuate those distinctions."[63] With the Pandora's box of communal representation thrown open, of course, there was no way of preventing other minority faiths from demanding the same treatment as the Muslims. Indeed, Clarke reported that Bombay's influential Jain and Eurasian communities petitioned him for precisely such "special consideration."[64] In the Punjab, the Sikhs naturally expected similar protection. Gokhale, however, publicly supported the separate electorate scheme in March, 1909, admitting that although it would weaken future political union, "we cannot pretend such union, however desirable, exists; moreover unless by special separate treatment soreness in minds of minorities is removed real union will be retarded; matter must be looked at in large way and practical spirit."[65]

In defending his policy before the Commons, Morley adopted the same line as Gokhale, and through his parliamentary undersecretary, T. R. Buchanan, argued: "If you start from our democratic theories of representative government, of course, all such special representation is an anomaly, but we have to deal with the practical problem which is before us—the best practical solution which is available. And the Mahomedans have a special and overwhelming claim upon us."[66] The problem of trying to decide just how many seats to reserve for Muslims remained a thorny one. The government of India had initially proposed reserving five seats at the center, but in July, 1909, raised that number to six, suggesting four seats for Bombay, and both Bengals at the provincial level. Muslims would thus always be able to ally themselves with the provincial official blocks "to prevent the other nonofficial members from carrying a contested question against the rest of the Council."[67] In addition, Muslims would be privileged to vote in other constituencies, for example landholders, and in municipalities, and could well win several seats other than those specially reserved for their community. If, however, they failed to win any additional seats, Minto was prepared to nominate two Muslims to the central legislative council, raising their total to eight out of some sixty. Provincial heads of government would similarly see to it that total Muslim representation was not less than proportional.

Amir Ali and the London branch of the Muslim League remained unsatisfied, interpreting the government's earlier "pledges" to mean that all Muslim members would be elected solely by Muslim constituencies, not by mixed electorates of any kind, and would not be appointed through nomination. Morison took up this cry, and drafted a note "Upon the Pledges given to the Muhamedans," which he submitted to Morley, charging that Minto's proposals were "absolutely inconsistent with these pledges."[68] Thanks to Gupta's presence on Morley's council by this time, however, Morison's special pleading could be countered at once by the cogent rejoinder: "In the first place, it must not be forgotten that Muhamedans ask special protection because they are in a minority. It follows, therefore, that in any province such as Eastern Bengal and Assam, where they have a very substantial majority, they cannot claim any special concession; but that on the contrary . . . the admittedly influential Hindu minority should receive special consideration."[69] In a supercilious "Postscript" to Gupta's note, Morison wrote that a "charge of ingenuity or subtlety in the interpretation of pledges is not one which the Government of India can afford to have levelled against it. All its dealings should be of such transparent candour as not to stand in need of elaborate justification; I should much rather see the Government of India err on the side of naive simplicity than of sophistical cleverness."[70] Gupta, however, was unabashed by so thinly veiled an attempt to put the "subtle Hindu" in his place, replying immediately that "it is hardly fair to characterise my main contention as subtle, ingenious, or savouring of sophistical cleverness; on the contrary, the point is so obvious that it should occur to every open mind. . . . true statesmanship requires that no *undue* favour is shown to one community at the *expense* of another."[71] Morley agreed, writing to inform Minto:

> I incline to rebel against the word "pledge" in our case. We declared our view and our intention at a certain stage. But we did this independently, and not in return for any "consideration" to be given to us by the M's., as the price of our intentions. This is assuredly not a "pledge" in the ordinary sense, where a Minister induces electors to vote for him, or members of Parliament to support his measures in the H. of C., by promising that if they will, he will do so and so. We shall have done the best we can according to the circumstances and conditions with which we have to deal, and by which we may be limited. That strikes me as the common sense of the thing. Pray don't scold me for being a pure Sophist.[72]

The more his own council debated the Muslim question, the more apparent it became to Morley that Morison "would rather have no Reforms at all than such as might be taken to place the M's at a disadvantage."[73] Other members[74] of the Council of India joined Morison in what was actually a "Muslim bloc" at Whitehall, whose special pleading and carping criticism of reform regulations gave Morley a sympathetic appreciation of why Cromwell was finally driven "to send his Counsellors packing."[75] The regulations as approved enfranchised all Muslims who were ordinary or honorary fellows of universities; or held "recognized" titles or government "honors"; or were pensioned, gazetted, or commissioned officers; or owned landed property, or paid income tax above certain specified minimums.[76]

Ironically enough, by November, 1909, when the regulations were published, Minto confessed his anxiety over "the excess of representation granted to Mahomedans": "I cannot see that they are in the least entitled to the number of seats that will now be allotted to them."[77] The agitation center of the cause he had championed mostly from motives of personal prestige and local pride had perversely been shifted from Simla to London in the past year, and the Viceroy now complained to Morley that "the Mahomedan agitation has been engineered from home and, from what you have told me, largely by Amir Ali and the Aga Khan, the former actuated to a great extent by personal reasons, whilst the latter although he has apparently a certain standing in English society, from all I have heard carries little, if any, weight at all in India."[78] The Viceroy was rudely awakened to find that the minority whose claims he had sponsored repaid him with neither loyalty nor gratitude, but, having grown to political maturity, naturally followed the path of its Congress sibling in gravitating toward the political power focus of empire at Whitehall. The Muslims had proved themselves more adept disciples of Roman political tactics than the British. Morley could hardly sympathize now with Minto's plight, reminding him "respectfully" that "it was *your* early speech about their extra claims that started the M. [Muslim] hare."[79] To his old friend Frederic Harrison, Morley sighed, "It passes the wit of man to frame plans that will please Hindus without offending Mahometans, and we shall be lucky if we don't offend *both*."[80] A month later, at its Lahore session, Congress resolved "its strong sense of disapproval of the creation of separate electorates on the basis of religion."[81]

In part because he expected less than Minto originally did from concessions to Muslim demands, and because he was more experienced in politics, with its pitfalls and pressures, Morley was less disappointed at the outcome of this facet of reforms. From his friend Chief Justice Jenkins he learned (too late to retract the concessions) that "many" in India who championed the Muslim demands did so "because they consider it the most effective mode of thwarting your scheme."[82] In a frustratingly inexplicit afterthought, moreover, Jenkins added a volatile ember to the charge that British duplicity might have been at the root of the Muslim deputation: "From all I hear,—and on the spot one is in a position to hear much—I incline to the view that the Mahomedan demand was prompted in the first instance from other sources, and has been skillfully engineered."[83] Morley, however, was relieved to note that the London press reacted so favorably to the Indian Councils Act, and felt "very sure" that "if we had not satisfied the Mahometans, we should have had opinion here—which is now with us—dead against us."[84] He accepted the separate electorate scheme, then, as the price of British public support, concluding that nothing "has been sacrificed for their [the Muslims'] sake that is of real importance."[85] But the importance of the precedent thus established would appear to indicate that Arthur Godley had better reason to congratulate Lee-Warner on how "skillfully" this particular matter was "managed" by the Muslim lobby[86] at Whitehall.

The communal electorate system, introduced in 1909, thereafter became a permanent feature of British India's constitution. The dilemma that plagued Morley haunted his Liberal successors at the India Office. In preparing the Government of India Bill in 1918, by which time Britain was openly committed to a policy of leading India toward the goal of parliamentary government, Montagu's reforms committee concluded "unhesitatingly" that "the history of self-government among the nations who developed it, and spread it through the world is decisively against the admission by the State of any divided allegiance; against the State's arranging its members in any way which encourages them to think of themselves primarily as citizens of any smaller unit than itself."[87] The communal electorate for Muslims was, therefore, denounced as "a very serious hindrance to the development of the self-governing principle."[88] Yet, for all the nobility of principle displayed by such statements, no attempt was made in 1919 to abolish the system. On the contrary, it was expanded to include Sikhs in the Punjab, and Eurasians elsewhere. The reasons in 1919 were the "settled facts" of Minto's promise of 1906 and the Act of 1909, but in addition, above and beyond these, just as in Morley's era, that the "Muhammadans regard separate representation and communal electorates as their only adequate safeguards."[89] The paradox Morley was unable to resolve could not be solved by Montagu either, and, though it is true that the precedent of 1909 added weight to the problem by 1919, it must also be remembered that Minto's *fait accompli* in 1906 had doomed Morley's attempt to formulate a territorial alternative scheme to the religious register virtually from the outset. By 1930 British brains had come no closer to finding a solution to India's foremost political problem, for, as the Statutory Commission concluded, although communal representation was "an undoubted obstacle in the way of the growth of a sense of common citizenship," the Muslims were not prepared to give it up; and, "Whatever view may be taken of the Muhammadan objection, the fact itself cannot be disputed, and it is one of the greatest possible gravity for all who are engaged in considering the constitutional future of British India."[90] Partition of the subcontinent alone removed this anomaly from the constitution, but then British India's communal conflict was transformed from an internal to an international one.

9

UNFINISHED SYMPATHY

> Education ... Often do I feel that here we have a far more important field for really fruitful work (if any of our work is destined to be fruitful) than all the political reforms in the world.
>
> Morley to Minto, July 24, 1908

The "great mischief"[1] of overcentralization was the most important Indian administrative problem to which Morley addressed himself, initiating proposals that reversed a half-century trend of bureaucratic centralization which had reached its apogee under Curzon. The Royal Commission upon Decentralisation in India, established during this era, completed its report[2] too late to affect significantly the administrative structure of India's government by 1910, but its recommendations were in good measure incorporated in the Government of India Act of 1919.[3]

Morley first proposed the creation of a parliamentary committee "to enquire into the distribution of local and centralised powers in India"[4] in December, 1906. He specifically recommended to Minto at the time that Indian members like Gokhale would be of special value to such a committee of both houses. Minto, however, protested against the launching of any investigation from England, and tried to undermine the idea. The Liberal House of Commons, on the other hand, had been urging Morley to set up a royal commission to investigate Indian unrest, and his decision to announce (in his budget message of June,

1907) the government's intention to appoint a royal commission on decentralization may be seen as a compromise course between the extreme favoring broader action at Westminster and that of bureaucratic inaction at Simla.

No sooner did Minto learn of Morley's promise to the Commons, however, than he rushed to appoint a "Viceregal Committee of Enquiry"[5] to study precisely the same question. But Morley, not to be diverted by Minto's hastily contrived attempt to whitewash the problem by empowering Simla's worst offenders of overcentralization to investigate themselves, insisted:

> The advantage of a *home* enquiry to my mind is not only that it would not burden the Indian servants of Government, but that it would or should let in a flood of new and fresh light from fresh minds. True, the business would turn upon details, and of details only Indian officials are in full and habitual possession. But these officials would be the witnesses, and their story would be the material, on which a small body of capable and open-minded outsiders, with experience of administration and public affairs, would build their conclusions. There would be the same kind of advantage in this as is supposed to come from taking a political Viceroy or Secretary of State from outside. . . . We should get new points of view, and your official Caste, for a Caste it is, would be all the better for having a good strong bull's eye turned upon them.[6]

By the end of June, 1907, Morley had decided that the commission's inquiry should encompass legislative and administrative relations between the central and provincial governments in India, and consider "whether, by measure of decentralization or otherwise, those relations can be improved, and the system of Government better adapted to meet the requirements and promote the welfare of the inhabitants of the different provinces."[7]

Personally predisposed to England's county council system of local autonomy, Morley favored administrative decentralization for India as well. With its vast area and extraordinary variety of conditions, India could hardly be ruled from any single center of administrative power. As Alfred Lyall advised Morley shortly before he proposed the commission to the Commons, "our policy should be to distribute the weight of government in such a vast empire as India by strengthening the local government," adding ironically (for Indian nationalists were strong advocates of decentralization), "this is the true interpretation of the maxim 'divide et impera.' "[8] Lyall favored the paternalism of early nineteenth-century British rule over the centralization of Curzonian bureaucratic "efficiency." He advocated, moreover, less rigid enforcement of the I.C.S. rule of retirement at fifty-five, noting[9] that Indians "invariably" respected older officials more than younger men. He cited the precedent of British practice in advocating the decentralization of such matters as education, police, excise, and sanitation, and concluded: "My own opinion is that the drawbacks to provincial decentralization, whatever they may be, can never be so serious as the evils of centralisation."[10]

Minto for once found himself "in sympathy" with Curzon, who, as was to be expected, led the attack in London against Morley's proposed commission. The Viceroy voiced concern about "the amount of power that can safely be deputed to Lieutenant-Governors and others."[11] Nor were his fears entirely baseless, as Morley himself admitted: "Do I want to transfer power from you to Lawley [Governor of Madras] or Lamington [Governor of Bombay]?"[12] In such cases, indeed, the lesser of evils resided at Simla. Or, as Gokhale later put it, "I certainly have no wish to see 'petty despotisms,' pure and simple, set up in place of the present Provincial Governments."[13] To be of true value, decentralization would have to be introduced together with some measure of popular responsibility and representative rule. Minto and his advisers understood full well that a royal commission's investigation might easily lead from mere mechanical devolution of administrative responsibility to a real revolution in provincial power. The government of India was, therefore, most forceful in remonstrating that it alone should be permitted to study its "Secretariat machinery," particularly insisting that "no Native"[14] was qualified to serve on a royal commission of the sort Morley had suggested. The conflict became so bitter an issue of rivalry that Morley finally wired the Viceroy, "requesting" him to suspend the entire operation of his committee until the royal commission was constituted "and its views and wishes ascertained."[15] To Godley, who could always be relied upon to convey the Secretary of State's mood in private correspondence to Minto, Morley wrote on the same day, "You remember in Lord Minto's last letter he described the wrath of his officials at our presuming to impose a Commission on them. This device [of creating a Simla committee] ... is evidently their way of countering the Commission by forestalling its operation. That must be withstood to the very death."[16]

The commission received its royal warrant on September 7, 1907, and left for India to begin investigations under the chairmanship of Charles E. H. Hobhouse,[17] Morley's parliamentary undersecretary of state. Romesh Dutt was the only Indian appointee, the other four members[18] being British: two from London, two from the government of India. Before long Minto began complaining that the commission was "inclined to go too far."[19] He first raised the ubiquitous specter of "unrest" to warn Morley that it was "all-important just now" to move cautiously. A month later the Viceroy challenged Hobhouse's power to interrogate the government of India about anything but the narrowest questions of financial and administrative relations between central and provincial governments. By deftly utilizing tactics of noncooperation, Minto and his government did their best to frustrate the labors of the commission and hinder its progress. Here again, as in so many instances of repression, the Secretary of State, from his distant vantage point, could do little more than cajole, berate, and wait. "I fear the Hobhouse Commission has provoked a good deal of criticism, not easy to distinguish from friction," Morley wrote ruefully to Clarke. "There seems to be a little touchiness in some quarters, and a little brusqueness in others."[20] In the tradition of his Bombay predecessors, Clarke was the strongest official advocate of decentralization. During its stay in Bombay the commission gathered evidence from nonofficial as well as official witnesses, most of which, as Clarke reported, "was of little value."[21] By far the weightiest evidence was the statement submitted by Gokhale, which the Governor himself considered important enough to summarize in a private letter to Morley:

> The scheme seems quite moderate, and in discussing it privately with me he [Gokhale] was most reasonable. As regards municipalities, he wishes the elected element to have a majority everywhere (as it has in Bombay and Poona) and to elect a President. The Government would retain the power of suppressing a municipality which proved wholly incompetent and of nominating a fresh body. I would not object to this. . . . Gokhale wishes for district councils with two-thirds of the members elected, and he defines the subjects on which a Collector should consult his council. If on these subjects the majority differed from the Collector, their views should be sent to the Government. I see no objection to this plan, but it does not commend itself to the official mind. . . . Gokhale desires to see a Provincial Advisory Council of 50, two-thirds elected on a rather elaborate system; but he admitted the difficulties at starting, and was inclined to favour my plan of 20 nominated members. If we establish such a council, the great point will be to show, at an early period, that we mean to ask its advice. I see no difficulty in doing this.[22]

Gokhale also urged the creation of village panchayats, so that local self-government[23] could be built upon India's true social base. He advocated statutory creation of panchayats for all villages with a population of over 500. The panchayats would be empowered to judge suits in which claims did not exceed Rs. 50 in value (some one-half of a total of 150,000 suits instituted annually in Bombay alone). The "next rung on the ladder" of local self-government consisted of taluka boards, created thanks to Ripon's initiative in 1882, but left to atrophy under official domination and because of inadequate funding. These boards were to be revitalized by making them wholly elective bodies and assuring them sufficient proceeds from district revenue (the 1-anna cess; i.e., a tax of $1/16$ of a rupee) so that they could initiate necessary reforms. Municipalities, like taluka boards, should be self-governing elective bodies. Finally, district boards and councils were to be given elective majorities, thus liberating them from "purely bureaucratic character" and, it was hoped, reducing the other major "evils of the present system"[24]—secrecy and departmental delays. "The cry of the people everywhere," concluded Gokhale, "is that the Car of Administration should not merely roll over their bodies but that they themselves should be permitted to pull at the ropes."[25]

Between November, 1907, and the following April, the commission examined some 307 witnesses and traveled more than 12,000 miles in India, returning to England with no less than nine volumes of evidence. The report itself was promised to Morley by November, 1908, since he was most anxious to incorporate its conclusions into his dispatch on reforms of that month. By January, 1909, however, it was still unfinished. "The delay approaches to a scandal," Morley wrote, "but I ought to have known that to put four Indian officials on the Commission was to ensure a mountain of superfluous writing—which no mortal man will read."[26] To get any business "actually done and finished," he groaned several weeks later, "appears to be the very last thing that these Scribes (and Pharisees) ever think of."[27]

Because of the bureaucratic delay, the commission's findings could not be incorporated into the act of 1909. The essence of its conclusions (mostly Gokhale's recommendations), however, was imparted by Morley to the government of India in his November 27, 1908, dispatch on reforms, which urged the necessity "to attempt without delay an effectual advance in the direction of local self-government."[28] Reaffirming Ripon's Liberal resolution of May 18, 1882, Morley noted: "It would be hopeless to expect any real development of self-government if the local bodies were subject to check and interference in matters of detail."[29] He advised, moreover, that since the village was India's "fundamental and indestructible" basic unit, it was essential to carry out a policy of local self-government reform through which the village would become the "starting point" of public life. Precisely half a century later, independent India officially adopted its policy of a village-based national system of panchayati raj.

The report of the Royal Commission upon Decentralisation, published in February, 1909, concluded that it was "most desirable to constitute and develop village *panchayats*"[30] which would be empowered with summary jurisdiction in petty legal cases and supported by some portion of the land cess. Subdistrict (taluka or tehsil) boards were to be "universally established"[31] and given substantial powers over education and rural sanitation. The commission recommended "a substantial majority of elected members"[32] for such boards, as well as for the more powerful district boards, whose members would be elected by the nonofficial members of the taluka boards. Municipal councils were also to have a working elective majority, and it was suggested that they should "usually elect their own Chairman."[33] Decentralization was generally recommended, moreover, in matters of finance and the administration of departments such as public works and forests.

When considered together with the expanded size of provincial legislative councils and the abolition of official majorities, the commission's report may be seen as a natural complement to Morley's program of political and administrative reform aimed at the introduction of responsible provincial rule for India, the logical prelude in all respects to the Act of 1919. To hasten the transition from provincial autocracy to democracy, Morley recommended[34] the creation of executive councils in provinces under lieutenant governor rule. Gokhale proposed[35] this change from the Bengal–United Provinces system of individual provincial rule to the Bombay-Madras executive method of a civilian governor in council. From his vantage point within the commission, Dutt also sponsored this radical change, and, in several personal letters to Morley, specifically argued[36] for the general introduction of provincial council government with at least one Indian member on each executive council of three or four. The commission's report advocated the same change, concluding that "the system of single Lieutenant-Governors is no longer suited to the larger Provinces. . . . We prefer a regular Council Government, such as exists in Madras and Bombay, with a Governor usually, but not invariably, appointed from Home. We think that all Council Governments should consist of not less than four members besides the Governor. . . . This enlargement would permit of the appointment of specially qualified natives of India."[37] Morley made this proposal the third clause of his councils bill, which, upon its second reading in the Lords, was attacked by Lord MacDonnell[38] (formerly an Indian lieutenant governor) as contrary to the "persistent opinion"[39] of Indian officialdom since 1868. An overwhelming majority of the Lords (59 to 18) voted to omit the clause in support of MacDonnell's motion. Curzon wrote to the *Times* that same day, defending his party's repudiation of "this great and startling change"[40] which he insisted Morley had "put forward only at the last moment and in a violent hurry." The clause was later replaced in modified form by the Commons, and finally accepted by the Lords, since it called only for the immediate creation of a council in Bengal, where the lieutenant governor had requested it, permitting subsequent councils to be created in other provinces provided neither house of Parliament objected during some sixty days of notification during any session. In 1915, when the next such council was proposed for the United Provinces, the Lords petulantly exercised their veto power.

By the end of his tenure at the India Office, Morley was convinced that, in matters of administrative reform, the "less striving after uniformity the better, and the more you leave to the local people and the extended bodies, the better."[41] He felt, as an unofficial adviser from Calcutta put it, that "Self-government must proceed by steps, first things first. In District Boards and Municipalities we have a splendid training ground. But these must have more power and less government interference. Let them gang their own gait."[42] Morley resolved in 1910 that if he remained at his post another year or two he would turn his attention primarily to the tasks of "working out the report of the Hobhouse Commission, for one, and a vigorous attempt to re-cast expenditure, for another."[43] On September 14, 1910, however, he submitted to the Prime Minister the last of what had reportedly been no less than twenty-three resignations[44] from his India Office secretaryship. Like Gladstone, Morley often resigned, it seemed, merely to be reassured that his continued service was strongly desired and properly appreciated. He apparently had no intention of being "taken at his word"[45] in 1910, but Asquith[46] surprised him by granting Morley's plea of release "on grounds of age, weariness, advent of a new Viceroy, etc."[47] Lord Crewe,[48] Rosebery's son-in-law, was shifted from the Colonial Office to succeed Morley on "the banks of the Ganges and the Brahmaputra," but showed little initiative in pressing forward the commission's recommendations on decentralization. As lord privy seal, Morley remained in the cabinet, and for several months in 1911, when Crewe was hospitalized[49] after a fall, he returned to the India Office, although as a temporary replacement he attempted no further policy innovations.

Perhaps because of his long and intimate association with political affairs, Morley well understood that political reforms alone would not suffice to transform and modernize Indian society. He was, therefore, alert to "all manner of suggestions of a non-political range"[50] of reform, encouraging Minto to be more flexible, more receptive to new ideas. Less than a month after taking office, for example, Morley advised the Viceroy to consider the possibility of appointing a really good sanitary expert as a member of his Executive Council, but Minto felt the suggestion premature, yet promised that "though it may not be possible to take it up immediately I will not lose sight of it."[51] Four years and countless millions of Indian deaths from plague, typhoid, and cholera later, nothing more was said or done by the Viceroy on this particular matter. Nor was Morley sufficiently alert to the disastrous dimensions of India's sanitation problems to prod his indifferent counterpart on the Indian scene to any more vigorous action. The mere combination of bureaucratic inertia and excessive daily burdens of routine work made it virtually impossible even for individuals with the best of intentions and the deepest of sympathy for Indian aspirations to do more than initiate change, as Morley did, in one or two areas at a time. It was not before December, 1907, for example, that Morley felt himself capable of "beginning to formulate ideas about education in India."[52] Early in 1908 he proposed to Minto the creation of a department of education to displace that of military supply on his council, but that suggestion was not realized until late in 1910. Appropriately enough, the member for education was given responsibility for affairs of local government as well.

An Oxford dropout himself, Morley never thought very highly of "Oxford training"[53] as preparation for Indian service. He favored legal training for all I.C.S. men, and spoke "very slightingly of the value of essays."[54] The major educational reforms he advocated were directed toward the encouragement of "more practical and technical instruction"[55] for Indians, and increased "comprehension of the ideals and traditions of the people"[56] of India by Englishmen. To further the former cause, Morley early sanctioned a recurring annual grant of Rs. 5 lakhs for expansion of the engineering college at Rurki; for the creation of an elementary school for handicrafts at Nagpur; for the development of the College of Science, the Victoria Technical Institution, and the School of Art in Bombay; and for the establishment of the Central Weaving School at Serampore in Bengal.[57] To stimulate British knowledge and understanding of India, Morley strongly supported the creation of a center for the study of oriental languages in London (known today as the School of Oriental and African Studies). Alfred Lyall was a member of Lord Redesdale's commission which proposed this singularly significant scholarly innovation in its report of 1909. Morley invited Lord Cromer to chair the committee established by government for implementation of the report through creation of a school for oriental languages at London University. Charles Hardinge, Minto's successor as viceroy, who was then still at the Foreign Office, agreed to join the Cromer Committee, since, as he wrote to Morley, "Having myself passed examinations some years ago both in Turkish and Russian, the question of the institution of a College for Oriental languages is one in which I take very great interest."[58] In supporting this proposal before the Lords, Morley noted: "It is very easy to talk, and we all of us talk, of the necessity of sympathy in dealing with the people of India. But sympathy means a good deal more than politeness and good manners, though that is something. . . . It means a knowledge and comprehension of the ideals and traditions of the people concerned. That is the point of view to which, I confess, I attach the highest value in the establishment of a College of this kind."[59]

Here again is the touchstone animating Morley's India policy—sympathy. Yet, unsupported as it was by firsthand experience in India or personal knowledge of Indian languages, it failed in areas of apolitical reform to probe effectively to the roots of India's complex problems and dynamically introduce the changes so urgently needed. What orders Morley issued, moreover, were left to be implemented by men in India who lacked his sympathetic motivation, and were themselves mostly ignorant of the languages and traditions of the country in which they served. Less than 2 million Indians knew any English at this time, and only 6 percent of the total population was sufficiently literate to write a brief letter in any language. Between British ignorance and Indian illiteracy yawned the chasm of violent unrest, militant discontent. As the Bishop of Lahore, whom Morley quoted as among "the most remarkable students of Indian matters it has ever been my fortune to come in contact with,"[60] put it:

A thoroughly good knowledge of an Eastern language is a primary condition that must be satisfied if a man is to come into easy and healthy contact with the people of the East, and . . . I feel perfectly certain that one cause of the difficulties that we are encountering in the present time in India is the failure on the part of so very many Englishmen out there to attain to any in the least accurate or scholarly knowledge of the vernaculars of that land, and the consequent impossibility of getting into close touch with the people.[61]

Like decentralization, however, Morley's educational reforms hardly matured, bearing little fruit of achievement by the end of his era. Yet, thanks to his foresight and interest, institutions were created both in India and in England designed to bridge the growing gulf of misunderstanding and distrust between Englishmen and Indians. Too little money was, however, invested in these educational experiments, for, nineteenth-century Liberal that he was, Morley believed as strongly in laissez faire as he did in parliamentary government.

10

LAISSEZ FAIRE VERSUS SVADESHI

Sufficient to the day is the work of the day. And I would say the same in reply to you, if you tell me that the time will come when India in the Councils will not stand the settlement of her budgets from this Office. I have long ago foreseen that such a result must come, and the insurgent Swadeshi will be transmogrified into a demand for a new tariff system, like the self-governing Colonies.
                Morley to Minto, April 19, 1910

The best description ever given of India was that it was a land of poverty-stricken people.
                J. Ramsay MacDonald to the House of Commons,
                July 26, 1910

Morley's economic and financial policy was a mid-Victorian mixture of laissez faire and retrenchment. His faith in the self-regulating "laws" of economics and finance helps explain his neglect of such questions throughout most of his tenure at Whitehall, despite the genuine conviction, as he early reported to Minto, that "questions of finance" were "according to my philosophy at the foundation of all things."[1] Good Gladstonian that he was, Morley paid more attention to retrenchment than to investment, publicly following, it would seem, the advice of Andrew Carnegie: "Take care of your Sixpences and the pounds will take care of themselves."[2] Only in his last year of office did Morley begin to appreciate the urgency and complexity of

India's economic plight, writing Minto then that he was "rather horrified to think that after all this long time of correspondence between us, I do not recall that you have ever spoken to me about Indian Finance."[3] The reproach was aimed as much at himself, for only a month later Morley confessed to Clarke, in speculating about topics of "future policy," "If the election, and my strength, and the stars, detain me where I am, it is upon Finance that I mean to concentrate."[4] Minto protested in self-defense, "I have never had a day without official work. . . . every letter I write to you is written under high pressure—so that if I have not broached Finance to you there is some reason for the omission!"[5] Problems of land revenue, settlements, and other such economic issues, moreover, were "amongst the most difficult problems with which the Government of India have to deal." Hence they were ignored.

Morley's failure to propose any meaningful economic reforms, and Minto's blatant disregard of the subject, which, since India's independence, has been the foremost concern of its government, offer more eloquent testimony to the inherent weakness and incapacity of British rule over India than did all the sound and fury raised about "unrest" and "repression." In no other realm of public affairs was the difference between British and Indian perspectives as wide, indeed as fundamentally irreconcilable, as in that of economic philosophy and financial policy. For India this was the dawn of an era of nationwide economic self-consciousness and agitation for economic self-sufficiency, the first flowering of the svadeshi (of our own country) movement.[6] Although Indian demands for fiscal reform, especially tariff protection for indigenous industries and opposition to the British "drain of wealth,"[7] long antedate the first partition of Bengal, it was only after 1905, in great measure as a reaction to Curzon's policy, that economic boycott and its natural counterpart svadeshi took root as popular movements under the leadership of Congress. Protection for indigenous industry became the "natural" economic interest of most articulate Indians, who viewed competition from Manchester as the major source of inhibition to Indian growth and development.

Morley's Liberal party, on the other hand, was not merely the traditional champion of laissez faire in Victorian Britain, but had, in good measure, come to power in the Edwardian era on its platform of economic freedom. Morley himself was among the most eloquent of his party's critics of Balfour's "Protective" policy, reminding the Commons, in 1904, that "the removal of protective duties has for more than half a century actively conduced to the vast extension of the trade and commerce of the realm and to the welfare of its population."[8] He cited the policy of free imports, following repeal of the Corn Laws, as the single most significant stimulus to Britain's industrial development, and hence "indispensable" to British commerce and human welfare. International economic competition free of all official restraints was seen as the healthiest incentive to national growth. The role of government was to pursue a policy of peace, retrenchment, and national education, and "leave as much freedom as possible for the application of capital, for the exercise of skill and industry, and the general operations of trade."[9] Such was the mainspring of Morley's economic philosophy, antipathetic in premise to that of India's svadeshi movement. There was really only one aspect of economic "reform" to which Morley addressed himself—retrenchment.

Retrenchment, of course, was a natural corollary of laissez faire, and Morley, like Gladstone, uncritically denounced "the mischiefs of the spirit of expenditure."[10] In typical pre-Keynesian fashion, he sought to "enrich" India through measures of "greater economy" which would allow government to "lighten taxation."[11] In guarding the public purse, he wrote of himself as "a real dragon, with horrible fangs and eyes of flame,"[12] and the savings he effected were hardly more realistic. His egalitarian conscience instinctively rebelled against the lavish waste of British-Indian pomp and princely pampering, and he admitted that, were he a backbencher rather than minister, "I would harry the government on such facts that the Durbar [held by Curzon at Delhi in 1903] cost India £360,000, and this year's visit of the Prince of Wales cost India £190,000."[13] On the eve of the Amir of Afghanistan's visit, he warned Minto against any exorbitant outlay of funds for mere ceremony, urging, "Let us put by for a *non*-rainy day."[14] Minto promised to keep expenditure on this entertainment "down" to within the equivalent of one year's subsidy to Afghanistan (Rs. 18 lakhs), but, after the visit, he wrote to apologize for having to present Morley with a "bill" amounting to almost a two-year subsidy, totaling some £230,000.[15] The government of India spent little more than this sum on all higher education for the year.[16] In 1908, when the Prime Minister of Nepal visited London, Morley insisted that the British Exchequer pay for his trip, since "Nepal is not India, and our hospitality to her Man is demanded by our noble Imperial instincts and interests. We spent a fortune last year upon our pampered Colonials at the Hotel Cecil and other quarters,—I never quite knew why.

The money extracted from India to pay for the Nepal P.M. will not be spent in India, but in England. So, in short, I have tackled Asquith [then chancellor of the exchequer]."[17]

Unfortunately, most of Morley's economy drives were of the "tuppeny-hapenny" variety. He vetoed Minto's attempt to add an extra gardener to Calcutta's Government House staff, for example, and denied the Viceroy's plea to raise the salary of his private secretary (Dunlop Smith) by Rs. 500 per month, insisting: "It is odious to me to play the skinflint... but after all we are trustees, and a trustee must harden himself."[18] He quite correctly came to feel, after some years of close contact with British India's "sun-dried" bureaucracy, that their salaries were "the most extravagant in the world,"[19] and spoke of the preretirement increase in Lawley's salary as "scandalous" and "unlawfully gotten plunder."[20] By appointing Fleetwood Wilson finance member of Minto's council, Morley introduced his own parsimonious "Treasury view" of expenditure into Simla's highly inflated atmosphere. The tragic misappropriation of India's meager revenue resources soon began to "haunt" the new minister of finance "day and night."[21] Whether he looked at the accounts of the Railway Board or of provincial governments, he found each and all of them "hopeless as to expenditure of public monies," noting that "Dane [Sir L. Dane, lieutenant governor of the Punjab] spent last year (when the province was all but declared famine-stricken and when the Punjab people were dying like flies) some £15,000 wrung from the taxpayers, and quasi-starving taxpayers on beautifying and enlarging his house. No wonder there is unrest."[22] Wherever possible, Wilson labored to reduce expenditure, strictly enforcing Morley's policy of keeping retirement salaries for British civil servants from being increased except for "very exceptional service" or "most exceptional merit."[23] He quickly became, as he knew, "the best hated man"[24] in British Indian society because of his "rigidly economical attitude," but, faced with near famine, trade depression, and falling revenue, Wilson labored desperately to balance his annual budget. The picture he drew of British luxury and extravagance at Simla, of the "absolutely indefensible" fortune lavished on homes like his Peterhof residence with ballroom, billiard room, and walnut-paneled dining room large enough to seat forty-two, and of the daily routine of "tennis and dancing" amid Indian poverty, famine, and plague, vividly revealed the gross imbalance of British India's economy. His well-intentioned efforts at retrenchment, like Morley's, were futile measures at pruning the extremities of a financial system, which should have been attacked at its deepest roots. The army, for one thing, continued to grow in size and expense, although time and again Wilson insisted[25] that its budget would have to be reduced if sanitation, education, and social reform were to receive anything like the necessary outlays of revenue each so urgently required.

Morley, as noted earlier (see chapter iv), hoped to effect significant retrenchment in military expenditure by reaching a rapprochement with Russia, but Simla raised the bugbear of unrest as soon as Whitehall had removed the specter of a Russian invasion. By 1906–07, practically all of India's £21.2 million of land revenue was consumed by military expenditure alone (£20.2 million).[26] Early in 1907, Morley's expert committee on special military expenditure, created to study Kitchener's scheme of army reorganization and strategic railway construction, reported that the five-year plan of special expenditure, launched in 1904 to counter "the possibility of hostile action by Russia,"[27] could safely be extended now over a ten-year period. The effect of thus prolonging the period of expenditure would be to allow an immediate reduction of some £.5 million per year in charges assigned against the revenue of India. Morley himself wanted to go further, to "stop strategical railways"[28] entirely, but even the mere suggestion of reduced military expenditure came as "a shock,"[29] which Minto and Kitchener tried their best to resist. Nonetheless, in his 1907 budget address[30] Morley was able to report the reduction in special military spending of some £500,000. A year later, however, he agreed to add £300,000 of Indian revenue to the cost of training English reservists by the War Office. Rarely was the economic inequity of India's subordination to Britain so clearly revealed as by this arbitrary extortion of Indian funds to help strengthen the imperial military machine, which kept her politically dependent. The added tribute to the War Office was made, moreover, in a year officially described as one of "famine and exceptional depression in trade"[31] for India. Had Morley been less sympathetic to Indian needs, less obsessive about retrenchment, less opposed to military expansion, or in a word, in any of these matters, less of a Liberal, his surrender to War Office demands would hardly have seemed surprising. Viewed in the light of his personal philosophy and other public actions, however, that capitulation can be explained only in terms of the most basic antipathy between British home and Indian interests.

In April, 1906, Morley was approached by his cabinet colleague

Richard Haldane,[32] who argued that India should pay more than £1 million per year (instead of £420,000) to the War Office for training British army reservists. When first reporting this War Office demand to Kitchener, Morley indicated the fundamental ambivalence of his own position: "It is my place, as the honest broker, to help to reconcile the general necessities of His Majesty's Government with the legitimate requirements of the India Department of that Government.... The difficulties are only too visible. The War Office wants more money from India. *I* want India to pay not more, but less, in military expenditure."[33] Minto readily conceded the justice in principle of the War Office claims, admitting that military expenditure "might, I should think, be distributed with greater regard to the pocket of Great Britain."[34] Surprisingly enough, however, Kitchener forcefully opposed Haldane's position, arguing that, although it was true that India relied upon support from reservists in England in time of war, it was equally true that "England regards the British Army in India as a potential assistance in time of need—as was shown in the case of South Africa."[35] Morley sent Kitchener's letter to the War Office, which replied in a memorandum that stated categorically: "India is a dependency of the British Crown, and our rule in India could not be maintained for a day without the moral and material support of the British Empire.... The principles of fair dealing enunciated by Lord Kitchener might be applicable enough to two independent states in alliance with each other. They are inapplicable to a dependency inhabited by alien races, our hold over which is not based on the general goodwill of those disunited races"[36] A home committee created (under Lord Justice Romer) to consider the matter agreed that India should pay more for British reservists' training; but the crucial question unresolved by 1908 was—how much? Haldane appealed to Morley in a personal letter, suggesting that "you and I close this case"[37] with an Indian payment of £350,000 in golden sovereigns to be added to the current India Office annual contribution. "I am so pressed for money that to secure a settlement I will drive this through," bargained the War Minister. Lionel Abrahams, financial secretary to the India Office, advised Morley that Haldane's demand was "unjustified" from a purely accounting expert's point of view, concluding that "to pay an additional £250,000 is extremely liberal."[38] A few weeks later, however, Morley and Haldane reached a "gentleman's agreement" to conclude their haggling by settling for an increase of £300,000 effective from May 1, 1908. The decision was clearly based solely on imperial–War Office needs, as naked an example of the plunder of Indian gold by British rule as any recorded since the days of Clive. With this one capricious surrender to British Cabinet interest, Morley abandoned most of the Indian revenue savings effected throughout his era by petty retrenchment.

Another example of the inexorable way in which India's dependent political status led to its financial exploitation may be seen in the negotiations between Morley and Sir Edward Grey[39] over the loan to Persia promised by the Foreign Office. Morley, who prided himself on being "not only that dismal creature, the Little Englander, but that even more dismal being, the Little Indian,"[40] favored, as already seen, a foreign policy of nonintervention and nonaggression for India. He saw no good reason for Indian diplomatic and military involvement in Persia, for one thing, and early sought to reduce or eliminate entirely India's contributions toward the support of Britain's ministerial establishment at Teheran, arguing, "I don't see why we should pay ½, for nothing."[41] The Shah's financial embarrassment, coupled with German diplomatic and commercial ambitions in Persia, led Grey to seek an agreement with Russia over Persia by which Britain and Russia would advance a substantial loan to the Shah in return for spheres of exclusive commercial interest. The Foreign Office, however, was as hard-pressed as the War Office to keep within its budgetary allotment, and Grey felt obliged to appeal for financial aid to the India Office. "The loan does not smile to me," Morley replied. "How can I—who am just opening a grand crusade for thrift at every turn—approve what may be a very risky speculation?"[42] Nonetheless, Morley conceded the "awkwardness" of driving Russia into Germany's arms in this area if Britain failed to come to the Shah's assistance, and therefore suggested that India would contribute money if the Anglo-Russian loan to Persia were made part of a more general Central Asian agreement. Thus, when Afghanistan and Tibet were tied to the Persian settlement under the Anglo-Russian Convention, India was committed to raise one half of Britain's half of the £4 million loan promised to Persia over a ten-year period as soon as the Shah would "pacify" his politically turbulent countrymen "with a Constitution."[43] Several months after the Persian parliament was convened in 1907, however, the Shah arrested his ministers, and the loan was therefore deferred. By 1908, when the Shah had revived hopes of a viable constitutional government, the question of the Anglo-Russian loan was revived as well, but by that time Morley admitted that had he been "rather more expert and wide-awake" when first promising Indian money to Grey, "I should have refused to let India risk a single rupee."[44] The Shah's treasury by then was empty, but India's financial position was hardly much stronger. Early in 1909 Grey pressed the India Office to meet its commitment, but Morley argued that "the question belongs to the F. O., and should be dealt with on your responsibility, without dragging in the poor untutored Indian."[45] A trenchant exchange of letters followed between the Foreign and Indian secretaries, in which Morley tried to release India from financial obligation to British imperial interests elsewhere, pleading, "I cannot feel disposed to use the money of my poor friends to extricate the Persian from his scrape."[46] He had considered the "great advantage" to India of the Persian portion of the Anglo-Russian Convention that securing the Seistan, Kerman, and Bunder Abbas triangle to British control would bring an "end" to India's Persian "engagements." He tried to present something of a legal brief on India's behalf: "One of the reasons why I did my best to help in the policy of the Anglo-Russian Convention was the expectation and implied promise (I mean in the facts of the policy) that India—after the settlement of the Seistan triangle—was done with Persia."[47] Grey replied that he would not have carried his negotiations "to the length he had with Russia"[48] except for Morley's promised support, and as a result, in 1909, India contributed £100,000 to the first installment of £400,000 of the international loan to Persia. In capitulating, however, Morley insisted that India would not be committed to any future payments designed to help bail out Britain's foreign dependents. "India ought not to find a rupee for the performance of a tune that India has not called, and has no particular taste or relish for,"[49] wrote Morley, as his final comment on the Persian loan fiasco.

Indeed, when Grey attempted to extract Indian financial support for subsidizing a British commercial combine in the Persian Gulf region to counter the threat of German competition from the Hamburg-Amerika line, Morley argued that "to ask India to contribute a half, or any other fraction, towards facilities for trade in the Gulf, is in fact to ask her to make things easier for her most formidable trade competitors."[50] He had successfully resisted attempts by the Admiralty to exact no less than an added £1.5 million annually from India for general "naval services," remarking, "Not one more pie or anna shall they have, unless they send the Dreadnought for it."[51] How then could he agree to ask "the Indian taxpayer" to support British commerce in the Gulf, a matter he was even less interested in "than he is in our general marine supremacy—to which we do not ask him to contribute?"[52] The inequity of this claim was so palpable that Morley concluded, "India ought not to contribute to anything in the Gulf except Muscat."[53] He came to sound much like the leaders of India's National Congress by the end of these negotiations, insisting that Britain had no right whatever to demand money from India "to keep German traders from competing with Manchester and Birmingham in the Gulf,—the Manchester and Birmingham traders being themselves, moreover, the great competitors in an overwhelming degree with the Indian trader."[54]

The inherent conflict of divided loyalties confronting Morley as His Majesty's minister for India extended in the realm of finance to India's opium production, which by this time had become the subject of international humanitarian concern. The official monopoly on opium production continued to provide India's government with one of its most lucrative sources of net income throughout this period.[55] Morley's closest friends in the Commons, including John Ellis, his first parliamentary under-secretary of state for India, were determined to press for the abolition of the opium trade, and, before this issue was debated in 1906, Morley cautioned Grey to be "very *non-committal* as to the views and intention's of H. M.'s government on the question of Indian Opium."[56] Grey, who was relieved to be unburdened of this matter, promptly replied "if you will take Opium (this sounds bad) I shall be delighted."[57] In April, 1906, Theodore Taylor moved in the Commons that "the Indo-Chinese opium trade is morally indefensible," and that government "take such steps as may be necessary for bringing it to a speedy close."[58] The motion was seconded by Dr. Rutherford, and received warm Liberal support. Morley himself admitted the deleterious medical effects of opium, and lauded the American decision to outlaw its use in the Philippines after 1908, but he opposed the motion on the grounds that India's economy could not afford the immediate loss of more than £3 million in revenue. "His honourable friends talked about retrenchment," Morley declaimed. "Nobody was more disposed to work ardently for retrenchment than he was. But let them get their retrenchment first and then give up opium."[59] He caustically asked if members of the house were prepared to have England's Exchequer shoulder the added revenue load. The answer was all too obvious. Morley then confessed that since his appointment to the India Office "the question of questions to him was whether a Parliamentary democracy would govern wisely and beneficently... so vast and complex a dependency as the Indian Empire?"[60] In concluding, he warned that they must be "very careful" not to allow their own "righteous sentiments" to "do wrong to the people living in India." Parliament had "no right," he insisted, "to place on them burdens, which, if they [the Indians] were represented here ... their interests and their habits and customs would predispose them not to accept."[61] Taylor's motion was carried, however, and after the debate Morley urged Grey to appeal to the Chinese government to seek more effectively to restrict opium imports and consumption. He also ordered the government of India to cut Bengal poppy cultivation back to the 1901 "standard" of 48,000 chests' worth, and welcomed America's invitation to join the international Opium Commission, which led to The Hague Opium Convention of 1912. Starting with 1908, Indian shipments of opium to China were reduced by more than 5,000 chests yearly, and in 1915 the trade was officially brought to an end for all but "medicinal purposes." Morley's role in helping end the poisonous trade was not insignificant, but he pursued his line with typical moderation and caution, summed up in his advice to the anti-opium delegation which called on him in 1907: "When you are at the top of the house and want to get to the bottom there are two ways of doing so," he said. "You can throw yourself out of a window, or you can go downstairs. *I* prefer to go downstairs."[62]

The most obvious and notorious economic conflicts of interest between Britain and India naturally centered on the "Home charges" and commerce and industry, or what were popularly referred to in India as the political and commercial "drains." By 1909 the concept of economic drain had become so widespread throughout India that the Undersecretary of State felt obliged to take note of it in his budget address to the Commons. The charge was "constantly made,"[63] he explained, that Indian poverty was due to an annual political drain of some £30 million, and a commercial drain of about £40 million. In attempting to refute the charge as without "foundation in fact," the Master of Elibank[64] noted that, over the past three years, the average annual "Home charges" actually came to no more than £21.2 million. Of this total, £5 million went to pensions and furlough pay for British civil and military officers; £9.5 million were required to service the British capital debt (some £265 million had been invested in railway construction alone up to the end of 1907); another £2.5 million were spent on stores purchased from England (mostly for the railways); and the remaining amount was divided between the sum remitted to defray capital charges in England and "miscellaneous" items. To the Indian nationalist these charges were exorbitant, largely unnecessary, and, so far as India's economy was concerned, unfruitful, especially with respect to the wealth showered on pensions and furloughs spent in a foreign land. The English official justification, on the other hand, was based on the formula of "payment for services rendered." Instead of some £40 million of commercial "drain," the Undersecretary insisted that the average annual amount of "private remittances" in British commercial profits and savings was only £2.7 million. The higher figure was based on the average value of Indian exports, mostly raw materials, in excess of the total annual value of imports, consisting mostly of manufactured goods from Britain. Once again, from the Indian perspective, this drain of food, cotton, jute, and so on was attributable to Britain's industrial advantage over India and British refusal to protect infant Indian industries by erecting tariff barriers against Manchester. Anglo-Indian law and official practice were seen as the cohorts of British private investors, the defenders of British capital, whose "free" and therefore naturally "unfair" competition had arrested India's industrial development, keeping the Indian economy overwhelmingly dependent upon the sole and precarious "industry" of agriculture. As even the most moderate of nationalist leaders, Dr. Rash Behari Ghose, put it: "The 'brightest jewel in the British Crown' must not be regarded merely as a market for British goods or a field for the safe investment of British capital or as opening a dignified career to 'our boys.' "[65] To British eyes, contrarily, British capital had been instrumental in "developing" India's commercial resources and "providing employment for the masses of people in that great continent."[66] An estimated total of some £350 million of British capital investment in India was seen as the foremost asset of India's economy, and the profit derived from that sum was hardly considered disproportionate.

There were, of course, many Britons in the Commons who recognized the economic roots of Indian unrest, and regularly inveighed against the economic inequities of British rule. Members like C. J. O'Donnell, F. C. Mackarness, Keir Hardie, and J. O'Grady called for radical reforms in taxation, pleading the Indian nationalist cause in Westminster. As O'Grady saw it, the first and greatest cause of "Indian unrest" was "poverty; then there was famine, plague, ignorance of the masses, excessive taxation, and certainly the discouragement of executive ability."⁶⁷ Mr. A. Lupton of Lincolnshire, Sleaford, was more explicit in his attack, arguing that the "first thing a good Government should do was to see that its people were well-fed and not half-starved; and how could the people be well-fed when the income of the natives over great parts of India was only ½ d. per day? That was the glorious Empire in India which the House was asked to uphold."⁶⁸ He then noted that in the past two decades the Indian land revenue had gone up some 32 percent; military expenditure had increased by 50 percent, and the cost of the civil service, by 51 percent. Indian wages on the average were one-fortieth of British wages, and India's total income was less than one-sixth that of the United Kingdom. No official challenged Lupton's statistics. Indeed, there was no conflict among Englishmen concerning the facts of Indian poverty. The years 1907–1909 were among the most depressed in the twentieth century,⁶⁹ with the specters of famine and plague stalking the heartland of north India's United Provinces and the Punjab, and a general depression of trade casting its economic shadow across the country. The trade depression in some measure attested to the success of the svadeshi and boycott movements, for, even after the famine of 1907–08 had ended, and food grains were exported most vigorously (the value of exports in 1909–10 was £123 million, compared with £100 million the year before), imports continued to fall (from some £86 million in 1908–09 to a new low of £82 million in 1909–10).⁷⁰ Members like J. D. Rees understood all too well what India's struggle for economic self-sufficiency meant to British pocketbooks, warning from the forum of the House: "Surendranath Bannerjee [sic] is again on the stump on the boycott. That means the exclusion of all British goods from India—cottons from Manchester, and so on. I should like to ask hon. Gentlemen who gained their seats as Free Traders how it is that they are strongly in favour of protection in India. Do their constituents know that it means no boots from Nottingham and no beer from Brentford?"⁷¹

The leader of the Congress "lobby" in the Commons, Sir Henry Cotton, openly charged, nonetheless, that the government of India's harshest repressive measures, especially its mass deportation in 1908 of Hindus from Bengal under the notorious act of 1818, were aimed not at stifling violence, but rather at crushing svadeshi, or what "is known in England as Tariff Reform. What is regarded as a patriotic movement in England is sedition in India," insisted Sir Henry. "The real offence of these men is that they were the leaders, the animators, of this movement in favour of encouraging the manufacture and consumption of country-made goods and the discouragement of foreign importations."[72]

Curzon himself, showing, Morley thought, "a most mischievous want of tact and decent judgment," admitted before the Lords "that Indian fiscal policy is settled and decided, not at all at Calcutta, but in Manchester: not in Indian interests, but English."[73] It would have been, as Morley feared, a "handsome present to make to Svadeshi" had any Indian nationalists been willing to risk the consequences of quoting their nemesis in support of their cause. The sacred cow of Anglo-Indian fiscal policy, of course, was that tariff should be levied only for "revenue purposes," never for "protection." The import duty of 3.5 percent ad valorem imposed on cotton manufactured goods was thus matched by an equal excise on cottons produced in India. The way in which pressures were exerted by British merchants and manufacturers to preserve "free" trade was seen in 1910, when, in order to balance the budget Indian customs duties had to be raised on liquor and tobacco. The increased tariff on imported liquor was immediately matched by an excise at precisely the same rate on India-made beer. Imported tobacco alone, however, was to be taxed an additional £420,000, for, as Montagu explained, Indian tobacco was of too "poor quality" to compete with the imported article. He felt obliged to promise, nonetheless, that "the desirability and possibility of a corresponding Excise will always be considered."[74] Morley, moreover, as he "expected," found that the increased tax on tobacco "has caused a bitter cry to reach my ears from the cigarette manufacturers at Bristol and Liverpool—orders from India cancelled, people thrown out of work, the British soldier in India to pay threepence a week instead of a penny for his innocent joys, and so forth."[75] The conflict was one of competing national interests in which British workers and even the most pro-Indian Labor party members of Parliament found themselves allied to Manchester's mill owners. Keir Hardie, for example, in urging state supervision of labor conditions in Bombay's textile mills, argued in the Commons: "The product of those mills was bound to be an increasing product and to come into increased competition with goods produced at home; therefore it was better from the point of view of the home industry that the condition of the Indians who were employed should not be such as to give an unfair advantage to the mill owners."[76] A deputation of Lancashire textile workers called upon Morley in 1906 to ask him to send a factory inspector from London to study labor conditions in Bombay's mills, where, as everyone knew, children were employed full time under the least healthy of conditions. Morley welcomed the suggestion for the "raising of standards"[77] from a humanitarian point of view, but, ironically enough, it was Minto who rightly pointed out that sending "an Inspector from home would be very unpopular amongst the section of the population represented by Gokhale and other Congress leaders. However bona fide in a benevolent sense the intention of such inspection might be, it would, I am afraid, be impossible here to avoid Indian opinion jumping to the conclusion that interested motives were at the bottom of it."[78] The paradoxical forces of imperial economics thus at times made strange bedfellows of Tory viceroys and Indian nationalists who found themselves allied against Socialist workers and Liberal M.P.'s in the camp of British industrialists.

The only measure of economic reform introduced by Morley which met with the approval of a broad segment of Indian opinion was reduction of the salt tax. Since 1888, when the tax on salt was sharply increased to make up for a deficit caused by the removal of several customs duties, Congress had annually called for the reduction of this tax, whose incidence fell most onerously upon the impoverished peasant population. Not until 1903, however, was any remission granted, when Curzon finally agreed to reduce the tax on Indian-made salt from Rs. 2.5 per maund (*ca.* 82 lbs. in Bengal) to Rs. 2. Congress tendered its "thanks,"[79] but pressed for further remission. For political as well as economic reasons, Morley favored lower taxation, which might naturally be seen as the other side of his retrenchment drive. The first such reduction he urged upon Minto was "total repeal" of the salt tax, to "make your government memorable, and your name great."[80] He called Minto's attention to scientific speculation concerning a possible link between the salt tax, which prevented "proper fish-curing,"[81] and leprosy. The government of India merely conceded a half-rupee reduction, but, at any rate, Morley was able to open his first budget address to the Commons by announcing that remission, stating he could no longer regard "with patience, the continuance at a high scale of a tax on a prime necessity of life."[82] Six months later Minto's Executive Council was willing to approve a further reduction of half a rupee on salt for 1907–08 since, as the Viceroy noted, "It is in itself good, but we felt too that it was necessary to get rid of some of our surplus to protect ourselves from the assumption by the anti-opium people that we are too wealthy to cavil at any reduction of our revenue."[83] By mid-1907, then, the salt tax was back to its low level of R. 1 per maund. There were, however, no further remissions, for the summer of 1907 was the start of a drought that cost the government of India more than £3 million in suspended land revenue and famine relief projects. Within the year almost 1 million people in the United Provinces alone were obliged to survive on famine relief, and more than 1 million more Indians died of bubonic plague.[84]

The tragically precarious dependence of India's economy on its monsoon rains grimly supported the svadeshi cry for indigenous industrial development. Although Minto paid lip service to the home industry movement by opening the second Industrial and Agricultural Exhibition at Calcutta in December, 1906 (the first had been held in 1901), the government of India's laissez-faire policy in this realm was made clear by the Viceroy's "promise of support" to all Indians "earnestly endeavouring to develop home industries in an *open market*" (emphasis added).[85] At best, the government offered mild encouragement to Indian entrepreneurs like J. N. Tata, who launched India's first iron and steel company in 1907 with all Indian capital totaling more than £1.5 million and an entirely Indian board of directors. The government promised to purchase some 20,000 tons of steel rails annually from Tata for ten years, but only if they met official specifications, subject to "competitive pricing."[86] It was not until five years later that Tata started his first blast furnace. Less wealthy, patient, and persevering Indians were generally unable to withstand British competition in the "open market," and many of those who actively joined in the boycott of British goods were harassed by officials, as Sir Henry Cotton noted.

British merchants and private investors warned Morley in 1908 that "investors are fighting shy of India,"[87] and less British capital was "being invested in its industries, and development, and retarding the commercial advancement of the country."[88] Some English businessmen were enlightened enough to prescribe the remedy of popular education in "self-government"[89] to allay the unrest which was making capital so "sensitive" about Indian risks that recent attempts to float private loans by the Calcutta Rangoon Port Trust and the Southern Punjab Railway "have fallen very flat."[90] The predominant feeling among British merchants and planters, however, was that "in oriental countries kindness is invariably interpreted as fear, and weakness is looked upon with contempt."[91] They advocated harsher measures of repression, including a general press act and licensing requirements for all private schools, to wipe out "hotbeds of sedition."[92] By 1909 the position of Indian securities on the London market had "altered for the worse," because (in the Bank of England's opinion) of the "recent unrest."[93] As a result of this depressed market, a £7.5 million loan of 3.5 percent stock, floated in London to provide funds for Indian railway construction and the discharge of debentures, had to be entirely underwritten at the exorbitant commission of 1.25 percent (£94,000), which was charged against Indian revenues. Several months later the market for government of India "Paper" had become so "dull" that the annual rupee loan of 2.5 crores (£1.66 million) could be raised at the Bank of Bengal only by offering the largest discount "on record"[94] for any 3.5 percent loan floated in British India. The total discount again was charged to Indian revenues, which, in this as all other eras of Indian history, meant primarily the land.

The high cost of India's civil and military establishment, coupled with the paucity of industrial development, placed the heaviest burden of Indian revenue upon its impoverished peasantry. With the exception of Bengal, where Cornwallis' permanent settlement of 1793 had fixed the government's claim on landowners in perpetuity, British demands upon the fruits of India's soil were subject to regular reassessment (usually every ten or thirty years). The pressure of increased population and the spread of irrigation extended and enhanced the value of Indian land throughout the epoch of British rule, and, since official policy was to treat the land revenue as a "rent" based on value, revenue assessments steadily increased with rising land values in proportion to increased agricultural assets. The deleterious effect of such a policy upon the peasant's initiative and the cultivator's desire to improve his holdings and maximize his output, thereby leaving him more vulnerable to tragedy in years of famine and more dependent upon moneylenders because of his inability to retain any reserve of crops or funds, had been annually called to the attention of the government of India by Congress resolutions since 1891.[95] Congress leaders like Romesh Dutt, who devoted their talents and energies to careful study of the land problem,[96] urged extension of the permanent settlement to all India as a practical first step in the fight against agricultural poverty. By 1906, however, no such action had been taken, and in this crucial matter Morley's policy showed no departure from Curzon's; in his first budget address he announced that the land revenue was to be raised by £1.5 million. Only three months earlier Gokhale had warned from the Viceroy's council at Calcutta:

> There is ample evidence to show that over the greater part of India—especially in the older Provinces—the agricultural industry is in a state of deep depression. The exhaustion of the soil is fast proceeding, the cropping is becoming more and more inferior, and the crop-yield per acre, already the lowest in the world, is declining still further. And such a deterioration in agricultural conditions is accompanied by an increase in the land-revenue demand of the State! The raiyat [peasant] staggers under the burden.[97]

Despite the famine years that followed, when land revenue was perforce suspended entirely in many districts, the total demand continued inexorably to rise: from £18.7 million in 1907–08 to £19.7 million in 1908–09 and to £21.3 million in 1909–10.[98] "I believe the prosperity of the country as well as the stability of our rule depend more on the quality and quantity of our land assessment than on anything else," warned Dunlop Smith in a "Note on Land Assessment in the Punjab" in 1907, urging Minto that "the time has come to reconsider our revenue policy."[99] The Viceroy sent the note to Morley, who wrote in red ink on the top margin, "Most important: making Policy, in its widest sense, the true test of administration—a principle that it is the very essence of Bureaucracy, even the best intentioned, to ignore."[100] Yet nothing was done to lighten the load on India's peasantry. Morley's failure to act in this matter, and the financial inability of British rule to function without reaping its revenue so heavily from Indian harvests of scarcity, were perhaps the clearest proof of the inherent failure of British imperialism in India. The monumental failure of the raj, for all its nobly exalted efforts and petty piecemeal reforms, and its ultimate destiny of historic fall, were pithily summarized in Ramsay MacDonald's statement to the Commons, after nearly one century of British paramountcy: "The best description ever given of India was that it was a land of poverty-stricken people."[101]

Morley's faith in "the self-adjustments of ordinary economic laws"[102] was hardly an adequate substitute for the sort of financial policy India required. He adhered to laissez faire, however, rather than embarking upon "a policy of excessive interference,"[103] as much out of desperation as conviction. When Fleetwood Wilson suggested in 1909 that government should undertake an inquiry into the general rise of prices, Morley frankly confessed that "for the moment we have as many things going in Indian government as we can manage, and this might start a new hare that would give us a long chase.... Questions of price bring us straight into questions of wage and salary and land revenues, and only the direct intervention of the Most High could keep currency out of the melting pot."[104] It was easier to leave such things alone. Perhaps, if he had been vouchsafed another five years at Whitehall, Morley would in fact have launched a program of economic and financial reforms as far-reaching as the political and constitutional measures to which he devoted most of his time and talent. He certainly recognized, by the end of his tenure, that India's economic plight could not be divorced from its political turmoil and unrest. In 1909 he wrote Minto: "it is a fixed belief with me that you almost always find an economic cause at the root of political discontent. And in Bengal, I am given to understand that the middle classes from which the politicians come, have in most or many cases fixed incomes, e.g. wages of Government and Zemindari [great landowner] services, and these people have been hard hit by the rise in prices, which of course is laid to the discredit of Government."[105]

By 1910, moreover, both Fleetwood Wilson and Chief Justice Jenkins, Morley's most trusted advisers in India, were alerting him to the need for radical economic reform. Jenkins indeed strongly advocated technical education for young Indians: "We should train them for productive occupations and pursue towards India a policy that will enable industries to come into existence; this I fear is heresy, for is it not Swadeshi? but the longer I am here the more I feel that it is only by a move in this direction that we can lay the demon that is amongst us."[106] There were equally practical and forthright suggestions in the Commons, like that of George Lloyd several months later: "You must step along the path of industrial development in India or you will be driven along it.... There is notably the case of the sugar industry. At the present moment India can grow any quantity of sugar, but as a matter of fact, the larger proportion of the sugar that is consumed comes from outside."[107] India's cry of svadeshi had thus found forceful spokesmen among Britons in London as well as Calcutta, but throughout this era official economic "policy" was really no more than a futile holding action, the tacit affirmation of an intolerable status quo.

11

THE PAST AS PROLOGUE

> No one supposes that under present conditions India could stand alone. She possesses all the materials for Self-Government; an ancient civilization; reverence for authority; an industrious and law-abiding population; abundant intelligence among the ruling classes. But she lacks training and organization. A period of apprenticeship is necessary, but that period need not be very long, if the leaders of the people set themselves to work in harmony. Hand in hand with the British people, India can most safely take her first steps on the new path of progress.
>
> William Wedderburn, Presidential Address to the Indian National Congress, Allahabad, December, 1910

On Monday afternoon, November 7, 1910, Morley handed the seals of his office to the Earl of Crewe and left Whitehall without fanfare, departing solitary in a modest hansom for his home at Wimbledon, beyond the Thames. None of the whirlwind series of farewell balls and glittering dinners which marked Minto's last weeks at Simla, nor the gun-booming pomp and pageantry which would welcome Hardinge to Calcutta's Government House two weeks later, accompanied the change of Whitehall's India Office guard. But long after the glitter of Minto's memory had faded in India, and the old soldier had returned to "my own Borderland," as he so appropriately phrased it, to "bury my head in the heather,"[1] Morley's legacy to India remained untarnished, his stature and fame continued to grow. "Every word you have uttered on this country is practically known by heart by every Indian in it," wrote Fleetwood Wilson to his friend in 1913. "They cling to every word you said when you were at the India Office, and I am telling you the simple truth when I say that you are as revered in this country as is the memory of Mr. Gladstone. It is impossible to say more."[2] We have but to look at the presidential addresses[3] to India's National Congress for half a decade following Morley's retirement for ample corroboration of Wilson's tribute.

The persistent power of Morley's impact upon India's intellectual elite, for all his shortcomings and failures, was more than a mere by-product of literary style or mental agility. The reverence he received from so many Indian leaders who lived through his era and appreciated the transition it marked in the history of Anglo-Indian relations was as well deserved as that which enshrined Allan Octavian Hume's memory[4] in the annals of Indian history. Just as Hume diagnosed the malignant condition of Indian frustrations in 1885 as potentially fatal to British India's body politic, founding the National Congress as a "safety-valve" for the expression of Indian political discontent and aspirations, thereby launching India's nationalist movement, so did Morley understand the explosive nature of Indian despair in the wake of Curzon's regime, and by his policy of reforms brought Congress' moderate leadership into direct association with India's government. Thus Wedderburn could remind India in 1910 that "Lord Morley's beneficent measures have followed Congress lines,"[5] and two years later, from the presidential rostrum of Congress as well, R. N. Mudholkar was able to say: "You want a Parliamentary form of Government. Your Legislative Councils are even now Parliaments *in embryo*. It rests with your representatives to secure their full growth."[6] To revolutionary nationalists, of course, Morley's achievement, like Hume's, was seen as hardly more than a diplomatic holding action of British duplicity, an administrative expedient that released the pressure of popular protests with "a crumb of bread tossed onto our body,"[7] as Tilak put it in denouncing what he called Gokhale's "politics of begging." Similar criticism, however, was, and indeed continues to be, levied against the acts of 1919 and 1935, which some Indians dismiss with the Act of 1909 as "equally devoid of any substance."[8] Yet each of these constitutional reforms helped prepare India in progressive stages for the self-government achieved in 1947 under Congress leadership.

The significance of Morley's achievement can perhaps best be appreciated through the perspective of changed relations between British officials and Indians at the beginning and end of this era. When reviewing Curzon's viceroyalty in December, 1905, Gokhale quite accurately noted, "Never was discontent in India more acute and widespread than when the late Viceroy laid down the reins of office."[9] Popular political aspirations were ignored entirely. Congress was contemned by the haughty Viceroy. The bureaucracy had never been more firmly entrenched and exalted. Morley's intimate association with moderate Congress leadership from the start of his tenure, his insistence upon a policy of legislative council reform, his appointments of Indians to the highest executive councils, his unremitting assault against bureaucracy and military autocracy—all served to restore faith and hope in the promises of British equality of opportunity among the most influential moderate leaders of Indian society. By 1910 the most hidebound of bureaucratic officials admitted that the "clouds are plainly lifting.... It is easier, than I have known it in 20 years, for loyal men to proclaim their loyalty.... The policy of the reforms has borne swift fruit."[10] The death of Edward VII in May, 1910, was followed in Calcutta by a mass demonstration of mourning which Minto himself found "most remarkable," for leaders of the svadeshi and antipartition movements like Surendra Nath Banerjea, Bhupendra Nath Basu, and Moti Lal Ghose were all "on bended knees before a picture of the King-Emperor!"[11] John Lewis Jenkins, the new Home member of Minto's council, informed the Viceroy in June, 1910, that "people who knew India five years ago are quite incapable of judging the present position; that the political change has been enormous.... He says that the fairly educated Indians and mercantile and business classes generally were thoroughly dissatisfied with the old order of things, and in answer to my question as to what would have happened if we had determined not to recognize the change, he replied we should have had a revolution."[12]

There is no way of ascertaining whether or not the alternative to Morley's policy of reforms would have been open warfare against the Indian population as a whole, although, with Kitchener's military machine and British experience gained since 1857, there could be little doubt concerning the outcome of any mass revolutionary assault against the raj at that time. The repressive measures taken against mere "unrest" were terrible enough, but some indication of how the government of India would have responded to revolution was given in

August, 1910, when Minto reported "the unravelling of a very old conspiracy and a very curious one which is only now coming to light. It is a story of an organized system of rebellion commencing as far back I think as 1905—a rebellion which if it had ever come to a head at all could as far as I can see have resulted in nothing but assassination and some tremendous retribution on our part. A rebellion in the Bengals without the assistance of the Army is an impossibility."[13] Fortunately, both for India and Britain, there was no need to test Minto's assurance in this matter. At the end of 1910, instead of rebellion raging through India, Congress met at Allahabad with Morley's old friend, Sir William Wedderburn, at its head concluding his speech with the promise, "Hand in hand with the British people, India can most safely take her first steps on the new path of progress."[14] Lord Hardinge, Morley's appointee as viceroy, then broke with the tradition of his predecessors by officially receiving a Congress deputation at Government House, an "act of kindness and grace," as the next president, Bishan Narayan Dhar, called it, which "was universally appreciated and applauded at the time and will always be gratefully remembered by the people."[15] The second session of the central legislative council then convened at Calcutta proceeded, as Hardinge wrote Morley in March, "extremely well and there seems to be a distinctly good feeling amongst all the Members of Council. I have given them the fullest opportunities for talking and blowing off steam."[16] Admittedly, with its official majority, the central legislative council remained little more than a forum from which Indians could voice their grievances, much as they had done before at Congress sessions. For some years, no doubt, the reforms at this center of power were more therapeutic and educational in value than politically effective. Hardinge frankly confessed as much, noting: "The non-official Members have put forward all sorts of resolutions during the past session, which is a useful indication of the trend of thought in this country. They knew perfectly well that their resolutions would not and could not be accepted, but it is a great safety-valve for them to be able to air their views."[17] Indeed, within half a year of Morley's resignation, so much had changed for the better in the atmosphere of India, thanks to the timely reforms introduced during Morley's era, that Hardinge was "quite convinced that, were Curzon to return to India, he would hardly recognize the present situation."[18]

Reforms, however, were but the bright side of this turbulent era, harsh repression its darker face. The deportation of Lajpat Rai without trial, and of Tilak after conviction for "sedition," cast a pall of repressive tyranny over the actions of the government of India in this half decade that no measures of constitutional concession would erase from Indian memory. Morley's personal conviction that both cases were unjust as well as unwise hardly exonerate him for tolerating the former as long as he did and taking no action whatever to reverse the latter. If anything, the dichotomy between his personal judgment and public inaction only add to his culpability, since it cannot even be said that he, unlike Ibbetson, Minto, and Clarke, believed such repression would silence revolutionary opposition. By sanctioning a series of harsh legislative measures against the press, free assembly, and the hard-won safeguards to individual freedom under common law, moreover, Morley closed his eyes to cherished principles of liberty and justice, as whose champion he had won worldwide fame and adulation. Throughout this era British Liberal and Labor leaders defended Indian freedoms with direct quotations from the writings and speeches of John Morley. Sir Henry Cotton, after quoting a blistering attack against Irish coercion bills, added, with most telling irony, "These are the words of our master ... that was the language used by Lord Morley."[19] Ramsay MacDonald concluded his brilliant eulogy on liberty of the press, which was strangled by the Indian Press Act of 1910, with a personal appeal to the "Secretary of State, one whom I for one honor myself by calling one of my teachers."[20] As has been seen, of course, Morley felt more keenly than anyone the bitter remorse of his surrender to the gods of "Reason of State," accepting his fall from the grace of Liberalism's conscience as the price of office. Nor did he tire of working to bridle by persuasion the bureaucracy over which he ruled, but, just as withholding political reforms might have driven India to open rebellion, so, too, might Morley's total veto over Simla's addiction to repression have driven Anglo-Indian officialdom to "revolt" against Whitehall. The most obvious immediate effect of any adamant refusal on Morley's part to permit the government of India to play its autocratic game would certainly have been retraction on the part of Minto and his council of all support for reform legislation. The House of Lords would then have made short work of any bills introduced by the Indian secretary. London's press, moreover, would have clamored for Morley's withdrawal from so sensitive an imperial post on the cabinet. Bureaucratic wrath and hostility might at the same time have goaded India to revolution, and Kitchener alone would then have been in a position to decide India's fate.

History, however, performs no "reruns" in which to test alternative courses of action. To understand what actually happened is difficult enough; to hypothesize about what might have been is impossible. Nor is the above speculation offered as an apology for, or vindication of, Morley's unprincipled action, but only as a possible explanation of why he chose the middle path of "order plus progress" rather than the latter extreme. After the Act of 1909 had passed the Lords, he was certainly less tolerant of Minto's repressive actions, ordering release of the nine Bengali deportees, and refusing absolutely to sanction further deportations. When a warrant was issued for Aurobindo Ghose's arrest in April, 1910, Morley at once informed Minto that the "summary of the article given in the *Times* does not seem to make it an incitement to murder,"[21] and soon after wrote: "So far as I can make out, the article (so far back as last X-mas) simply paraded passive resistance and abstention from taking part in public life. That may be as odious and objectionable as you please. But it is at least doubtful whether any decent court will find it to be *sedition*. . . . Nothing will induce me to defend such work. As for deportation, I will not listen to it."[22] To mark the coronation of George V, Morley recommended a general amnesty for all political prisoners in India as "Clemency of the Crown,"[23] but Minto could "only say that under existing conditions it is an impossibility."[24] So the struggle between Whitehall and Simla continued to the bitter end, Minto righteously insisting, "We are not tyrants in India! The Raj has always proudly relied on its reputation for justice!"[25]

By 1910, however, for all the repressive weapons that remained in the arsenal of India's government, the spirit of sympathy and equality of opportunity which Morley had labored to instill in the bureaucracy he was unable to overthrow had clearly begun to make itself felt. Although Minto admitted that "Indian official opinion is naturally conservative, and the views of a Collector or Commissioner . . . are not likely to be based upon a broad political outlook,"[26] the proven capacity of men like Sinha and Gupta served to establish "the principle that qualified Indian ability can fairly look forward to a share in the executive government of this country."[27] The executive councils of Bombay, Madras, and Bengal each had Indian members as well now, and, although racial prejudice dies slowly in any country, Curzon's exaltation of "White supremacy" had at least been overthrown "in principle" during Morley's era. Then, too, instead of elevating Anglo-India's most powerful bigot, Lord Kitchener, to the viceroyalty, Morley replaced Minto with as liberal and broad-minded a viceroy as India had known since the reign of Ripon. Lord Hardinge at Simla and Edwin Montagu at Whitehall were indeed not the least of Morley's legacies to India. The I.C.S., however, continued to throw up men who attained positions of power, like J. L. Jenkins, the Home member, for whose promotions Morley confessed, "I ought to be impeached (like Warren Hastings)."[28] He could "only hope," as he wrote to Hardinge, "that a powerful Viceroy and a courageous Legislative Council will teach your mimic Scroggs or Jeffreys to mend his manners. It rejoices my heart to read in your letter to Crewe, how you pulled Jenkins up for his culpable folly about the Night Searches [in Eastern Bengal and Assam]."[29] While Minto's insistence that the partition of Bengal could not be reversed without destroying Indian faith in British judgment had strongly influenced Morley in his blunder of leaving partition "a settled fact," Hardinge had the wisdom and courage to report by August, 1911, that "the bitterness of feeling engendered by the Partition of Bengal is both widespread and unyielding,"[30] which led in December to Bengal's reunification by royal proclamation at Delhi.

Morley's policy of decentralization and the self-governing potential established by his revolutionary overthrow of official majorities in provincial legislative councils was soon made the explicit goal of British policy by both his heirs to Indian power. Hardinge's dispatch to Whitehall of August 25, 1911, stated:

It is certain that in the course of time, the just demands of Indians for a large share in the Government of the country will have to be satisfied, and the question will be how this devolution of power can be conceded without impairing the supreme authority of the Governor-General in Council. The only possible solution of the difficulty would appear to be, gradually to give the provinces a larger measure of self-government, until at last India would consist of a number of administrations autonomous in all provincial affairs with the Government of India above.[31]

Montagu publicly supported this policy in his speech at Cambridge in February, 1912, insisting: "That statement shows the goal, the aim towards which we propose to work.... At last and not too soon a Viceroy has had the courage to state the trend of British policy in India and the lines on which we intend to advance."[32] That trend had been initiated by Morley. Begun in his era, it bore fruit through the patient and faithful pursuit of his policies by his young disciples. Although Curzon continued desperately to fight against Montagu's efforts at home, the prow of British imperial policy, whose Liberal direction was set toward the shore of Indian self-government by Morley, could never again be reversed by Tory reaction.

Yet, for all the beneficent reforms he introduced to India, and for all the bloodshed and tragedy he may have averted both within and beyond its frontiers, Morley's capitulation to the separate electorate demand of Muslims only helped intensify communal tensions and conflict, while his failure to sponsor economic reforms did nothing to alleviate Indian poverty. In the balance of history, that which is left undone may at times outweigh the sum total of any statesman's noble as well as ignoble actions, and for Morley this indeed was true of the missing factor of economic innovation. His decision on communal electorates was, like his sanctioning of repressive measures, based on the expedient acceptance of politics as at best a second best. His lack of an economic policy, however, was rooted in imperial self-interest, Liberal and Tory alike. The most sympathetic, hardworking, and Liberal (in every sense of that word) statesman ever to rule over the Indian Empire was thus "powerless" to improve, in any meaningful way, the impoverished status of the some 300 million subjects whose destinies he guided. His failure in this regard underscores the historic incompatibility of Britain and India and the ultimate untenability of British imperial rule. Or, as Morley himself confessed in one of his last official letters to Hardinge (during Crewe's illness), "I am never quite sure that if Clive had been beaten at Plassey, 't might have been no bad thing either for Indians or English."[33]

REFERENCE MATERIAL

ABBREVIATIONS

BM	British Museum
HD	The Diary of Frederick Arthur Hirtzel, Vols. I–IV, VI (clippings), India Office Library, Home Miscellaneous Series, 864
HPDHC	Hansard's Parliamentary Debates, House of Commons
HPDHL	Hansard's Parliamentary Debates, House of Lords
IO	India Office
JM	John Morley
JMP	John Morley Papers, India Office Library, MSS Eur. D. 573
JSM	Collection of Papers and Correspondence of John Stuart Mill, British Library of Political and Economic Science
MB	John Morley, *Edmund Burke: A Historical Study* (London, 1867)
MG	John Morley, *The Life of William Ewart Gladstone* (3 vols.; London, 1903)
MIS	John Morley, *Indian Speeches, 1907–1909* (London, 1909)
MOC	John Morley, *On Compromise* (London, 1910)
MR	John Morley, *Recollections* (2 vols.; New York, 1917)
PRO	Public Record Office, Chancery Lane, London
UBL	Library of the University of Birmingham, Birmingham, England

Short Titles Used in Notes

Early Life	Francis W. Hirst, *Early Life and Letters of John Morley* (2 vols.; London, 1927)
Golden Days	Francis W. Hirst, *In the Golden Days* (London, 1947)
Reminiscences	Arthur Godley, *Reminiscences of Lord Kilbracken* (London, 1931)

NOTES

NOTES TO INTRODUCTION

[1] A poem signed C. J. D. appeared in the *Pall Mall Gazette* III (April, 1908), 37 (clipping preserved in HD, VI):
> When Morley said, "Let's end the Lords—
> Or, at the least, let's mend 'em"—
> We little thought what pregnant words
> Composed that vague addendum.
> To-day we learn how much they meant—
> His Majesty—as I count—
> Improves the Peers by ten per cent,
> In making John a Viscount.

[2] Mary, Countess of Minto, *India, Minto and Morley, 1905–1910* (London, 1934); John Buchan, *Lord Minto: A Memoir* (London, 1924).

[3] Especially Syed Razi Wasti, *Lord Minto and the Indian Nationalist Movement, 1905 to 1910* (Oxford, 1964).

[4] Sidney Lee, *King Edward VII: A Biography* (2 vols.; London, 1925–1927), II, 53. The chair vacated by Acton in 1902 went to Bury instead because Balfour refused to accept JM for political reasons.

[5] See John H. Morgan, "The Personality of Lord Morley," *Quarterly Review*, CCXLI (Jan., 1924), 175, re the conversation of June 24, 1922.

[6] *Ibid.*

NOTES TO CHAPTER I

[1] JM to Frederic Harrison, Aug. 25, 1906, Frederic Harrison Collection, British Library of Political and Economic Science, Box 3, letter 6.

[2] Sir Edward Boyle has left a moving, unpublished personal note, written on March 17, 1930, of his memory of John Morley's final appearance at Newcastle-on-Tyne, in which he recalls that "long before the proceedings were to begin, the large and rather dingy Town Hall was packed to overflowing," and that long after Morley was seated "the audience continued to cheer, to stand in their places and to lean over the galleries, in order to see him better. And then Morley rose, and the audience, as one man, rose with him. . . . it was undoubtedly a personal triumph and a tribute to character such as I never expect to see again" (JMP, 43a; see also J. Ramsay MacDonald, "John Morley," *Contemporary Review*, CXXXI [March, 1927], 285 ff.).

[3] *Early Life*, I, 19.

[4] G. P. Gooch, "Lord Morley," *Contemporary Review*, CXXIV (Nov., 1923), 545, notes that Mill's portrait by Watts hung over Morley's library mantelpiece at "Flowermead," his last home, in Wimbledon. The library, which was 40 feet square, contained some 11,000 volumes, now forming the Morley Collection at Manchester University. The house itself no longer stands.

[5] *MR*, I, 53.

[6] MacDonald, *op cit.*, p. 285.

[7] *MR*, I, 63.

[8] JM to Henry Crompton, Aug. 1, 1870, Crompton Papers.

[9] JM to John Stuart Mill, March 21, 1873, JSM, item 50, fol. 580.

[10] HD, Nov. 25, 1907, VI, 100, clipping from *Westminster Gazette*.

[11] JM wrote to Harriet Taylor from Puttenham on May 10, 1873, as soon as he learned the news (JSM, vol. 5).

[12] JM, "John Stuart Mill," *Times Literary Supplement*, May 18, 1906, p. 199.

[13] John Stuart Mill, *Autobiography* (New York, 1924), p. 169.

[14] JM, "John Stuart Mill," p. 203.

[15] JM, "Philosophers and Politicians," in *Modern Characteristics* (London, 1865), p. 196 (hereafter cited as *MC*).

[16] JM to Joseph Chamberlain, Jan. 7, 1876, Microfilm of Letters, Reel I, UBL.

[17] See especially JM to Lord Lytton, Feb. 28, 1879, Lytton Papers, 10, MSS Eur. E. 218, Vol. VII and Vols. VII–VIII *passim*.

[18] JM to Lord Lytton, Dec. 24, 1878, *ibid.*, Vol. VI.

[19] *MB*, p. 22.

[20] *Ibid.*, p. 29.

[21] *Ibid.*, p. 50.

[22] *Ibid.*, p. 70.

[23] *Ibid.*

[24] *Ibid.*, p. 129.

[25] *Ibid.*

[26] *Ibid.*, p. 130.

[27] *Ibid.*, p. 217.

[28] For this period see Warren Staebler, *The Liberal Mind of John Morley* (Princeton, 1943); Francis W. Knickerbocker, *Free Minds: John Morley and His Friends* (Cambridge, 1943); Mrs. W. L. Courtney, *The Making of an Editor: W. L. Courtney, 1850–1928* (London, 1930).

[29] John H. Morgan, "The Personality of Lord Morley," *Quarterly Review*, CCXLI (Jan., 1924), 183.

[30] *Golden Days*, Aug. 22, 1899, at Hawarden, p. 175.

[31] JM to Joseph Chamberlain, Aug. 29, 1875, Microfilm of Letters, Reel I.

[32] JM to Joseph Chamberlain, Aug. 22, 1873, *ibid.*
[33] JM to Joseph Chamberlain, Aug. 11, 1873, *ibid.*
[34] JM to Henry Crompton, June 17, 1873, Crompton Papers.
[35] H. W. Massingham, "Lord Morley's Place in History," *Current History Magazine*, XIX (Nov., 1923), 211.
[36] JM to Joseph Chamberlain, March 12, 1874, Microfilm of Letters, Reel I.
[37] *MOC*, p. 17.
[38] For this period see J. W. Robertson-Scott, *The Life and Death of a Newspaper* (London, 1952).
[39] In *MG*, III, 295n, Morley insists he had not come around to home rule until 1885, "a few days before the fall of the Tory Government."
[40] The quotation is from Cobden's letter to a friend written Oct. 16, 1857, in JM, *The Life of Richard Cobden* (2 vols.; London, 1881), II, 207.
[41] JM to Joseph Chamberlain, Dec. 22, 1873, Microfilm of Letters, Reel I: "I see there is a vacancy now for Newcastle. Do you think Sir I. Cowen's son will stand? ... If young Cowen does not want to go before the General Election, I shall not mind trying my chance for the interim. I should well like to be in the House." But on Dec. 24, 1873, he wrote again: "As it is, of course, I shan't move." He meant he would not contest the election, as Joseph Cowen did stand and was Morley's colleague in the constituency in 1883. JM was sworn into Commons on Feb. 27, 1883.
[42] *Golden Days*, Sept. 13, 1889, p. 181.
[43] Morgan, *op. cit.*, p. 179.
[44] Justin M'Carthy, *British Political Portraits* (New York, 1903), pp. 131–133.
[45] Carnegie quipped: "A hero surely is 'Honest John' Morley" (Andrew Carnegie, *Autobiography* [London, 1920], p. 22).
[46] *MG*, III, 295.
[47] *MR*, II, 8.
[48] Henry Fowler to JM, Dec. 23, 1886, in Edith H. Fowler, *The Life of Henry Hartley Fowler, First Viscount Wolverhampton* (London, 1912), pp. 212–213.
[49] JM, "Liberalism and Social Reforms," speech given at the Eighty Club Dinner, Nov. 19, 1889, at St. James Hall, in *The Eighty Club: 1890* (London, 1890), p. 13.
[50] JM to Sir A. Godley, March 5, 1883, Correspondence of Lord Kilbracken, BM, Add. MS 44902, Vol. III.
[51] Morley also edited the Macmillan series of more than forty volumes in print (by 1893), with the promise of "other volumes to follow" of "English Men of Letters." Reprinted 1890, 1893, John Morley, *Walpole* (London, 1890).
[52] See Robert R. James, *Rosebery: A Biography of Archibald Philip, Fifth Earl of Rosebery* (London, 1963), p. 237.
[53] JM to Joseph Chamberlain, Dec. 31, 1875, Microfilm of Letters, Reel I.
[54] JM to Henry Crompton, Jan. 25, 1876, Crompton Papers.
[55] *Journals and Letters of Reginald Viscount Esher*, ed. Maurice V. Brett (4 vols.; London, 1934–1938), April 3, 1891, I, 151 (hereafter cited as *Esher Journals*).
[56] Sir Henry Robinson, *Memories, Wise and Otherwise* (London, 1923), p. 100.
[57] Henry W. Lucy, *A Diary of the Home Rule Parliament, 1892–1895* (London, 1896).

[58] James, *op. cit.*, p. 310.
[59] JM to Charles W. Dilke, March 5, 1894, Dilke Papers, BM, Add. MS 43895, Vol. XXII, fol. 185.
[60] *MR*, II, 19.
[61] JM to Leonard Courtney, July 28, 1895, Courtney Collection, British Library of Political and Economic Science, R.(S.R.) 1003, Vol. VI.
[62] JM to Henry Campbell-Bannerman, Nov. 18, 1895, Campbell-Bannerman Papers, BM, Add. MS 41223, Vol. XVIII, "Letters from John Morley, 1885–1907," p. 40.
[63] JM to C. W. Dilke, Dec. 20, 1898, Dilke Papers, Vol. XXII, fol. 206.
[64] JM to Leonard Courtney, July 10, 1898, in Courtney, *op. cit.*, p. 167.
[65] *Golden Days*, Sept. 22, 1899, p. 189.
[66] Within five years of publication, more than 120,000 copies of the three editions of Morley's biography of Gladstone had been sold (HD, Oct. 26, 1908, III, 94).
[67] JM to Arthur Godley, July 15, 1902, Correspondence of Lord Kilbracken, Vol. III, fols. 71–73.
[68] JM to C. W. Dilke, Sept. 29, 1900, Dilke Papers, Vol. XXII, fol. 232.
[69] *HPDHC*, May 23, 1901, 4th ser., Vol. XCIV, col. 1088.
[70] JM to Campbell-Bannerman, Jan. 3, 1903, Campbell-Bannerman Papers, Vol. XVIII, pp. 121–122.
[71] JM, "An Address to Young Liberals," March 20, 1905, published by the National League of Young Liberals as *Pamphlet No. 4*, pp. 2–3.
[72] J. A. Spender, *Life, Journalism and Politics* (2 vols.; London, 1927), I, 132, insists that "quite early in his career he [JM] had come under the tacit ban ruling in both parties which decreed that certain kinds of politicians had an inherent disqualification for this office [Foreign Office] . . . in the Liberal party . . . impenitent members of the Manchester school who were supposed to hold strong little-England or anti-Imperialist views . . . [like] Morley."
[73] *Esher Journals*, Dec. 1, 1905, II, 121–122.
[74] JM to Charles W. Dilke, Dec. 10, 1905, Dilke Papers, Vol. XXII, fol. 259.
[75] HD, Dec. 12, 1905, I, 1.
[76] See H. W. Nevinson, *More Changes, More Chances* (London, 1925), p. 228, re his visit to JM's office, Sept. 25, 1907.
[77] JM to Frederick Harrison, March 20, 1906, Frederick Harrison Collection, Box 3, letter 6.
[78] JM to Lord Minto, March 8, 1906, JMP, Morley to Minto, Vol. I.

Notes to Chapter II

[1] HD, March 22, 1907, II, 29.
[2] HD, May 18, 1909, IV, 40; see also HD, Aug. 29, 1906, I, 74.
[3] St. John Brodrick to Ampthill, Dec. 8, 1904, Ampthill Collection, IO, MSS Eur. E. 233/11. Curzon later attributed all his "troubles" to Brodrick's "jealousy and vanity" (HD, Oct. 29, 1906, I, 92).
[4] Lord Minto to JM, Dec. 20, 1905, JMP, Minto to Morley, Vol. I.
[5] A. Godley to JM, May 12, 1906, Kilbracken Collection, IO, MSS Eur. F. 102/8.

NOTES

[6] St. John Brodrick to Ampthill, June 2, 1905, Ampthill Collection, E. 233/11.
[7] Sir G. Clarke's "Note on Indian Military Administration," Aug. 5, 1904, to the prime minister, Arthur J. Balfour, PRO, Cabinet Papers: Committee of Imperial Defense (hereafter cited as CID), Correspondence and Manuscript Papers, Cab. 17/40.
[8] St. John Brodrick's memo, Nov. 11, 1904, to His Majesty on Kitchener's army reorganization scheme, Royal Archives, Windsor Castle, W/3/2; Kitchener's "Note on the Military Policy of India," July 19, 1905, Kitchener Collection, PRO 30/57, no. 30.
[9] St. John Brodrick to Ampthill, Dec. 30, 1904, Ampthill Collection, E. 233/11.
[10] Lord Esher to Kitchener, March 2, 1905, Kitchener Collection, no. 33.
[11] Especially Stedman, Clarke, and Esher. See Stedman to Kitchener, June 16, July 21, Aug. 4, 11, 1905, Kitchener Collection, no. 33; Sir G. Clarke to Kitchener, Jan. 30, Dec. 22, 1905, *ibid.*, no. 32; Esher to Kitchener, Dec. 21, 1905, *Journals and Letters of Reginald Viscount Esher*, ed. Maurice V. Brett (London, 1934–1938), II, 131–132 (hereafter cited as *Esher Journals*).
[12] St. John Brodrick to Ampthill, March 10, 1905, Ampthill Collection, E. 233/11.
[13] Military [Secret] Despatch, no. 66, May 31, 1905, JMP, 39h.
[14] *Reminiscences*, p. 181.
[15] Stedman to Kitchener, June 16, 1905, Kitchener Collection, no. 33.
[16] Arthur J. Balfour to JM, March 2, 1906, Balfour Papers, BM, Add. MSS 49778, 49962.
[17] St. John Brodrick to Knollys, Aug. 5, 1905, Royal Archives, W/4/14.
[18] HD, Oct. 29, 1906, I, 92.
[19] Dated only "Thursday," although from internal evidence clearly after Aug. 20, 1905, to "My dear Lord K.," misfiled among some letters from Lady Minto to Lord Kitchener; unsigned though obviously from Lady Curzon because it begins "Our Nathan tells me . . . ," Kitchener Collection, no. 33.
[20] See Syed Razi Wasti, *Lord Minto and the Indian Nationalist Movement, 1905 to 1910* (Oxford, 1964); M. N. Das, *India under Morley and Minto* (London and New York, 1964); K. K. Aziz, *Britain and Muslim India* (London, 1963), chaps. 3, 4; Z. H. Zaidi, "The Political Motive in the Partition of Bengal," *Journal of the Pakistan Historical Society*, XII, Pt. II (April, 1964); Sufia Ahmed, "Some Aspects of the History of the Muslim Community in Bengal, 1884–1912" (unpublished Ph.D. thesis, University of London, 1961).
[21] Lord Curzon to JM, Feb. 19, 1906, JMP, Envelope K.
[22] A. H. L. Fraser's note to JM, March 25, 1907, JMP, 43a.
[23] Lord Minto to JM, Dec. 13, 1905, JMP, Minto to Morley, Vol. I.
[24] Lord Minto to JM, Jan. 3, 1906, *ibid.*
[25] Lord Curzon to Hamilton, Nov. 18, 1900, Hamilton Papers, IO, MSS Eur. D. 510/6, vol. 18.
[26] Lord Curzon to Hamilton, April 23, 1900, *ibid.*, vol. 17.
[27] Lord Curzon to Hamilton, Aug. 29, 1900, *ibid.*
[28] A. Godley to JM, May 12, 1906, Kilbracken Collection, F. 102/8; also HD, May 10–11, 1906, I, 43.
[29] Lord Curzon to Hamilton, Sept. 17, 1902, Hamilton Papers, vol. 23.
[30] Lord Curzon to Hamilton, June 4, 1903, *ibid.*, vol. 26.
[31] Sir George Clarke to JM, July 7, 1909, JMP, 42.
[32] Lord Curzon to Hamilton, June 4, 1903, Hamilton Papers, vol. 26.

[33] Sir Alfred Lyall to JM, June 15, 1907, JMP, 43c.
[34] A. J. Balfour to St. J. Brodrick, Oct. 28, 1903, Balfour Papers, Add. MS 49720.
[35] As per Secret Despatch no. 58, Dec. 2, 1904, Secretary of State to Viceroy, in Ampthill Collection, E. 233/11.
[36] St. J. Brodrick to Ampthill, Feb. 3, 1905, *ibid.*
[37] St. J. Brodrick to Ampthill, March 24, 1905, *ibid.*
[38] Curzon to Brodrick, Feb. 18, 1905, telegram quoted in Brodrick to Ampthill, Feb. 24, 1905, *ibid.*
[39] Brodrick to Ampthill, March 17, 1905, *ibid.*
[40] Lord Ampthill, whose noble father had been an eminent statesman, wrote, with supreme aristocratic contempt for Curzon, to Godley: "If Lord Curzon were not the first of his family to rise to any sort of eminence and distinction he would have been guided by traditions which would have saved him from many mistakes. As it was, the motto of his family, 'Let Curzon holde what Curzon helde,' was well exemplified on his voyage home for he flew the Viceregal flag as far as Suez!" (Ampthill to Godley, Dec. 21, 1905, Kilbracken Collection, F. 102/39).
[41] *Lord Curzon in India* (London, 1906), p. 585.
[42] John Gore, *King George V: A Personal Memoir* (London, 1941), p. 207. The exchange occurred after the Calcutta state dinner of January 1, 1906, when Gokhale was presented to the Prince of Wales by Walter Lawrence (see Lawrence's report to Knollys, Jan. 3, 1906, Royal Archives, W/4/14).
[43] Ampthill to Godley, Nov. 23, 1905, Kilbracken Collection, F. 102/39; see also Minto to Godley, April 3, 1906, *ibid.*, F. 102/25.
[44] Ampthill to Godley, Nov. 17, 23, 1905, *ibid.*, F. 102/39.
[45] Minto to Godley, April 3, 1906, *ibid.* In December, 1905, Curzon tried to scotch talk of the slight by attributing it to Brodrick in a letter to Knollys, Royal Archives, W/4/11.
[46] JM to Minto, Nov. 2, 1906, JMP, Morley to Minto, Vol. I.

Notes to Chapter III

[1] See Thomas R. Metcalf, *The Aftermath of Revolt in India, 1857–1870* (Princeton, 1964).
[2] Duke of Argyll to Government of India, Nov. 24, 1870, cited in C. H. Phillips, ed., *The Evolution of India and Pakistan, 1858 to 1947* (London, 1962), p. 13.
[3] Élie Halévy's overall title for the era 1905–1914. See vol. 6 of his *A History of the English People in the Nineteenth Century*, trans. from French by E. I. Watkin (London, 1961).
[4] JM to Minto, June 23, 1906, JMP, Morley to Minto, Vol. I.
[5] JM to Minto, Jan. 16, 1906, *ibid.*
[6] JM to Minto, Jan. 25, 1906, *ibid.*
[7] This was what Morley told his private secretary, Hirtzel, "he cared most about" (HD, Sept. 13, 1906, I, 79).
[8] JM to Minto, June 6, 1906, JMP, Morley to Minto, Vol. I.
[9] John Buchan, *Lord Minto: A Memoir* (London, 1924), p. 222; Mary, Countess of Minto, *India, Minto and Morley, 1905–1910* (London, 1934), *passim*;

H. Dodwell, "Lord Minto as Viceroy," *National Review*, LXXXV (March-Aug., 1925), 300–303; John H. Morgan, "The Personality of Lord Morley," *Quarterly Review*, CCXLI (Jan., 1924), 180–181; Syed Razi Wasti, *Lord Minto and the Indian Nationalist Movement, 1905 to 1910* (Oxford, 1964), pp. 20, 36 ff.

[10] Sir Malcolm Seton, *The India Office* (London and New York, 1926), p. 80.

[11] Ampthill to Godley, Oct. 17, 1905, Kilbracken Collection, IO, MSS. Eur. F. 102/39.

[12] J. Ramsay MacDonald, "John Morley," *Contemporary Review*, CXXXI (March, 1927), 285 ff.

[13] JM to Minto, Sept. 19, 1907, JMP, Morley to Minto, Vol. II.

[14] Gen. Sir E. Barrow to Curzon, July 27, 1907, Curzon Papers, IO, MSS Eur. F. 111/426. Barrow's letter continues: "I had a highly placed Simlaite friend here last week and he was most despondent about things both official and social . . . nothing but an atmosphere [in Simla] of suspicion and intrigue. I was amused by one story he related.—The P.W.B. Punjab have just made a broad carriage road round Sumer Hill. When H.E. returned to Simla and saw it, he was furious as his best ride and walk had been spoilt. They protested that he had himself approved the plans, and sure enough his initials were there, so either he had signed the papers without looking at them or had not understood them."

[15] On May 6, 1907, JM wrote Godley, "I think he [no explanation of whom] hits the nail on the head when he says that Lord M. [Minto] does not keep up communication with his lieutenants" (Kilbracken Collection, F. 102/8). Sir G. Clarke to JM, May 26, 1909: "The real defect (in G. of I. "machine") in which I see danger, is the utter lack of coordination" (JMP, 42); and again, Clarke to JM, June 2, 1909: "The Viceroy has never consulted me on any matter" (*ibid.*). Sir J. Hewett (Lt. Gov. Punjab) to Curzon, Feb. 9, 1910: "The Viceroy . . . has a wretchedly weak council, but he has never been in the habit of consulting it" (Curzon Papers, F. 111/428).

[16] Minto to JM, Jan. 9, 1908, JMP, Minto to Morley, Vol. VIII.

[17] HD, Aug. 22, 1906, I, 73. See also *Journals and Letters of Reginald Viscount Esher*, ed. Maurice V. Brett (London, 1934–1938), Jan., 1908, II, 275 (hereafter cited as *Esher Journals*).

[18] HD, June 15, 1908, III, 56.

[19] *Ibid.*, Nov. 12, 1908, p. 99.

[20] JM to Guy Fleetwood Wilson, Jan. 13, 1909, Fleetwood Wilson Papers, IO, MSS Eur. E. 224/11; re Minto's council, see also JM to Minto, April 15, 1908, JMP, Morley to Minto, Vol. III.

[21] JM, "British Democracy and Indian Government" (hereafter cited as JMBD), *Nineteenth Century and After*, 69 (Feb., 1911), 202. See also JM to Sir G. Clarke, Sept. 18, 1908, JMP, 42: "Yes—you may well say that governments become careless whenever the governed are voiceless. That's the very root of liberalism in its widest and deepest sense. Let us stick to that."

[22] JMBD, pp. 198–199.

[23] JM at Arbroath, *Times*, Oct. 22, 1907 (clipping in HD, VI).

[24] JM to Minto, Sept. 19, 1907, JMP, Morley to Minto, Vol. II; see also JM to Minto, Jan. 24, 1907, *ibid.*; JM to Clarke, May 15, 1908, JMP, 42; JM to Minto, June 17, 1908, JMP, Morley to Minto, Vol. III.

[25] See JM to Minto, Feb. 9, 1906, JMP, Morley to Minto, Vol. I; CID paper 68B and minute 3 of 83d meeting, Feb. 15, 1906, CID Papers, PRO 2/2/1,

Cabinet Papers; HD, Sept. 4, 1906, I, 77; JM to Minto, Nov. 9, 1906, JMP, Morley to Minto, Vol. I; JM to Minto, Nov. 30, 1906, *ibid.*; JM to Minto, July 6, 1906, *ibid*,; JM to Minto, April 4, 1907, *ibid.*, Vol. II; JM to Minto, June 24, 1908, *ibid.*, Vol. III; JM to Minto, July 28, 1910, *ibid.*, Vol. V.

26 Minto to Godley, Oct. 17, 1906, Kilbracken Collection, F. 102/25.
27 Minto to JM, Nov. 3, 1909, JMP, Minto to Morley, Vol. XVI.
28 Minto to JM, May 27, 1908, *ibid.*, Vol. XV. On June 11, 1908, Minto wrote: "travelling M.P.'s! . . . I don't at all like any of them" (*ibid.*, Vol. XVI).
29 JM to Minto, June 17, 1908, JMP, Morley to Minto, Vol. III.
30 Minto to JM, May 27, 1908, *ibid.*
31 JM to Minto, June 17, 1908, *ibid.*
32 JM to Minto, April 15, 1908, *ibid.*
33 JM to Minto, April 30, 1908, *ibid.*
34 JM to Minto, Sept. 10, 1908, *ibid.*
35 JM to Minto, July 28, 1910, *ibid.*, Vol. V.
36 JM to Minto, Oct. 19, 1910, *ibid.*
37 JM to Minto, April 26, 1907, *ibid.*, Vol. II.
38 JM to Minto, May 9, 1907, *ibid.*
39 JM, "On Presenting the Indian Budget," House of Commons, June 6, 1907, *MIS*, p. 2.
40 JM to Minto, Oct. 8, 1907, JMP, Morley to Minto, Vol. II.
41 JM to Minto, Nov. 22, 1907, *ibid.*
42 JM to Clarke, May 15, 1908, JMP, D42.
43 JM to Minto, July 10, 1908, JMP, Morley to Minto, Vol. III.
44 JM to Minto, Oct. 3, 1907, *ibid.*, Vol. II.
45 JM to Minto, Aug. 15, 1907, *ibid.*
46 *Ibid.*
47 JM's quote from Mill's *Representative Government* in his Budget Speech of June 6, 1907, *MIS*, p. 19.
48 JM to Minto, March 14, 1907, JMP, Morley to Minto, Vol. II.
49 The formula is Sir Alfred Lyall's (Lyall to JM, May 28, 1907, JMP, Bundle C).
50 "The prevailing feeling, especially in Bengal, Madras, and Bombay, is distrust in the Government,—despair of getting any real popular reforms,—estrangement and bitterness," wrote R. C. Dutt to JM, Feb. 22, 1908, JMP, G.
51 Minto to JM, July 24, 1907, JMP, Minto to Morley, Vol. VI.
52 *MB*, p. 222.
53 JM to Minto, Jan. 18, 1907, JMP, Morley to Minto, Vol. II.
54 JM to Minto, May 7, 1908, *ibid.*, Vol. III.
55 JM to Godley, July 31, 1908, Kilbracken Collection, F. 102/08; JM to Minto, Sept. 3, 1908, JMP, Morley to Minto, Vol. III.
56 JM to Minto, Jan. 19, 1910, JMP, Morley to Minto, Vol. V.
57 G. Fleetwood Wilson to Judge Fletcher, Aug. 10, 1909, Fleetwood Wilson Papers, E. 224, no. 2.
58 Sir Charles Comyn Egerton, general of the Indian Army, had joined the Bengal Staff Corps in 1871, and had subsequently served as assistant adjutant general, Punjab Frontier Force, 1886–1893; assistant quartermaster general, Bengal, 1895; ADC to the Queen, 1896; and commandant of Secunderabad Division, 1904.
59 JM to Minto, May 9, 1907, JMP, Morley to Minto, Vol. II.
60 Sir Harvey Adamson had served in various capacities in Burma from 1875,

when he was appointed to the Foreign Service, until 1903, when he was made an additional member of the governor-general's Legislative Council. He returned to Burma as a chief judge in 1905, and was later (1906) appointed member of the governor-general's council.

[61] JM to Minto, June 17, 1909, JMP, Morley to Minto, Vol. IV.

[62] JM to Minto, May 31, 1907, ibid., Vol. II.

[63] JM to Minto, Jan. 28, 1909, ibid., Vol. IV.

[64] Sir Denzil Charles Ibbetson, appointed to the service after the examination of 1868, served during the period 1870–1883 in the Punjab in many positions. Later he filled the posts of secretary to the government of India, Department of Revenue and Agriculture (1896), chief commissioner of the Central Provinces (1898), temporary member of the governor-general's council (1899), and lieutenant governor of the Punjab (1905). Once, in writing to his former chief, Ibbetson referred to "that *hateful* India Office" (Ibbetson to Curzon, June 14, 1907, Curzon Papers, F. 111/428).

[65] JM to Minto, June 13, 1907, JMP, Morley to Minto, Vol. II.

[66] JM to Minto, July 5, 1907, *ibid*.

[67] Sir Lancelot Hare arrived in India in 1873. In 1904 he served as a member of the Legislative Council of Bengal. In 1906 he officiated briefly as lieutenant governor of Bengal and was then appointed lieutenant governor of East Bengal and Assam.

[68] Minto to JM, Aug. 1, 1906, JMP, Minto to Morley, Vol. III.

[69] Minto to JM, Aug. 2, 1906, *ibid*.

[70] JM to Minto, Jan. 10, 1907, JMP, Morley to Minto, Vol. II.

[71] Minto to JM, Jan. 15, 1908, JMP, Minto to Morley, Vol. VIII.

[72] JM to Minto, July 15, 1909, JMP, Morley to Minto, Vol. IV.

[73] JM to Minto, Feb. 6, 1908, *ibid.*, Vol. III.

[74] JM to Minto, March 19, 1908, *ibid*.

[75] JM to Minto, Dec. 31, 1908, *ibid*.

[76] Esher to M. V. Brett, Jan. 14, 1910, *Esher Journals*, II, 437.

[77] Seton, *op. cit.* p. 73.

[78] Sir Arthur Godley, K.C.B., undersecretary of state for India, was educated at Rugby and Balliol College, Oxford. He was called to the bar at Lincoln's Inn, 1876. He served as private secretary to the first lord of the treasury in 1872–1874 and again in 1880–1882, as commissioner of inland revenue in 1882–83, and became permanent undersecretary at the India Office in 1883.

[79] HD, Dec. 13, 1907, II, 105.

[80] *Ibid*.

[81] HD, Jan. 3, 1908, III, 9.

[82] *Reminiscenses*, p. 233.

[83] Ritchie was permanent undersecretary of state for India, 1909–1912 (see P. Leigh-Smith, *Record of an Ascent: A Memoir of Sir Richmond T. Ritchie* [Cambridge, 1961]; also see HD, May 25, 1908, III, 50).

[84] Asquith, the prime minister, said "Godley had ruled India for 25 years, but added, 'but doesn't *now!!*'" (HD, May 25, 1908, III, 50).

[85] "I cannot say how grateful I am to you. . . . I assure you I thankfully rely upon your discretion as to anything I may ever write to you, and it is a very great help to me to know that I have you at the India Office whom I may confidentially consult" (Minto to Godley, April 25, 1906, Kilbracken Collection, F. 102/25).

[86] JM to Kilbracken, Feb. 25, 1918, Correspondence of Lord Kilbracken, BM, Add. MS 44902, Vol. III, fol. 148.
[87] Kilbracken to Lee-Warner, Aug. 5, 1910, Lee-Warner Collection, IO, MSS Eur. F. 92/2.
[88] Kilbracken to Lee-Warner, Aug. 7, 1910, *ibid*.
[89] Sir William Lee-Warner, a graduate of St. John's College, Cambridge, arrived in India in 1869. He served as private secretary to the governor of Bombay (1873–74), as acting director of public instruction, Bombay (1885), as political agent in Kolhapur (1886), as secretary of the political, judicial, and educational departments of Bombay (1887–1893), and also held other posts. He became a member of the Council of India in 1902.
[90] See HD, May 31, 1906, I, 49.
[91] *Ibid.*, July 17, 1906, p. 62.
[92] Lee-Warner was undersecretary to the governor of Bombay, a post he held for one year in 1875. The clipping (with no date) from an Anglo-Indian newspaper reporting the assault is preserved in the Lee-Warner Collection, F. 92, Box 1.
[93] "Assault on Sir W. Lee Warner by a Hindu Student," in Judicial and Political Records, PRO, 1909, vol. 915, no. 318.
[94] Sir Edward, arriving in Bengal in 1873, had served in several posts including lieutenant governor and inspector general of police. He returned from India in 1900 and became assistant commissioner of London's Metropolitan Police in 1901, and commissioner in March, 1903.
[95] *HD*, Feb. 5, 1909, IV, 11.
[96] Since Hirtzel alone kept a diary that has been preserved, his influence may in fact appear somewhat more exalted than it was, though sufficient independent testimony by Morley (in letters to Minto and the Prime Minister) seems to corroborate the accuracy of Hirtzel's own estimate of his influence.
[97] JM to Minto, Oct. 7, 1909, JMP, Morley to Minto, Vol. IV.
[98] This was JM's description of Hirtzel, not Hirtzel's of himself (HD, June 25, 1909, IV, 51).
[99] HD, July 3, 1906, I, 58.
[100] See HD, Sept. 3, 1906, I, 76; May 9, 1907, II, 43; Nov. 4, 1907, II, 94; Feb. 21, 1908, III, 23; April 19, 1909, IV, 31; June 11, 1909, IV, 47.
[101] HD, Sept. 3, 1906, I, 76.
[102] HD, May 9, 1907, II, 43.
[103] JM to Campbell-Bannerman, June 14, 1907, Campbell-Bannerman Papers, BM, Add. MS 41223, XVIII, 251.
[104] HD, June 25, 1909, IV, 51.
[105] George Sydenham Clarke (Baron Sydenham of Combe), *My Working Life* (London, 1927), p. 219. This autobiography suffers from the bitter tone of Lord Sydenham's later years.
[106] JM to Minto, Oct. 3, 1907, JMP, Morley to Minto, Vol. II.
[107] JM to Minto, Nov. 19, 1908, *ibid.*, Vol. III.
[108] JM to Clarke, Feb. 7, 1908, JMP, D42.
[109] Clarke to JM, Simla, May 6, 1909, *ibid*.
[110] Clarke to JM, "Most Private," undated but necessarily, since it is from Simla, written sometime in May or June, 1909, *ibid*.
[111] Clarke to JM, Simla, May 26, 1909, *ibid*.
[112] *Ibid*.
[113] Clarke to JM, Simla, June 2, 1909, *ibid*.

[114] Clarke to JM, Simla, June 11, 1909, *ibid*.
[115] Clarke to JM, Simla, June 2, 1909, *ibid*.
[116] *Ibid*.
[117] JM to Clarke, June 18, 1909, JMP, D42.
[118] *Ibid*.
[119] Clarke to JM, May 6, 1909, *ibid*.
[120] See his letters to Minto, March 8, 1906, JMP, Morley to Minto, Vol. I; August 23, 1907, *ibid*., Vol. II; Aug. 19, 1908, *ibid*., Vol. III.
[121] Minto to JM, "Private," Sept. 23, 1909, JMP, Miscellaneous.
[122] HD, Sept. 27, 1909, IV, 78.
[123] JM to Clarke, Oct. 19, 1909, JMP, D42.
[124] HD, Feb. 17, 1909, IV, 14.
[125] JM to Clarke, Nov. 14, 1909, JMP, D42.
[126] JM to Clarke, June 10, 1909, *ibid*.
[127] JM to Minto, March 17, 1910, JMP, Morley to Minto, Vol. V.
[128] JM to Clarke, June 14, 1910, JMP, D42.
[129] The Council of India met every Tuesday of the year (at least five members required) at 11 A.M. in the elegant room on the first floor of the India Office, a spacious square room modeled after the old Court of Directors Chamber at Leadenhall Street. In front of the marble mantelpiece stood the highbacked, red velvet chair that every secretary of state since 1858 had used. The secretary faced the original mahogany doors of the company's room. The procedure of the India Office has been described as "intolerably cumbrous and dilatory," and it is clear that the terms of the act of 1858 did not make for extreme speed in the conduct of business. Only the secretary could initiate new business into the council, and any proceedings taken in his absence required his approval in writing. As president, the secretary appointed and regulated the committees of the council, appointed one member as vice-president, and had the power to cast a vote. Recalling Morley's relations with the council, Hirtzel wrote: "Campbell told me that J.M. had been getting into hot water with Council. . . . he had been irritated with them and had talked of their flaccid good nature. . . . They were getting sick and objecting to being 'treated like a pack of schoolboys' " (HD, Sept. 23, 1909, IV, 77).
[130] JM to Clarke, Dec. 12, 1907, JMP, D42.
[131] Clarke to JM, Dec. 27, 1907, *ibid*.
[132] JM to Clarke, April 24, 1908, *ibid*.
[133] JM to Minto, Jan. 28, 1909, JMP, Morley to Minto, Vol. IV.
[134] L. Jenkins to JM, June 3, 1909, JMP, H.
[135] *Ibid*.
[136] L. Jenkins to JM, July 18, 1909, *ibid*.
[137] L. Jenkins to JM, July 14, 1909, JMP, 43H.
[138] Minto to JM, March 17, 1909, JMP, Minto to Morley, Vol. XIII.
[139] HD, June 7, 1909, IV, 46.
[140] JM to Minto, June 10, 1909, JMP, Morley to Minto, Vol. IV.
[141] JM to Minto, March 19, 1908, *ibid*., Vol. III.
[142] Sir Herbert Hope Risley (1851–1911) joined the I.C.S. in 1873. He held the following posts in the service: undersecretary to the government of India's Home Department (1879); acting financial secretary (1898); director of ethnography for India (1901); secretary to the home government (1902). He returned to England in 1910.
[143] JM to Minto, May 7, 1908, JMP, Morley to Minto, Vol. III. Among the

"other people" was Clarke, who wrote JM on March 18, 1908: "Crime . . . goes on and gives rise to bitter complaints. Meanwhile, I wait vainly for a reply to my urgent letter to the Government of India which may, like another letter on police matters, require eleven months of Sir H. Risley's consideration. It is very galling and it really is not safe" (Clarke to JM, JMP, D42). JM subsequently thought of Risley as "the incarnation in a peculiarly obnoxious or equivocal form of the spirit of bureaucratic caste" (JM to Minto, Nov. 5, 1908, JMP, Morley to Minto, Vol. III). In April, 1910, however, when Risley returned home and Morley met him for the first time, he changed his appraisal: "He is really first-rate. I am enormously impressed by his qualities" (JM to Minto, April 1, 1910, ibid., Vol. V).

[144] Almeric Fitzroy, *Memoirs* (2 vols.; London, 1925), July 27, 1908, I, 357.

[145] HD, Dec. 21, 1908, III, 110.

[146] HD, Feb. 17, 1909, IV, 14.

[147] JM introduced them; see his letter to Fleetwood Wilson, Feb. 5, 1909, Fleetwood Wilson Papers, E. 224; and see L. Jenkins to Fleetwood Wilson, June 22, 1909, *ibid*.

[148] G. Fleetwood Wilson to Jenkins, July 6, 1909, *ibid*.

[149] A. Godley to JM, Dec. 12, 1905, Curzon-Kitchener Conflict, IO, MSS Eur. D. 555.

[150] Fleetwood Wilson's note to the Home Department, government of India, June 17, 1909, Fleetwood Wilson Papers, E. 224.

[151] *Ibid*.

[152] Dunlop Smith to Fleetwood Wilson, June 8, 1909, *ibid*.

[153] HD, June 28, 1909, IV, 52.

[154] A rabid dog had attacked Lady Minto's pet, and Lord Minto, who had had contact with it, was advised by his doctor to undergo the Pasteur treatment (see Minto to JM, May 13, 1909, JMP, Minto to Morley, Vol. XIV).

[155] G. Fleetwood Wilson to Judge Fletcher, "very private," Aug. 10, 1909, Fleetwood Wilson Papers, E. 224.

[156] *Ibid*.

[157] Minto to Godley, Aug. 19, 1909, Kilbracken Collection, F. 102/35.

[158] G. Fleetwood Wilson to Judge Fletcher, Aug. 10, 1909, Fleetwood Wilson Papers, E. 224.

[159] *Times* (London), July 27, 1910.

[160] JM to Minto, Oct. 11, 1906, JMP, Morley to Minto, Vol. I.

[161] JM to Minto, Jan. 16, 1908, *ibid*., Vol. III.

[162] HD, April 28, 1908, III, 42.

[163] JM to Minto, May 7, 1908, JMP, Morley to Minto, Vol. III.

[164] Minto to JM, May 27, 1908, JMP, Minto to Morley, Vol. IX.

[165] JM to Minto, June 17, 1908, JMP, Morley to Minto, Vol. III.

[166] HD, Aug. 22, 1906, I, 73.

[167] Minto to JM, March 13, 1907, JMP, Minto to Morley, Vol. V.

[168] HD, April 2, 1907, II, 32.

[169] JM to Minto, April 4, 1907, JMP, Morley to Minto, Vol. III.

[170] See JM to Minto, June 29, 1906, JMP, Morley to Minto, Vol. I; see also HD, May 10, 1907, II, 43; and JM to Minto, May 9, 1907, JMP, Morley to Minto, Vol. II. On September 4, 1907, JM wrote to Minto: "When you renew your plans for a general Press Law, be sure to send me a very full set of the reports and other material of every kind on which you found the case for more stringent

means of countering the seditious papers. You cannot send me too much 'chapter and verse' " (JM to Minto, Sept. 4, 1907, JMP, Morley to Minto, Vol. II).

[171] "I am writing under great difficulties. . . . Dunlop Smith laid up with a sharp attack of fever. . . . Pandemonium. In the midst of this, your telegram. . . . Please do not think me pig-headed or nervous. . . . It is impossible to convey to you in letters or despatches the knowledge the Government of India possess. . . . It is quite impossible" (Minto to JM, Oct. 21, 1909, JMP, Minto to Morley, Vol. XVI). "I am simply worked off my legs. There seems never to be a spare moment to settle down to think" (Minto to JM, Nov. 19, 1909, *ibid.*). "The Secretary of State is troublesome beyond words" (Minto to Kitchener, Feb. 1, 1910, Kitchener Collection, PRO 30/57, no. 33). See also Minto to his wife, April 10, 1907, quoted in Mary, Countess of Minto, *India, Minto and Morley, 1905–1910* (London, 1934), p. 118.

[172] JM to Godley, July 30, 1907, Correspondence of Lord Kilbracken, BM, Add. MS 44902, fol. 119.

[173] JM to Minto, June 28, Sept. 26, 1907, JMP, Morley to Minto, Vol. II. See also Godley to Lee-Warner, Oct. 4, 1907, Lee-Warner Collection, F. 92/2.

[174] JM to Minto, Aug. 23, 1907, JMP, Morley to Minto, Vol. II.

[175] Morley's sarcasm here was certainly wasted on John Buchan, who completely misread or perversely misinterpreted JM's meaning (see John Buchan, *Lord Minto: A Memoir* [London, 1924], p. 223).

[176] JM to Minto, Nov. 22, 1907, JMP, Morley to Minto, Vol. II.

[177] JM to Minto, Nov. 12, 1908, *ibid.*, Vol. III.

[178] JM to Minto, April 15, 1908, *ibid.*

[179] JM to Minto, May 15, 1908, *ibid.*

[180] JM to Minto, Jan. 27, 1910, *ibid.*, Vol. V.

[181] JM to Minto, Feb. 3, 1910, *ibid.*

[182] Report of the Royal Commission upon Decentralisation in India, Parliamentary Papers, 1909, I (Cd. 4360), 7.

[183] Sir Alfred Lyall, in HD, May 15, 1909, IV, 39; see also *Esher Journals*, Oct. 28, 1908, II, 353.

[184] Sir J. Hewett (lieutenant governor of United Provinces) to Curzon, Feb. 9, 1910, Curzon Papers, F. 111/428.

[185] JM to Clarke, Oct. 19, 1909, JMP, D42.

[186] In February, 1910, Montagu was appointed parliamentary undersecretary of state for India. This was the beginning of a close connection with India which lasted for the remaining fourteen years of his life. He held the post until 1914, having twice visited India during his tenure. In July, 1917, he became secretary of state, a position he held until March, 1922. It had been his ambition to succeed Hardinge and later Chelmsford as viceroy.

[187] Montagu's Budget Speech, July 26, 1910, *HPDHC*, 5th ser., Vol. XIX, 6th vol. of Session 1910, 11 July–3 Aug. 1910, cols. 1950 ff., 1962.

[188] *Ibid.*, cols. 1983–1984.

[189] *Ibid.*, col. 1984.

[190] *Times*, July 27, 1910, p. 11.

[191] Lovat Fraser to Lee-Warner, July 31, 1910, Lee-Warner Collection, F. 92/2.

[192] These minutes, by H. W. Woodman, dated Aug. 19, 1910; by A. Earle, Aug. 20, 1910; by J. L. Jenkins [not related to Sir Lawrence], Aug. 22, 1910; by Minto, Sept. 2, 1910; and by Guy Fleetwood Wilson, Sept. 9, 1910, are all preserved in Fleetwood Wilson Papers, E. 224/4.

193 HD, May 17, 1906, I, 45; July 4, 1906, I, 58; JM to Minto, Sept. 19, 1907, JMP, Morley to Minto, Vol. II; HD, March 20, 1908, III, 31; JM to Minto, April 2, 1908, JMP, Morley to Minto, Vol. III; JM to Clarke, May 15, 1908, JMP, D42.

194 JM to Minto, July 28, 1910, JMP, Morley to Minto, Vol. V.

195 JMBD, p. 193.

196 Sir John Prescott Hewett, a graduate of Balliol College, Oxford, was appointed to the I.C.S. after the examination of 1875. He was chief commissioner of the Central Provinces in 1902; member of the governor-general's council in 1904, and lieutenant governor of the United Provinces in 1907.

197 Sir J. Hewett, Government House, Lucknow, to Curzon, "confidential," Feb. 9, 1910, Curzon Papers, F. 111/428.

198 "India under Lord Morley," *Quarterly Review*, CCXIV (Jan., 1911), 213.

199 *Ibid.*, p. 214.

200 JMBD, p. 199.

Notes to Chapter IV

1 In one letter to Godley, Lord Ampthill claimed that the "great victory" was not really Kitchener's at all, but "has really been won by the young lions of Army Headquarters who work Lord Kitchener for their own ends. It is a case of the triumph of obscure wire-pullers of whom the principal is the man Mullaly. He has really run the whole business including the writing and the advertising, and his success is all the more remarkable as he is not a man of real talent" (July 4, 1905, Kilbracken Collection, IO, MSS Eur. F. 102/39). This may well be true, yet vis-à-vis Curzon it is still quite historically sound to speak of "Kitchener's victory."

2 HD, I, 1.

3 Godley (citing JM's earlier letter) to JM, Dec. 20, 1905, Curzon-Kitchener Conflict, IO, MSS Eur. D. 555.

4 Brodrick to Ampthill, June 2, 1905, Ampthill Collection, IO, MSS Eur. E. 233/11.

5 HD, I, 1.

6 JM's "Memorandum" on "Indian Army Administration," Feb. 5, 1906, JMP, 39G. On December 13, 1905, Minto wrote to JM: "Kitchener told me yesterday . . . that if there was any idea of reverting to the former system of dual control he should feel bound to resign" (JMP, Minto to Morley, Vol. I).

7 Blunt noted on June 4, 1899, "Morley is very fierce against Kitchener" (Wilfred S. Blunt, *My Diaries: Being a Personal Narrative of Events, 1888–1914* [2 vols.; London, 1920], I, 397). And Morgan, who knew JM in the last years of his life, noted, "I think he underestimated Lord Kitchener, of whom he once said, 'A stupid face'" (John H. Morgan, "More Light on Lord Morley," *North American Review*, CCXXI [March, 1925], 488).

8 Ampthill to Godley, Jan. 30, 1906, Kilbracken Collection, F. 102/39.

9 *Ibid.*

10 Minto to JM, Dec. 20, 1905, JMP, Minto to Morley, Vol. I. See also Minto to JM, Dec. 13, 1905, *ibid.*

11 Minto to Godley, Dec. 28, 1905, Kilbracken Collection, F. 102/25.

12 Minto to Godley, Jan. 2, 1906, *ibid.*, 35.

13 *Ibid.* See also Minto to JM, Feb. 1, 1906, JMP, Minto to Morley, Vol. I.

NOTES 253

[14] Minto to JM, Jan. 10, 1906, *ibid.*
[15] G. Clarke to Kitchener, Jan. 5, 1906, Kitchener Collection, PRO 30/57, no. 34.
[16] Military [Secret] Despatch no. 18, entitled "Indian Army Administration." The draft was sent by JM to the cabinet on February 5, 1906, and is preserved in JMP, 39G; the final dispatch of February 9, 1906, is kept in 39f.
[17] JM's covering letter sent with the above-mentioned dispatch to Knollys, Feb. 9, 1906, Royal Archives, Windsor Castle, W/4/67.
[18] Mesopotamia Commission Report, Parliamentary Papers (Cd. 8610) (1917), p. 98 ff.
[19] JM subsequently explained his position in the remarkably illuminating statement of August, 1914, published as *Memorandum on Resignation* (London, 1928).
[20] Minto to JM, March 1, 1906, JMP, Minto to Morley, Vol. I. Minto had apparently been won over quite recently by Kitchener on this point. See his letter to JM, Dec. 13, 1905, *ibid.*, in which he takes JM's position on separation of powers.
[21] JM to Minto, March 14, 1907, JMP, Morley to Minto, Vol. II.
[22] See JM to Minto, Sept. 14, 1906, *ibid.*, Vol. I; JM to Minto, March 28, 1907, *ibid.*, Vol. II.
[23] JM to Minto, March 28, 1907, *ibid.*, Vol. II. See also JM to Minto, March 14, 1907, *ibid.*
[24] JM to Minto, Sept. 19, 1907, *ibid.* See also Minto to JM, Nov. 23, 1907, JMP, Minto to Morley, Vol. VII.
[25] JM to Minto, Nov. 29, 1907, JMP, Morley to Minto, Vol. II.
[26] JM to Minto, Oct. 1, 1908, *ibid.*, Vol. III.
[27] JM to Minto, March 15, 1906, *ibid.*, Vol. I.
[28] As late as June 18, 1907, Minto wrote to JM: "I am not at all sure that we do not underrate the possibility of a Russian army advancing on the Hindu Kusk [*sic*] meeting with little opposition and possible sympathy. . . . For how many years has one talked of this Russian invasion!—still the danger is not diminishing" (JMP, Minto to Morley, Vol. VI).
[29] See St. John Brodrick's memo to His Majesty, Nov. 11, 1904, Royal Archives, W/3/2; Kitchener's "Note on the Military Policy of India," Secret, Simla, July 19, 1905, Kitchener Collection, no. 30; Mowatt Committee Report, Feb. 15, 1907, JMP, 38a.
[30] JM to Minto, Feb. 16, 1906, JMP, Morley to Minto, Vol. I.
[31] JM to Minto, July 11, 1907, *ibid.*, Vol. II.
[32] Eighty-fifth meeting of the Committee of Imperial Defense (hereafter cited as CID), March 9, 1906, CID Papers, PRO 2/2/1, Cabinet Papers.
[33] Direct quotation from Grey in J. A. Spender, *The Life of the Rt. Hon. Sir Henry Campbell-Bannerman, G.C.B.* (2 vols.; London, 1923), II, 362.
[34] JM to Minto, Nov. 2, 1906, JMP, Morley to Minto, Vol. I.
[35] Minto to JM, Feb. 15, 1906, JMP, Minto to Morley, Vol. I. See also Minto to JM, April 9, 1906, *ibid.*, Vol. II.
[36] Minto to JM, Sept. 3, 1906, *ibid.*, Vol. III.
[37] Minto to JM, June 12, 1906, *ibid.*, Vol. II.
[38] JM to Minto, July 6, 1906, JMP, Morley to Minto, Vol. I.
[39] Minto to JM, Sept. 3, 1906, JMP, Minto to Morley, Vol. III.
[40] JM to Lamington, April 12, 1906, Lamington Papers, IO, MSS Eur. B. 159/1, 2, 3, Vol. III.

⁴¹ JM to Minto, Aug. 29, 1906, JMP, Morley to Minto, Vol. I.
⁴² JM to Minto, March 7, 1907, *ibid.*, Vol. II.
⁴³ JM's Indian Budget, June 6, 1907, *MIS*, p. 8.
⁴⁴ JM to His Majesty, Feb. 14, 1907, Royal Archives, W/4/108.
⁴⁵ Minto to JM, Feb. 14, 1907, JMP, Minto to Morley, Vol. V.
⁴⁶ JM to Minto, Feb. 15, 1907, JMP, Morley to Minto, Vol. II.
⁴⁷ Minto to JM, Jan. 2, 1907, JMP, Minto to Morley, Vol. V.
⁴⁸ Minto to His Majesty, Jan. 24, 1907, Royal Archives, W/4/105.
⁴⁹ JM to Minto, March 14, 1907, JMP, Morley to Minto, Vol. II. See also Mary, Countess of Minto, *India, Minto and Morley, 1905–1910* (London, 1934), p. 91.
⁵⁰ Minto to JM, March 19, 1908, Minto quoting from the report of his Kabul agent, Fakir Saiyid IstiKar-ud-Din, JMP, Minto to Morley, Vol. VIII.
⁵¹ Minto to JM, March 17, 1909, *ibid.*, Vol. XIII.
⁵² JM (reporting McMahon's "Secret" memo "On the Present Situation in Afghanistan") to Sir E. Grey, July 8, 1909, Grey Papers, Foreign Office Library, Cornwall House, Vol. LIX.
⁵³ Referred to by Minto in his report to His Majesty, June 18, 1908, Royal Archives, W/5/42a.
⁵⁴ E. Grey to A. Nicolson, April 1, 1907, Grey Papers, Vol. XXXIII.
⁵⁵ Convention between the United Kingdom and Russia (1908), Parliamentary Papers (Cd. 3753). See also Russia, no. 1 (1907), "Convention signed on August 31, 1907, between Great Britain and Russia, containing Arrangements on the subject of Persia, Afghanistan and Thibet" (*ibid.*, Cd. 3750).
⁵⁶ JM to Minto, May 24, 1907, JMP, Morley to Minto, Vol. II.
⁵⁷ "The Military Problems of India," note prepared by Sir G. Clarke for the CID, April 16, 1907, JMP, 37a.
⁵⁸ JM's own description of himself, HD, May 1, 1907, II, 40.
⁵⁹ JM to Minto, Jan. 2, 1907, JMP, Morley to Minto, Vol. II. See also HD, Jan. 8, 1907, II, 8.
⁶⁰ JM to Campbell-Bannerman, Jan. 6, 1907, Campbell-Bannerman Papers, BM, Add. MS 41223, XVIII, 213.
⁶¹ The report, dated May 1, 1907, was submitted to the full CID on May 30, 1907 (JMP, 37:3).
⁶² CID Papers, 98D, *ibid.*
⁶³ JM to Minto, May 31, 1907, JMP, Morley to Minto, Vol. II.
⁶⁴ JM to Minto, Sept. 19, 1907, *ibid.*
⁶⁵ JM to Minto, April 19, 1906, *ibid.*, Vol. I.
⁶⁶ JM to Minto, Sept. 19, 1907, *ibid.*, Vol. II.
⁶⁷ JM to Minto, Oct. 3, 1907, *ibid.*
⁶⁸ JM to Minto, June 15, Aug. 15, Sept. 14, Oct. 11, 1906, *ibid.*, Vol. I.
⁶⁹ JM to Minto, March 28, 1907, *ibid.*, Vol. II.
⁷⁰ HD, Feb. 6, 1908, III, 19.
⁷¹ "Some one at Balmoral told JM that during a game of billiards he had with his own eyes seen Kitchener alter the score in his own favor when he thought no one was looking" (HD, Oct. 16, 1907, II, 89). JM wrote to Minto, "I want nothing more than to get on with Kitchener, but such pranks . . . fill me with disgust. . . . it would be monstrous if there were the least departure from absolute straightness on his part" (JM to Minto, Sept. 4, 1907, JMP, Morley to Minto, Vol. II). On the eve of his departure from India, Kitchener was again a subject of curious controversy. His farewell speech in India, written for him by General

B. Duff, turned out to contain plagiarized portions of Curzon's famous Byculla Club speech (see Minto to JM, Sept. 30, Oct. 14, 1909, JMP, Minto to Morley, Vol. XVI). "The only explanation that I can think of," wrote JM, "is that the draftsman employed by Kitchener, to save himself trouble, carelessly borrowed Curzon's language and points, not guessing that the act of plunder was sure to be discovered. . . . Curzon yesterday, when the thing appeared, came and ate his luncheon at the Athenaeum at the table next to mine. . . . When he read Kitchener's speech, he told me, he thought it sensible and well put. No wonder. By and by he seemed to recollect his own language" (JM to Minto, Sept. 22, 1909, JMP, Morley to Minto, Vol. IV).

[72] Philip Magnus, *Kitchener: Portrait of an Imperialist* (London, 1958), pp. 225–226.

[73] JM to Minto, Aug. 28, 1907, JMP, Morley to Minto, Vol. II.

[74] *Ibid*.

[75] HD, Aug. 28, 1907, II, 74. After Lady Minto's visit to Whitehall in 1908, Hirtzel noted she was "very much galled because everyone thinks Ld. M. [Minto] is in Kitchener's pocket" (HD, March 12, 1908, III, 29).

[76] HD, Nov. 1, 1907, II, 93.

[77] JM to Kitchener, March 30, 1909, JMP, 39t.

[78] The Mowatt Committee's report of February 15, 1907, is preserved in JMP, 38a. L. Abrahams, secretary, Finance Department, IO, and General Sir E. Stedman, secretary, Military Department, IO, were the other members of the committee.

[79] Clarke to JM, Nov. 14, 1907, JMP D42. See also A. Lyall to JM, Dec. 6, 1907, JMP, 43C.

[80] JM to Minto, March 12, 1908, JMP, Morley to Minto, Vol. III.

[81] Military (Secret) Despatch no. 50, March 20, 1908, JMP, 37f.

[82] HD, March 5, 1908, III, 27.

[83] Despatch no. 33, March 1, 1907. See Minto to JM, May 13, 1908, JMP, Minto to Morley, Vol. IX.

[84] Minto to JM, March 19, 1908, *ibid.*, Vol. VIII.

[85] Minto to JM, April 8, 1908, *ibid.*, Vol. IX.

[86] JM to Clarke, June 12, 1908, JMP, D42.

[87] Minto to JM, April 18, 1906, JMP, Minto to Morley, Vol. II.

[88] Speech at Forfar, entitled "Back to Lord Lawrence," Oct. 4, [1898?], *MIS*, p. 205. See also JM's speech at Arbroath called "The Forward Policy," Sept. 28, 1897, *MIS*, pp. 195–196.

[89] JM to Minto, March 29, 1906, JMP, Morley to Minto, Vol. I.

[90] Curzon to JM, Dec. 24, 1905, JMP, 41.

[91] Minto to JM, Jan. 17, 1906, JMP, Minto to Morley, Vol. I. See also Minto to Godley, Jan. 2, 17, 1906, Kilbracken Collection, F. 102/25.

[92] Minto to JM, April 18, 1906, JMP, Minto to Morley, Vol. II.

[93] Minto to JM, Feb. 18, 1907, *ibid.*, Vol. V.

[94] Minto to JM, July 15, 1907, *ibid.*, Vol. VI.

[95] JM to Minto, Sept. 26, 1907, Morley to Minto, JMP, Vol. II.

[96] Sir Harold A. Deane, lieutenant colonel in the Indian Army, and Leslie M. Crump, I.C.S., 1897–1908.

[97] JM to Minto, Jan. 8, 1908, JMP, Morley to Minto, Vol. III.

[98] Minto to JM, Jan. 29, 1908, JMP, Minto to Morley, Vol. VIII.

[99] HD, Jan. 27, Feb. 6, 1908, III, 16, 19. For Minto's reaction see Minto to JM, Feb. 6, 1908, JMP, Minto to Morley, Vol. VIII.

[100] *Ibid.*
[101] JM to His Majesty, March 2, 1908, Royal Archives, W/5/37.
[102] JM to Clarke, March 5, 1908, JMP, D42.
[103] Clarke to JM, March 26, 1908, *ibid.*
[104] Minto to Kitchener, April 12, 1908, Kitchener Collection, no. 33.
[105] Minto to JM, May 13, 1908, JMP, Minto to Morley, Vol. IX.
[106] HPDHL, 4th ser., Vol. CXCI, 9th vol. of Session 1908, June 30, 1908, col. 527.
[107] JM to Minto, Sept. 10, 1908, JMP, Morley to Minto, Vol. III.
[108] HD, May 19, 1909, IV, 40.
[109] Secretary of State to Viceroy, Dec. 28, 1905, Private Telegram, JMP, 28.
[110] JM to Minto, Dec. 28, 1905, JMP, Morley to Minto, Vol. I.
[111] See JM's speech at Manchester, May 13, 1904, *The Issues at Stake* (London, 1904), p. 11; and JM to Minto, March 23, 1906, JMP, Morley to Minto, Vol. I. See also HD, after May 26, 1906, I, 3.
[112] Walter Lawrence's report to Knollys on the Prince of Wales's visit, Jan. 3, 1906, Royal Archives, W/4/64.
[113] Minto to JM, Jan. 3, 1906, JMP, Minto to Morley, Vol. I.
[114] See Minto's letters to JM, Jan. 3, 10, 17, 1906, *ibid.*
[115] Viceroy to Secretary of State, Feb. 2, 1907, Private Telegram, JMP, 28.
[116] Secretary of State to Viceroy, Feb. 6, 1907, *ibid.*
[117] JM to Minto, Feb. 8, 1907, JMP, Morley to Minto, Vol. II.
[118] Convention between the United Kingdom and Russia, 1908, Part III.
[119] Convention between the United Kingdom and China Respecting Tibet, signed at Peking, April 27, 1906, IO, Records, Treaty Series, 1906, vol. 136, no. 9, p. 119 ff.
[120] JM to Minto, Jan. 3, 1908, JMP, Morley to Minto, Vol. III.
[121] HD, Feb. 7, 1908, III, 19.
[122] O'Connor to Curzon, Quetta, May 5, 1908, Curzon Papers, IO, MSS Eur. F. 111/430.
[123] JM to Minto, March 3, 1910, JMP, Morley to Minto, Vol. V.
[124] JM to Minto, March 9, 1910, *ibid.*
[125] JM to Minto, March 17, 1910, *ibid.* Morley was even more emphatic on this point later, writing to Minto on June 30, 1910: "The Dalai Lama is a pestilent animal, as he proved himself to the Chinese in Peking, and he should be left to stew in his own juice" (*ibid.*).
[126] JM to Minto, March 3, 1910, *ibid.*
[127] JM to Minto, March 23, 1910, *ibid.*
[128] JM to Minto, July 18, 1910, *ibid.*
[129] *Ibid.*
[130] JM to Grey, March 22, 1909, Grey Papers, LIX.
[131] HD, Sept. 4, 1906, I, 77. See also JM to Minto, July 6, 1906, JMP, Morley to Minto, Vol. I.
[132] Minto to JM, Oct. 17, 1906, JMP, Minto to Morley, Vol. III.
[133] JM to Minto, March 4, 1908, JMP, Morley to Minto, Vol. III. JM reiterates this position again a year later; see JM to Minto, June 3, 1909, *ibid.*, Vol. IV.
[134] Kitchener's cable quoted by JM in JM to Minto, Sept. 20, 1906, *ibid.*, Vol. I.
[135] *Ibid.*
[136] Minto to Godley, Oct. 17, 1906, Kilbracken Collection, F. 102/25.
[137] JM to Minto, July 30, 1908, JMP, Morley to Minto, Vol. III. See also JM to Grey, Sept. 4, 1906, Grey Papers, LIX.

[138] JM to Lamington, March 23, 1906, Lamington Papers, B. 159/1, 2, 3.
[139] JM to Lamington, April 12, 1906, *ibid.*
[140] A. Godley to Lamington, April 6, 1906, *ibid.*
[141] JM to Lamington, May 4, 1906, *ibid.* See also JM to Minto, May 3, 1906, JMP, Morley to Minto, Vol. I.
[142] Meeting of Feb. 1, 1906, CID Papers, 68B, 70B, Cabinet Papers.
[143] JM to Minto, Feb. 9, 1906, JMP, Morley to Minto, Vol. I.
[144] Viceroy to Secretary of State, Private Telegram, Feb. 5, 1906, JMP, 28.
[145] JM to Minto, May 31, 1907, JMP, Morley to Minto, Vol. II. The quoted allusion dates back to a letter JM sent to Minto on December 21, 1906, in which he wrote: "Chamberlain, who was for some months at Washington in search of a Fishery Treaty long ago, used to give rather evil accounts of Americans as negotiators—'so extremely *practical*,' he said, with a somewhat sardonic accent."
[146] Minto to JM, Sept. 9, 1909, JMP, Minto to Morley, Vol. XVI.
[147] *Journals and Letters of Reginald Viscount Esher*, ed. Maurice V. Brett (London, 1934–1938), May 12, 1910, III, 3.
[148] JM to Minto, June 15, 1910, JMP, Morley to Minto, Vol. V.
[149] C. H. Hardinge, *My Indian Years: 1910–1916* (London, 1948), p. 4.
[150] V. Chirol to "My dear T [?]," April 28, 1910, Grey Papers, LXVII.
[151] Minto to JM, Feb. 25, 1909, JMP, Minto to Morley, Vol. XIII.
[152] Chirol to "T," April 28, 1910, Grey Papers, LXVII.
[153] JM to Minto, Jan. 8, 1908, JMP, Morley to Minto, Vol. III.

Notes to Chapter V

[1] Government of India Despatch 7 of 1907, March 21, 1907, no. 3, JMP, 32:2. For a detailed study of Indian politics at this time see M. N. Das, *India under Morley and Minto: Politics behind Revolution, Repression and Reforms* (London and New York, 1964), pp. 88–146.
[2] JM's Budget Speech, July 20, 1906, HPDHC, 4th ser., vol. 161 of Session 1906. col. 586.
[3] "Benares Presidential Address," in G. K. Gokhale, *The Speeches of Gopal Krishna Gokhale* (3d ed.; Madras, 1920), p. 708.
[4] Government of India Despatch 7 of 1907, March 21, 1907, no. 3. For the history of partition see Z. H. Zaidi, "The Political Motive in the Partition of Bengal," *Journal of the Pakistan Historical Society*, XII, Pt. II (April, 1964); Sufia Ahmed, "Some Aspects of the History of the Muslim Community in Bengal, 1884–1912" (unpublished Ph.D. thesis, University of London, 1961); Syed Razi Wasti, *Lord Minto and the Indian Nationalist Movement, 1905 to 1910* (Oxford, 1964).
[5] Budget Speech, June 6, 1907, *MIS*, p. 11.
[6] Minto to Morley, Dec. 20, 1905, JMP, Minto to Morley, Vol. I.
[7] HD, Jan., 1906, I, 6.
[8] JM's reply to Roberts' Amendment of the Address, Feb. 26, 1906, HPDHC, 4th ser., vol. 152 of Session 1906, cols. 843–844.
[9] JM to Minto, March 8, 1906, JMP, Morley to Minto, Vol. I.
[10] Minto to JM, March 29, 1906, JMP, Minto to Morley, Vol. I.
[11] JM to Minto, April 19, 1906, JMP, Morley to Minto, Vol. I.
[12] JM to Minto, April 25, 1906, *ibid.*

[13] JM to Minto, May 3, 1906, *ibid*.
[14] JM to Godley, April 14, 1906, Kilbracken Collection, IO, MSS Eur. F. 102/8.
[15] JM to Minto, May 3, 1906, JMP, Morley to Minto, Vol. I.
[16] Minto to JM, May 24, 1906, JMP, Minto to Morley, Vol. II.
[17] Minto to JM, May 9, 1906, *ibid*.
[18] HD, May 14, 1906, I, 43.
[19] JM to Lamington, May 18, 1906, Lamington Papers, IO, MSS Eur. B. 159/3.
[20] *Ibid*.
[21] JM to Minto, June 6, 1906, JMP, Morley to Minto, Vol. I.
[22] Viceroy to Secretary of State, June 25, 1906, Private Telegram, JMP, 28.
[23] Viceroy to Secretary of State, June 30, 1906, Private Telegram, *ibid*.
[24] HD, July 2, 1906, I, 58.
[25] Fuller's reply to Minto, July 15, 1906, and Risley's letter to Fuller, July 5, 1906, provoking the reply, are both enclosed with Minto to JM, July 25, 1906, JMP, Minto to Morley, Vol. III.
[26] According to P. Lyon, chief secretary to the government of Eastern Bengal and Assam, "It was certainly unexpectedly accepted" (Lyon to Curzon, Oct. 8, 1906, Curzon Papers, IO, MSS Eur. F. 111/429). Hirtzel recorded that "he [Fuller] had said to his Secretary [Lyon]—'I will bet you what you like that they won't accept it, they daren't!' And was thunderstruck when the acceptance came" (HD, Sept. 12, 1906, I, 78–79).
[27] Minto to JM, July 25, 1906, JMP, Minto to Morley, Vol. III. Minto wrote Godley that "we have been extremely lucky in getting rid of him as we have done" (Aug. 16, 1906, Kilbracken Collection, F. 102/25).
[28] Morley (signing himself "M.P.") answered one letter sent by Sir W. Ward to the *Times* (*Times*, Aug. 27, 1906, p. 6).
[29] HD, Oct. 26, 1906, I, 91. Curzon's introduction of Sir B. Fuller at a meeting of the Royal Colonial Institute (*Times*, June 9, 1909; clipping in JMP, miscellaneous). See Curzon to JM, June 20, 1909, JMP, envelope 12. In 1957 I met an "Old India Hand" who had been in Sir B. Fuller's service, and the first thing he said upon learning of my interest in India's nationalist movement was, "Yes, well, Morley started all that nonsense by firing Sir B. Fuller—worst mistake we made in India!"
[30] P. Lyon to Curzon, Oct. 8, 1906, Curzon Papers, F. 111/429.
[31] JM to Minto, Aug. 15, 1906, JMP, Morley to Minto, Vol. 1.
[32] HD, July 26, 1906, I, 65.
[33] *Ibid*.
[34] JM to Minto, July 27, 1906, JMP, Morley to Minto, Vol. I.
[35] JM to Minto, Aug. 2, 1906, *ibid*.
[36] JM to Minto, Aug. 6, 1906, *ibid*.
[37] Minto to JM, Aug. 15, 1906, JMP, Minto to Morley, Vol. III. See also Minto to Godley, Aug. 16, 1906, Kilbracken Collection, F. 102/25.
[38] Marked in red ink in JM's own hand "Most Secret," these enclosures are with Minto to JM, Sept. 10, 1906, JMP, Minto to Morley, Vol. III.
[39] O'Donnell to Banerjea, March 2, 1906, enclosed with *ibid*.
[40] Hirtzel's quote from JM re O'Donnell, HD, July 1, 1907, II, 58.
[41] JM to Godley, Sept. 21, 1906, Kilbracken Collection, F. 102/8.
[42] JM, June 30, 1908, *HPDHL*, 4th ser., vol. 191, 9th vol. of Session 1908, col. 525.
[43] JM to Minto, Jan. 24, 1907, JMP, Morley to Minto, Vol. II.

NOTES

44 HD, April 17, 1907, II, 36; Dec. 2, 1908, III, 105; June 8, 24, 1909, IV, 46, 51.
45 Lord MacDonnell, who had served on the IO reforms committee (HD, Nov. 5, 1908, III, 97).
46 HD, June 28, 1908, III, 59.
47 JM to Minto, April 9, 1908, JMP, Morley to Minto, Vol. III.
48 Romesh C. Dutt (1848–1909), whom Morley called "the most satisfying Indian that I have yet seen." (JM to Minto, July 27, 1906, *ibid.*, Vol. I), passed the I.C.S. examination in 1869. He served as divisional commissioner in Orissa, 1894–1895. He was lecturer in Indian history at University College, London, and in 1899 presided over the Indian National Congress. He served Baroda State as revenue minister from 1904 to 1906, and became prime minister of that state in 1909.
49 JM to Minto, Oct. 5, 1906, JMP, Morley to Minto, Vol. 1.
50 Minto to Godley, Jan. 3, 1907, Kilbracken Collection, F. 102/25.
51 IO Records, Public Letters from India, 1907, no. 10. Minor Judicial and Public Letters, government of India to JM, May 16, 1907. Ordinance no. 1 of 1907 read: "The District Magistrate may at any time, by order in writing . . . prohibit any meeting in a proclaimed area [East Bengal and Assam and the Punjab] if in his opinion such meeting is likely to promote sedition or disaffection or to cause a disturbance of the public tranquility."
52 Budget Address, June 6, 1907, *MIS*, p. 17 ff.
53 Viceroy to Secretary of State, Aug. 1, 1907, IO Records, Judicial and Public, 1907, vol. 817, no. 2570; Viceroy to Secretary of State, Sept. 3, 1907, *ibid.*, vol. 821, no. 3002.
54 *Ibid.*, 1908, vol. 843, no. 511; vol. 852, collection 992.
55 R. C. Dutt to JM, Feb. 22, 1908, JMP, 43g.
56 R. C. Dutt to JM, April 24, 1908, *ibid.*
57 IO Records, Judicial and Public, 1908, vol. 866, no. 1961.
58 HD, Nov. 12, 1908, III, 99.
59 See the regulation's wording. See also "Deportation of 9 Indian Leaders of Sedition under Regulation III of 1818," IO Records, Judicial and Public, 1909, vol. 908, collection 26.
60 HD, March 15, 1909, IV, 22.
61 L. Jenkins to JM, June 3, 1909, JMP, 43H.
62 JM to Indian Probationers, June 13, 1908, *MIS*, p. 141.
63 Charles Hardinge, *My Indian Years: 1910–1916* (London, 1948), p. 11. For an explanation of this dramatic reversal of policy see Z. H. Zaidi and F. Eustis, II, "Crown, Viceroy and Cabinet," *History* (June, 1964).
64 JM to Clarke, April 28, 1910, JMP, D42.
65 Minto to JM, March 5, 1907, JMP, Minto to Morley, Vol. V.
66 HD, Feb. 16, 1907, II, 19.
67 Minto to JM, Feb. 18, 1907, JMP, Minto to Morley, Vol. V.
68 JM to Minto, April 26, 1907, JMP, Morley to Minto, Vol. II.
69 Budget Speech, June 6, 1907, *MIS*, p. 15. JM relied on information received from Minto in Viceroy to Secretary of State, Private Telegram, May 7, 1907, JMP, 28.
70 R. C. Dutt to JM, April 24, 1908, JMP, 43G.
71 Minto to JM, Aug. 7, 1907, JMP, Minto to Morley, Vol. VI.
72 Viceroy to Secretary of State, Private Telegram, May 5, 1907, JMP, 27.
73 *Ibid.*
74 HD, May 27, 1907, II, 48.

75 This "most unfortunate case" was reported by Minto in his letter to JM of October 9, 1907 (JMP, Minto to Morley, Vol. IV).
76 Curzon to Hamilton, Sept. 17, 1902, cited in C. H. Philips, ed., *The Evolution of India and Pakistan, 1858 to 1947* (London, 1962), p. 72.
77 Viceroy to Secretary of State, May 7, 1907, Private Telegram, JMP, 27.
78 Secretary of State to Viceroy, May 6, 1907, Private Telegram, *ibid.*
79 Viceroy to Secretary of State, May 7, 1907, Private Telegram, *ibid.* This telegram informed JM of the issue of warrants. A copy was sent to the King (Royal Archives, Windsor Castle, W/4/116).
80 As noted in chap. iii (HD, May 10, 1907, II, 43).
81 HD, May 11, 1907, II, 43.
82 Wired on May 15, 1907 (HD, II, 44).
83 Minto to JM, May 16, 1907, JMP, Minto to Morley, Vol. V.
84 Minto to Lamington, May 27, 1907, Lamington Papers, B. 159/1.
85 Minto to JM, May 21, 1907, JMP, Minto to Morley, Vol. V.
86 HD, May 23, 1907, II, 47.
87 Budget Speech, June 6, 1907, *MIS*, pp. 16–17.
88 Editorial comment on JM's speech (*Times*, June 7, 1907, p. 9).
89 JM to Minto, Dec. 26, 1907, JMP, Morley to Minto, Vol. II.
90 Letter of June 15, 1907, printed in *Times*, June 18, 1907, p. 16.
91 JM to Minto, June 13, 1907, JMP, Morley to Minto, Vol. II.
92 JM to Minto, July 18, 1907, *ibid.*
93 JM to Lamington, July 12, 1907, Lamington Papers, B. 159/3.
94 JM to Minto, Aug. 23, 1907, JMP, Morley to Minto, Vol. II.
95 See his letters to Minto, Aug. 28, Oct. 3, 25, 1907, JMP, Morley to Minto, Vol. II.
96 HD, Oct. 26, 1907, II, 91.
97 HD, Oct. 28, 1907, II, 92.
98 HD, Oct. 30, 1907, II, 92.
99 Minto to Morley, Nov. 5, 1907, JMP, Minto to Morley, Vol. VII.
100 Minto to Godley, Nov. 7, 1907, Kilbracken Collection, F. 102/25.
101 Report of J. R. Dunlop Smith's interview with Gokhale of October 20, 1907, enclosed in Minto to JM, Oct. 29, 1907, JMP, Minto to Morley, Vol. VII.
102 JM to Minto, Nov. 29, 1907, JMP, Morley to Minto, Vol. II.
103 JM to Minto, April 15, 1908, JMP, Morley to Minto, Vol. III.
104 *Ibid.*
105 JM to Minto, April 23, 1908, JMP, Morley to Minto, Vol. III.
106 HD, May 14, 1908, III, 47.
107 *Ibid.*, May 15, 1908.
108 "Indian Civil Service," *MIS*, p. 70.
109 JM to Minto, Feb. 27, 1908, JMP, Morley to Minto, Vol. III.
110 JM to Minto, May 7, 1908, *ibid.*
111 D. H. Kingsford, chief presiding magistrate, Calcutta. He was educated at Haileybury College and Trinity College, Oxon., and was appointed after the examination of 1893, serving in Bengal as assistant magistrate and collector until 1904.
112 HD, May 4, 1908, III, 44. This led for a while to "a distinct cloud over our relations," Hirtzel soon noted, explaining that "what he said involved 4 monstrous assumptions (1) that there was in fact a connexion between the outrage and the alleged floggings (2) that there had been flogging for sedition (3) that Kingsford had acted illegally (for JM said 'of course, *it may be that*

he acted within the law') (4) that he deserved to be blown up!" (HD, May 7, 1908, III, 45).

[113] HD, July 31, 1906, I, 66.
[114] HD, Nov. 4, 1907, II, 94.
[115] HD, Feb. 27, 1908, III, 25.
[116] JM to Minto, May 7, 1908, JMP, Morley to Minto, Vol. III.
[117] The quotation is taken from an article in the *Sandhya* sent by Risley to Godley on January 16, 1908, from the government of Bengal's report no. 104 (IO Records, Judicial and Public, 1908, vol. 843, no. 425).
[118] See Stanley A. Wolpert, *Tilak and Gokhale: Revolution and Reform in the Making of Modern India* (Berkeley and Los Angeles, 1962), pp. 157–240.
[119] Clarke to JM, May 7, 1908, JMP, D42.
[120] This power, enjoyed by local governments until 1899, was withheld from them at that time, and all such prosecutions could be initiated only after approval from the central government (see IO Records, Judicial and Public, 1907, vol. 809, nos. 1546, 1743, 1771).
[121] Viceroy to Secretary of State, Telegram, June 1, 1907, *ibid.*, no. 1771.
[122] Clarke to JM, May 10, 1908, JMP, D42.
[123] Tilak was believed by some to be the avatara "Kalki," the tenth manifestation in terrestrial form of Vishnu.
[124] Clarke to JM, June 9, 1908, JMP, D42.
[125] Clarke to JM, Jan. 16, 1908, *ibid.*
[126] *Ibid.*
[127] JM to Clarke, Feb. 11, 1908, *ibid.*
[128] JM to Clarke, April 24, 1908, *ibid.*
[129] Clarke to JM, April 30, 1908, *ibid.*
[130] Clarke to JM, May 22, 1908, *ibid.*
[131] Clarke to JM, May 27, 1908, *ibid.*
[132] Clarke to JM, June 9, 1908, *ibid.*
[133] Clarke to JM, June 24, 1908, *ibid.*
[134] JM to Clarke, July 3, 1908, *ibid.*
[135] Clarke to JM, July 6, 1908, *ibid.*
[136] JM to Minto, July 16, 1908, JMP, Morley to Minto, Vol. III.
[137] JM to Clarke, July 17, 1908, JMP, D42.
[138] HD, July 24, 28, 1908, III, pp. 67–68.
[139] JM to Minto, July 24, 1908, JMP, Morley to Minto, Vol. III.
[140] Clarke to JM, July 31, 1908, JMP, D42.
[141] *Ibid.*
[142] Clarke to JM, Aug. 6, 1908, *ibid.*
[143] JM to Clarke, July 31, 1908, *ibid.*
[144] JM to Clarke, Aug. 7, 1908, *ibid.*
[145] JM to Clarke, Aug. 19, 1908, *ibid.*
[146] Minto to His Majesty, Aug. 20, 1908, Royal Archives, W/5/46.
[147] JM to Minto, Aug. 20, 1908, JMP, Morley to Minto, Vol. III.
[148] JM to Clarke, Sept. 3, 1908, JMP, D42. For the Tinnevelly riots see IO Records, Judicial and Public, 1908, vol. 852, no. 993, collection entitled "Riots at Tinnevelli and Tuticorin."
[149] Extract from the Proceedings of the Council of the Governor General for Making Laws and Regulations, Simla, June 8, 1908, *ibid.*, vol. 870, no. 2363. The text of the Press Act (VII of 1908) is in Parliamentary Papers, House of Commons (Cd. 4152), LXXIV, 919.

[150] JM to Minto, May 28, 1908, JMP, Morley to Minto, Vol. III.
[151] IO, Records, Judicial and Public, 1908, vol. 870, no. 2363.
[152] JM to Clarke, May 29, 1908, JMP, D42. For House of Commons questions on the press law see IO, Records, Judicial and Public, 1908, vol. 866, no. 1934.
[153] "Indian Civil Service," July 1908, MIS, pp. 71–72.
[154] Ibid., p. 73.
[155] Minto to Godley, Aug. 27, 1908, Kilbracken Collection, F. 102/25.
[156] Fraser arrived in India in 1871, and was appointed lieutenant governor of Bengal in November, 1908.
[157] JM to Minto, Nov. 12, 1908, JMP, Morley to Minto, Vol. III.
[158] The year's list of "Anarchical Offences" was telegraphed to Morley by Minto, Dec. 13, 1908, IO, Records, Judicial and Public, 1908, vol. 904, no. 4642.
[159] HD, Nov. 30, 1908, III, 104.
[160] Ibid.
[161] IO, Records, Judicial and Public, 1908, vol. 908, no. 26. The entire volume is entitled "Deportation of 9 Indian Leaders of Sedition under Regulation III of 1818."
[162] Secretary of State to Viceroy, Dec. 15, 1908, in ibid.
[163] Dec. 17, 1908, ibid.
[164] Referred to by JM to Minto in his letter of May 6, 1909 (JMP, Morley to Minto, Vol. IV): "Some 150 Members of Parliament have written to Asquith protesting against Deportation. . . . you will not be able to deport any more of your suspects—that is quite clear."
[165] HD, May 25, 1909, IV, 42.
[166] Minto to JM, Feb. 4, 1909, JMP, Minto to Morley, Vol. XIII.
[167] Minto to JM, Jan. 21, 1909, ibid.
[168] Minto to JM, Feb. 16, 1909, ibid.
[169] Enclosed with letter from B. S. Dutt to Stuart, secretary to government of India, Home Department, June 28, 1909, IO, Records, Judicial and Public, 1909, vol. 908, no. 26.
[170] JM to Minto, June 3, 1909, JMP, Morley to Minto, Vol. IV.
[171] IO, Records, Judicial and Public, 1909, vol. 920, no. 855.
[172] Clarke to JM, March 31, 1909, JMP, D42.
[173] Clarke to JM, July 1, 1908, ibid.
[174] Clarke to JM, March 31, 1909, ibid.
[175] Sir William H. Curzon-Wyllie, born in 1848, entered the Indian Staff Corps in 1869. In 1879 he was appointed to the Political Department of the government of India, and from then until his appointment in 1901 as A.D.C. to the secretary of state he served in several capacities throughout central India.
[176] JM to Clarke, July 9, 1909, JMP, D42.
[177] Jenkins to JM, July 4, 1909, JMP, H.
[178] Statement of Chanjeri Rao in enclosure from weekly letter (Feb. 1, 1910) of the secretary of the Home Department, Bombay, sent by Clarke to JM, Feb. 10, 1910, JMP, D42.
[179] HD, July 7, 24, 1909, IV, 54, 59.
[180] HD, Nov. 24, 1908, III, 102.
[181] HD, May 18, 1907, II, 45.
[182] HD, Oct. 15, 1908, III, 88.
[183] HD, Oct. 15, Nov. 26, 1908, III, 91, 103.
[184] HD, July 17, 1909, IV, 57.
[185] HD, July 5, 1909, IV, 54.

[186] *Ibid.*
[187] Sir John David Rees (1854–1922), appointed to I.C.S. in 1873, served from 1886 to 1891 as private secretary to the governor of Madras; he was a member of the governor-general's Legislative Council from 1895 to 1897 and again in 1898. He retired in 1900.
[188] July 30, 1907, IO, Records, Judicial and Public, 1907, vol. 817, no. 2559.
[189] See *Rex v. Aldred: London Trial, 1909; Indian Sedition: Glasgow Sedition Trial, 1921,* ed. Guy A. Aldred (Glasgow, 1948).
[190] JM to Clarke, Sept. 17, 1909, JMP, D42.
[191] JM to Minto, Oct. 14, 1909, JMP, Morley to Minto, Vol. IV.
[192] Minto to JM, Nov. 19, 1909, JMP, Minto to Morley, Vol. XVI.
[193] Clarke to JM, Aug. 17, 1910, JMP, D42.
[194] Minto to JM, Dec. 30, 1909, JMP, Minto to Morley, Vol. XVI.
[195] "Indian Criminal Law (Amendment) Act, 1908," IO, Records, Judicial and Public, 1909, vol. 909, no. 32.
[196] "Note on One of Many Repressive Bills," Jan. 5, 1910, Fleetwood Wilson Papers, IO, MSS Eur. E. 224/13. Jenkins soon noted that "there can be no doubt that the secret procedure of the recent Act gives great opportunities for the manufacture of false evidence, and I am able to say this from what has recently come under my own observation" (Jenkins to JM, May 24, 1910, JMP, H).
[197] JM to Clarke, Jan. 7, 1910, JMP, D42.
[198] JM to Minto, Jan. 27, 1910, JMP, Morley to Minto, Vol. V.
[199] An admission with which Fleetwood Wilson agreed. See his note on "Wholesale Deportation," Feb. 12, 1910, Fleetwood Wilson Papers, E. 224/13.
[200] JM to Clarke, Feb. 2, 1910, JMP, D42.
[201] JM to Minto, Feb. 3, 1910, JMP, Morley to Minto, Vol. V. For the official rationale behind the act and an explanation of what it does see Montagu's Budget Speech, July 26, 1910, HPDHC, 5th ser., vol. 19, 6th vol. of Session 1910, col. 1968 ff. For the text of the act see Parliamentary Papers, 1910 (Cd. 5269), LXVIII, 1, Indian Press Act.
[202] Among them the Bihar Planters Association; Darjeeling Planters Association; Dehra Doona Tea Planters Association; Duars Planters; India Tea Association; Surma Valley Branch; Assam Branch; Karachi Chamber of Commerce, and many others, all of whom signed an "open letter" to JM, received December 12, 1908, advocating new press legislation such as the above (IO, Records, Judicial and Public, 1908, vol. 904, no. 4650; also see *ibid.,* 1909, vol. 909, no. 32).
[203] Feb. 4, 1909, IO, Records, Finance, 1909, vol. 1531, no. 531.
[204] L. Jenkins to JM, Feb. 14, 1910, JMP, 43H.
[205] JM's speech at Arbroath, Oct. 21, 1907 (*Times*, Oct. 22, 1907; HD, VI).
[206] Curzon's Debate, June 30, 1908, HPDHL, 4th ser., vol. 191, 9th vol. of Session 1908, col. 529. The London organ of the INC, *India,* wrote on April 9, 1909, that "if a Liberal Secretary of State has allowed India to be chastised with whips, a Tory in the place of Lord Morley would have scourged her with scorpions."
[207] Arbroath Speech, Oct. 21, 1907, HD, VI.
[208] *Ibid.*
[209] JM to Minto, Aug. 15, 1907, JMP, Morley to Minto, Vol. II.
[210] JM to Minto, April 2, 1908, *ibid.,* Vol. III.
[211] JM to Minto, Oct. 31, 1907, *ibid.,* Vol. II.
[212] "Indian Civil Service" speech, July, 1908, *MIS*, p. 66.

Notes to Chapter VI

[1] Certainly not mere adjustments of "the machinery of British Government to the changed circumstances in India," as S. R. Mehrotra calls them ("The Politics behind the Montagu Declaration of 1917," in C. H. Philips. ed., *Politics and Society in India* [London, 1963], pp. 71–74).

[2] R. B. Ghose's Presidential Address at Madras Conference, December, 1908 (copy preserved in IO, Records, Judicial and Public, 1909, vol. 916, no. 497).

[3] J. Ramsay MacDonald, *The Awakening of India* (London, 1910), p. 270. More extreme radicals like Wilfred Blunt, however, contended they were "a great flourish of trumpets about a very small matter" (Wilfred S. Blunt, *My Diaries: Being a Personal Narrative of Events, 1888–1914*, Feb. 25, 1909 [2 vols.; London, 1920], II, 242).

[4] "On Proposed Reforms," Dec. 17, 1908, HPDHL, 4th ser., vol. 198, 1908, col. 1974.

[5] *Ibid.*, col. 1985.

[6] Proceedings of the Legislative Council of the Governor-General of India, Jan. 25, 1910, XLVIII, 49. Minto had earlier told his Legislative Council much the same thing at the conclusion of the budget debate on March 29, 1909 (see Mary, Countess of Minto, *India, Minto and Morley, 1905–1910* [London, 1934], pp. 290–291).

[7] "India under Lord Morley," *Quarterly Review*, CCXIV (Jan., 1911), 215.

[8] Mary, Countess of Minto, *op. cit.*, p. 111. Countess Minto entitled her twenty-fourth chapter "Minto's Reform Scheme" (p. 212).

[9] John Buchan, *Lord Minto: A Memoir* (London, 1924).

[10] See H. H. Dodwell, ed., *The Cambridge History of India* (Cambridge, 1932), VI, 296. See also *ibid.*, p. 560; R. Coupland, *The Indian Problem, 1833–1945* (Oxford, 1942), p. 25; James Pope-Hennessey, *Lord Crewe, 1858–1945: The Likeness of a Liberal* (London, 1955), p. 84.

[11] Minto to JM, May 28, 1906, JMP, Minto to Morley, Vol. II.

[12] *Ibid.*

[13] Coupland, *op. cit.*, p. 25.

[14] Even so eminent a historian as Knaplund was sufficiently deceived to write a grossly distorted appraisal, stating that the "Conservative Viceroy [Minto] was in fact readier to make concessions than was his Liberal Chief" (Paul Knaplund, *The British Empire, 1815–1939* [London, 1942], p. 760).

[15] JM to Minto, June 6, 1906, JMP, Morley to Minto, Vol. I.

[16] JM to Minto, June 15, 1906, *ibid.*

[17] Gokhale to Dravid, July 6, 1906, quoted in Stanley A. Wolpert, *Tilak and Gokhale: Revolution and Reform in the Making of Modern India* (Berkeley and Los Angeles, 1962), p. 184.

[18] E.g., "Dr. Pollen" (see HD, July 25, 28, Aug. 1, 1906, I, 64–66). See also intelligence report by G. Fell, deputy secretary, government of India, Home Department, Nov. 15, 1906, in IO, Records, Judicial and Public, 1907, vol. 796, no. 616; Minto to Godley, Aug. 16, 1906, Kilbracken Collection, IO, MSS Eur. F. 102/25; and especially Minto to JM, Aug. 22, 1906, JMP, Minto to Morley, Vol. III.

[19] JM sent Minto an extract of a letter from Gokhale as late as September 29, 1910, urging that prompt attention be paid to the particular grievance reported

(JM to Minto, Sept. 27, 1910, with postscript dated Sept. 29, JMP, Morley to Minto, Vol. V).

[20] JM to Minto, June 15, 1906, *ibid.*, Vol. I.

[21] Resolution III of 1885 stated: "That this Congress consider the reform and expansion of the Supreme and existing local Legislative Councils, by the admission of a considerable proportion of elected members essential; and holds that all Budgets should be referred to these Councils for consideration, their members being moreover empowered to interpellate the Executive in regard to all branches of the administration" (Report of the Indian National Congress, 1885, in Philips, *op. cit.*, p. 151).

[22] Lord Elgin was secretary of state for the colonies, and Fowler was in charge of the Duchy of Lancaster, but both men might just as easily have been sent up to the India Office, since Elgin, as governor-general from 1894 to 1899, had had long Indian experience, while Fowler had already served as Indian secretary (1893–1894).

[23] JM to Minto, June 22, 1906, JMP, Morley to Minto, Vol. I.

[24] HD, July 5, 1906, I, 59.

[25] JM, Nov. 19, 1889, at the Eighty Club dinner, "Liberalism and Social Reform." *The Eighty Club: 1890* (London, 1891), p. 12.

[26] The Fifth Marquess of Lansdowne, Henry Clark Keith Petty-Fitzmaurice (1845–1927), was leader of the Conservative party in the House of Lords from 1902 to 1916. He was undersecretary of state for India in 1880 and viceroy of India from 1888 to 1894.

[27] JM to Minto, March 28, 1907, JMP, Morley to Minto, Vol. II.

[28] Viceroy to Secretary of State, July 14, 1906, Private and Confidential Telegram, JMP, 28.

[29] Minto to JM, Sept. 2, 1908, JMP, Minto to Morley, Vol. XI. This letter was written in response to JM to Minto, Aug. 10, 1908, JMP, Morley to Minto, Vol. III.

[30] JM to Minto, Oct. 31, 1907, *ibid.*, Vol. II.

[31] JM's Budget Speech, July 20, 1906, *HPDHC*, 4th ser., vol. 161, 1906, cols. 587–588.

[32] In his Presidential Address to the Benares Congress in December, 1905, Gokhale said: "In my humble opinion, our immediate demands should be:—(1) a reform of our Legislative Councils, i.e., raising the proportion of elected members, requiring the Budget to be formally passed by the Councils, and empowering the members to bring formal amendments" (G. K. Gokhale, *The Speeches of Gopal Krishna Gokhale* [3d ed.; Madras, 1920], p. 705).

[33] Note by T. Morison, added to the resolutions of the Secretary of State's Special Committee on Reforms, April 18, 1907, JMP, 32.

[34] JM's Despatch to the Government of India, May 17, 1907, par. 20, *ibid.*

[35] Technically, these continued to be only one council, the Central Executive Council. To the Executive Council of the governor-general were added not less than six nor more than twelve members when assembled for the purpose of making laws and regulations. Of these additional members, not less than half were to be nonofficials and several were Indians nominated by the viceroy. Initially, the presidencies of Bombay and Madras alone were given legislative councils with not more than eight additional members appointed by each governor. The act, however, allowed for the creation of such councils in other provinces when desired, so that in 1862 one was established in Bengal and in 1886 another was established in the United Provinces.

[36] Lord Cross to Lord Lansdowne, June 30, 1892, par. 3, Lansdowne Papers, IO, MSS Eur. D. 558, II, B(c).

[37] In 1897 two new legislative councils were inaugurated in the Punjab and Burma, and in 1905, with its creation, East Bengal and Assam was given a legislative council.

[38] The maximum number of additional members added to the councils of Madras, Bombay, and Bengal (and after 1905, of East Bengal and Assam as well) was twenty, while that for the United Provinces, Punjab, and Burma was fixed at fifteen.

[39] "Report on the Subject of Provincial Councils," by G. Chesney, C. U. Aitchison, and J. Westland (MacDonnell, secretary), Oct. 10, 1888, IO, Records, Public Letters from India and General Letters from Bengal, 1888, vol. 9, pp. 1173–1183. See also B. Martin, Jr., "New India, 1885: A Study of British Official Policy and the Emergence of the Indian National Congress" (unpublished Ph.D. thesis, University of Pennsylvania, 1964).

[40] Report of the 14th Madras Provincial Conference, June 20–22, 1906, with Appendixed Memorials to the Secretary of State for India, IO, Records, Judicial and Public, 1907, vol. 811, no. 1902.

[41] Rt. Hon. Sir Henry Hartley Fowler, born May 16, 1830; educated at Woodhouse Grove School; Mayor of Wolverhampton (1863); M.P. for Wolverhampton from 1880; undersecretary of state, Home Department (1884–1885); financial secretary to treasury (1886); secretary of state for India (1894–1895).

[42] Rt. Hon. Lord George Francis Hamilton, born Dec., 1845; educated at Harrow; M.P. for Middlesex (1868–1885); undersecretary of state for India (1874); first lord of the admiralty in the Marquis of Salisbury's first and second administrations (1885–1886) and (1886–1892); secretary of state for India (1895–1903).

[43] Rt. Hon. St. John Brodrick, educated at Eton and Balliol College, Oxford; M.P. for West Surrey (1880–1885); financial secretary to the War Office (1886–1892); undersecretary of state for foreign affairs (1898–1900); secretary of state for war (1900–1903); secretary of state for India (1903–1905).

[44] Rt. Hon. Victor Alexander Bruce, Earl of Elgin and Kincardine, born May, 1849; succeeded his father, who had been viceroy of India (1862–1863), in the earldom in 1863; educated at Eton and Balliol College, Oxford; treasurer of Her Majesty's household and joint commissioner of works in Gladstone's third administration (1886); viceroy of India (1894–1899).

[45] The Rt. Hon. George Nathaniel, Lord Curzon of Keddleston, educated at Eton and Balliol College, Oxford; fellow of All-Souls College (1883); M.A. (1884); private secretary to Lord Salisbury (1885–1886); undersecretary of state for India (1891–1892); undersecretary of state for foreign affairs (1895–1899); created baron in the peerage of Ireland; viceroy of India (1899–1905).

[46] Minto's minute of Aug. 15, 1906, enclosed in Minto to JM, Aug. 15, 1906, JMP, Minto to Morley, Vol. III.

[47] Viceroy to Secretary of State, Aug. 20, 1906, Private Telegram, JMP, 27.

[48] Minto to JM, Oct. 4, 1906, JMP, Minto to Morley, Vol. III.

[49] The report, dated Simla, Oct. 12, 1906, is preserved in JMP, 32:1 (hereafter cited in text by paragraph and referred to as Report).

[50] JM to Minto, Nov. 23, 1906, JMP, Morley to Minto, Vol. I.

[51] Minto to JM, Dec. 19, 1906, JMP, Minto to Morley, Vol. IV.

[52] Minto to JM, Jan. 23, 1907, *ibid.*, Vol. V.

[53] Viceroy to Secretary of State, Feb. 17, 1907, Private Telegram, JMP, 27.
[54] JM to Minto, Feb. 22, 1907, JMP, Morley to Minto, Vol. II. JM had earlier cabled Minto (Secretary of State to Viceroy, Feb. 18, 1907, JMP, 27).
[55] JM to Minto, Feb. 22, 1907, JMP, Morley to Minto, Vol. II.
[56] *Ibid.*
[57] Government of India Despatch 7, 1907, March 21, 1907, JMP, 32:2 (hereafter cited in text by paragraph).
[58] JM to Minto, March 28, 1907, JMP, Morley to Minto, Vol. II.
[59] Note by Sir D. Barr, April 11, 1907, JMP, 32:8.
[60] JM had written to Godley in 1888 about Theodore Morison, whose father had been a friend of JM's, "He is barely 24. He has some means, but wants something to do.... [Might] some use ... be made of him at the India Office? [He] is a capital fellow, and did his work excellently in India."
[61] Appended "Note by Mr. T. Morison" to Resolutions of the Secretary of State's Special Committee of April 18, 1907, JMP, 32:11.
[62] *Ibid.*
[63] Note by H. S. Barnes, April 15, 1907, JMP, 32:4.
[64] Note by H. S. Barnes, April 23, 1907, JMP, 32:5.
[65] Note by J. Edge, April 11, 1907, JMP, 32:3.
[66] The proposed amendments by Sir W. Lee-Warner and T. Morison are preserved in JMP, 32:9. See also Resolutions, par. 14, JMP, 32:11.
[67] Resolution no. 17, *ibid.*
[68] Note by T. Morison, JMP, 32:11.
[69] JM to Minto, April 17, 1907, JMP, Morley to Minto, Vol. II.
[70] *Ibid.*
[71] JM, "British Democracy and Indian Government" (hereafter cited as JMBD), *Nineteenth Century and After*, 69 (Feb., 1911), 190.
[72] Rt. Hon. Sir Alfred Comyns Lyall, educated at Haileybury, was appointed to the Bengal Civil Service in 1855. He spent 32 years in the I.C.S. and in 1888 retired from India to be a member of the Council of India. He was vice-president of that body from 1895 to 1896, retiring in 1903.
[73] JM to Minto, Feb. 8, 1907, JMP, Morley to Minto, Vol. II.
[74] Most of the letters from Lyall to JM are notes confirming luncheon engagements between them in London (see JMP, 47, 48).
[75] A. Lyall to JM, "Easter Sunday," 1907, JMP, 48.
[76] A. Lyall to JM, April 11, 1907, *ibid.* The remaining quotations in the text on Lyall's opinion of the dispatch are from this letter.
[77] *Ibid.*
[78] JM to Minto, May 9, 1907, JMP, Morley to Minto, Vol. II.
[79] *Ibid.*
[80] *Ibid.*
[81] No copy of the original draft has been preserved. It can now be "read" only in the fragments cited by Lyall in his critique (see A. Lyall to JM, May 8, 1907, JMP, 48).
[82] Secretary of State's Secret Despatch 71 of 1907, May 17, 1907, par. 2, JMP, 32:12 (hereafter cited by paragraph).
[83] JM to Minto, May 16, 1907, JMP, Morley to Minto, Vol. II.
[84] R. C. Dutt to JM, Sept. 7, 1906, JMP, 50.
[85] JM to Minto, Aug. 6, 1906, JMP, Morley to Minto, Vol. I.
[86] Minto to JM, June 18, 1907, JMP, Minto to Morley, Vol. VI.
[87] Minto to JM, Oct. 3, 1907, JMP, 43a.

[88] Despatch No. 21, 1908, Home Department, Government of India to Secretary of State, Oct. 1, 1908, pars. 4–8, JMP, 33:2.
[89] Secretary of State's Despatch, Nov. 27, 1908, to Governor-General in Council, pars. 2–4, JMP, 33:11.
[90] "On Preserving the Indian Budget," June 6, 1907, *MIS*, p. 26.
[91] Par. 10 of Government of India's "Circular to Local Governments and Administrators," Aug. 24, 1907, JMP, 32:13.
[92] Clarke to JM, March 26, 1908, JMP, 42.
[93] H. H. Risley to JM, May 7, 1908, JMP, 45.
[94] H. H. Risley to JM, May 14, 1908, *ibid*. Risley mentioned in this same letter that Minto had ample time for more "talk with Scindia about the Imperial Advisory Council."
[95] Compare Risley to Dunlop Smith, May 12, 1908, JMP, 45, with Despatch 21, 1908, Oct. 1, 1908, Home Department, Government of India to Secretary of State, JMP, 33:2.
[96] H. H. Risley to JM, April 30, 1908, JMP, 45.
[97] JM to Minto, April 30, 1908, JMP, Morley to Minto, Vol. III. The latter allusion is to J. S. Mill's famous formula elaborated in his *Representative Government* (London, 1861).
[98] Rt. Hon. Frederick Sleigh, Earl Roberts (field marshal) served at the siege and capture of Delhi during the mutiny. He also served from 1878 to 1880 during operations in Afghanistan, commanded the Kuran Valley field force, and subsequently commanded the Kabul field force at the occupation of Kabul. He was commander in chief at Madras, and, in 1881, a member of the governor's council. He was commander in chief for India and a member of the governor-general's council from 1885 to 1893. From 1900 to 1904 he served as commander in chief of Army Headquarters. In this letter JM referred to Roberts as "a man of unsurpassed experience in India" and went on to quote Roberts (JM to Minto, May 7, 1908, JMP, Morley to Minto, Vol. III).
[99] *Ibid*.
[100] Minto to JM, June 4, 1908, JMP, Minto to Morley, Vol. X.
[101] Minto to JM, July 1, 1908, *ibid*.
[102] JM to Minto, May 21, 1908, JMP, Morley to Minto, Vol. III.
[103] JM to Minto, Aug. 6, 1908, *ibid*.
[104] JM to Minto, Aug. 10, 1908, *ibid*.
[105] *Ibid*. Italics in the original.
[106] "Speaking broadly, most of the reforms that we have been advocating . . . aim at securing for our people a larger and larger share in the administration and control of our affairs" (G. K. Gokhale's Presidential Address to the Benares Congress, in Gokhale, *op. cit.*, p. 705).
[107] JM to Clarke, Sept. 3, 1908, JMP, 42.
[108] JM to Minto, Sept. 10, 1908, JMP, Morley to Minto, Vol. III.
[109] JM to Minto, Sept. 18, 1908, *ibid*.
[110] HD, May 22, 1908, III, 49; JM to Minto, June 12, 1908, JMP, Morley to Minto, Vol. III; JM to Clarke, June 12, 1908, JMP, 42; HD, July 6, 1908, III, 62.
[111] JM to Clarke, June 12, 1908, JMP, 42.
[112] Italics in original. JM to Lamington, June 20, 1907, Lamington Papers, IO, MSS, Eur. B. 159/3. Rt. Hon. Charles Wallace Alexander Napier Cochrane-Baillie, Baron Lamington, was educated at Eton and Christ Church College, Oxford. He was assistant private secretary to the Marquis of Salisbury in 1885–

NOTES

1886. He served as M.P. from St. Pancras, 1886–1890; governor of Queensland, 1895–1901; governor of Bombay from 1903.

[113] Despatch No. 21, 1908, pars. 22–56, JMP, 33:2.

[114] JM, "Order of Reference," question 8, JMP, 33:3.

[115] The "Report of the Special Committee," appointed October 5, 1908, dated October 12, 1908, is preserved in JMP, 33:4.

[116] Lee-Warner's "Note on Constitutional Reforms in India," par. 2, JMP, 33:9.

[117] JM to Minto, Oct. 7, 1908, JMP, Morley to Minto, Vol. III.

[118] JM told this to his private secretary (HD, Oct. 19, 1908, III, 92).

[119] HD, Oct. 27, 1908, III, 94.

[120] *Ibid.*

[121] *Ibid.*, Oct. 29, 1908, p. 95.

[122] See *ibid.*, Oct. 19, 1908, p. 92. By publishing the entire proclamation as an appendix to his *Recollections*, II, 369–372, JM tacitly acknowledged his authorship of the famous document.

[123] Sir Lawrence Jenkins prepared a précis of the dispatch for him on November 4, and Hirtzel sent along his own suggestions as well (see HD, Nov. 4, 1908, III, 96).

[124] Sir James Thomson, whom Morley came to consider "no good at all" (HD, Oct. 29, 1908, III, 95), was made a member of the Council of India in 1908. Hirtzel noted their dissent (HD, Nov. 26, 1908, III, 103). Thomson was educated at Aberdeen grammar school and University. He was appointed to the I.C.S. after the examination of 1869, and arrived in India in 1871. He served in several posts in Madras until 1885 and later (until 1889) in Godavari. He served as member of the Revenue Board (1897), additional member of the Legislative Council of Madras (1898), ordinary member of the Legislative Council of Madras (1901–1906), and acting governor of Madras (1904). He retired from the service in 1906 and became a member of the Council of India in 1908.

[125] See Wolpert, *op. cit.*, pp. 210–240.

[126] Minto to JM, Jan. 5, 1908, JMP, Minto to Morley, Vol. VIII.

[127] JM to Clarke, Dec. 27, 1907, JMP, 42.

[128] HD, Dec. 2, 1908, III, 105.

[129] Secretary of State's Despatch, Nov. 27, 1908, pars. 18–19, JMP, 33:11.

[130] *HPDHL*, 4th ser., vol. 198, 1908, cols. 1974–1975.

[131] *Ibid.*, col. 1985.

[132] Lansdowne's speech Feb. 16, 1909, IO, Records, Judicial and Public, 1909, vol. 918, no. 693.

[133] R. B. Ghose's "Presidential Address," Madras, 1908, *ibid.*, vol. 916, no. 479. The Indian National Congress also passed a formal resolution thanking Morley and Minto for the reform proposals (Resolution II, "Reform Proposals," *ibid.*).

[134] Minto to JM, Dec. 24, 1908, JMP, Minto to Morley, Vol. XII.

[135] Chimanlal H. Setalvad to "Sir Lawrence" [Jenkins?], Jan. 5, 1909, JMP, 51.

[136] HD, Jan. 5, 1909, IV, 2.

[137] JM to Clarke, Jan. 7, 1909, JMP, 42.

[138] Mill, *Representative Government*, esp. chaps. iv, xvi.

[139] JM to Fleetwood Wilson, Jan. 13, 1909, Fleetwood Wilson Papers, IO, MSS, Eur. E. 224/2.

[140] JM to Minto, Jan. 13, 1909, JMP, Morley to Minto, Vol. IV.

141 JM to Minto, Feb. 4, 1909, *ibid.*
142 *Ibid.*
143 V. K. Iyer to "Dear Sir William" [Wedderburn], Feb. 21, 1909, JMP, 51.
144 The Indian Councils Act, 1909 [9 Edward VII, ch. 4], preserved in JMP, 33.
145 Viceroy to Secretary of State, Feb. 8, 1909, Telegram, JMP, 33:13.
146 Secretary of State to Viceroy, Telegram, Feb. 10, 1909, *ibid.*
147 Minto to JM, Feb. 9, 1909, JMP, Minto to Morley, Vol. XIII.
148 *Ibid.*
149 House of Lords debate on the second reading of the bill, *Times*, March 5, 1909, p. 6.
150 *Ibid.*
151 Curzon's letter of March 5, 1909, to the *Times*, March 6, 1909 (clipping preserved in JMP, 54).
152 Telegram from Madras Mahajana Sabha to JM, March 8, 1909, IO, Records, Judicial and Public, 1909, vol. 921, no. 919.
153 Telegram from Motilal Nehru to JM, March 9, 1909, *ibid.*, no. 920.
154 Telegram from Pherozeshah Mehta to JM, March 12, 1909, *ibid.*, no. 953.
155 Minto to JM, March 11, 1909, JMP, Minto to Morley, Vol. XIII.
156 JM to Minto, March 12, 1909, JMP, Morley to Minto, Vol. IV.
157 Earl Percy in debate on the second reading of the bill in the House of Commons, *Times*, April 2, 1909, p. 6.
158 Arthur Balfour in debate on the second reading of the bill in the House of Commons, April 1, 1909, *India*, April 9, 1909 (clipping preserved in JMP, 54).
159 *Ibid.*
160 *Ibid.*
161 JM to Minto, April 2, 1909, JMP, Morley to Minto, Vol. IV.
162 JM to Clarke, May 7, 1909, JMP, 42.
163 JM to Minto, May 21, 1909, JMP, Morley to Minto, Vol. IV.
164 JM to "Indian Probationers," Oxford, June 13, 1909, *MIS*, p. 140.
165 L. Jenkins to JM, July 18, 1909, JMP, 46.
166 "JM saw Jenkins, who is preparing a precis on which JM is to base his 'reforms' despatch" (HD, Nov. 4, 1908, III, 96).
167 A. Lyall to JM, Aug. 12, 1909, JMP, 49.
168 Italics in original. JM to Minto, Dec. 6, 1909, JMP, Morley to Minto, Vol. IV.
169 JM to Clarke, Dec. 8, 1909, JMP, 42.
170 G. Fleetwood Wilson's "Note on One of Many Repressive Bills," Jan. 5, 1910, Fleetwood Wilson Papers, E. 224/2.
171 Proceedings of the Legislative Council of the Governor-General of India, Vol. XLVIII, Jan. 25, 1910.
172 The heading given over this letter to the editor (*Times*, March 2, 1909, p. 12). The letter was dated February 26, 1909.
173 JMBD, p. 202.
174 *Ibid.*, p. 197.
175 *Ibid.*, pp. 197–198.
176 Sir Richard Burn (1871–1947) was educated at Christ Church College, Oxford, and joined the I.C.S. in 1891. He served as undersecretary to the government of the United Provinces (1897), superintendent of the census, and, subsequently, editor of the *Imperial Gazetteer of India* (1900–1905). He was

secretary to the government of India (1910), chief secretary (1912), commissioner (1918), and retired from the service in 1927.

[177] *Times*, Nov. 3, 1928.
[178] *Ibid.*, Nov. 9, 1928, p. 12.
[179] *Ibid.*, Nov. 17, 1928, p. 8.
[180] HD, Feb. 12, 1909, IV.
[181] Minto to JM, March 17, 1909, JMP, Minto to Morley, Vol. XIII.
[182] Secretary of State to Viceroy, April 14, 1909, Telegram, JMP, 33:13.
[183] HD, IV, April 5, 1909.
[184] Viceroy to Secretary of State, May 3, 1909, JMP, 33:13.
[185] Secretary of State to Viceroy, May 11, 1909, *ibid.* As a result of this sweeping formula (adopted as paragraph 7(i) of the regulations outlined in the Government of India's Despatch No. 12, July 22, 1909, to Secretary of State). The dispatch is preserved in JMP, 34:1. N. C. Kelkar, Tilak's lieutenant and editor of the *Mahratta*, in Poona, was disqualified for election in 1910.
[186] JM to Minto, Oct. 14, 1909, JMP, Morley to Minto, Vol. IV.
[187] JM to Minto, Oct. 29, 1909, *ibid.*
[188] "Regulations for Giving Effect to the Indian Councils Act of 1909" (9 Edward VII, ch. 4), Parliamentary Papers, East India (Executive and Legislative Councils) (Cd. 4987) (London, 1910). See Appendix B.
[189] Resolution IV, "Council Reform," in *Indian National Congress* (Madras, 1917), Resolutions Appendix, p. 133.
[190] Montagu's Budget Speech, July 20, 1910, *HPDHC*, 5th ser., vol. 19, cols. 1978–1981.

Notes to Chapter VII

[1] Thomas R. Metcalf, *The Aftermath of Revolt in India, 1857–1870* (Princeton, 1964).
[2] See "The Indian Charter Act of 1833," in Ramsay Muir, *The Making of British India, 1756–1858* (Manchester, 1923), pp. 301–304, esp. par. 87; "Queen Victoria's Proclamation," Nov. 1, 1858, in C. H. Philips, ed., *The Evolution of India and Pakistan, 1858 to 1947* (London, 1962), pp. 10–11.
[3] S. Gopal, *The Viceroyalty of Lord Ripon, 1880–1884* (London, 1953).
[4] Benares Presidential Address, Dec., 1905, in G. K. Gokhale, *The Speeches of Gopal Krishna Gokhale* (3d ed.; Madras, 1920), p. 701.
[5] *Ibid.*
[6] Resolution IV of the Twenty-first Congress, 1905, Benares, in *The Indian National Congress* (Madras, 1917), Resolution Appendix, p. 115.
[7] JM's speech at Arbroath, Oct. 21, 1907 (*Times*, Oct. 22, 1907).
[8] JM to Minto, May 3, 1906, JMP, Morley to Minto, Vol. I.
[9] JM to Minto, May 11, 1906, *ibid.*
[10] *Ibid.*
[11] Minto to JM, July 5, 1906, JMP, Minto to Morley, Vol. II.
[12] Minto to JM, July 11, 1906, *ibid.*
[13] From the report of a missionary sent to Morley by the Archbishop of Canterbury (JM to Minto, Aug. 28, 1907, JMP, Morley to Minto, Vol. II).
[14] Quoted in Minto to JM, Sept. 26, 1906, JMP, Minto to Morley, Vol. IX.

[15] HD, July 13, 1906, I, 61.
[16] JM to A. Godley, July 13, 1906, Correspondence of Lord Kilbracken, BM, Add. MS 44902, Vol. III, fols. 62–154.
[17] HD, July 17, 1906, I, 62.
[18] JM to Minto, Aug. 2, 1906, JMP, Morley to Minto, Vol. 1.
[19] JM to Minto, Aug. 29, 1906, *ibid.*
[20] Report of Arundel's Committee, Oct. 12, 1906, JMP, 32:1.
[21] JM to Minto, Nov. 23, 1906, JMP, Morley to Minto, Vol. I.
[22] Minto to JM, Dec. 12, 1906, JMP, Minto to Morley, Vol. IV.
[23] Minto to JM, Feb. 18, 1907, JMP, Minto to Morley, Vol. V.
[24] JM to Minto, Jan. 24, 1907, JMP, Morley to Minto, Vol. II.
[25] Government of India Despatch 7 of 1907, March 21, 1907, JMP, 32:2.
[26] The six members were Kitchener, Richards, Scott, Adamson, J. F. Finley, and J. O. Miller.
[27] HD, April 2, 1907, II, 32.
[28] A. Lyall to JM, Easter Sunday, 1907, JMP, 43c.
[29] A. Lyall to JM, April 11, 1907, *ibid.*
[30] Quoted in a letter from Lady Minto to Lord Minto, April 4, 1907, in Mary, Countess of Minto, *India, Minto and Morley, 1905–1910* (London, 1934), p. 115.
[31] JM to Minto, April 12, 1907, JMP, Morley to Minto, Vol. II.
[32] May 16, 1907, Mary, Countess of Minto, *op. cit.*, p. 138. See also HD, April 23, 1907, II, 38.
[33] JM to Minto, Sept. 24, 1908, JMP, Morley to Minto, Vol. III.
[34] Secretary of State to Viceroy, April 16, 1907, Private Telegram, JMP, 28.
[35] *Ibid.*
[36] Viceroy to Secretary of State, April 19, 1907, *ibid.*
[37] *Ibid.*
[38] JM to Minto, May 3, 1907, JMP, Morley to Minto, Vol. II.
[39] Minto to JM, June 5, 1907, JMP, Minto to Morley, Vol. VI.
[40] There were several other minor changes as well, including reduction of council members' salaries from £1,200 to £1,000 and reduction of the term of office from ten to seven years, but the bill's *raison d'être* was to increase maximum membership to fourteen (Council of India Bill, Aug. 15, 1907, IO, Records, Judicial and Public, 1907, vol. 817, no. 2482).
[41] Secretary of State to Viceroy, July 25, 1907, Private Telegram, JMP, 28.
[42] JM to Minto, June 13, 1907, JMP, Morley to Minto, Vol. II.
[43] Krishna Gobinda Gupta was educated at Calcutta University and appointed to the I.C.S. after the examination of 1871. He served in Bengal as magistrate and collector. He became secretary to the Board of Revenue in May, 1890, and commissioner of excise in 1893. He was a member of the Board of Revenue from 1905 to 1906. After his retirement in 1908, he was made a member of the Council of India.
[44] Saiyid Husain Bilgrami, the Nawab Imad-ul-Mulk, was in the Nizam's employ until 1902, serving Hyderabad in many capacities. In 1902 he became a member of the governor-general's Legislative Council and, in 1907, member of the Council of India.
[45] HD, July 22, 1907, II, 64.
[46] JM to Minto, May 21, 1908, JMP, Morley to Minto, Vol. III.
[47] JM's speech at Arbroath, Oct. 21, 1907, (*Times*, Oct. 22, 1907).
[48] JM to Minto, March 12, 1908, JMP, Morley to Minto, Vol. III.

NOTES

[49] JM to Minto, March 26, 1908, *ibid.*
[50] JM to Minto, May 21, 1908, *ibid.*
[51] JM to Minto, June 4, 1908, *ibid.*
[52] Satyendra P. Sinha (1864–1928), barrister at Lincoln's Inn, 1886. He became advocate-general of Bengal in 1905, and was law member of the Executive Council from 1909 to 1910. He was president of the Indian National Congress, 1915, and parliamentary under-secretary of state for India in 1919. From 1920 to 1921 he was governor of Bihar and Orissa.
[53] "On Proposed Reforms," Dec. 17, 1908, *MIS*, p. 92.
[54] HD, Jan. 10, 1909, IV.
[55] JM to Minto, Jan. 21, Feb. 4, 1909, JMP, Morley to Minto, Vol. IV.
[56] JM to Minto, Jan. 28, 1909, *ibid.*
[57] Minto to JM, Jan. 12, 1909, JMP, Minto to Morley, Vol. XIII.
[58] JM to His Majesty, Edward VII, March 10, 1909, Royal Archives, Windsor Castle, W/5/66.
[59] His Majesty to JM, March 12, 1909, *ibid.*, W/5/68.
[60] JM to His Majesty, March 17, 1909, *ibid.*, W/5/69.
[61] JM to Minto, April 7, 1909, JMP. Morley to Minto, Vol. IV.
[62] Secretary of State to Viceroy, Dec. 19, 1906, Private Telegram, JMP, 28.
[63] Secretary of State to Governor of Bombay (Rt. Hon. Sir Charles Wallace Alexander Napier, Baron Lamington), Jan. 14, 1907, *ibid.*
[64] JM to Minto, March 22, 1907, JMP, Morley to Minto, Vol. II.
[65] See Report of the Commissioners, Royal Commission on the Public Services in India (Cd. 8382) (London, 1916).
[66] JMP, 43:6.
[67] "Indian Civil Service," examination of 1909 in IO, Records, Judicial and Public, 1909, vol. 919, no. 752.
[68] See Keir J. Hardie, *India: Impressions and Suggestions* (London, 1909), chapter entitled "The Colour Line."
[69] Sir B. Fuller's statement quoted by JM to Minto, March 19, 1908, Morley to Minto, JMP, Vol. III.
[70] JM to Minto, Aug. 28, 1907, *ibid.*
[71] Minto to JM, July 31, 1907, JMP, Minto to Morley, Vol. VI.
[72] JM to Minto, Dec. 5, 1907, JMP, Morley to Minto, Vol. II.
[73] Minto to JM, Sept. 10, 1906, JMP, Minto to Morley, Vol. III.
[74] Under the chairmanship of Sir David Barr, the committee, which met from October 5 to October 12, 1909, included the following members of the Council of India: Sir James La Touche, Sir James Thomson, Sir Lawrence Jenkins, Mr. K. G. Gupta, Sir Walter Lawrence, and Syed Husain Bilgrami. The only outside member was Lord Anthony MacDonnell.
[75] JM's "Order of Reference" to his Special Committee on "Reform Scheme," Oct., 1908, par. 11, JMP, 33:3.
[76] JM's "Summary of Reforms Despatch, telegraphed privately to Viceroy," Nov. 20, 1908, JMP, 33:10. This Public Despatch no. 193, IO, Records, Judicial and Public, 1908, vol. 908, no. 3910, is preserved in JMP, 33:11.
[77] Viceroy to Secretary of State, Feb. 8, 1909, par. 14; Secretary of State to Viceroy, Feb. 10, 1909, JMP, 33:13.
[78] JM to Minto, Nov. 9, 1906, JMP, Morley to Minto, Vol. I.
[79] JM to Minto, Nov. 19, 1908, *ibid.*, Vol. III.
[80] JM to Minto, July 15, 1909, *ibid.*, Vol. IV.
[81] Clarke to JM, May 26, 1909, JMP, D42.

[82] G. Fleetwood Wilson to Sir L. Jenkins, July 6, 1909, Fleetwood Wilson Papers, IO, MSS Eur. E. 224/2.
[83] JM to G. Fleetwood Wilson, July 29, 1909, *ibid.*, no. 1.
[84] G. Fleetwood Wilson to Judge Fletcher, Aug. 10, 1909, *ibid.*, no. 2.
[85] Sir L. Jenkins to JM, Aug. 15, 1909, JMP, H.
[86] Syed Ali Imam was called to the bar in the Middle Temple in 1890. He was a member of the governor-general's Legislative Council in 1910 and temporary member of the governor-general's Executive Council for Law.
[87] JM to Minto, April 19, 1910, JMP, Morley to Minto, Vol. V.
[88] JM to Clarke, April 24, 1910, Sydenham Papers, BM, Add. MSS 50831–50841, Vol. III.
[89] JM to Minto, July 18, 1910, JMP, Morley to Minto, Vol. V.
[90] Mirza Abbas Ali Baig joined the service in 1882 as deputy educational inspector in Bombay. From 1886 to 1890 he was employed in Janjira State. In 1893 he went on special duty in Junagadh State, and late in that year was appointed official oriental translator to the government. He was dewan of Junagadh from 1906 to 1910, when he was appointed a member of the council of the secretary of state for India.
[91] JM to Clarke, July 1, 1910, JMP, D42.
[92] Sir L. Jenkins to JM, July 18, 1909, JMP, H.
[93] *Ibid.*
[94] *MR*, Sept. 1, 1910, II, 336.

Notes to Chapter VIII

[1] For general background on Hindu-Muslim communalism, see W. Norman Brown, *The United States and India and Pakistan* (rev. and enl. ed., Cambridge, 1963); W. C. Smith, *Modern Islam in India: A Social Analysis* (London, 1946), Pt. II; Rajendra Prasad, *India Divided* (Bombay, 1946); S. M. Ikram, *Muslim Civilization in India*, ed. A. T. Embree (New York and London, 1964); S. R. Sharma, *The Crescent in India* (Bombay, 1937); Asoka Mehta and Achyut Patwardhan, *The Communal Triangle in India* (Kitabistan, 1942).

[2] See Syed Razi Wasti, *Lord Minto and the Indian Nationalist Movement, 1905–1910* (Oxford, 1964), pp. 22–88; M. N. Das, *India under Morley and Minto* (London and New York, 1964), pp. 147–182; R. C. Majumdar, *History of the Freedom Movement in India* (Calcutta, 1963), II, 218–250; K. K. Aziz, *Britain and Muslim India* (London, 1963), pp. 62–75.

[3] Majumdar, *op cit.*, II, 258.
[4] Das, *op cit.*, p. 242.
[5] Wasti, *op. cit.*, p. 12.
[6] *Ibid.*, p. 13.
[7] Nawab Mohsin-ul-Mulk (1837–1907), was connected with Sir Sayed Ahmed Khan in the Aligarh Movement from 1863 and succeeded him as honorary secretary of the college in 1898. From 1874 to 1894 he was in the service of the Nizam of Hyderabad.
[8] Mohsin-ul-Mulk to Archbold, Aug. 4, 1906, enclosed in Minto to JM, Aug. 8, 1906, JMP, Minto to Morley, Vol. III.
[9] Minto to JM, Aug. 8, 1906, *ibid.*
[10] Secretary of State to Viceroy, Aug. 27, 1906, Telegram, JMP, 27.

NOTES

[11] Minto to JM, Aug. 29, 1906, JMP, Minto to Morley, Vol. III.

[12] Mohsin-ul-Mulk to Archbold, Aug. 18, 1906, in Wasti, *op. cit.*, App. V, p. 232.

[13] According to Lady Minto there were "about seventy delegates" in the deputation (Mary, Countess of Minto, *India, Minto and Morley, 1905–1910* [London, 1934], p. 45), but the address itself was signed by only thirty-five persons (JMP, 35). For the list of names see Wasti, *op. cit.*, App. II, pp. 222–223.

[14] Aga Sultan Mahomed Shah, third Aga Khan (1875–1958), head of the Khoja (Isma'ili) sect; graduate of Aligarh College; president of Bombay's Mohammedan Educational Conference, 1903; member of the Imperial Legislative Council, 1903; permanent president of the Muslim League, 1908–1913.

[15] JMP, 35; excerpts are reprinted in C. H. Philips, ed., *The Evolution of India and Pakistan, 1858–1947* (London, 1962), pp. 190–193.

[16] JMP, 35; excerpts of this reply in Mary, Countess of Minto, *op. cit.*, pp. 46–47.

[17] See the Chesney Committee Report on Provincial Councils, under Lord Dufferin's administration, Oct., 1888, in Philips, *op. cit.*, p. 60 ff.

[18] *Ibid.*, par. 7.

[19] Minto to JM, Oct. 4, 1906, JMP, Minto to Morley, Vol. III.

[20] Minto's reply, Oct. 1, 1906, JMP, 35.

[21] JM to Minto, Oct. 26, 1906, JMP, Morley to Minto, Vol. I.

[22] Theodore Morison, educated at Westminster and Trinity College, Cambridge. In 1886–1887 he was tutor to the Maharaja of Chhatarpur. He became a professor at Aligarh in 1889 and principal of the college in 1899, a post he held until 1905. He served from 1903 to 1904 as a member of the Governor-general's Legislative Council and also as a member of the Council of India (1906).

[23] JM to Minto, Dec. 21, 1906, JMP, Morley to Minto, Vol. I.

[24] JM to Minto, Jan. 24, 1907, *ibid.*, Vol. II.

[25] At least by Feb. 11, 1908 (see HD, III, 20).

[26] JM to Minto, Oct. 11, 1906, JMP, Morley to Minto, Vol. 1.

[27] JM to Minto, Nov. 23, 1906, *ibid.*

[28] Arundel Report, Oct. 12, 1906, pars. 57–59, JMP, 32:1.

[29] Government of India Despatch, March 21, 1907, pars. 52–58, JMP, 32:2.

[30] Secretary of State's Despatch, May 17, 1907, par. 26, JMP, 32:12.

[31] W. Lee-Warner, Note of April 18, 1907, JMP, 32:10.

[32] *Ibid.*

[33] Minto to JM, March 19, 1907, JMP, Minto to Morley, Vol. V.

[34] For Congress factional strife at this time see Stanley A. Wolpert, *Tilak and Gokhale: Revolution and Reform in the Making of Modern India* (Berkeley and Los Angeles, 1962), chap. vi.

[35] Gokhale's report in a conversation with Dunlop Smith on October 20, 1907, enclosed in Minto to Morley, Oct. 29, 1907, JMP, Minto to Morley, Vol. VII.

[36] Government of India Despatch 30, Oct. 1, 1908, JMP, 32:2.

[37] Resolutions adopted at the All-India Muslim League meeting, Dacca, Dec. 30, 1906, IO, Records, Judicial and Public, 1907, vol. 796, no. 614.

[38] Resolution on Reform Proposals, March 24, 1908, Aligarh, Enclosure XXVI in Government of India's letter, Oct. 1, 1908, East India Advisory and Legislative Councils, Parliamentary Papers (Cd. 4436).

³⁹ Syed Amir Ali, author, barrister, and political leader, first Indian member of the Judicial Committee of His Majesty's Privy Council and founding head of the London branch of the All-India Muslim League, 1908. Author of *The Spirit of Islam; Mohammedan Law;* and *A Short History of the Saracens.*

⁴⁰ JM's "Order of Reference" to guide his select committee of Council on Reforms, Oct., 1908, JMP, 33:3.

⁴¹ Secretary of State to Viceroy, Summary of Reforms Despatch, Nov. 20, 1908, JMP, 33:10.

⁴² Morley wrote: "Let it be supposed that the total population of Province is 20 millions, of whom 15 millions are Hindus and 5 millions are Mohamedans; and the number of members to be elected 12. Then . . . , 9 Hindus should be elected to 3 Mohamedans. In order to obtain these members, divide the Province into three electoral areas, in each of which 3 Hindus and 1 Mohamedan are to be returned. Then, in each area constitute an electoral college, of say 100 members . . . 75 of these should be Hindus and 25 Mohamedans. . . . Out of those offering themselves and obtaining votes, the 75 Hindus who obtained the majority of votes should be declared members of the College, and the 25 Mohamedans who obtained the majority should similarly be declared elected. If the Mohamedans did not provide 25 members . . . the deficiency would be made good by nomination. . . . [Now the] Electoral College would be called on to elect 3 representatives for Hindus and 1 for Mohamedans; each member of College would have only one vote" (Secretary of State's Despatch to Viceroy, Nov. 27, 1908, JMP, 33:11).

⁴³ Viceroy to Secretary of State, Jan. 8, 1909, JMP, 35.

⁴⁴ Memo from Ibni Ahmad to Under-secretary of State for India, Jan. 25, 1909, IO, Records, Judicial and Public, 1909, vol. 914, no. 298.

⁴⁵ HD, Jan. 11, 1909, IV, 4.

⁴⁶ JM to Muslims, *MIS*, p. 105 ff.

⁴⁷ HD, Feb. 2, 1909, IV, 10.

⁴⁸ A. Lyall to JM, Feb. 4, 1909, JMP, E. See also Lyall to JM, Feb. 15, 1909, *ibid.*

⁴⁹ Viceroy to Secretary of State, Feb. 8, 1909, JMP, 33:13.

⁵⁰ Clarke to JM, Oct. 22, 1908, JMP, 42.

⁵¹ Viceroy to Secretary of State, Feb. 8, 1909, JMP, 33:13.

⁵² JM to Clarke, Feb. 12, 1909, JMP, 42.

⁵³ JM to Minto, Feb. 18, 1909, JMP, Morley to Minto, Vol. IV.

⁵⁴ JM to House of Lords, Feb. 23, 1909, JMP, 35. Also see *MIS*, p. 126 ff.

⁵⁵ JM to House of Lords, Feb. 23, 1909, JMP, 35.

⁵⁶ See R. Nathan to Curzon, Dec. 28, 1907, Curzon Papers, IO, MSS Eur. F. 111/430. See also Z. Hare's enclosure of Sept. 2, 1906, in Minto to JM, Sept. 10, 1906, JMP, Minto to Morley, Vol. III.

⁵⁷ Nawab of Dacca to Curzon, Feb. 24, 1909, Curzon Papers, F. 111/430.

⁵⁸ Punjab Muslim League, Lahore, March 6, 1909, IO, Records, Judicial and Public, 1909, vol. 920, no. 893.

⁵⁹ Secretary of State to Viceroy, April 27, 1909, JMP, 33:13.

⁶⁰ HD, March 25, 1909, IV, 25.

⁶¹ Minto to JM, April 29, 1909, JMP, Minto to Morley, Vol. XIV.

⁶² India Association to JM, Feb. 27, 1909, IO, Records, Judicial and Public, 1909, vol. 919, no. 798; Lahore to JM, Feb. 28, 1909, *ibid.*, vol. 920, no. 807; Mahajana Sabha, Madras to JM, March 8, 1909, *ibid.*, vol. 921, no. 919; Fyzabad and Ajudhia to JM, March 10, 1909, *ibid.*, vol. 921, no. 931; Agra to JM, March

12, 1909, *ibid.*, vol. 921, no. 987; Gonda to JM, March 13, 1909, *ibid.*, vol. 921, no. 989.

[63] Lajpat Rai to the editor, *Times*, March 4, 1909, p. 6.
[64] Clarke to JM, April 30, 1909, JMP, 42.
[65] Minto's telegraphic summary of Gokhale's council statement, Viceroy to Secretary of State, March 31, 1909, JMP, 33:13.
[66] Buchanan to House of Commons, April 1, 1909, JMP, 35.
[67] Government of India Despatch 12 of 1909, July 22, 1909, JMP, 34:1.
[68] Note by Sir T. Morison, Aug. 3, 1909, JMP, 34:6.
[69] Gupta's Note on "Muhamedan Representation," Aug. 3, 1909, JMP, 34:7.
[70] T. Morison's "Postscript to the Note Upon the Pledges," JMP, 34:8.
[71] "Further Note by Gupta on Muhamedan Representation," Aug. 10, 1909, JMP, 34:9.
[72] JM to Minto, Aug. 6, 1909, JMP, Morley to Minto, vol. IV.
[73] JM to Minto, Aug. 20, 1909, *ibid.*
[74] The other members were Lee-Warner, La Touche, Bilgrami, and Edgerley (see the Raleigh Committee Proposals on the revisions of Regulations, JMP, 34:13).
[75] JM to Minto, Aug. 20, 1909, JMP, Morley to Minto, Vol. IV.
[76] The minimum amounts for Muslim electors to the Imperial Legislative Council were payment of land revenue on landed income of not under Rs. 750 from both Bengals; Rs. 3,000 from Madras; and Rs. 10,000 from the United Provinces; or of income tax on income over Rs. 6,000 (Rs. 10,000 for the U.P.). For electors of Muslim members of provincial councils, the regulations required a minimum income of Rs. 500 from land, or nonlanded income of Rs. 2,000 in Madras; landed income of Rs. 100 or above, and nonlanded income of Rs. 1,000 from Bombay (though double that amount was required for Bombay City); landed income of from Rs. 31 to Rs. 125 in various districts of Bengal, or monthly income of Rs. 25 (for Calcutta the landed income was Rs. 2,000 and the monthly salary Rs. 50); and Rs. 3,000 from both landed and nonlanded income for the United Provinces (see Viceroy to Secretary of State, Oct. 12, 1909, JMP, 34:3).
[77] Minto to Morley, Nov. 11, 1909, JMP, Minto to Morley, Vol. XVI.
[78] *Ibid.*
[79] JM to Minto, Dec. 6, 1909, JMP, Morley to Minto, Vol. IV.
[80] JM to Frederic Harrison, Nov. 4, 1909, Frederic Harrison Collection, British Library of Political and Economic Science, R.(S.R.) 1003, 3/6.
[81] Resolution IV, Twenty-fourth Congress, 1909 (Lahore, *The Indian National Congress* [Madras, 1917], Resolution Appendix, p. 133).
[82] Sir L. Jenkins to JM, Sept. 15, 1909, JMP, H.
[83] *Ibid.*
[84] JM to Minto, Nov. 18, 1909, JMP, Morley to Minto, Vol. IV.
[85] *Ibid.*
[86] Godley to Lee-Warner, Dec. 20, 1909, Lee-Warner Collection, IO, MSS Eur. F. 92/2.
[87] Report on Indian Constitutional Reforms, Parliamentary Papers, East India (Constitutional Reforms) (London, 1918) (Cd. 9109), p. 187.
[88] *Ibid.*, p. 188.
[89] *Ibid.*
[90] Report of the Indian Statutory Commission, Vol. II, Recommendations, Parliamentary Papers (London, 1939) (Cd. 3569).

Notes to Chapter IX

[1] JM's Budget Speech to House of Commons, June 6, 1907, *HPDHC*, 4th ser., vol. 175, col. 882.

[2] Great Britain, East India, Report of the Royal Commission upon Decentralisation in India (Cd. 4360), 1909, April 2, 1909, IO, Records, Judicial and Public, 1909, vol. 919, no. 748.

[3] Great Britain, East India, Report on Indian Constitutional Reforms, Parliamentary Paper (Cd. 9109), 1918, p. 158 ff.

[4] JM to Minto, Dec. 7, 1906, JMP, Morley to Minto, Vol. I.

[5] Viceroy to Secretary of State, June 8, 1907, Telegram, JMP, 27.

[6] JM to Minto, June 13, 1907, JMP, Morley to Minto, Vol. II.

[7] Secretary of State to Viceroy, June 27, 1907, Telegram, JMP, 28.

[8] A. Lyall to JM, May 8, 1907, JMP, bundle C.

[9] A. Lyall to JM, May 28, 1907, *ibid.*

[10] A. Lyall to JM, June 15, 1907, *ibid.*

[11] Minto to JM, June 18, 1907, JMP, Minto to Morley, Vol. VI.

[12] JM to Minto, June 21, 1907, JMP, Morley to Minto, Vol. II.

[13] G. K. Gokhale, "Note on Decentralisation," in G. K. Gokhale, *The Speeches of Gopal Krishna Gokhale* (3d ed.; Madras, 1920), App. II, p. 188.

[14] Viceroy to Secretary of State, July 4, 1907, Telegram, JMP, 30.

[15] Secretary of State to Viceroy, July 26, 1907, *ibid.*

[16] JM to Godley, July 26, 1907, Kilbracken Collection, IO, MSS Eur. F. 102/8.

[17] Charles Edward Henry Hobhouse was educated at Eton and Christ Church, Oxford, and at Sandhurst. From 1889 to 1890 he served as lieutenant with the 60th Rifle Brigade. In 1892 he served in the House of Commons as member for East Wiltshire and later became private secretary to the undersecretary of state for the colonies. In 1900 he was returned to the house from East Bristol and then was elected a member of the Thames Conservancy Board (1904). It was in January, 1907, that he became parliamentary undersecretary of state for India.

[18] The two members from London were W. L. Hickens and Sir Frederick S. P. Lely; the two from the government of India, Sir Steyning Edgerley and William S. Meyer.

[19] Minto to JM, Nov. 30, 1907, JMP, Minto to Morley, Vol. VII.

[20] JM to Clarke, Feb. 7, 1908, JMP, D42.

[21] Clarke to JM, March 12, 1908, *ibid.*

[22] *Ibid.*

[23] Sir Hugh Tinker, *The Foundations of Local Self-Government in India, Pakistan and Burma* (London, 1954), pp. 64–105. See also Gokhale's "Note on Decentralisation," in Gokhale, *op. cit.*, pp. 191–199.

[24] Gokhale's "Note on Decentralisation," p. 196.

[25] *Ibid.*, p. 199.

[26] JM to Minto, Jan. 6, 1909, JMP, Morley to Minto, Vol. IV.

[27] JM to Minto, Jan. 21, 1909, *ibid.*

[28] Reforms Despatch, Nov. 27, 1908, par. 33, JMP, 33:11.

[29] *Ibid.*

[30] Report of the Royal Commission upon Decentralisation in India, Conclusions, par. 85, p. 297 ff.

[31] *Ibid.*, par. 91.
[32] *Ibid.*, par. 109.
[33] *Ibid.*, par. 126.
[34] Reforms Despatch, par. 39, JMP, 33:11.
[35] Gokhale's "Note on Decentralisation," in Gokhale, *op. cit.*, p. 188.
[36] Romesh Dutt to JM, Feb. 22, April 24, 1908, JMP, 43G.
[37] Report of the Royal Commission upon Decentralisation in India, par. 28.
[38] Rt. Hon. Sir Anthony Patrick MacDonnell (1844–1925), whom Morley had earlier tried to win over by appointing him to his reforms committee, but in December, 1908, JM wrote: "MacDonnell, a hard-mouthed brute, . . . combines the defects of an Irishman, with those of a tip-top Indian Civilian, and those two qualifications combined may lead a man very close to malignity" (JM to Minto, Dec. 18, 1908, JMP, Morley to Minto, Vol. III). MacDonnell arrived in India in 1865. He served in Bengal in many capacities and, in 1893, became acting lieutenant governor of the province. In that year he also became a member of the governor-general's council. In 1902 he was made a privy councillor, and from 1903 to 1905 was a member of the Council of India.
[39] *Times*, March 5, 1909, p. 6.
[40] Curzon's letter to the editor, March 5, 1909, *Times*, March 6, 1909, preserved in JMP, 43A.
[41] JM to Minto, May 27, 1909, JMP, Morley to Minto, Vol. IV.
[42] Tremearne to JM, June 20, 1909, JMP, 43A.
[43] JM to Minto, Jan. 13, 1910, JMP, Morley to Minto, Vol. V.
[44] J. A. Spender, *The Life of the Rt. Hon. Sir Henry Campbell-Bannerman*, G.C.B. (2 vols.; London, 1923), I, 148.
[45] *Journals and Letters of Reginald Viscount Esher*, ed. Maurice V. Brett (London, 1934–1938), Oct. 28, 1910, III, 28–29.
[46] Herbert Henry Asquith, first Earl of Oxford and Asquith (1852–1928), the son of a Lancashire weaver, entered Balliol College, Oxford, in 1870. He became a fellow there in 1874, and was called to the bar from Lincoln's Inn in 1876. While struggling to establish his legal career he wrote articles and became involved in politics. In 1886 he was sent to the House of Commons from East Fife. Gladstone made him Home secretary of state in his 1892 cabinet, which lasted until 1895. During his eleven years out of office, Asquith earned a fortune at the bar. He served as chancellor of the Exchequer, 1905–1908, and after Campbell-Bannerman's death, became prime minister, 1908–1916.
[47] H. Asquith to Crewe, Sept. 14, 1910, in James Pope-Hennessey, *Lord Crewe, 1858–1945: The Likeness of a Liberal* (London, 1955), p. 85.
[48] Robert O. A. Crewe-Milnes, second Baron Houghton, Marquess of Crewe, (1858–1945); viceroy of Ireland, 1892–1895; lord president of the council, 1905–1908, 1915–1916; lord privy seal, 1908–1911, 1912–1915; colonial secretary, 1908–1910; secretary of state for India, 1910–1915.
[49] See Spender, *op cit.*, I, 150; Pope-Hennessey, *op. cit.*, p. 90; and Charles Hardinge, *My Indian Years: 1910–1916* (London, 1948), p. 21.
[50] JM to Minto, July 30, 1908, JMP, Morley to Minto, Vol. III.
[51] Minto to JM, Jan. 17, 1906, JMP, Minto to Morley, Vol. I.
[52] HD, Dec. 3, 1907, II, 102.
[53] *Ibid.*, Dec. 4, 1907.
[54] HD, April 27, 1908, III, 42.

55 Montagu's Budget Speech, *Times,* July 27, 1910, p. 11.
56 JM to the House of Lords, Sept. 27, 1909 (quoted in *Times,* Sept. 28, 1909), preserved in HD, VI.
57 Secretary of State to Governor General in Council, April 19, 1907, IO, Records, Judicial and Public, Despatch to India, 1907, vol. 28, Public Despatch no. 56. See also Montagu's Budget Speech, *Times,* July 27, 1910, p. 11.
58 Charles Hardinge to JM, Nov. 2, 1909, JMP, 43E.
59 JM to the House of Lords, Sept. 27, 1909 (*Times,* Sept. 28, 1909).
60 *Ibid.*
61 *Ibid.*

Notes to Chapter X

1 JM to Minto, May 18, 1906, JMP, Morley to Minto, Vol. I.
2 A. Carnegie to JM, Oct. 10, 1905, JMP, 66.
3 JM to Minto, Sept. 22, 1909, JMP, Morley to Minto, Vol. IV.
4 JM to Clarke, Nov. 14, 1909, JMP, 42.
5 Minto to JM, Oct. 14, 1909, JMP, Minto to Morley, Vol. XVI.
6 For a general survey of the movement see R. C. Majumdar, *History of the Freedom Movement in India* (Calcutta, 1963), II, 29–174.
7 See Dadabhai Naoroji, *The Poverty of India* (London, 1878); Romesh Dutt, *Economic History of India in the Victorian Age* (London, 1956).
8 JM's speech on "Amendment to the Address in Reply to the King's Speech," Feb. 8, 1904, in JM, "Free Trade v. Protection," speech delivered by the Rt. Hon. John Morley, M.P., in the House of Commons (London, 1904), p. 1.
9 *Ibid.,* p. 9.
10 *MG,* II, 92.
11 JM to the Commons, Feb. 26, 1906, *HPDHC,* 1906, 4th ser., vol. 152, p. 846.
12 JM to Minto, Nov. 2, 1906, JMP, Morley to Minto, Vol. I.
13 JM to Minto, March 2, 1906, *ibid.*
14 JM to Minto, Aug. 29, 1906, *ibid.*
15 Minto to JM, Dec. 19, 1906, JMP, Minto to Morley, Vol. IV.
16 Fifteen rupees equaled £1 at this time. Total government expenditure for arts and professional colleges for 1908–09 was £354,197 (Parliamentary Papers, Great Britain, East India, "Statistical Abstract Relating to British India from 1908–09 to 1917–18" [London, 1920] [Cd. 725], p. 120).
17 JM to Minto, Jan. 24, 1908, JMP, Morley to Minto, Vol. III.
18 JM to Minto, June 4, 1908, *ibid.*
19 JM to Minto, July 8, 1910, *ibid.,* Vol. V. The viceroy received a salary equal to $83,000 with additional "allowances"; governors of Bombay and Madras received about $40,000 plus allowances; lieutenant governors received about $33,000 plus allowances; members of the viceroy's council received $26,700; the president of the Railway Board, $20,000; chief commissioners, from $11,000 to $20,000; secretaries to government departments, from $10,000 to $16,000; political residents to princely states, from $11,000 to $16,000. The total salaries paid to Europeans (including soldiers) in India at this time was some £4 million.
20 JM to Minto, June 1, 1910, *ibid.*
21 G. Fleetwood Wilson to Judge Fletcher, Aug. 10, 1909, Fleetwood Wilson Papers, IO, MSS Eur. E. 224/2.

[22] *Ibid.*
[23] Minute on denying "6000 Rs. for Registrar Revenue & Accounts Department on Retirement," Feb. 2, 1910, *ibid.*, E. 224/4.
[24] Fleetwood Wilson to "My dear Friend," Sept. 9, 1909, *ibid.*, E. 224/2.
[25] Fleetwood Wilson's note on "Inspector of Cantonements," Aug. 11, 1910, *ibid.*, E. 224/4. See also note of June 21, 1910, *ibid.*; "Minute on Army Expenditure," May, 1910, *ibid.*; and note of Sept. 13, 1910, *ibid.*
[26] Great Britain, East India (Income & Expenditure), House of Commons Return, April 25, 1910, Accounts and Papers, Vol. LXVII.
[27] Report of the Mowatt Committee, Feb. 15, 1907, JMP, 38. The members were Sir F. Mowatt, chairman; Mr. L. Abrahams, financial secretary of the India Office; General Sir E. Stedman, military secretary of the India Office.
[28] HD, March 5, 1908, III, 27.
[29] Minto to JM, March 19, 1908, JMP, Minto to Morley, Vol. VIII.
[30] JM's Budget Speech to the Commons, June 6, 1907, in *HPDHC*, 4th ser., vol. 175, col. 867.
[31] Master of Elibank's Budget Address, Aug. 5, 1909, *ibid.*, 4th ser., vol. 8, col. 1956.
[32] Richard Burdon Haldane (1856–1928), Liberal M.P. from East Lothian (1885–1911); created viscount, 1911; secretary of state for war (1905–1912); lord chancellor (1912–1915).
[33] JM to Kitchener, April 6, 1906, JMP, 39t.
[34] Minto to JM, May 2, 1906, JMP, Minto to Morley, Vol. II.
[35] Kitchener to JM, Aug. 22, 1906, JMP, 40e.
[36] Fourth War Office Memorandum, Oct. 10, 1906, *ibid.*
[37] Haldane to JM, March 18, 1908, JMP, 40d.
[38] L. Abrahams to JM, March 20, 1908, *ibid.*
[39] Sir Edward Grey, third baronet, and Viscount Grey of Fallodon (1862–1933); Liberal M.P. from Berwick-on-Tweed (1885–1916); parliamentary undersecretary of Foreign Office (1892–1895); foreign secretary, 1905–1916.
[40] JM to Minto, March 4, 1908, JMP, Morley to Minto, Vol. III.
[41] JM to Minto, Aug. 23, 1906, *ibid.*, Vol. I.
[42] JM to Sir E. Grey, Sept. 4, 1906, Grey Papers, Foreign Office Library, Vol. LIX.
[43] Grey to JM, Feb. 3, 1909, *ibid.*
[44] JM to Minto, July 30, 1908, JMP, Morley to Minto, Vol. III.
[45] JM to Sir E. Grey, Feb. 3, 1909, Grey Papers, Vol. LIX.
[46] JM to Sir E. Grey, March 22, 1909, *ibid.*
[47] JM to Sir E. Grey, March 30, 1909, *ibid.*
[48] HD, March 31, 1909, IV, 26.
[49] JM to Minto, April 15, 1909, JMP, Morley to Minto, Vol. IV.
[50] JM to Minto, July 30, 1908, *ibid.*, Vol. III.
[51] JM to Minto, Aug. 23, 1907, *ibid.*, Vol. II.
[52] JM to Minto, March 4, 1908, *ibid.*, Vol. III.
[53] HD, July 14, 1908, III, 64.
[54] JM to Minto, April 15, 1909, JMP, Morley to Minto, Vol. IV.
[55] In 1905–06, the net return from opium was 3,572,944 rupees; in 1906–07, 3,643,773; in 1907–08, 3,571,948; in 1908–09, 4,645,113; and in 1909–10, 4,195,614 (Great Britain, East India (Income & Expenditure), House of Commons Return, April 25, 1910, Accounts and Papers, Vol. LXVII; Great Britain, East India, "Statistical Abstract Relating to British India from 1908–09 to 1917–18" [Lon-

don, 1920] [Cd. 725], p. 52). For a general history of the opium trade see D. E. Owen, *British Opium Policy in China and India* (New Haven, 1934); J. Rowntree, *The Imperial Drug Trade* (London, 1905).

[56] JM to Sir E. Grey, March 17, 1906, Grey Papers, Vol. LIX.
[57] Sir E. Grey to JM, March 17, 1906, *ibid.*
[58] Mr. Theodore Taylor, M.P., Lancashire, *HPDHC*, 4th ser., vol. 158 of 1906, p. 494.
[59] JM to the House of Commons, *ibid.*, p. 510.
[60] *Ibid.*, p. 511.
[61] *Ibid.*
[62] HD, Aug. 21, 1907, II, 73.
[63] Master of Elibank's Budget Address, *HPDHC*, 4th ser., vol. 175, col. 1990.
[64] Alexander William Charles Oliphant Murray, master of Elibank (1870–1920), Liberal M.P. for Midlothian, 1900–1905; for Peebles and Selkirk, 1906–1910; for Midlothian, 1910–1912; made baron in 1912; undersecretary of state for India, 1909–1910; parliamentary secretary to the treasury, 1910–1912. He was considered by Morley second only to Hardinge for Minto's replacement in 1910.
[65] Dr. R. B. Ghose's Presidential Address to Surat Congress, 1907, *The Indian National Congress* (Madras, 1917), p. 879.
[66] Master of Elibank's Budget Address, cols. 1991–1992.
[67] J. O'Grady, M.P., June 6, 1907, *HPDHC*, 4th ser., vol. 175, col. 919.
[68] A. Lupton, M.P., July 22, 1908, *ibid.*, vol. 193, cols. 217–218.
[69] The gross revenue in 1904–05 was £84.8 million (*ibid.*, vol. 161, col. 637); in 1907–08 it was £71 million; in 1908–09, £69.7 million; in 1909–10, £74.6 million; in 1910–11, £80.7 million; in 1912–13, £86.8 million; in 1916–17, £98 million; in 1917–18, £112.6 million ("Statistical Abstract Relating to British India from 1908–09 to 1917–18," p. 47).
[70] Edwin Montagu's Budget Address, *HPDHC*, 4th ser., vol. 175, col. 1952.
[71] *HPDHC*, 5th ser., Aug. 5, 1909, vol. 8, col. 2054.
[72] *Ibid.*, col. 2072.
[73] JM to Clarke, May 20, 1908, JMP, 42.
[74] Montagu's Budget Address, col. 1961.
[75] JM to Minto, March 9, 1910, JMP, Morley to Minto, Vol. V. In 1911 the tobacco duty was reduced by one-third over strenuous Indian opposition. "We have been most careful not to let it appear that the reduction was in any sense due to instructions from home," Hardinge wrote Morley, "but is it generally known" (Hardinge to JM, March 16, 1911, JMP, 26).
[76] Keir Hardie to House of Commons, July 26, 1906, *HPDHC*, 4th ser., vol. 161, col. 597.
[77] JM to Lamington, March 23, 1906, Lamington Papers, IO, MSS Eur. B. 159/3.
[78] Minto to JM, April 3, 1906, JMP, Minto to Morley, Vol. I.
[79] Resolution VIII, Madras Session, 1903 (*The Indian National Congress*, "Congress Resolutions," p. 105).
[80] JM to Minto, April 19, 1906, JMP, Morley to Minto, Vol. I.
[81] JM to Minto, April 11, 1906, *ibid.*
[82] JM to House of Commons, July 20, 1906, *HPDHC*, 4th ser., vol. 161, col. 575.
[83] Minto to JM, Dec. 19, 1906, JMP, Minto to Morley, Vol. IV.
[84] Buchanan's Budget Address, July 22, 1908, *HPDHC*, 4th ser., vol. 193, cols. 117–124.

[85] Minto's speech enclosed in Minto to JM, Dec. 26, 1906, JMP, Minto to Morley, Vol. IV.
[86] "Tata Iron and Steel Works," Moral and Material Progress of India Report, 1911–12, pp. 281–282, quoted in C. H. Philips, ed., *The Evolution of India and Pakistan, 1858 to 1917* (London, 1962), p. 687.
[87] Tremearne to JM, Calcutta, June 20, 1908, JMP, 43.
[88] "Open Letter" to JM, Dec. 12, 1908, from large group of planters' associations, chambers of commerce, and the like, IO, Records, Judicial and Public, 1908, vol. 904, no. 4650.
[89] Tremearne to JM, June 20, 1908.
[90] *Ibid.*
[91] "Open Letter" to JM, Dec. 12, 1908.
[92] *Ibid.*
[93] Lionel Abrahams, corresponding secretary of Finance Department, IO, to JM, Feb. 4, 1909, IO, Records, Financial, 1909, vol. 1531, no. 531.
[94] Sir William Meyer, financial secretary to government of India, to L. Abrahams, May 27, 1909, *ibid.*, vol. 1534, no. 3281.
[95] "Increasing Poverty of India," Resolution III, Nagpur Congress, 1891, in *The Indian National Congress*, "Congress Resolutions," p. 23. For later resolutions see pp. 31, 37, 40, 50, 56, 57, 76, 87, 94, 102, 108, 119, 125, 131.
[96] Dutt, *op. cit.*, chaps. iii–vii, pp. 262–516.
[97] Gokhale's Budget Speech at Meeting of Imperial Legislative Council, March 28, 1906, in R. P. Patwardhan and D. V. Ambekar, eds., *Speeches and Writings of Gopal Krishna Gokhale* (Poona, 1962), I, 102.
[98] "Statistical Abstract Relating to British India from 1908–09 to 1917–18," p. 48.
[99] J. R. Dunlop Smith, "Note on Land Assessment in the Punjab," July 21, 1907, in JMP, Miscellaneous.
[100] *Ibid.*
[101] J. Ramsay MacDonald to House of Commons, July 26, 1910, *HPDHC*, 5th ser., vol. 19, col. 1999.
[102] JM to G. Fleetwood Wilson, Feb. 5, 1909, Fleetwood Wilson Papers, E. 224/2.
[103] S. S. Despatch, Revenue, no. 56, May 21, 1909, IO, Records, Finance, 1909, vol. 1531, no. 682.
[104] JM to G. Fleetwood Wilson, Feb. 5, 1909, Fleetwood Wilson Papers, E. 224/2.
[105] JM to Minto, Jan. 13, 1909, JMP, Morley to Minto, Vol. IV.
[106] L. Jenkins to JM, Feb. 14, 1910, JMP, 46.
[107] George Lloyd to House of Commons, July 26, 1910, *HPDHC*, 5th ser., vol. 19, cols. 2029–2031.

Notes to Chapter XI

[1] Minto to JM, Aug. 3, 1910, JMP, Minto to Morley, Vol. XIX.
[2] G. Fleetwood Wilson to JM, June 19, 1913, Fleetwood Wilson Papers, IO, MSS Eur. E. 224.
[3] See Wedderburn's address of 1910, in *The Indian National Congress* (Madras, 1917), p. 1001; Dhar's address of 1911, *ibid.*, pp. 1020–1022, 1036, 1040, 1043;

Mudholkar's address of 1912, *ibid.*, pp. 1072–1073; Mohammed's address of 1913, *ibid.*, p. 1141; Basu's address of 1914, *ibid.*, pp. 1173–1175; Sinha's address of 1915, *ibid.*, p. 1196; Mazumdar's address of 1916, *ibid.*, pp. 1237–1239.
[4] See William Wedderburn, *Allan Octavian Hume: Father of the Indian Congress, 1829–1912* (London, 1913), esp. p. 49.
[5] Wedderburn's Presidential Address, Allahabad Congress, 1910, *The Indian National Congress*, p. 1001.
[6] R. N. Mudholkar's Presidential Address, Bankipore Congress, 1912, *ibid.*, p. 1079.
[7] "The Confusion of the Honourable Gokhale," editorial in *Kesari*, Feb. 12, 1907, p. 4.
[8] V. B. Kulkarni, *British Statesmen in India* (Bombay, 1961), p. 279.
[9] Gokhale's Presidential Address, Benares Congress, 1905, *The Indian National Congress*, p. 793.
[10] Harcourt Butler, "Note on the Political Outlook in India," April 20, 1910, enclosed in Minto to JM, April 28, 1910, JMP, Minto to Morley, Vol. XVIII.
[11] Minto to JM, May 26, 1910, *ibid.*
[12] Minto to JM, June 2, 1910, *ibid.*
[13] Minto to JM, Aug. 11, 1910, *ibid.*
[14] W. Wedderburn in *The Indian National Congress*, p. 1007.
[15] B. N. Dhar's Presidential Address, Calcutta Congress, 1911, *ibid.*, p. 1011.
[16] Hardinge to JM, March 23, 1911, JMP, 26.
[17] Hardinge to JM, March 29, 1911, *ibid.*
[18] Hardinge to JM, May 11, 1911, *ibid.*
[19] Sir H. Cotton to House of Commons, Aug. 5, 1909, *HPDHC*, 5th ser., vol. 8, col. 2073.
[20] R. MacDonald to House of Commons, July 26, 1910, *ibid.*, vol. 19, col. 2008.
[21] JM to Minto, April 7, 1910, JMP, Morley to Minto, Vol. V.
[22] JM to Minto, May 5, 1910, *ibid.*
[23] JM to Minto, May 12, 1910, *ibid.*
[24] Minto to JM, June 2, 1910, JMP, Minto to Morley, Vol. XVIII.
[25] Minto to JM, Sept. 22, 1910, *ibid.*
[26] Minto to JM, May 12, 1910, *ibid.*
[27] *Ibid.*
[28] JM to Hardinge, March 24, 1911, JMP, 6.
[29] JM to Hardinge, March 17, 1911, *ibid.*
[30] Quoted from Government of India's Despatch, Aug. 25, 1911, to the Secretary of State, in Dhar's Presidential Address, *The Indian National Congress*, p. 1013.
[31] Quoted by R. N. Mudholkar in his Presidential Address, *ibid.*, p. 1074.
[32] E. Montagu, quoted in *ibid.*, p. 1075.
[33] JM to Hardinge, April 11, 1911, JMP, 6.

BIBLIOGRAPHY

PRIMARY SOURCES

Manuscripts

India Office

John Morley Papers. MSS Eur. D. 573. (A complete catalogue of the Morley Collection, compiled by M. C. Poulter, was published by the India Office in 1965.) Five volumes of letters from Morley to Minto; nineteen volumes of letters from Minto to Morley; two volumes of Hardinge-Morley letters; five volumes of telegrams; files on specific subjects; eight bundles containing miscellaneous correspondence, notes, and clippings; envelopes A–Q containing miscellaneous correspondence and notes; a tin trunk full of miscellany.
Ampthill Collection. MSS Eur. E. 233.
Curzon Papers. MSS Eur. F. 111.
Curzon-Kitchener Conflict. MSS Eur. D. 555.
Fleetwood Wilson Papers. MSS. Eur. E. 224.
Hamilton Papers. MSS Eur. D. 510/6.
The Diary of Frederick Arthur Hirtzel. Home Miscellaneous Series, no. 864.
Kilbracken Collection. MSS Eur. F. 102.
Lamington Papers. MSS. Eur. B. 159.
Lansdowne Papers. MSS Eur. D. 558.
Lee-Warner Collection. MSS Eur. F. 92.
Lytton Papers. MSS. Eur. E. 218.
"The Life of Edwin Montague." Unpublished, 2-vol. MS by Sir David Waley. MSS Eur. D. 591/1–2.

BRITISH MUSEUM
Balfour Papers. Add. MSS 49683–49962.
Campbell-Bannerman Papers. Add. MSS 41213, 41214, 41223.
Dilke Papers. Add. MS 43895.
Correspondence of Lord Kilbracken. Add. MS 44902.
Sydenham Papers. Add. MSS 50831–50841.

PUBLIC RECORD OFFICE
Kitchener Collection. PRO 30/57. Archives File no. 7283.

OTHER LIBRARIES AND COLLECTIONS
Royal Archives of King Edward VII. Windsor Castle. R.A. W/3/1–72, W/4/1–22, W/5/108, and X/14/1–33.
Crompton Papers. Thirty-one letters from JM to Henry Crompton in the possession of Gustavo Duran, New York.
Courtney Collection. British Library of Political and Economic Science. R.(S.R.) 1003. 41 vols.
Mill Collection. British Library of Political and Economic Science.
Frederic Harrison Collection. British Library of Political and Economic Science, Rare Book Room.
Grey Papers. Foreign Office Library, Cornwall House.
Minto Papers. National Library of Edinburgh.

RECORDS

INDIA OFFICE
India: Public Proceedings, July, 1905–Dec., 1910. 16 vols.
Political and Secret Records (Home Correspondence), 1906–1910. 7 vols.
Public Letters from India, 1906–1910. 5 vols.
Public Despatches from England, 1906–1910. 5 vols.
India: Confidential Proceedings, Political, July, 1907–Dec., 1910. 5 vols.
India: Legislative Council Proceedings, 1905–1910.
Political Files. Vols. 1–20, 1906; vols. 1–10, 1907.
Political and Secret Department: Letters from India, 1905–1910.
India: Public Proceedings, Jan., 1906–Dec., 1911.
India: Political Proceedings, July, 1907–July, 1910.
Judicial and Public Department: Letters and Despatches, 1906–1910, Register and Index.
East India: Progress and Condition; Statistics exhibiting the moral and material progress of India—1905–06; 1906–07; 1907–08; 1908–09.
Hansard's Parliamentary Debates, House of Commons and House of Lords, 1905–1910 *passim*. Indian Affairs. Parliamentary Papers, 1905–1910, *passim*. East India Titles.

PUBLIC RECORD OFFICE
Cabinet Papers: Committee of Imperial Defense, 1901–1910, *passim*.
Cabinet Papers: Defence of India, 1900–1910; Colonial/Overseas Defense Committee Remarks, 1904–1910; Defense Schemes, 1885–1910; Proceedings and Memoranda, 1907; Correspondence and Miscellaneous Papers, 1903–1909.

Books

Works of John Morley

Books

> *Edmund Burke: A Historical Study.* London, 1867. Reprinted by Macmillan, London, 1921.
> *Indian Speeches (1907–1909).* London, 1909.
> *Life of Richard Cobden, The.* London, 1881. 2 vols.
> *Life of William Ewart Gladstone, The.* London, 1903. 3 vols. Popular Abridged Edition, London, 1929.
> *Modern Characteristics.* A series of short essays from the *Saturday Review* (Morley, though author, did not allow his name to appear on this work). London, 1865.
> *On Compromise.* London, 1910. This work was first published in 1874, and another edition appeared in 1886.
> *Oracles on Man and Government.* London, 1923.
> *Politics and History.* London, 1923.
> *Recollections.* New York, 1917. 2 vols.
> *Speeches on Indian Affairs.* Madras, n.d.
> *Studies in Conduct.* Short essays from the *Saturday Review* (published anonymously). London, 1867.

Pamphlets, Speeches, and Articles

> "An Address to Young Liberals" (delivered at a Liberal demonstration, held in the Queen's Hall, Monday, March 20, 1905, under the auspices of the National League of Young Liberals). Published by the National League of Young Liberals as *Pamphlet No. 4.*
> "British Democracy and Indian Government," *Nineteenth Century and After,* 69 (Feb., 1911), 189–209.
> "Free Trade v. Protection," speech delivered by the Rt. Hon. John Morley, M.P., in the House of Commons, on Feb. 8, 1904. London: Liberal Publications Department, 1904.
> "Issues at Stake, The," speech delivered by the Rt. Hon. John Morley, M.P., together with a speech delivered by Mr. Winston Churchill, M.P., on May 13, 1904, at Manchester. London: Liberal Publications Department, 1904.
> "Liberalism and Social Reforms," speech given at the Eighty Club Dinner on Nov. 19, 1889, at St. James Hall, published in a pamphlet entitled *The Eighty Club: 1890.*
> "Machiavelli," the Romanes Lecture, delivered in the Sheldonian Theatre, June 2, 1897. London, 1897.
> "Memorandum on Resignation," Aug., 1914, with preface by Guy Morley and introduction by F. W. Hirst. London, 1928.
> "Signs of the Times in India," *Edinburgh Review,* CCVI (1907), 305.
> "Three Policies for Ireland: Coercion, Compromise, Conciliation," Mr. John Morley's Election Address. London: British Home Rule Association Publication, n.d.

WORKS OF OTHER WRITERS

Balfour, Arthur James. *Chapters of Autobiography.* Ed. Mrs. E. Dugdale. London, 1930.
Brodrick, William St. John. *Records and Reactions: 1856–1939.* London, 1939.
Blunt, Wilfred S. *My Diaries: Being a Personal Narrative of Events, 1888–1914.* London, 1920. 2 vols.
Carnegie, Andrew. *Autobiography.* London, 1920.
Clarke, George Sydenham (Baron Sydenham of Combe). *My Working Life.* London, 1927.
Journals and Letters of Reginald Viscount Esher. Ed. Maurice V. Brett. London, 1934–1938. 4 vols.
Fitzroy, Almeric. *Memoirs.* London, 1925. 2 vols.
Godley, Arthur (Lord Kilbracken). *Reminiscences of Lord Kilbracken.* London, 1931.
Grey, Edward (Viscount Grey of Fallodon). *Twenty-five Years, 1892–1916.* London, 1925. 2 vols.
Hardinge, Charles (Lord Hardinge of Penshurst). *My Indian Years: 1910–1916.* London, 1948.
Hirst, Francis W. *In the Golden Days.* London, 1947.
Lord Curzon in India: Being a Selection from His Speeches as Viceroy and Governor-General of India, 1898–1905, and with an Introduction by Sir Thomas Raleigh. London, 1906.
Minto, Mary, Countess of. *India, Minto and Morley, 1905–1910.* London, 1934.
Private Diaries of the Rt. Hon. Sir Algernon West. Ed. Horace G. Hutchinson. London, 1922.

SECONDARY SOURCES

BOOKS

Asquith, H. H. *Fifty Years of Parliament.* London, 1926. 2 vols.
Ayyar, Sir S. S. *Constitutional Reforms.* Madras, 1917.
Aziz, K. K. *Britain and Muslim India.* London, 1963.
Bassett, Arthur T. *The Life of the Rt. Hon. John Edward Ellis, M.P.* London, 1914.
Benn, Alfred W. *The History of English Rationalism in the Nineteenth Century.* London, 1914. 2 vols.
Bevan, Edwyn. *Indian Nationalism: An Independent Estimate.* London, 1913.
Braybrooke, Patrick. *Lord Morley: Writer and Thinker.* London, n.d. [after 1923].
Buchan, John. *Lord Minto: A Memoir.* London, 1924.
Cecil, Algernon. *Six Oxford Thinkers.* London, 1909.
Chailley, Joseph. *Administrative Problems of British India.* Trans. from French by Sir William Meyer. London, 1910.
Churchill, Winston. *Great Contemporaries.* London, 1937.

Correspondence of Mr. Justice Holmes and Harold J. Laski, The. Ed. Mark de W. Howe. Cambridge, 1953. 2 vols.
Cotton, Sir Henry. *Indian and Home Memories.* London, 1911.
Coupland, R. *India: A Restatement.* London, 1945.
———. *The Indian Problem, 1833–1945.* Oxford, 1942.
Courtney, Mrs. W. L. *The Making of an Editor: W. L. Courtney, 1850–1928.* London, 1930.
Creagh, Gen. Sir O. *Indian Studies.* London, n.d.
Cross, Cecil. *The Development of Self-Government in India, 1858–1914.* Chicago, 1922.
Das, M. N. *India under Morley and Minto: Politics behind Revolution, Repression and Reforms.* London and New York, 1964.
Davidson, W. L. *Political Thought in England: The Utilitarians from Bentham to J. S. Mill.* New York, n.d.
Dodwell, H. H., ed. *The Cambridge History of India.* Vol. VI. Cambridge, 1932.
Dugdale, Blanche E. *Arthur James Balfour.* London, 1937.
Durand, Mortimer. *Life of the Rt. Hon. Sir Alfred Comyn Lyall.* London, 1913.
Dutt, Romesh. *Economic History of India in the Victorian Age.* 8th impression. London, 1956.
Elliott, Murray K., 4th Earl of Minto. *Speeches by Minto, 1905–1910.* Calcutta, 1911.
Fowler, Edith H. (Mrs. R. Hamilton). *The Life of Henry Hartley Fowler, First Viscount Wolverhampton.* London, 1912.
Fraser, Lovat. *India under Curzon and After.* London, 1911.
Fuller, J. B. *Some Personal Experiences.* London, 1930.
Furniss, Harry. *Some Victorian Men.* London, 1924.
Gardiner, A. G. *The Life of Sir William Harcourt.* London, 1923. 2 vols.
Garvin, James L. *The Life of Joseph Chamberlain.* London, 1932, 1933, 1934, 1951. 4 vols.
Gladstone, Herbert. *After Thirty Years.* London, 1929.
Gokhale, G. K. *The Speeches of Gopal Krishna Gokhale.* 3d ed. Madras, 1920.
Gooch, G. P. *The Life of Lord Courtney.* London, 1920.
Gopal, S. *The Viceroyalty of Lord Ripon, 1880–1884.* London, 1953.
Gore, John. *King George V: A Personal Memoir.* London, 1941.
Grey, Sir Edward. Anonymous biography. London, 1915.
Griesinger, W. *German Intrigues in Persia, Afghanistan and India.* London, 1918.
Habib Allah, Amir of Afghanistan. *My Life: From Brigand to King.* London, 1936.
Hamilton, George. *Parliamentary Reminiscences and Recollections, 1886–1906.* London, 1922. 2 vols.
Hardie, Keir J. *India: Impressions and Suggestions.* London, 1909.
Harper, George M. *John Morley and Other Essays.* Princeton, 1920.
Hirst, F. W. *Early Life and Letters of John Morley.* London, 1927. 2 vols.
Hirst, F. W., By His Friends. London, 1958.
Hobhouse, L. T. *Democracy and Reaction.* London, 1905.
———. *Liberalism.* London, 1911.
Indian National Congress, The. An account of its origin and growth, of all

Congress resolutions, extracts from the welcome addresses, notable utterances on the movements, portraits of all congress presidents. 2d ed. Madras, 1917.
James, Robert R. *Rosebery: A Biography of Archibald Philip, Fifth Earl of Rosebery.* London, 1963.
Kabir, Humayin. *Muslim Politics, 1906–1942.* Calcutta, 1944.
Khan, H. H. the Aga. *India in Transition: A Study in Political Evolution.* London, n.d.
———. *The Memoirs of Aga Khan: World Enough and Time.* New York, 1954.
Knaplund, Paul. *The British Empire, 1815–1939.* London, 1942.
Knickerbocker, Francis W. *Free Minds: John Morley and His Friends.* Cambridge, 1943.
Lee, Sidney. *King Edward VII: A Biography.* London, 1925–1927. 2 vols.
Leigh-Smith, P. *Record of an Ascent: A Memoir of Sir Richmond T. Ritchie.* Cambridge, 1961.
Lucy, Henry W. *A Diary of the Home Rule Parliament, 1892–1895.* London, 1896.
M'Carthy, Justin. *British Political Portraits.* New York, 1903.
MacDonald, J. Ramsay. *The Awakening of India.* London, 1910.
Magnus, Philip. *Kitchener: Portrait of an Imperialist.* London, 1958.
Major, E. *Viscount Morley and Indian Reforms.* London, 1910.
Majumdar, R. C. *History of the Freedom Movement in India.* Vol. II. Calcutta, 1963.
Mallick, Q. A. *His Royal Highness Prince Aga Khan, Guide Philosopher and Friend of the World of Islam.* Karachi, 1954.
Mehrotra, S. R. *India and the Commonwealth, 1855–1929.* New York, 1965.
Mehta, A., and Achyut Patwardhan. *The Communal Triangle in India.* Allahabad, 1942.
Meredith, George. *George Meredith on John Morley: Glasgow University Rectorial Election, 1902.* Winchester, 1936.
Metcalf, Thomas R. *The Aftermath of Revolt in India, 1857–1870.* Princeton, 1964.
Mill, John Stuart. *Autobiography.* New York, 1924.
———. *Dissertations and Discussions, Political, Philosophical and Historical.* London, 1859–1876. 5 vols.
———. *On Liberty.* London, 1859.
Morgan, John H. *John, Viscount Morley: An Appreciation and Some Reminiscences.* Boston and New York, 1924.
Muir, Ramsay. *The Making of British India, 1756–1858.* Manchester, 1923.
Nateson, G. A. *Sir Henry Cotton.* Madras, 1912.
Nevinson, H. W. *More Changes, More Chances.* London, 1925.
———. *New Spirit in India.* London, 1908.
Nicolson, Harold. *King George V: His Life and Reign.* London, 1952.
O'Donnell, C. J. *The Causes of Present Discontent in India.* London, 1908.
Philips, C. H., ed. *The Evolution of India and Pakistan, 1858 to 1947: Select Documents.* London, 1962.
Pope-Hennessey, James. *Lord Crewe, 1858–1945: The Likeness of a Liberal.* London, 1955.
Prasad, Bisheswar. *The Origins of Provincial Autonomy.* Allahabad, 1951.
Prasad, Rajendra. *India Divided.* Bombay, 1946.
Rai, Lajpat. *The Story of My Deportation.* Lahore, 1908.

——. *Young India.* New York, 1917.
Robertson-Scott, J. W. *The Life and Death of a Newspaper.* London, 1952.
Robinson, Sir Henry. *Memories, Wise and Otherwise.* London, 1923.
Seton, Sir Malcolm. *The India Office.* London and New York, 1926.
Sirdar, Ali Khan Syed. *Life of Lord Morley.* London, 1923.
——. *Lord Curzon's Administration of India: What He Promised? What He Reformed?* Bombay, 1905.
——. *The Unrest in India.* Bombay, 1907.
Somervell, D. C. *English Thought in the Nineteenth Century.* New York, 1936.
Spender, J. A. *Life, Journalism and Politics.* London, 1927. 2 vols.
——. *The Life of the Rt. Hon. Sir Henry Campbell-Bannerman, G.C.B.* London, 1923. 2 vols.
Staebler, Warren. *The Liberal Mind of John Morley.* Princeton, 1943.
Stephen, Leslie. *The English Utilitarians.* Vol. III. London, 1900.
Strachey, G. L. *Characters and Commentaries.* London, 1933.
Titus, Murray J. *Islam in India and Pakistan.* Rev. ed. Calcutta, 1959.
Ward, Sir A. W., and G. P. Gooch, eds. *The Cambridge History of British Foreign Policy, 1783–1919.* Cambridge, 1922–1923. 3 vols.
Wasti, Syed Razi. *Lord Minto and the Indian Nationalist Movement, 1905 to 1910.* Oxford, 1964.
Wilson, S. G. *Modern Movements among Muslims.* London, 1916.
Wolpert, Stanley A. *Tilak and Gokhale: Revolution and Reform in the Making of Modern India.* Berkeley and Los Angeles, 1962.
Young, G. M. *Victorian England: Portrait of an Age.* 2d ed. Oxford, 1953.
Zacharias, H. C. E. *Renascent India from Ram Mohan Roy to Mohandas Gandhi.* London, 1933.

Articles

A. A. B. "Morley and Gladstone," *Spectator*, CXXXVIII (March 5, 1927), 355–356.
——. "Lord Morley in the Making," *Saturday Review*, CXLIII (Jan. 29, 1927), 146–147.
A. G. G. "Honest John," *The Nation and the Athenaeum*, XXXIII (Sept. 29, 1923), 799–800.
Allen, H. M. "A 'Double First': Lord Morley," *Bellman*, XXV (Dec. 21, 1918), 686–690.
Ameer, Ali. "The Unrest in India: Its Meaning," *Nineteenth Century and After*, 61 (June, 1907), 873–885.
Brooks, Sidney. "John Morley," *Harper's Weekly*, XLVIII (Oct. 1, 1904), 1498–1499.
Cecil, Algernon. "Mr. Morley," *Monthly Review*, XXIII (April, 1906), 5–17.
——. "Two Distinguished Gladstonians," *Quarterly Review*, CCXXIX (Jan., 1918), 205–221.
Dodwell, H. H. "Lord Minto as Viceroy," *National Review*, LXXXV (March-Aug., 1925), 291–303.
Duchesne, A. E. "The Situation in India. Part II: The Indian Muhammadans and the 'Reforms,'" *Empire Review*, XVII (May, 1909), 254–263.
Ford, Issac M. "John Morley in Politics," *Outlook*, XC (Sept. 26, 1908), 212.

Fortnightly Review. Ed. John Morley. N.s., Vols. VII, VIII, IX, X, *passim*.
Fraser, Sir Andrew. "Lord Morley's Indian Reforms," *Empire Review*, XVII (March, 1909), 101–110.
———. "The Situation in India. Part I: Indians and Executive Councils," *Empire Review*, XVII (May, 1909), 249–254.
"Gladstone-Morley Administration, The," *Quarterly Review*, CLXII (April, 1886), 544–580.
Gooch, G. P. "Lord Morley," *Contemporary Review*, CXXIV (Nov., 1923), 545–555.
Harris, Muriel. "Two Victorian Portraits," *North American Review*, CCXII (Sept., 1920), 404–411.
"India under Lord Morley," *Quarterly Review*, CCXIV (Jan. 1911), 203–224.
"John Morley: A Study," *Century Illustrated*, n.s., XXXVI (Oct., 1899), 874–880.
Johnstone, W. J. "Mr. Morley and Ireland," *Westminster Review*, CLXV (May, 1906), 476–480.
Knickerbocker, F. W. "Legacy of John Morley," *Sewanee Review*, 47 (April, 1939), 145–151.
Laski, Harold. "Review of Morley's *Reminiscences*," *New Republic*, 13 (Jan., 5, 1918), 286.
"Lord Morley and His Colleagues," *New Statesman and Nation*, 44 (Nov. 3, 1928), 167–168.
"Lord Morley of Blackburn's Indian Speeches," *Spectator*, CIII (Dec. 4, 1909), 947–948.
MacDonald, J. Ramsay. "John Morley," *Contemporary Review*, CXXXI (March, 1927), 282–289.
Massingham, H. W. "Lord Morley's Place in History," *Current History Magazine*, XIX (Nov., 1923), 209–214.
More, Paul E. "Viscount Morley," *Unpopular Review*, IX (Jan.-March, 1918), 265–285.
Morgan, John H. "More Light on Lord Morley," *North American Review*, CCXXI (March, 1925), 486–494.
———. "The Personality of Lord Morley," *Quarterly Review*, CCXLI (Jan., 1924), 175–192; (April, 1924), 342–367.
Morison, John Lyle. "John Morley: A Study in Victorianism," *Bulletin of the Department of History and Political and Economic Science*, Queens University, Ontario, Canada, no. 34 (Jan., 1920). 16 pp.
"Morley's Fears for His Life," *Literary Digest*, LXXX (Jan. 12, 1924).
Pall Mall Gazette. Vol. XXXII, nos. 4870, 4871, 4872, 4947.
Parker, Henry. "Lord Morley and Albrecht Dürer," *Modern Language Review*, 40 (April, 1945), 129.
Ratcliffe, S. K. "Most Eminent of the Liberal Elders," *New Statesman*, 10 (Nov. 24, 1917), 186–187.
Samuel, Herbert: "The Cobden Centenary and Modern Liberalism," *Nineteenth Century and After*, 55 (June, 1904), 898–909.
Shepard, W. J. "The Indian Councils Act," *American Political Science Review*, III (Nov., 1909), 552–556.
Spender, J. A. "Lord Morley: Last of the Victorian Liberals," *Living Age*, 319 (Nov., 1923).
Steward, H. L. "Lord Morley's Relation to History, to Theology and to the

Churches," *American Journal of Theology*, XXIII (April, 1919), 165–188.
Strachey, J. St. L. "Lord Morley: A Personal Recollection," *Spectator*, CXXXI (Sept. 29, 1923), 415–416.
"Study in Character: The Rt. Hon. John Morley, M.P.," *New Review*, VIII (April, 1893), 430–438.
Walsh, W. "Apostles of World Unity," *World Unity*, VIII (June, 1931), 162–171.
Zaidi, Z. H. "The Political Motive in the Partition of Bengal," *Journal of the Pakistan Historical Society*, XII, Pt. II (April, 1964).
Zaidi, Z. H., and F. Eustis, II. "Crown, Viceroy and Cabinet," *History* (London) (June, 1964).

DISSERTATIONS

Ahmed, Sufia. "Some Aspects of the History of the Muslim Community in Bengal, 1884–1912." Unpublished Ph.D. thesis, University of London, 1961.
Chakravarty, S. "The Evolution of Representative Government in India, 1884–1909, with Reference to the Central and Provincial Legislative Councils." Unpublished Ph.D. thesis, University of London, 1954.
Ghosh, S. "The Influence of Western, Particularly English Political Ideas on Indian Political Thought with Special Reference to the Political Ideas of the Indian National Congress, 1885–1919." Unpublished Ph.D. thesis, University of London, 1950.
Hassan, R. B. M. R. "The Educational Movement of Sir Syed Ahmed Khan, 1858–1898." Unpublished Ph.D. thesis, University of London, 1960.
Jones, I. M. "The Origins and Development to 1892 of the Indian National Congress." Unpublished M.A. thesis, University of London, 1947.
McLane, J. R. "The Development of Nationalist Ideas and Tactics and the Policies of the Government of India, 1897–1905." Unpublished Ph.D. thesis, University of London, 1961.
Stelzner, Herman G. "Ethical Qualities in John Morley's Speaking on Irish Home Rule, 1885–1921." Unpublished Ph.D. thesis, University of Illinois, 1957.
Zakaria, R. A. "Muslims in India: A Political Analysis, 1885–1906." Unpublished Ph.D. thesis, University of London, 1948.

INDEX

Adamson, Sir Harvey, 120–121, 246–247 n. 60
Aden, 95
Afghanistan, 38, 81 ff., 84, 90
Aga Khan, 178, 188, 189, 192, 275 n. 14; and John Morley, 195
Agnew, Patrick, 108
Amir Ali, 192, 195, 197
Amir of Afghanistan: visit to India, 81 ff.; loses power, 83; cost of visit of, 213
Ampthill, Lord: on Minto's appointment, 43; on Curzon, 244 n. 40
Anglo-Japanese Agreement (1905), 95
Anglo-Russian Convention (1907), 80–86 *passim*, 92, 94, 217, 218
Archbold, W. A. J., 186
Arundel, Arundel T., 136, 137
Arundel Committee, 136; proposals of, 137–138; on native member, 170–171; recommends separate electorates, 190
Arya Samaj, 107, 109
Asquith, Herbert Henry (Lord), 23, 27, 207, 214, 279 n. 46

Baig, Mizra Abbas Ali, 184, 274 n. 90
Baker, Sir Edward Norman, 67, 137, 141, 157, 181
Balfour, Arthur James, 15, 26, 30, 32, 37, 212; reaction of, to Reform Bill, 158
Banerjea, Surendra Nath, 100, 103, 191, 231
Barnes, Sir Hugh S., 141
Barr, Sir David W. K., 140, 273 n. 74

Barrow, Sir Edmund, 32; on Minto at Simla, 43
Basu, Bhupendra Nath, 231
Bengal, 226; partition of, 2, 33–35, 99–104, 106, 212, 235
Bengal Provincial Conference (1906), 100
Bilgrami, Saiyid Husain, 176, 272 n. 44; appointed to Council of India, 175; leaves England, 181
Biswas, Ashutosh, 123
Bose, Khudiram, 105
Boycott, 191–192, 222
British investment in India, 225–226
Brodrick, St. John, 30, 31, 32, 76, 136, 266 n. 43
Buchan, John, 130
Buchanan, T. R., 64
Burke, Edmund, 15 ff.
Burn, Sir Richard, 162, 270 n. 176

Campbell-Bannerman, Sir Henry, 13, 25, 26, 28
Carnegie, Andrew, 184, 211
Central Legislative Council, 135 ff., 232
Chamberlain, Joseph, 13, 15, 19, 25
China, 93
Chirol, Sir Valentine, 106
Clarke, Sir George (Lord Sydenham), 36, 57, 68, 114–116, 181, 204; on Simla and government of India, 57–60; on unrest, 116; and Tilak's trial, 116–119; on legislative council expansion, 147; opposes electoral college scheme, 194

295

INDEX

Clive, Robert, 47, 217, 236
Cobden, Richard, 20
Committee on Imperial Defense (CID), 84
Communal electorates. *See* Separate electorates
Communalism, 185-200 *passim*
Congress. *See* Indian National Congress
Cotton, Sir Henry, 103, 225, 233; reaction of, to Reform Bill, 158; on *svadeshi*, 222
Council of India, 52, 62, 249 n. 129; Muslim bias of, 198
Council of India Act (1907), 174, 272 n. 40
Courtney, Leonard, 24, 104
Creagh, General Sir O'Moore, 96, 180
Crewe, Robert O. A. (Lord), 61, 207, 229, 279 n. 48
Cromer, Evelyn Baring (Lord), 209
Curzon, George Nathaniel (Lord), 1, 5, 35-36, 45, 79, 136, 207, 212, 213, 230, 236, 255 n. 71, 266 n. 45; as viceroy, 30-33; and partition of Bengal, 34; and diplomacy, 37-38; leaves India, 39; opposes reforms, 155-157; opposes decentralization commission, 203; on Indian finance, 223
Curzon, Lady, 32
Curzon-Wyllie, Sir William, 262 n. 175; murder of, 124

Dane, Sir Louis, 38, 214
Davar, Justice D. D., 183
Decentralization, 201-210 *passim*
Dhar, Bishan Narayan, 232
Dhingra, Madan Lal, 124
Dilke, Charles, 19, 25
Disraeli, Benjamin, 15
Divide and rule, 33, 34, 186, 187, 191, 202
Drains, political and commercial, on Indian economy, 220 ff.
Dunlop Smith, J. R., 65, 186; on land revenue, 227
Dutt, Romesh Chandra, 52, 104, 105, 144, 170, 175, 176, 192, 204, 206, 226, 259 n. 48

Eastern Bengal and Assam, 99, 105
East India Company, 41
Edge, Sir John, 141
Edward VII, King, 32, 55, 151-152; opposes native member, 176, 177; Indian reaction to death of, 231
Egerton, Sir Charles Comyn, 49, 246 n. 58
Elections, India's first nationwide, 165
Electoral college scheme, 193-195

Elgin, Victor Alexander (Lord), 136, 174, 266 n. 44
Ellis, John, 219

Fawcett, Henry, 19
Finlay, James, 51
Fiscal policy, 223
Fleetwood Wilson, Guy Douglas Arthur, 63-66, 227, 228; on government of India, 64-66; on John Morley and Reform Bill, 160; on Sinha at Simla, 181; on British extravagance in India, 214-215; tribute of, to John Morley, 230
Fortnightly Review, 17
Fowler, Sir Henry Hartley, 3, 136, 174, 266 n. 41
Fraser, Lovat, 72
Fraser, Sir Andrew, 34, 50, 121
Fuller, Sir Bampfyllde, 100-103

Ghose, Aurobindo, 234
Ghose, Moti Lal, 231
Ghose, Rash Behari, 153, 176, 221
Gladstone, William Ewart, 19, 21, 23 ff., 42
Godley, Sir Arthur (Lord Kilbracken), 26, 40, 52-53, 199, 247 n. 78
Gokhale, Gopal Krishna, 1, 34, 39, 52, 53, 55, 98-99, 112, 132, 133, 145, 149, 150, 152, 156, 178, 192, 201, 203, 206, 224, 230, 265 n. 32; on racial domination, 168; supports separate electorates, 196; on decentralization, 204-205; on land revenue, 227; on Curzon, 231
Government of India Act (1919), 201
Grey, Sir Edward, 10, 20, 23, 27, 28, 80, 217, 218; on opium, 219
Gupta, Krishna Gobinda, 176, 178, 180, 272 n. 43; appointed to Council of India, 175; on separate electorates, 197-198

Habibullah Khan. *See* Amir of Afghanistan
Haldane, Richard, 216
Hamilton, George (Lord), 30, 31, 266 n. 42
Harcourt, Sir William, 23, 25
Hardie, Keir, 46, 221, 223
Hardinge, Charles (Lord), 61, 96, 209, 235; receives Congress deputation, 232
Hare, Sir Lancelot, 50-51, 247 n. 67
Henry, Sir Edward R., 54, 248 n. 94
Hewett, Sir John Prescott, 47, 73, 252 n. 196
Hirst, Francis Wrigley, 25

INDEX

Hirtzel, Frederic Arthur, 69, 111, 164, 248 n. 96, 260 n. 112; influence of, on John Morley, 55
Hobhouse, Charles Edward, 203, 278 n. 17
Hobhouse Commission. *See* Royal Commission upon Decentralisation in India
House of Commons, 3; reactions of, to repression, 122–123; opium motion in, 219–220
Hume, Allan Octavian, 5, 230

Ibbetson, Sir Denzil Charles, 50, 101, 107, 109, 112, 137, 176, 247 n. 64
Ilbert Bill, 168, 171, 172, 173
Imam, Syed Ali: replaces Sinha, 183, 274 n. 86
Indian Councils Act (1909), 7, 129, 133, 150 f., 181; origins of, 129–135; Arundel Commission and, 136–138; Minto's reform dispatch and, 138–140; Morley's reform dispatch and, 143–147 *passim*; considered by Council of India, 151; in House of Lords, 152–154, 157; Indian reactions to, 153–154; provisions, 154–157 *passim*; in House of Commons, 158; disqualifications under, 163 ff.; regulations issued, 165
Indian National Congress, 1, 35, 133, 143–144, 152, 185, 219, 230, 232; support of, in House of Commons, 42; reaction of, to reforms, 165; demands racial equality, 168; opposes separate electorates, 192; economic demands of, 212; resolutions of, on land revenue, 226 f.
Inverarity, J. D., 117
Islington Committee on the Public Services in India, 178
Iyer, Krishnaswamy, 154

Jackson, Arthur M. T.: murder of, 126
Japan, 82; and India, 95
Jenkins, John Lewis, 231
Jenkins, Sir Lawrence, 62, 106, 127; on situation in India, 62–63; reaction of, to reforms, 156–160; on Sinha, 182–183; on racism in India, 184; on separate electorates, 199; on economic reforms, 228
Jinnah, M. A., 191

Kimberley, Lord, 3, 24
Kingsford, D. H., 113, 114, 260 n. 111
Kitchener, Lord, 4, 5, 32, 43, 61, 69, 85–90 *passim*, 94–97 *passim*, 109, 182, 215, 216, 233, 234, 252 n. 1, 254 n. 71; and Curzon, 31–32; on John Morley, 85; reputation of, as racist, 169

Krishnavarma, Shyama, 125

Lamington, Lord, 50, 95, 268 n. 112
Lansdowne, Lord, 80, 153, 173; supports reforms, 156
Lawley, Sir Arthur, 69, 169
Lee-Warner, Sir William, 53–55, 72, 141, 152, 176, 191, 199, 248 n. 89; opposes reforms, 151; influences John Morley against Indians, 170
Liberalism, 1, 3
Literary Gazette, 12
London Colonial Conference (1907), 47
Lupton, A.: on Indian economics, 222
Lyall, Sir Alfred C., 37, 38, 144, 172, 194, 202–203, 209; influence of, on John Morley, 142–143
Lytton, George Bulwer (Lord), 15, 35

MacDonald, J. Ramsay, 13, 227, 233
MacDonnell, Sir Anthony (Lord), 149–150, 207, 279 n. 38
MacKarness, F. C., 221
Mehta, Pherozeshah, 157
Military reorganization, 76 ff.
Mill, John Stuart, 12, 13, 15
Milner, Sir Alfred, 25, 32
Minto, Lady, 6, 130
Minto, Lord, 4, 33; on Curzon, 30–31; on partition of Bengal, 34, 101–102; arrival of, in India, 39–40; description of, 43–44; opposes John Morley's trip to India, 60–61; and Kitchener, 76–77; on Russia and Afghanistan, 81; reaction of, to Anglo-Russian Convention, 84–85; frontier policy of, 88–89; on Tilak trial, 120; attempted assassination of, 126; claims initiative for reforms, 130; appoints reforms committee, 136; prepares reforms dispatch, 138–140; on Congress split, 152; and Reform Bill, 153, 155, 160–161; and native member, 169, 173; on "natives" in high posts, 180; receives Muslims, 187–190; pledges separate electorates, 189; reaction of, to electoral college scheme, 193–194; reverses position on Muslims, 198 f.; opposes decentralization commission, 201–203; reaction of, to threat of revolution, 232
Mohsin-ul-Mulk, 186, 187, 274 n. 7
Montagu, Edwin S., 5, 72, 223, 235, 251 n. 186; on reforms, 166
Morison, Theodore, 140, 162, 190, 197, 275 n. 22
Morley, John (Lord): early years of, 10; rejects clergy in favor of literary career,

12; influence of J. S. Mill on, 13 ff.; marriage of, 13–14; early political failures of, 14; on Burke, 16 ff.; as editor and author, 17–20; and Ireland, 20, 21 ff., 23 ff.; first election of, to House of Commons, 20 ff.; writes *Life of Gladstone*, 25 ff.; offered India Office, 27; visits America, 27; on Curzon, 40; on bureaucracy, 48–49, 51; on Egerton, 49; on Adamson, 49; and Hirtzel, 55–57; abortive visit of, to India, 60–61; on Kitchener, 61, 252 n. 7, 254 n. 71; failure of, to control repression, 69–71, 121–122; on Lajpat Rai, 70; on government of India, 73; on military administration, 76 ff.; and Anglo-Russian Convention, 80–82; on racism in India, 85–86; on military expenditure, 86–87; frontier policy of, 87–92 *passim*; on China, 93; on Persia, 94; on Hardinge, 96; and partition of Bengal, 99–104, 106; on Fuller, 100–101; on repression and preventive detention, 109–114 *passim*, 127–128; on Ibbetson, 110–111; on Tilak, 115–119; outlines reforms to Minto, 132; appoints reforms committee, 140; prepares reforms dispatch, 143 ff.; on raj, 145, 151; on expansion of legislative councils, 146–147; on Gokhale, 150; on Congress, 152; presents reforms to House of Lords, 152–153; on Reform Bill, 159–161; and racial equality, 168 ff.; and native member, 169–176; on employment of "Natives," 177–179; on Negroes in America, 184; and electoral college scheme, 193–195; and decentralization, 201–210 *passim*; on Indian sanitation, 208; on Indian education, 208–210; economic policy of, 211–228 *passim*; on free trade, 212 ff.; and retrenchment in India, 213 ff.; and Grey, 217–220; on opium trade, 219–220; on land revenue, 226 f.; economic and financial failures of, 227–228; leaves Whitehall, 229; on Risley, 250 n. 143

Morley-Minto conflicts: on role of House of Commons in Indian affairs, 45–47; on selection of officers, 67–68; on Russian policy, 94; on Council of Princes, 145–146; on disqualification of elected council members, 163 ff.

Morley-Minto reforms. *See* Indian Councils Act

Mountbatten, Louis (Lord), 5, 177

Mowatt Committee on Military Expenditure, 86–87

Mudholkar, R. N., 230

Mukherji, Asutosh, 176

Murray, Alexander, 282 n. 64

Muslim League, 1, 175, 185–186, 192, 195–197 *passim*; first policy statement by, 188–189; opposes electoral college scheme, 193–195

Naoroji, Dadabhai, 144

Native judges, 178

Native member, 168–177 *passim*

Nehru, Motilal, 157

Nicolson, Sir Arthur, 83

O'Connor, W. F., 91–93

O'Donnell, C. J., 103, 221

O'Grady, J., 221

Opium trade, 219–220

Pakistan, 1

Pal, Bepin Chandra, 69, 191

Percy, E., 158

Persia, 83, 217–218; and India, 93–94

Press prosecutions, 114 ff.

Preventive detention, 105–106, 112, 122

Provincial executive councils: attempt to integrate, 180–181

Provincial legislative councils, 135 ff., 155; powers broadened, 136; expansion of, under reforms, 146–147, 156 ff.; abolition of official majority in, 155; first national election to, 165 ff.

Punjab: unrest in, 106–109

Punjab Alienation of Land Act, 107

Punjab Colonisation Bill, 107

Racial prejudice, 179–180

Rai, Lala Lajpat, 70, 112, 196, 232; arrest and deportation of, 109–110; release of, 112

Ranade, M. G., 53, 170

Rau, Benegal N., 179

Rees, Sir John David, 222, 263 n. 187

Reforms. *See* Indian Councils Act

Repressive measures: Explosive Substances Act (1908), 120 ff.; Newspapers (Incitements to Offences) Act (1908), 120 ff.; Criminal Law (Amendment) Act XIV (1908), 126

Richards, Sir Earle, 137, 177

Ripon, Lord, 5, 168, 174

Risley, Sir Herbert Hope, 64, 104, 131, 147–148, 149, 249 n. 142, 249–250 n. 143

Ritchie, Richmond Thackeray, 52

Roberts, Lord, 31, 38, 148, 268 n. 98

Romer, Lord Justice, 216

Rosebery, Lord, 23–25

INDEX

Royal Commission upon Decentralisation in India, 71, 201–207 *passim*
Russia, 215; in Indian foreign policy, 79–86 *passim*; Anglo-Russian Convention, 80 ff.

Salisbury, Lord, 41
Salt tax: reduction of, 224–225
Saturday Review, 12
Savarkar, Ganesh Damodar (Veer), 123–124
Scott, Major General C. H., 79
Separate electorates, 7, 185–200 *passim*, 236; genesis of, 186–190; approved by John Morley, 195; Hindu agitation against, 196
Shah of Persia, 217 f.
Shams ul-Alam: assassination of, 183
Simla, 2, 57–60
Singh, Ajit, 108, 109
Sinha, Satyendra P., 162, 164, 176, 273 n. 52; appointed to Viceroy's Executive Council, 177; resigns, 181 ff.
Sino-British Convention (1906), 92
Smith, Dunlop. *See* Dunlop Smith

Stephens, Fitzjames, 13
Svadeshi, 34, 212, 222, 225, 228
Svaraj, 34, 144
Sydenham, Lord. *See* Clarke, Sir George

Tashi Lama: in India, 91–92
Tata, J. N., 225
Taylor, Harriet, 13
Thomson, Sir James, 152, 269 n. 124
Tibet, 37–38, 91–93
Tilak, Bal Gangadhar, 1, 4, 114–119, 183, 191, 230, 233

War Office, 215–216
Waziristan, 88–89
Wedderburn, Sir William, 229, 230, 232
West Bengal, 99
White, Sir George, 32
Wilson, Fleetwood. *See* Fleetwood Wilson

Younghusband, Col. Sir Francis, 37–38

Zakka Khel expedition, 88–90

DATE DUE